SUMMIT

Mary Ellen Blackburn

SUMMIT

A Gold Rush History of Summit County, Colorado

By Mary Ellen Gilliland

Designed by Diane Adams. Cover painting by Stuart Goldman. Printed in the United States of America.

Library of Congress Catalog Card Number: 80-65781
ISBN 0-960-3624-0-1 (pbk.)
ISBN 0-960-3624-1-X

2nd Edition, 1987

Alpenrose Press
Box 499
Silverthorne, Colorado 80498

For the people of Summit County,
past and present,
and particularly, for Larry

Contents

Acknowledgments

A hearty "thank you!" goes to all who lent their knowledge, time and talent to help launch this book. I wish to thank my husband, Larry, for his unwavering support, and my children, Sheliah and Matthew, for patience beyond their years. To my copy editors, Jack and Elsa Gilliland, I offer my gratitude for a sharp editorial eye and tireless effort. My friend Slyvia McGhie gave me the gift of time by caring for a pre-school child. Maureen Nicholls generously shared her boundless knowledge of the Breckenridge area. Verna Sharp, Montezuma, Howard Giberson, Frisco, and Penny Lewis, Copper Mountain, who read sections of the book to verify historical accuracy, expressed a contagious enthusiasm for *Summit* that renewed my own. Max and Edna Dercum read chapters, counseled and cared. Elizabeth Culbreath kindly critiqued the chapter on Breckenridge. My genuine thanks go also to Naomi Fleming of the Summit Historical Society for concerned guidance with research materials. The Frisco librarians, Alice Meister, Janice Rumberger and Lynn Amstutz, with Dillon's Vanessa Woodford and the Western History Department librarians at the Denver Public Library, provided invaluable aid. I also wish to thank Rev. Mark Fiester, whose book *Blasted, Beloved Breckenridge* revealed so much of that area's rich past.

M.E.G.

Author's Note

An 1881 Colorado mine town newspaper made this editorial jab at visiting journalists: ". . . when the scribblers come here, they attempt to take the town in a day or so, and following natural vicious instinct or taste, never get farther than the gambling halls and variety theatres."

This history of Summit County during its mineral rush heyday strives for accuracy, breadth and balance. But reaching this goal isn't always easy. Along with the profusion of tall tales and lively legends come blurred memories of past events and rapidly diminishing physical remnants of ghost towns and mine structures. Our picture of Summit's past is fading like an old photograph. Details become difficult to discern. To restore the photograph to clarity requires painstaking research and delicate weighing of fact. A big job. Hopefully, this book will provide a start in recapturing the whole Summit scene.

The author hopes readers — both local residents and visitors — will enjoy the parade of Summit's colorful past and that the story will enrich a day, week, or lifetime spent here.

This is Summit County

Located at the top of the Rockies, with its south and southeast boundaries on the soaring Continental Divide, Summit County lies 75 miles west of Denver via Interstate Highway 70 and the Eisenhower Tunnel. Summit ranked as one of 1861 Colorado Territory's original 17 counties. A huge Summit County expanse then stretched from the Divide to the Utah border and from Fremont and Hoosier Passes to the Wyoming line. Six counties later divided from this early Summit: Grand, Routt, Eagle, Garfield, Moffat and Rio Blanco.

Today's Summit boundaries with neighboring Clear Creek, Park, Lake and Eagle counties are marked by mountain ranges. Grand County alone offers easy access, with a route unblocked by mountains. The county today encompasses 391,680 acres with 77 percent in public lands managed by the U.S. Forest Service and Bureau of Land Management, and 23 percent in private land.

Relics remain in testimony to the cash crop of rich mines that sprouted all over Summit County. Here, the New York Mine, just southeast of Montezuma.

1

Summit's salient features include the beautiful Blue River, its roiling waters generating three times the flow of any other Colorado River contributing basin. The Denver Water Board seized advantage of this peak water flow to dam the Blue and create 2,970-acre Dillon Reservoir in the early 1960's. Green Mountain Reservoir, north of Silverthorne, also utilizes Blue River flow to provide power and irrigation capability to northern Summit County ranchlands.

The Blue River and its tributaries, the Snake and the Ten Mile, define the county's contours with their respective basins cutting deep valleys in the area's mountainous terrain.

Summit's most outstanding feature is its skyscraping altitude, from a low 7,750 feet above sea level at Green Mountain Reservoir to a spiraling 14,270 feet at Gray's Peak. This high and dry climate creates powdery snow to bless Summit's four ski mountain operations at Arapahoe Basin, Breckenridge, Copper Mountain and Keystone. These ski areas issued 1,886,852 lift tickets during the 1978-79 ski season, more than popular Vail or famous Aspen.

County residents number close to 8,000. Second-home owners and visitors swell population during the busy ski and summer recreation seasons.

It all began 70 million years ago, with the creation of Colorado's 240-mile mineral belt. Boiling fountains of gold, silver and other precious minerals seamed mountains of granite and gneiss.

Later, during the glacial age, advancing rivers of ice crumbled rock to release nuggets, then melted to form streams that deposited grains of gold along pristine creeks. High country trappers, from 1810-1840, saw the glittering metal, but kept its secret, lest a swarm of prospectors disrupt tranquil beaver ponds. Ute Indians pointed out placer gold to a few isolated alpine explorers, but somehow the news of gold never filtered back from this remote mountain wilderness to the United States. Finally, in 1858, an Indian named Fall Leaf showed a pouch of placer nuggets to frontier townsmen in Lawrence, Kansas. Gold fever flashed through the border towns. About the same time, prospector John Beck, who had panned Colorado gold in 1850 while enroute to California with the Cherokee Indians, organized a group of Georgia prospectors to come to Colorado. News of discoveries on Denver's Cherry Creek swept an economically-depressed United States. Hordes of gold-hungry adventurers arrived in Denver and by summer,

1859, scaled the snow-encrusted Continental Divide to the gold-rich valley of the Blue River. This gentle valley, today part of Colorado's historic Summit County, was catapulted from tranquil isolation into the gold rush days.

Mine camps mushroomed amid the lofty pine forests lining the Blue River and

its tributaries. Prospectors found gold all over fabled French Gulch, dazzling Gold Run, mineral-laced Georgia and many other gulches.

A cry of "Silver!" soon echoed against the cliffs of Montezuma Canyon, near today's Keystone Resort, and its reverberation began Colorado's first silver rush in 1863.

A parade of colorful characters, some scoundrels (like Pug Ryan) and a few saints (like Methodist itinerant preacher John Lewis Dyer) marched across the pages of Summit County's gold rush history. Bustling new towns exploded into being. Some, like Parkville, the first county seat, lapsed into ghost town status. Others, like Breckenridge, Montezuma, Frisco and Dillon, flourished during the days of mining prosperity. These towns clung to life during the grim years after the mines played out, and now hum with the beehive activity of Summit County's booming tourism.

The stories of Summit's key communities gain significance as each launches its centennial celebration of incorporation: Frisco in 1980, Breckenridge in 1980, Montezuma in 1981 and Dillon in 1983.

Before the Rush Began

The Rocks That Made the Rockies

Hundreds of millions of years ago, long before the present Rocky Mountains took shape, an earlier continental divide began to rise. Colorado's first Front Range, part of this ancient system, soared to a staggering 20,000 feet. A giant trough had formed across a large Western region including Colorado, and in this depression gathered the waters of a vast inland sea. This watery waste once submerged an area stretching from western Utah to the Missouri River. It was no flash flood — Colorado remained underwater more than 65 million years.

A towering Front Range, plus the skyscraping Saguache Mountains, pierced these waters to rise as sentinel islands. Western shores of the massive Front Range island probably touched at Breckenridge, Frisco, Dillon and Montezuma. The waters lapped relentlessly at the rocky shoulders of the Front Range mountains and, over millions of years, caused their erosion. Silt and clay crumbled from the mountain range to form thick deposits of muddy sediment impregnated with the remains of marine fossils on the ocean floor. Fossil-rich Pierre

Glaciers carved 600-million-year-old Pre-Cambrian rock to create Montezuma's valley.

Shale, embedded with the remains of ammonites (shell fossils), swimming reptiles and fish, today stands 4,000 feet thick in the Snake River Valley near Keystone. The sedimentary Minturn Formation, created 300 million years ago while the coal swamps formed in Pennsylvania, gradually thickens from Dillon to Breckenridge, then deepens rapidly toward Hoosier Pass, indicating that the rich muds gathered there in a once-low area south of Breckenridge. The red color of this sedimentary rock, and that seen so clearly on Vail Pass, came from the oxidation of iron contained in the mud-turned-rock.

Motorists driving the Dillon Dam Road can view the results of Front Range erosion recorded in the road cut just beyond the south end of the dam. There, deposits from the Morrison Formation, laid down by a receding ocean, hark back to the Jurassic Age when dinosaurs roamed. And a layer of Dakota sandstone, derived from beach sands of a Cretaceous Sea, also remains as a testament to an ancient age when a diminished and forgotten Rocky Mountain chain eroded endlessly into a rising ocean floor.

Suddenly, the monotony ended. Seventy million years ago, a rumble emitted from the sediment-thick floor of the Cretaceous Sea. The massive sea floor began to buckle, bend and arch! The earth's crust had shifted. A dense Pacific plate rammed beneath a lighter Continental plate to cause a violent upheaval. Convulsive forces shoved and lifted here, crumpled and crushed there. A new Rocky Mountain range arose. Huge ledges thrust upward. Giant slabs of rock folded. Collision piled up mountains of granite. The strain of intense folding tilted the layer of sedimentary sea floor, thousands of feet thick, and split the 600 million-year-old Pre-Cambrian rock beneath it into a mosaic of fractures. When the earth floor cracked, volcanoes erupted to spew out fiery lava. Into the fractured Pre-Cambrian rock flowed molten intrusions of gold, silver, lead, zinc, copper, and molybdenum solutions. As boiling lava cooled and cracked, its fissures too eventually filled with hot water and gases bearing mineral-rich molten material. The 600-million-year-old rock of the Gore, Ten Mile and Front Range was permeated by gleaming fingers of gold and silver and other precious metals. The sedimentary rock of Breckenridge received intrusions of igneous molten rock, bearing rich gold and silver. At Farncomb Hill, molten gold honeycombed fissured sedimentary rock to create Breckenridge's famous wire gold.

This upheaval, called the Laramide Orogeny, over eons created the 10-35 mile wide Colorado mineral belt. Dazzling mine camps sprang up after 1859 across the mineral belt, which stretched from the mountains behind Boulder and Lyons diagonally through Breckenridge to Leadville. The camps that blossomed along that belt — Gold Hill, Idaho Springs, Central City, Black Hawk, Empire, Silver Plume, Georgetown, Montezuma, Breckenridge and Leadville — rank as legendary in the annals of fabulous mineral finds.

Other sensational discoveries of gold and silver, such as the electrifying news of Cripple Creek's riches and the silver-seamed San Juans, resulted from mineral deposits from later volcanic activity (the San Juan deposits are a youthful 35 million years old). Geologists separate these camps from the Colorado mineral belt.

5

During the Ice Age, a snowbound Summit County looked much like glaciated areas of Alaska today. A 1,000-foot thick river of ice lumbered through today's Blue Valley, hewing out valley contours and leaving behind a 45 to 90-foot-thick layer of terrace gravels that form the base of the gentle vale. Dredge boats mined these deep gravels for bedrock gold from the early 1900's through 1942.

Rivers of ice carved the gorge-like Ten Mile Canyon as well as the scenic Swan and Snake River valleys. Glaciers sculpted sheer, steep walls in Montezuma Canyon, with its abundance of slide areas. Cirques (amphitheater-like depressions on mountainsides) formed at the headwaters of glacial valleys. Glacial lakes, popular with high-country fishermen, filled depressions blocked by a "dam" of glacial gravel deposits. Uneva, Cataract and Chihuahua exemplify these glacial lakes.

Bulldozer ice worked at inchworm pace. Summit County lay locked in slow-moving ice from 100,000 years ago to 20,000 or 10,000 years ago.

The glaciers not only sculpted the spectacular mountain valley playground we enjoy today. They also scraped and sandpapered the ancient granite and sedimentary rock to reveal the gold hidden in its stony vault. The glaciers grated the gold into dust, flakes and nuggets. Ice, frozen in rock, shattered stone and released gold imprisoned there. Tumbling streams washed the glittering mineral down from the mountainsides. Gold, a heavy material, worked its way down through glacial gravels to finally rest at the stream's bedrock base. Streams and rivers changed their courses through the centuries. Ancient stream beds, covered over by earth and vegetation, concealed as much placer gold as those discovered by the first gold-panning prospectors.

Sometimes, glacial scraping exposed a vein of gold-bearing quartz embedded in ancient granite, an eye-opener for the lucky lode miner to discover tens of millions of years later.

Mother Earth, in fiery rage, had flung from her treasure trove gold, silver and other mineral riches. Hidden in the craggy caverns of the rugged and challenging Rocky Mountains, the treasure waited for men who would dare to seek.

First Footfalls

Who were the first white men to penetrate the isolated reaches of the mountain-bound Blue River Valley? We know that the Spanish explored Colorado during Coronado's 1541 expedition, a futile search for the fabled "Seven Cities of Gold". But these Spaniards probably never entered the Blue Valley. The first recorded visit of a Frenchman to Colorado came in 1724 with the sojourn of explorer Bourgmount. The Dominguez-Escalante expedition of 1776 entered the mountains in search of a route to California. Zebulon Montgomery Pike first viewed his lofty namesake, Pikes Peak, in November, 1806, and Major Stephen Long explored Colorado in 1820. But these white men never scaled the Divide to reach Summit County.

In 1803, the Louisiana Purchase stretched U.S. holdings westward from the

Mississippi River to the crest of the Rockies. Then in 1848, President James Polk acquired the western portion of Colorado in the Mexican cession. These moves helped to open the West to exploration, and set the stage for trappers and explorers to cross the Divide and discover the Blue Valley.

In 1811, a Missourian, Ezekiel Williams, led a party of 19 men to what is now Colorado to trap beaver. By 1812, they had penetrated South Park and reached the headwaters of the South Platte on Hoosier Pass. Half of Williams' party crossed the pass to the Western Slope (presumably into Summit County) and were never seen or heard from again! Summit's first white visitors encountered some hair-raising adventures.

To make matters worse, Ezekiel Williams suffered the fate of capture by hostile Arapahoe Indians. He and two companions endured a wretched two years as unwilling guests of the Arapahoe before his escape and return to Missouri. But the wily Mr. Williams had cached his party's yield of pelts before his capture. The next spring Williams re-crossed the plains to Colorado, hazarded the journey into the mountains, retrieved his hidden furs and plodded back to the States to exchange his "hairy banknotes" for cash!

Farnham's Oregon Dragoons, an emigrant society from Peoria, Illinois, provided the first written record of a visit to the Summit in 1839. Originally a party of 18 young men led by Thomas Jefferson Farnham, the group dwindled to five by the time the men reached the Summit. They were: Farnham, a 35-year old former Vermonter; Joseph Wood; Obadiah Oakley; Sidney Smith; and William Blair. (Farnham had hired a guide at Bent's Fort, a Kentucky blacksmith named Kelley, who brought them over what became Boreas Pass and down the Blue River.)

Farnham's diary records the first, history-making description of a virgin Blue Valley:

> The face of the country along the morning's trail was much the same as that passed over the day before; often beautiful, but more often sublime. Vast spherical swells covered with buffalo, and wild flowering glens echoing the voices of a thousand cascades, and countless numbers of lofty peaks crowding the sky, will perhaps give some idea of it.

In 1842, Summit County's first tourist, Rufus B. Sage, traveled the Blue Valley enroute to South Park. Sage was stretching the summer tourist season a bit — the date being December 10. On December 12, 1842, a fierce storm caught Sage atop Hoosier Pass and swept the disgruntled vacationer down into blustery South Park. But Sage's adventures did not go wasted. He wrote a book on his 1841-1844 western sojourn entitled *Scenes in the Rocky Mountains,* published in 1846. Public attention focused on the West through this and other similar books, laying ground work for the mass scramble to Colorado that would follow the discovery of gold.

Famous "Pathfinder" John C. Fremont led an 1843 U.S. government expedition through Summit County with legendary Kit Carson, William Gilpin and Thomas Fitzpatrick as guides. Fremont mapped and surveyed the West in three trips, 1842, 1843 and 1845, for the Army Corps of Topographical Engineers.

His party of 40 men, mostly Creoles and French Canadians, included a Negro (probably the first in Summit County), a Prussian drill sergeant (who manned Fremont's 12-pound howitzer) and talented cartographer Charles Pruess. Pruess, a German who created the first good map of Summit County, later published his book, *Exploring with Fremont*.

Along with the hefty howitzer, Fremont's mountain touring equipment included 12 carts and a large rubber boat.

Colonel Fremont entered Summit County from the north and followed the Blue River to its head on Hoosier Pass, then crossed Hoosier to South Park, on June 22, 1844. His journal details his impressions of a pine-forested valley abounding with buffalo:

We halted to noon under the shade of the pines, and the weather was most delightful. The country was literally alive with buffalo; and the continued echo of the hunter's rifles on the other side of the river made me uneasy, thinking perhaps they were engaged with Indians; but in a short time they came into camp with the meat of seven fat cows.

During the earlier part of the day's ride, the river had been merely a narrow ravine between high piney mountains, backed on both sides, but particularly on the west, by a line of snowy ridges; but, after several hours ride, the stream opened out into a valley with pleasant bottoms. In the afternoon the river forked into three apparently equal streams;* broad buffalo trails leading up the left hand, and the middle branch indicating good passes over the mountains; but up the right hand branch . . . there was no sign of a buffalo trace. Apprehending from this reason the character of the mountains which are known to be extremely rugged, and that the right hand branch led to no pass, I proceeded up the middle branch, which formed a flat valley bottom between timbered ridges on the left and snowy mountains on the right, terminating in large buttes of naked rock. The trail was good, and the country interesting; and at nightfall we encamped in an open place among the pines, where we built a strong fort . . .

At dark, we perceived a fire in the edge of the pines, on the opposite side of the valley . . . In the morning, they were found to be a party of six trappers, who had ventured out among the mountains after beaver. They informed us that two of the number with which they started had been already killed by the Indians . . . by the Arapahoes we had lately seen . . .

In the afternoon, we continued our road — occasionally through open pines, with a very gradual ascent. We surprised a herd of buffalo, enjoying the shade at a small lake among the pines; and they made the dry branches crack, as they broke through the woods. In a ride of about three quarters of an hour, and having ascended perhaps 800 feet, we reached the summit of the dividing range,** which would this have an estimated height of 11,200 feet.

* The three rivers area (today's Dillon)
** Hoosier Pass summit

Finally, in 1855, Sir St. George Gore, a rich Irish baronet, strode into Summit County to slaughter its abundant game in a high-rolling hunting safari that massacred thousands of bear, buffalo, elk, deer, antelope, fish and birds. The titled huntsman sipped vintage wines in a portable "castle" after the day's sport. His story, too rich to capsule here, appears in Chapter 17.

Did these bold adventurers notice bright yellow flecks in creek sands or stream beds? Did they have any inkling of the riches buried beneath their boots?

James Purcell, probably the first white American on the Western Slope, had confided the story of Colorado gold to Zebulon Pike during Pike's 1807 visit to Santa Fe. Friendly Ute Indians spoke freely of gold (which was fine if you spoke the Ute language; otherwise you nodded and smiled). Lord Gore's cook brought him a bottle of gold dust, but the avid huntsman suppressed the story, threatening his cook to silence. Gore feared news of gold spreading among his retinue of servants, marksmen and attendants would spoil his grand safari.

So the secret remained, and the land lay in tranquility . . . waiting.

The Skin Game

Beaver men, the trappers who penetrated remote mountain wilderness in search of pelts, did America a great service: They opened the West. Despite the dangers of scalp-seeking Indians, enraged grizzlies, fierce mountain lions or harsh high country storms, these mountain men tramped every glen and canyon. George Ruxton, who visited the Colorado Rockies in 1847-48 spent much of his time in South Park on the other side of Summit's Hoosier Pass. Of the trappers, Ruxton wrote: "All this vast country, but for the daring enterprise of these men, would be even now a *terra incognita* to geographers, as indeed a great portion still is; but there is not an acre that has not been passed and repassed by the trappers in their perilous excursions."

The object of the trappers' profit-oriented scramble was the world's second largest rodent, the beaver. Descendant of the giant Castorides, a 700-pound beaver that stalked the wetlands one million years ago, the industrious beaver can alter the ecology of an entire area by his dam-building activity. Usually living about 12 years, the four-foot-long, 40 to 60 pound average beaver sports a handy 12 to 16 inch tail which serves as a rudder and diving plane while swimming. This versatile tail, considered a gourmet delicacy by the trappers, also served the beaver as a stabilizing "third leg" when he perched upright to fell a tree.

Evolution did great things for the beaver. This admirable animal developed a transparent eyelid that allows him to see while swimming, with no risk of debris in the eye. His mouth is similarly adapted with flaps that close over the beaver's sharp teeth. He can gnaw bark while submerged, without collecting a mouthful of water! Highly efficient lungs allow the beaver to remain underwater for as long as eight minutes, during which time his porpoise-like "deep dive syndrome" slows heartbeat and sends blood to vital organs to protect life functions.

When he is not munching on his eclectic diet of Columbine flowers (Colorado State Flower), Indian paint brush, skunk cabbage, ferns, bulbs or mushrooms, the beaver aims his incisors at aspen trees, willows and alder. The trees he neatly fells by cutting triangular chips, working deeper into the trunk until the tree falls (toward his pond, of course!).

While he cuts, the wary beaver must keep a sharp nose alert for the scent of coyote, wolverine, bobcat and mountain lion, for his land-lubbering waddle is nothing to match his deft agility in the water.

Neither coyote nor bobcat could destroy the resourceful beaver, but man, trapping beaver families, even the kits, nearly exterminated the aquatic mammal.

Adolphus Wislizenus, who traveled over nearby Tennessee Pass during his 1839 visit to the Colorado Rockies, said ". . . constant hunting has very much reduced the number of beavers." However, just as the beaver faced his demise, the popular beaver fur hat met a similar fate. Elegant silk top hats became the rage. Beaver trapping nearly ceased. And the beaver remained on the Western Slope.

Biggest years for those who trapped the beaver had been 1810-1840, the years when every fashionable American and European gentleman broadcast his affluence to the world by wearing a beaver fur hat. But trapping in the West began earlier. In 1773, Scotsmen James Finlay and Alex McLeod sent long strings of canoes West every spring. Their trappers "penetrated much of the Rocky Mountains above the Missouri headwaters," according to writer Mari Sandoz.

Lewis and Clarke's reports from early 1800's expeditions detail the presence of British and French trappers in Ute territory on "the other side of the mountains". The Spaniards launched mountain beaver hunts from their New Mexico and Louisiana towns between 1763 and 1802. (Spaniard Vincente de Zaldivar of Ornate had camped near Denver about 1598 and named the South Platte the "Rio do Chato".) The Hudson Bay trappers reportedly were "trapping the ponds and streams west of the Divide to the last kit" to discourage American

Early 1800's trappers found Summit's beaver ponds a rich source of lucrative furs. Artist Frederic Remington depicts caravan of hunters enroute to the Rockies, above. Trappers toted "Platte River Punch" for Indian consumption. The recipe: 1 gallon alcohol, 1 lb. molasses, 1 lb. plug black-twist tobacco, handful Spanish peppers, 10 gallons river water and 2 rattlesnake heads per barrel.

invasion and eventual settlement.

But the musky scent of beaver profit filled the nostrils of American entrepreneurs and their trappers came, under the auspices of powerful fur trade companies like John Jacob Astor's empire-building American Fur Company. Founded in 1808, "the Company", as frontiersmen called it, earned the distinction of becoming the first American business monopoly. (Astor sold the St. Louis/Western branch of the American Fur Company to Pierre Chouteau, Jr. in 1834.)

The little companies organized to compete with Astor's giant were dubbed "the Opposition". One of these, General William Ashley's successful Rocky Mountain Fur Company made a valiant stab at competing with "the Company". Ashley's roster of mountain men included Jim Bridger, Jim Beckwourth, Thomas Fitzpatrick, Louis Vasquez and Jedediah Smith — all famous names in the his-

11

tory of the West. Ashley became rich during three short years in the fur trade, 1824-1827, and retired to wear beaver hats himself.

Trappers hired by the fur companies either accepted an outfit (horses, beaver traps, a gun, powder and lead) from the trading company and worked for meager pay, or they supplied their own outfits and sold the pelts to company agents at rendezvous time for a previously set price. Some "freelance" trappers sold pelts to agents for current market prices. Trappers could make up to $1,000 yearly, prize wages in the early 1800's, even for "hazardous duty". But they gambled and drank the entire year's profit during the annual rendezvous spree and returned, on company credit, for another year's trapping after that bawdy event.

Ruxton relates the story of an old French Canadian trapper who made an eye-popping $15,000 during a 20-year beaver trapping career. Every year he planned to return to Canada to retire, with a year's profit providing ample cash to "purchase and stock a farm and enjoy himself in ease and comfort the remainder of his days". However, after the final rendezvous, the old trapper "had not even credit sufficient to buy a pound of powder".

While trapping proved lucrative during the peak years of beaver pelt demand,

Author George Frederick Ruxton, who camped nearby in 1847-48, told chilling tales of mountaineers scalped by Indians, mauled by grizzlies and trapped by forest fires.

it also proved tough work for the beaver man. Indians ambushed and plundered the trappers, taking their flowing hair as trophy. "One of our fellow travelers," reported Wislizenus in 1839, "who had gone to the mountains for the first time nine years ago with about 100 men, estimates that by this time half the number had fallen victim to the tomahawks of the Indians." Mauling attack by bears, the surprise of a screaming mountain cougar on his back, the dangerous melee of the buffalo hunt, the spectre of freezing or starving during a surprise high country storm all endangered the trapper.

Ruxton told of a mountain man horribly mutilated by an enraged bear. A companion shot the bear, but left the bleeding victim, far more dead than alive, to his fate. The wounded man, with half his face taken off and gouges from arms, back and legs, not only managed to stay alive but survived a winter with no real shelter or provisions. He lived to confront his fair weather friend many months later.

The trappers wore buckskin, though they preferred woolen pants and shirts. Wool was warmer, even when wet, but it shredded after a few month's hard use. Buckskin proved durable and available — a trapper could buy his dressed, fringed buckskin shirt, porcupine-quill decorated pantaloons and a pair of moccasins from Indian squaws. Buckskin had its drawbacks: It stretched till saggy when wet and shrank in drying. When dry, it hardened to a stiff, abrasive hide that chafed the skin. Because buckskin failed to provide adequate warmth, the trapper's heavy sleeping blanket often doubled as a makeshift overcoat.

Getting wet (and cold) provided a constant challenge to the trapper because he worked in the icy beaver pond to set his traps. He set the traps, baited with castoreum, four inches below the water surface. In this shallow water an adult beaver could drag a five pound trap to shore and release himself by chewing off his own foot. So the trapper planted a stake in deep water and chained the trap to this stake. The panicky beaver would dive into deep water when trapped. Then the trap's weight would drag him below to drown. When the trapper discovered a beaver lodge, he set his trap at the edge of the dam, where the animal passes from deep to shoal water.

The hunter set his traps at dusk. He returned at dawn to retrieve his catch. The trapper skinned the animals immediately, then packed the skins to camp where they were stretched over a hoop of osier or willow for two to three days to dry. Scraping the skin followed; then the trapper stamped skins with a trader's mark, folded them square and tied then in 10 to 20-skin bundles. Periodic airing and shaking kept the pelts marketable till rendezvous time.

(If the trapper had a squaw, all this work would fall on her shoulders. The trapper would relax, smoke his pipe and survey her labors.)

Mountain men carried little gear not absolutely essential to survival. George Ruxton described this gear in *Ruxton of the Rockies*:

> Over his left shoulder and under his right arm hangs his powder horn and bullet pouch in which he carries his balls, flint and steel and odds and ends of all kinds. Round the waist is a belt, in which is stuck a large butcher knife in a sheath of buffalo hide, made fast to the belt by a chain or guard of steel, which also supports a little buckskin case containing a whetstone.

The trapper's skinning and butchering knife, also used as a weapon, often came from a Green River, Massachusetts craftsman who stamped "G.R." on the blade just below the handle. The trapper's expression "up to Green River" meant he had plunged the blade to the hilt, or, in a more general sense, "to go all the way".

A "possibles" sack hung round the trapper's neck. Pipe and tobacco, "medicine" for baiting beaver traps (oil from the animal's sex glands), spare parts for rifle lockwork and perhaps a Jew's harp bulged in this pouch. Some huntsmen wore a special pipe bag. This bag, often heart-shaped and "garnished with beads and porcupine quills", was "a triumph of workmanship by a squaw wife". The mountain man stretched his meager supply of tobacco by smoking only at night. Even then, he often had to mix a dwindling supply of pipe tobacco with the ground inner bark of the red willow.

A long heavy rifle (St. Louis' Hawken rifles were the finest) and a tomahawk, provided protection and fresh meat.

Pack animals (usually mules because Indians loved to steal horses) lugged a bag crammed with beaver traps plus sacks of flour and salt, a kettle, and trade goods for the Indians. The animals also toted the bundles of dried, dressed beaver skins and the trapper's buffalo robe "mattress".

Picky eaters couldn't survive the rugged West. Mountain men supped on gourmet puppy stew with friendly Indian tribes, sampled rattlesnake in the Southwest, learned to love broiled beaver tail in the high country. ("Tender as a young raccoon" raved Ruxton about an old gray-headed beaver whose tail once provided a dainty entree.) In general, the trapper ate meat, the only fresh and available fare, sometimes eight pounds in a single day.

Lonely trappers sought wives in the West, either pretty Mexican girls to return to each winter at Taos, or the less alluring Indian squaw. Trappers treated their Indian wives as badly as the Indian braves did. In his book, *A Journey to the Rocky Mountains*, Wislizenus writes:

> He (Fleming, a trapper) had a squaw with him, one of the tribe of the Eutaws (Utes), whom he had bought at one time for $500, but was disposed to sell for half the purchase price. She was a little, unshapen bundle of fat, but (he) recommended her: "She is young, gentle, easy and in first rate order."

Wislizenus said: "The trappers seem, unfortunately, to have adopted from the Indians the habit of looking on their Indian wives as chattels, not persons, and the squaws themselves seem to desire no other position."

Today's mountain dwellers joke that the only thing higher than the altitude is the cost of living. But the trapper, too, winced at mountain prices. One pound of beaver skins usually purchased $4 worth of goods at trading post or rendezvous. But prices were high. Grain meal cost $1 a pint; coffee, beans, cocoa beans and sugar, $2 a pint; a diluted alcohol (the only available spirits) $4 a pint. A hunk of common tobacco cost $2. These prices shocked people in the 1830's, when five cents bought a basket of vegetables.

Summer finally came to the high country and beaver fur grew too thin to entice the trapper. Rendezvous time had arrived! With a whoop and a holler, frisky trappers set off to the rendezvous site. The revelers, only too glad to pay inflated prices, wallowed in the delights of flour, sugar and coffee after an all-meat diet. Carousing trappers forgot their hardships in the glow of bad whiskey. Wislizenus reported:

> With their hairy bank notes, the beaver skins, they can obtain all the luxuries of the mountains and live for a few days like lords. Coffee and chocolate is cooked; the pipe is kept aglow day and night; the spirits circulate; and whatever is not spent in such ways the squaws coax out of them; or else it is squandered at cards. Formerly single trappers on such occasions have often wasted a thousand dollars.

LaBonte's Hole, an old rendezvous site here in Summit County, drew 1800's mapmakers to note the site on early maps, according to Douglas S. Walters' "Historic Sites in Summit County". Located at the confluence of the Snake, Ten Mile and Blue Rivers (the site of early Dillon), LaBonte's Hole supposedly took the name of a trapper named LaBonte who was reportedly killed about 1838-40. Hundreds of trappers and Indians gathered for the annual blow-out. Scenic LaBonte's Hole, where today's Dillon Reservoir is located, would have provided the perfect scene for the summer frolic.

General William Ashley concocted the idea of the rendezvous as a mild-mannered business affair designed to exchange merchandise and barter for beaver pelts. The general's eyeballs might have popped had he witnessed the hair-rising event his idea spawned.

Tall tales, wrestling, horse racing and drinking rotgut whiskey made for high hilarity. But gambling, with beaver skins as currency, became the number one sport. The cry of "There goes hos and beaver" cut the air as another drunken gamester lost his year's profit to euchre, poker or seven-up. Mules, rifles, shirts, breeches and wives were recklessly staked when trappers lost all else. "Daring gamblers make the round of the camp," Ruxton wrote, "challenging each other to play for the trapper's highest stake — his horse, his squaw (if he had one) and, as once happened, his scalp."

"Bloody duels" erupted from these gambling sprees. ". . . over their cups and cards no men are more quarrelsome than your mountaineers," Ruxton advised.

Tales of famous trappers punctuate the history of the West. Men like Jedediah Strong Smith, Thomas Fitzpatrick, Jim Bridger and Kit Carson used their mountain expertise in later service as guides for explorers, mapmakers and railroad builders.

These heroic figures often failed to fit the image-maker's mold. They, and the trappers who came to the Blue Valley, a prime beaver area, failed to fit our romantic image of the mountain men. "Savage" is the adjective Ruxton chose to describe most beaver men. "The trappers of the Rocky Mountains belong to a 'genus' more approximating to the primitive savage than perhaps any other class of civilized men," he stated. ". . . they . . . destroy human as well as animal life with as little scruple and as freely as they expose their own." Ruxton sums up the trappers' characteristics as ". . . revengeful, bloodthirsty, drunkards and gamblers". But this devotee of Kit Carson claimed that exceptions existed. ". . . I *have* met honest mountain men", he affirms.

Kit Carson, short in stature, but long on daring, was one of these. Of Carson who looked mild, but was "an incarnate devil in an Indian fight," Ruxton wrote:

> Last in height, but first in every quality that constitutes excellence in a mountaineer, whether of indomitable courage or perfect indifference to death or danger — with an iron frame capable of withstanding hunger, thirst, heat, cold, fatigue and hardships of every kind — (with) wonderful presence of mind, and endless resource in time of peril — with the instinct of an animal and the moral courage of a man — who was "taller" for his inches than Kit Carson, paragon of pioneers.

The beaver men shared a secret: Colorado gold. Traveler Rufus Sage witnessed the Arapahoes battle enemies with golden bullets bursting forth from their rifles. James Purcell told Zebulon Pike at Santa Fe in 1807 his tales of finding gold at the headwaters of the Platte. But the beaver men feared an influx of gold-hungry prospectors trampling their tranquil beaver haunts. They sealed a pact of silence.

The Utes:
Dwellers of the Turquoise Sky

In 4,800 B.C., almost 6,800 years ago, a proud caravan of nomad mountain Indians, the free-roaming Utes, scaled Vail Pass from the west. Open meadows at the summit provided the Indians with a rich hunting ground. They set up their hunting camp at the top, built fires and chipped out stone weapon points for an upcoming game hunt.

The dark-skinned Utes, short, stocky and muscular hunters, would later descend the Pass into Summit's Ten Mile Canyon enroute to the favorite camping spots in the Blue River Valley, a gentle land they called "Nah-oon-kara". From there, an age-old trail led over Hoosier Pass toward South Park and its vast buffalo herds. The Utes roamed all over Summit County, which formerly encompassed a huge area, stretching all the way to the present Utah border.

"The Black Indians" were expert horsemen, fierce enemies, loyal allies. Age-old dwellers, Indians camped on Summit's Snake River 10,000 years ago.

17

Centuries later, in the year 1881, another caravan of Utes plodded dejectedly west toward the Colorado-Utah border, urged forward by United States militia. The Indians had inhabited their high country homeland for at least 10,000 years, according to documented recent archeological discoveries. Incredible, but true, the friendly Utes were driven out by gold-seeking white prospectors within about 20 years of their 1859 gold rush arrival in the Indians' ancestral homeland. The White River Utes, who inhabited our Blue River Valley, departed their Colorado home forever in September, 1881, for final encampment in Utah's Uintah Indian Reservation.

Perhaps they whispered a last good-bye to Nah-oon-kara, translated roughly as "where the river of blue rises". There nature had provided for the Utes in abundance. In what is now Summit County, elk, antelope, mountain sheep, deer, beaver, bear, rabbit, squirrel, grouse abounded. Trout crowded swift mountain streams.

The Indians found more than small game and fish here. Buffalo, the mainstay of Indian life, roamed Summit County in large herds. ("The country was literally alive with buffalo," U.S. Army Corps of Topographical Engineers explorer Colonel John Fremont reported in his diary while passing through the Blue Valley in 1843.) But nearby South Park hosted even greater herds of the much-used beast. (The presence of salt marshes in South Park, deposited by an ancient inland sea, plus the proliferation of buffalo grasses in cold months when plains grasses withered or rotted, made South Park a buffalo habitat.)

Nature also shared her bounteous garden with the wandering Utes. Mountainsides blossomed forth wild raspberries, strawberries, gooseberries, currants and rose hips, which the Utes combined with dried powdered meat for the winter's supply of pemmican.

Scientists Carbon-date Ute Campsites

Until recently, little was known of Ute history in Summit County. But the Indians left an archeological record at their Vail Pass campsite and I-70 highway archeological advance crews unearthed it. Utes hunted elk, deer and antelope at the summit for thousands of years before the time of Christ. Their hearth fires, layered one atop another over centuries, provided evidence for today's scientists. (Radio carbon tests on these hearth's charcoal in 1975 proved the ancient beginnings of the continuously-used 10,580-foot Vail Pass camp, highest known site of Indian activity in Colorado.) Also uncovered at the stratified Indian campsite were bone fragments of elk, deer and bison, arrowheads, Indian ceramics and tool fragments. A test excavation produced fragmented wood scrapers, knives, hammerstones and choppers.

Archeologist John Gooding, who supervised the Vail Pass dig for the Colorado Department of Highways, speculated in a local newspaper that Indian hunting bands traveled to Vail Pass, killed and dressed an abundance of game and returned home with their meat. Bone fragments from big game animals remained in great number. Indians broke down animal bones to remove the nutritious bone marrow, Gooding said. They left the fragments over the one-quarter mile camp area now the site of an Interstate 70 highway rest area. The archeological site, protected by rest area construction, may soon display signs to inform travelers of the Stone Age history of the campsite, used regularly from about 4,800 B.C. till about 1760 A.D.

Colorado Ute huntsmen hailed from the heritage of a proud Shoshone nation which spread widely over the Rocky Mountain region from Canada to Mexico. As a branch of the big Shoshone family, their language resembled that of Shoshone-speaking Indians of Arizona and California. The Utes had some very cultured Shoshone cousins, the Aztecs, who rose to heights of civilization never attained by the struggling Utes. While the Aztecs drew from the rich cultural milieu of the South and organized a stable agricultural society, the isolated Utes wandered the mountains seeking food. Their early life was a constant battle to survive. Thus, they remained in a semi-savage state, failing to develop the intellectual acumen of their Aztec brothers.

Because they never farmed, the Utes became nomads of necessity. In the early years, before the Indians acquired horses, the Utes tribal organization centered on the family group. Each family maintained a known circuit of travel, covering its own berry patches, hunting grounds and trout streams, gathering edible roots and seeds, corn, piñon nuts, wild potatoes and grass seeds wherever available. Each family needed a large area in which to forage for an often-scarce food supply. The rare times when families united with their tribe came in autumn for the annual hunt and in spring for the ritual of the Bear Dance. If danger or war threatened at other times, Indian leaders could easily round up other migrating families on their habitual routes to form an attack group.

The Utes wandered across northeast Utah, northwest New Mexico and northeast Arizona. When winter winds swept with icy vengeance down from Boreas Pass to chill the Blue River Valley, Summit County Utes took down their tipi poles, lashed them to their horses (or their squaws before the Spaniards introduced the Indians to the horse), and traveled to warmer climes. While some Ute groups traveled south, the hardy White River Utes of our area wintered along the White, Colorado and Wyoming's Green Rivers.

The early Utes wandered with large family groups. Those were the primitive Ute nomads that camped here thousands of years ago.

An archeological site typical of this primitive era was recently discovered in Summit County, east of Keystone. Littered with wood and stone relics of food preparation, habitation and tool manufacture, the site had hearths that carbondated to 8,000, even 10,000 years old!

By the time the gold rush influx arrived, the Ute lifestyle had changed. When the Spaniards brought horses to Ute territory, the Indian began to band together for big group hunts on horseback. Gradually, the Ute nation united. Tribes gathered into confederations.

Eighteen-fifty-nine gold seekers found three Ute confederations in Colorado: the Southern Utes, led by Ignacio; the Uncompahgre Utes, led by Ouray; and the Northern or White River Utes, who roamed the Blue River Valley, led by Nevava. Seven major bands had united into these three groups, numbering about 1,000 families, according to an early observer, 1839 explorer Thomas Farnham. The migrant tribe never exceeded more than 10,000, Ute historian Wilson Rockwell has stated.

Utes Welcome Gold Seekers

The single most outstanding (and astounding) Ute characteristic important to historians was the Ute's warm friendliness to whites. To prepare for their first Summit winter, panicky prospectors at Breckenridge hastily threw up a log stockade, Fort Meribeh (also called Fort Mary B., Fort Mary Bigelow) to protect their tiny colony from Indian attack. But the placid Utes failed to provide the expected threat. No milk toast tribe, the Utes made vicious enemies. But, for some curious reason, they accepted whites as their friends.

Jesuit missionary Jean Pierre de Smet in 1841 encountered the "Utaws", whom he estimated to number about 4,000: "Mildness, affability, simplicity of manners, hospitality toward strangers, constant union among themselves, form the happy traits in their character," Father de Smet wrote.

Pioneer Breckenridge prospector William A. Smith wrote on June 9, 1860 to the *Rocky Mountain News*: "Some five or six hundred Utah Indians visited us a few days ago; they manifested no ill will toward the whites, but passed off towards Tarryall very quietly and friendly."

"Ute Indians were very neighborly . . . a good deal higher grade of Indian than I had supposed," wrote nationally-known journalist Samuel Bowles of his Summit County sojourn in his 1869 book, *Colorado: Its Parks and Mountains.*

Bowles contemporary, William H. Brewer, who visited Summit County and wrote an 1869 book entitled *Rocky Mountain Letters,* spoke of the Indians: "They are the Utes, long perfectly peaceful towards the whites, but of course, enemies of rival tribes of Indians. They are very intelligent, and their friendship has been greatly to their advantage in many ways." (When the whites drove away the Plains Indians, bitter enemies of the Utes, they allowed the mountain Indians to emerge from the mountains onto this formerly taboo terrain.)

Bayard Taylor, noted writer and lecturer, traveled to Breckenridge in 1866. While on the Blue River trail he looked up aghast to notice a traveling companion riding towards him across a meadow chaperoned by a fiercely-painted Indian on each side. But Taylor breathed a sigh of relief: "As they were Utes, there was no trouble to be feared, and we supposed they were guiding him toward Breckenridge."

Early writers who visited Summit County almost all affirmed the friendliness of the Utes. Only one, Henry Villard, charged the Indians with savagery. Villard wrote: "They are a bloodthirsty tribe. They steal and murder whenever they can do so with impunity. During the winter, several hundred of them were, however, reported to have camped for weeks in the Blue River diggings without giving the miners any trouble."

So, early reports describe the Utes as downright docile in their acceptance of the white miner. (There were a few bloody reprisals against whites in later years, however.) They maintained friendly ties with a few Indian tribes too. The Utes opened warm arms to the Snakes, Shoshone, Bannocks and Piutes of the West. And, of course, their neighbors and friends, the Jicarilla Apaches roamed Ute territory at will. Linked by centuries of intermarriage, the Utes mingled freely with this southern Apache tribe. But the Utes had a long black list of enemies.

Plains Indians: Bitter Enemies

While they generally claimed the mountain areas of Colorado and ranked as the state's oldest residents, the Utes had to share Colorado with the Arapahoes and Cheyennes, Plains Indians who lived east of the Continental Divide. The Plains Indians, of Algonquin stock and driven west over the years from New England by enemy tribes who took over their territory, were relative newcomers. The Utes stood as deadly enemies of these East Slope residents and waged ferocious war against them during their frequent invasions of Ute territory. When the Plains Indians ventured into the mountains during the hot summer months to hunt the buffalo that had retreated to cool upland parks, terrible battles ensued. The Cheyenne and Arapahoe came only on business — to hunt, to divest the Utes of their scalps or to steal ponies — and they usually wound up "getting the business", for the Utes lost few battles.

Colonel John C. Fremont, "The Pathfinder", whose 1843 expedition camped north of today's Silverthorne, wrote:

> We saw today the returning trail of an Arapahoe party which had been sent forth from the village to look for Utahs in the Bayou Salade (South Park): and it being probable that they would visit our camp with the desire to return on horseback, we were more than usually on the alert.

Several days later the Arapahoe found the Utes in South Park. Fremont witnessed their clash.

Ute inhospitality took on a fiendish note. Though the Cheyenne, Arapahoe and Apaches gained fame for their savagery, they failed to match the devilish Utes. Journalist Horace Greeley observed in 1859:

> The Utes . . . are stronger and braver than any one of the three tribes . . . though hardly a match for them all, are at war with them. The Arapahoe Chief, Left Hand, assures me that his people were always at war with the Utes; at least he has no recollection, no tradition, of a time when they were at peace.

Journalist Samuel Bowles also wrote about the lack of cordiality between the Utes and the Plains Indians. "Though the Utes are quite peaceful and even long suffering towards the whites, they bear eternal emnity to the Indian tribes of the Plains and are always ready to have a fight with them."

After all, the Cheyennes and Arapahoes ranked as latecomers to Colorado and as such deserved a poison-arrow snub from the centuries-old resident Utes. These "squatters" acquired their Plains land after years of scrapping over territory with the Kiowas. An 1840 Indian treaty granted the Cheyenne and Arapahoe an 80,000 square mile region north of the Arkansas River and east of the mountains. Ample room to roam for the 5,000 Cheyenne-Arapahoe population.

Other lowland Indians penetrated the mountains to hunt — the Kiowas, Comanches, Sioux and Pawnees — and the Utes regarded these tribes with equal animosity.

21

Guilt over their ungracious treatment of Plains enemies never haunted the spitfire Utes. They felt righteous about their hostile behavior, because enemies played a vital role in Indian culture. A young Ute brave could not marry, sit in council or feast until he had proven his mettle by touching or killing an enemy in battle.

The isolated Utes probably even looked a bit diabolic to their flatlands neighbors. Called "the Black Indians" by other tribes, they were surprisingly dark-skinned. Short, hardy and muscular, Ute braves proved strong and agile in both battle and the hunt. The Utes adapted over centuries to punishing high country winters in drafty tipis. They *had* to be strong. But Samuel Bowles reported in 1869 that the Utes he met in Summit County failed to measure up to this strapping image; in fact, to him the short-in-stature Utes appeared sickly:

> They look frailer and feebler than you would expect; I did not see a single Indian who was six feet high or would weigh over one hundred and seventy-five pounds; they are all, indeed, under size and no match in nervous or physical force for the average white man.

Indian Downfall: White Man's White Sugar

Bowles also lamented the fact that the Utes "gobbled up" the white man's sugar and were using patent medicines: "To make matters worse, they have got hold of our quack medicines and are great customers for Brandreth and other pills, with the vain hope of curing their maladies." Bowles commented that "Coughs are frequent and dyspopsia; sickness and deaths are quite common among the children." Bowles blamed the white man's food and medicine for "sapping their vitality at its fountains".

Before the white man came with white flour, white sugar and firewater, the Utes ate earth food — meat, wild vegetables, including corn and potatoes, berries, roots and seeds. Dried berries and fruits, crushed fine and mixed with hot melted buffalo fat, bone marrow and pounded dried meat, made a rich and nutritious pemmican. The mixture was poured into a skin bag or container — a light weight and portable "complete meal".

Colorful dress marked the typical Ute. The Ute warrior never cut his hair, which hung in long braids over his thick-set shoulders. He wore no headgear, except his feathered headdress for dancing. He painted his smooth cheeks (Utes were beardless) vivid yellow and black for battle. Men's clothing consisted of a shirt or robe and leggings and breech-cloth made of dressed skins (deer, antelope, mountain sheep or buffalo). The garments were stitched with thread made from buffalo sinew, a substance strong as catgut. Fringe, paint, elk teeth and embroidery added lively accents to the Ute brave's clothing until the white man's bright beads were introduced. Then the Ute squaws became skillful at creating intricate beadwork designs.

Young unmarried Ute women dressed in fresh, clean, belted leather gowns with row upon row of elk teeth at yoke and sleeve. Leggings, moccasins and a basket cap completed the maiden costume. The older women wore greasy, dirty leather dresses and cared poorly for their personal grooming. But the old squaw's disheveled appearance comes as no surprise. She was a workhorse, toiling at heavy labor from dawn to dark, gathering food, cooking, hauling water and firewood.

Indian finery displayed bright color and intriguing accessories. An Indian gathering in Denver boggled the young mind of William Brewer in 1868. He wrote home about a 1,000-strong Indian fete, "the most picturesque crowd by far I have ever seen. A Tyrolese fair, even, cannot compare with it . . ."

> Swarms were out decked in their very best, from the infant, whose only costume would be a pair of earrings and a few strings of beads, to the brave warrior, with painted face, seemingly burdened with his trappings, his buckskin leggings, his moccasins covered with beads, his feathers, bright colors, earrings — in fact everything that could ornament them.

> Belles in all the glory of embroidery, gay colors, beads, feathers, jewelry (such as it is) laid on with a profusion equal to that of their more civilized sisters, perhaps less tasty, but certainly more picturesque by far, and it seemed so in keeping with these nomadic savages.

Utensils for daily living came from the world around. The Utes fashioned vessels and containers from the paunch or intestines of animals. They carved bowls and platters from wood. Animal horns provided spoons. Squaws sewed bags from buckskin.

Utes depended on the buffalo for a myriad of sundries. Tipi covers were buffalo hide, blankets were buffalo fur. The bowstring and sinew thread came from the buffalo as did horn glue and large skin storage bags. Moccasins also could be crafted from buffalo skin. And buffalo meat, especially the tender hump, provided a vital food source.

Long centuries of nomad search for food, before Ute hunters owned horses, kept the mountain Indians from developing any noteworthy expertise in crafts. Ute bead work in later years ranked with that of cultured tribes. And Ute basketry was good. But Ute squaws never mastered the art of pottery.

Squaws Sole Indulgence: White Man's Beads

Beads had to be bought from the white man. Brewer reported on these transactions: "In the stores they were eager purchasers, but very sharp in their bargains, except where beads were bought — for these they had a weakness, and paid the best prices in skins." He watched a Ute husband purchase beads for his wife. "An hour later, I saw her sitting on the sidewalk, dangling the treasures in her hands and contemplating them with looks of happy satisfaction."

A wandering Ute lifestyle demanded a handy mobile home and the conical tipi was just the thing — easily erected and disassembled. Both Utes and Plains Indians used the lodgepole pine (named for its tipi use), available only at 8,000-10,000 feet above sea level. The Utes chose 20-foot poles, usually about two and one-half inches in diameter. To erect the tipi, the poles were tied together about two or three feet from the top, forming a triangular base. Then 16-18 additional poles, set in a circle, provided stability and shape. The Ute squaw covered this pole framework with buffalo skins which she had tanned and sewn together. A flap at the top allowed smoke to escape; another at the bottom provided a door.

The squaw carried all of the bedding, buffalo robes and other family belongings into the newly-constructed tipi and piled them around the sides. Then she dug a small pit in the center of the earth floor to build her fire. (The squaw erected the tipi and labored to make it comfortable with no help from her Ute warrior husband.)

When the Utes traveled, the squaw took down the tipi, bundled up the buffalo skins and fastened the skins to the two collections of poles tied to either flank of the horse. Babies and small children rode atop this cushioned litter as the caravan moved along steep, rock-strewn mountain trails.

The Utes, and the Plains Indians, who also traveled in this manner, faced a continual annoyance: Their tipi poles, constantly dragged along the trail, soon wore down. The Plains Indians had to replace these lodgepoles in the mountains — and that usually meant a hair-raising encounter with the Utes.

Brewer wrote about the pageantry of Ute travel:

> They must carry their lodgepoles with them, small poles, sometimes a dozen or more tied to a horse, one end securely fastened about the pack-saddle, the other trailing behind on the ground, while on top of the load would be a child, clinging on like a monkey. They seem to be born on horseback, grow there, and almost to become a part of the animal.

Early Ute saddles consisted of a simple skin bag stuffed with grass and peaked high in front and back with elk horn prongs. But most Ute braves disdained the saddle, rode bareback, especially during the hunt or battle. The Indian rider used a rope of twisted horse or buffalo hair tied around the horse's jaw as reins.

Ute Arrow: Swift, Silent, Lethal

The bow and arrow, silent and deadly, allowed the Ute to outshoot the white man's revolver in speed and effectiveness. At 40-70 feet, the bow's surest range, the Ute made a fearful enemy.

Painstakingly constructed of juniper or hickory (or sometimes straight lengths of horn, spliced and glued), the sinew-wrapped bow measured three to five feet in length. Twisted sinew provided a bowstring. Arrows were crafted from shoots of cherry, currant or tough willow, peeled, straightened and dried. The Ute brave meticulously split and trimmed turkey or buzzard feathers, then glued the feathers to his arrow. (An arrow's sure flight depended on these feathers.) Arrow tips, first made of jasper, stone flint or bone, became metal after the white man arrived. Barrel hoops provided a good source for arrow tip metal.

The Ute arrow had to be sure, especially for the dangerous buffalo hunt. Buffalo bulls could measure six feet high and weigh a ton. A wounded buffalo was a menace.

Narrow mountain valleys functioned as a natural trap for the antelope hunt. The Indians drove an antelope herd into a pen at the termination of a V-shaped valley. Samuel Bowles reported that the Utes he met in Summit County had recently snared 4,000 antelopes during their annual three-week hunt, probably using the V-shaped trap. They built similar V-shaped artificial traps, chutes to trap buffalo, also. Often, the Utes killed large numbers of buffalo by driving them over a cliff at the point of the V-shaped trap.

After the hunt, victorious braves rested while the squaws scrambled to skin and dress the animals, and dry strips of meat for jerky.

Game Slaughter Angers Utes

For the Ute, hunting proved vital both to raw survival and also to the brave's cultural role. But white prospectors, boring into gold-rich hillsides and platting towns in green valleys, killed off and drove away Ute game. "They live on the game they can find in the parks and among the mountains," Bowles wrote in 1869. "It is altogether even a precarious and hard reliance; the game is fast disappearing — save of trout we have not seen enough in all our travels among the mountains to feed our small party . . . "

But Bowles reported the local trout fishing as first-rate! "The river before us offered good fishing, but better was to be found in Williams Fork, a smaller stream a few miles below, where half a day's sport brought back from 40-60 pounds of as fine speckled trout as ever came from brooks or lakes of New England."

The buffalo was the Indian's mainstay. As the buffalo disappeared, the Ute way of life began to crumble. White buffalo harvesters, who killed the huge beasts for $2-$3 per hide, and left the carcasses to rot, managed to reduce the millions-strong buffalo herds to near-extinction.

Huge wagonloads of game and birds were hauled to the feverish mine camps where miners busy digging gold could buy needed meat. In Kokomo, the newspaper reported in 1879: "Three wagonloads of elk came in from Green Mountain yesterday and were offered for sale at five and ten cents a pound." One account casually mentioned a catch of "2,500 trout in a few hours". And a group on Trout Creek "amused themselves with fishing for a time with extraordinary success. They caught about 200 pounds."

And, of course, the ignoble nobleman Lord Gore, with his arsenal of hunting weapons and entourage of servants, managed to decimate thousands of Colorado game animals during his 1855 safari.

This slaughter made the Utes angry. The Indians willingly shared their land, but wild game massacre made Ute blood boil.

The Utes retaliated against plundering whites by setting spite fires, conflagrations which have changed the Summit County landscape as well as other nearby mountain terrain. (The Vail Ski Area would never boast its magnificent back bowls were it not for Ute spite fires destroying thick forest cover there.) Noted author Bayard Taylor, during his 1866 lecture tour encountered the desolation of a Blue Valley ravaged by fire:

> Being now but four miles from Breckenridge, we spurred our weary animals forward, taking a trail which led for a long distance through a burned forest. It was scenery of the most hideous character. Tens of thousands of charred black poles, striped with white where the bark had sprung off, made a wilderness of desolation which was worse than a desert. The boughs had been almost entirely consumed; the sunshine and the blue of the sky were split into a myriad of parallel slices, which fatigues and distracted the eye, until one almost became giddy in riding through. I cannot recall any phase of mundane scenery so disagreeable as this.

Sometimes Ute fires devoured miles of verdant forest land, creating a roaring ocean of engulfing flame. George Ruxton, early 1800's explorer, experienced the horror of such a conflagration in South Park:

> When I awoke the sun had already set; but although darkness was fast gathering over the mountain, I was surprised to see a bright light flickering against its sides. A glance assured me that the mountain was on fire and starting up, I saw at once the danger of my position . . . a mass of flame shot up into the sky and rolled fiercely up the stream, the belt of dry brush on its banks catching fire and burning like tinder. The mountain was already invaded by the devouring element, and two wings of flame spread out from the main stream which roaring along the bottom with the speed of a racehorse, licked the mountainside, extending its long line as it advanced . . . The fire had extended at least three miles on each side of the stream, and the mountain was one sheet of flame.

Hard-working squaws and a plentiful supply of narrow Lodgepole pine tipi stakes provided the wandering Ute with snug portable home. Squaws dug hearth inside.

Ruxton knew whom to blame. "I had from the first no doubt but that the fire was caused by the Indians . . . hoping to secure the horses and mules in the confusion, without the risk of attacking the camp."

Common practice among Ute raiding parties, departing an enemy camp in haste with a band of stolen horses, was to set a timber fire to cover their retreat. In 1874, for example, the Utes crept into a 1,500-strong camp of a Sioux and Cheyenne hunting party, stampeded their horses and escaped with 200 fine ponies. A fire would certainly be a useful deterrent to what could prove a blood-thirsty pursuit by angry Sioux and Cheyenne.

U.S. politicians named loyal Ouray Ute Chief in 1873, though Ute tradition excluded tribal chiefs. Wife Chipeta poses with Ouray here, while babies cry.

The Dating Game

But, then, all's fair in love and war. And if the Utes failed to act fairly in war, they did only slightly better in love and marriage. Though polygamous in early centuries, the 1800's Utes married for life at age 18 for men and 14-16 for maidens.

The Ute miss knew something was afoot when a painted and feather-bedecked young warrior, his best clothes laden with beads and ornaments, arrived at the family tipi. He ignored the maiden, even to the point of not answering when she spoke, but carried on a lively conversation with everyone else. If the young man believed his suit favorable, he killed a deer and brought it to the girl's home, hanging the animal on a tree branch. Again, he visited, with

27

the same "cold shoulder" to the maiden. If she went out to water and feed his horse, take down the deer, care for the meat and cook some to share with him, he knew that he had snared a squaw. (And she knew she'd won a lifetime's hard work.) The decision belonged to the maiden. Her parents could encourage or discourage, but that was all.

The pair moved in with the bride's family until the number of their offspring rendered tipi life a bit chaotic. Then the couple built their own tipi.

Promises and "Pokantee"

The Utes cherished children, never cuffed or slapped them. A gentle people, they offered free-handed hospitality to all, including strangers. Even an enemy could not go hungry in the Ute camp. The Indians allowed no feasting in one house and starving in another. Possessed with great fortitude as a tribe, the Utes held strong to the virtue of loyalty. A Ute never broke his word.

If a promise was broken, especially the medicine man's promise to heal, the consequences proved harsh. For "malpractice", the medicine man paid with his life. When a man established himself as a healer, the Utes gave him implicit trust. They parted with fine horses and many blankets to reward his services. In return, the medicine man offered his "pokantee", a magic procured from dead Utes who visited him at night from the Happy Hunting Grounds. (The healer himself visited Indian heaven during trances.) Eagles, bears, various birds and animals also shared their magic secrets with the medicine man. Amulets and charms based on their power, along with the use of root and herb remedies numbered among his prescriptions. A bath in one of the mountains' many hot springs (such as Hot Sulphur Springs, now part of Grand County), followed by an icy plunge into the snow was another "cure".

The medicine man's position in tribal life was prestigious, but tricky. Not only did he have to cure his patients, he had to read correctly the omens that would portend a victory in battle.

A mystical people, the Utes performed sacred dances to celebrate spiritual events. These rituals included the Dog Dance, performed by men only as a war dance, and the Tea Dance, for both men and women, featuring incantations for health. The Lame Dance dramatized the action of squaws who participated in looting after a battle. Hauling their heavy load of war bounty, they mimed gathering the spoils of victory.

Brewer watched a Scalp Dance near Denver in 1868. Thirty to forty warriors in a close line, shoulders touching, wailed a bizarre chant to the beat of a drum . . . "keeping such perfect time on the drums that for a time I thought there was but one."

> Facing them were the squaws, sometimes in one row, sometimes in two, dressed in their gayest dresses, red, trimmed with beads, silver — everything that could possibly adorn. One or more of them carried a warrior's shield and another a pole with the precious scalp . . . The long hair of the big scalp was waving in the night air, like a black banner. Indian dogs barked. Old Indians looked on, and I suppose, talked of other days, while over all, the bright moon shone, until I could hardly believe I was in a civilized land.

The entire confederation gathered each March for the Utes' biggest, the Bear Dance, an elaborate festival that celebrated Spring. Sacred dancing helped the sleeping bear emerge from his cave, protected dancers from dangerous bears, provided food for living bears and spirit bears in the Happy Hunting Grounds as well. Four days of dancing preceded a great feast. The Utes timed their weddings, parties and other social functions with the festival to add to the spree.

Ritual Torture: The Sun Dance

The time of the full moon in June signalled celebration of the Sun Dance, a sacrificial ceremony to ward off evil. The full moon cured ailments, according to Ute tradition. Secret rites during the one-to-four day ritual included fasting and torture. Example: Skewers driven under the skin of a Ute man's back attached him to a buffalo skin which he dragged about in ascetic exercise.

The Sun Dance's public performance took place in the Utes' special Sun Dance Lodge. Singing and music on wooden flutes, plus willow and skin drums provided accompaniment.

The sun played a vital role in Ute religious belief. According to Sidney Jocknick's *Early Days on the Western Slope of Colorado*, "All good Indians go to the sun when they die. There they behold the Great Spirit who lives in the sun."

Subordinate to the Great Spirit and representing his power on earth were gods of War, Peace, Blood (who heals the sick), Thunder, Lightning and Flood, Jocknick states.

". . . the Great Spirit breathes out his love for all the Indians whom he desires should become mighty hunters and brave warriors." No Ute feared death because all Indians, good or bad, entered the Happy Hunting Grounds. There all men were strong, all women beautiful and no sickness dwelt. Life in this happy land was an endless round of hunting, feasting, dancing and merrymaking. "Merrymaking" might include gambling, a fond Ute pastime.

("Happy Hunting Grounds," like "medicine man", is an American expression, not an authentic translation of the Indian word in any way.)

Horses must accompany the Ute warrior to his eternal reward. They were killed and buried with him in a cliff cave. Father Pierre de Smet in 1841 witnessed the cremation of a Ute chief with his horses. "The moment that the smoke rises in thick clouds," he wrote, "they think that the soul of the savage is flying toward the region of spirits, borne by the manes of his powerful coursers."

After Nevava died around 1870, the Northern Utes who camped in Summit County never paid allegiance to another strongman. (Again, the word "chief" is our expression, the Indians didn't need authorities.) While lesser Ute leaders gained and lost repute or regional power — Antelope, Douglas, Jack, Colorow, Johnson, Bennet — one "chief", chosen by the white man emerged as leader of the Colorado Ute nation.

His name was Ouray. He was to become the Utes' most famous chief.

Ouray: From Shepherd to President's Friend

Born at Taos, New Mexico in 1833 to a Tabeguache Ute father and a Jicarilla Apache mother, Ouray spent his childhood herding sheep for Mexican ranchers.

He learned Spanish and preferred it to his native Ute. He mastered some English.

At age 18, he rejoined the Ute Tabeguache band led by his father. Until he reached 27, the stocky 5'7" Ouray hunted and made war like any Indian. In 1859, he chose a wife, named Chipeta, a Tabeguache maiden he would love throughout his life.

During an 1863 Ute buffalo hunt near Fort Lupton on the Platte River, Cheyennes surprised Ouray's hunting camp and kidnapped his five-year old son, a tragedy that long haunted the Ute chief.

It was in 1863 also that Ouray emerged as primary Ute spokesman during Tabeguache Treaty negotiations with Washington. His friendliness to whites, his knowledge of the English language, his gentle manners and courtly bearing endeared him to government agents. (Washington officials later discovered that few of them could match the quick-thinking Ouray.) "The most intelligent man I have ever conversed with," stated President McKinley of the Ute leader. In 1873, Washington magnanimously appointed Ouray "Chief of all the Utes" and awarded him a $1,000 annual stipend for life.

While the government made and broke treaties guaranteed to last "as long as the rivers flow and the grass grows green," Ouray remained steadfast in his loyalty to the whites.

When Antelope shot a South Park settler named Marksberry who attempted to retrieve his horse stolen by Antelope, Ouray gave up the offending Ute to justice. When Utes in 1866 began to raid settlers on Huerfano Creek, Ouray sent runners to warn neighboring homesteaders. Later he captured the Ute attackers and dispatched them to Fort Garland. At Meeker, Colorado, the Utes retaliated against an oafish White River Indian agent, Nathan Meeker, who tried to force the Utes to take up farming. Meeker threatened to "cut every Indian down to bare starvation point if he will not work". In his pique at their refusal, agent Meeker plowed one of the Utes' favorite pony racing tracks. Ouray's quick action is credited with containing the Meeker Massacre, preventing its bloody spread across Colorado.

Ouray remained steadfast. Even when Ute lands disappeared around him, Ouray on September 13, 1873, could mildly say:

> We have many friends among the people in this territory, and want to live in peace and on good terms with them . . . We are perfectly willing to sell our mountain land, and hope the miners will find heaps of gold and silver, and we have no wish to molest them or make trouble. We do not want they should go down into our valleys, however, and kill or scare away our game.

Ouray died in 1880 of Brights disease at age 47. Chipeta lived 40 years longer, becoming totally blind before her death at 81. She lived to march with her tribe under U.S. Army command from her Colorado homeland to the wastelands of eastern Utah. After her funeral (where a U.S. Congressman eulogized the famous Ute woman), her body was removed from its first burial site and reburied in Montrose, Colorado as a tourist attraction. Ouray's grave, too, was disturbed 45 years after his death. His grave in a traditional Ute mountain cave was moved to a burial ground in Ignacio, Colorado. Squabbles resulted in officials placing his body half in the Protestant, half in the Catholic sections of adjoining cemeteries.

Colorow, dressed in his finest, glares at camera. This Comanche-born Ute was renegade.

"Chief" Colorow: A Scallywag

A street in Dillon commemorates a fat, blustering coward named Colorow who was never really a Ute Indian at all. Colorow, a Comanche, was captured as a child by the Northern Utes. He has earned the labels "treacherous by nature", "ponderous, over-rated, sub-chief", "scallywag" and "lazy no-good reprobate" by historians.

Colorow certainly did little for Summit County. He once shot a settler in the Gore Range when the man refused to cook Colorow's dinner. He set a spite fire in the Blue River Valley in 1879 to retaliate against Colorado Governor Pitkin's refusal to replace White River Indian Agent Meeker.

The leader of a group of young Ute renegades, Colorow proved himself no hero. He led a group of Utes who joined Crook's army to fight the hostile Sioux. When the army reached Sioux country, Colorow announced, "Ponies heap tired, no can go" and hightailed it back to Colorado.

Wolfe Londoner, who later became a mayor of Denver, once reluctantly entertained Colorow at dinner in his California Gulch cabin "to keep on his good side". Londoner's wife reacted with horror to the invitation, pointing to her bare pantry. But she managed to create a soup.

Colorow arrived with an entourage of three or four of his squaws. Said Londoner:

> I gave the old devil the head of the table. *They* got the soup, but we did not get any soup that day. He would take a spoonful of soup and then spit. He would spit alongside the table. It was the most villainous thing I ever encountered, but durst not say a word.

31

Colorow then weighed about 275 pounds. He later darkened the door of Londoner's store, moaning, "Injun heap sick . . . Eat too much . . . You give me medsin."

Londoner gave him Epsom Salts, in a dosage he felt would be effective for Colorow's size. Of the Indian's health the next morning, Londoner reported: "While he had weighed probably 275 pounds the day before, he now looked like an umbrella cover."

"No good," moaned Colorow. "White man heap bad, heap sick, pretty near die, no more medsin."

A doctor later informed Londoner that a tin cup full of Epsom Salts was "enough to kill an elephant".

"Well, it haint killed Colorow," Londoner replied.

Colorow eventually died of causes other than Epsom Salts poisoning. But not before he earned ill-repute in the Thornburg ambush. He passed away in 1908, age undetermined, but at a weight recorded at 300 pounds.

A Bizarre "Ball"

Even though Colorow's personal grooming distressed the fastidious, he and other Utes mingled with Summit County citizenry. The highlights of a smash soiree in the Montezuma Canyon community of Decatur are detailed in this September 30, 1882, social note from the Montezuma *Millrun* reprinted in Verna Sharp's *A History of Montezuma, Sts. John and Argentine*:

> Decatur gave a ball last Saturday evening . . . All the elite and ton of Decatur, Chihuahua and the rest of the Snake River country were present and helped to form an assemblage which for beauty and refinement has never been equaled in our lovely hamlet.

> Everything was most recherche, chic and utterly one, two, three . . . Mrs. Chipeta Ouray (wife of the Ute chief) wore a dress of lyonaise velvet and a seal-skin sack . . . Colorow, who accompanied Chipeta, wore a Prince Albert coat, made of an old army blanket, and buckskin breeches. His hair was dressed a la Oscar Wilde or an Indian herb doctor . . .

Blue River residents never needed to fear the Utes except shortly after the Meeker Massacre.

The mountain-dwelling Utes had never farmed throughout their tribal history. The braves recoiled at the idea of farm labor as beneath their culturally-instilled "macho" status. This infuriated not only the crusading Indian agent Meeker but other white Colorado residents as well.

During the precarious period of the Meeker Massacre, Breckenridge families panicked at the rumor that the Utes were on the warpath. Women and children scurried for Denver. But Methodist preacher Father John Dyer, famous "Snowshoe Intinerant", sent word that no danger existed. "The Indians were not within 100 miles," he wrote. Chief Ouray exerted a similar cooling influence on hot Ute tempers.

Nevertheless, the Meeker Massacre gave impetus to a growing consensus among whites: "The Ute Must Go!" After talking the Utes into retiring to a reservation near Grand Junction, Governor Pitkin decided fertile reservation land was wasted on the Indians: "The number of Indians who occupy this reservation is 3,000 . . . I believe that one able-bodied settler would cultivate more land than a whole tribe of Utes . . ."

The Ouray *Times* asked why "non-productive, semi-barbarious" people occupied land that "intelligent, and industrious citizens" could use.

And the Denver *Times* ponderated: "Either they (the Utes) or we must go, and *we* are not going . . . Western Empire is an inexorable fact. He who gets in the way of it will be crushed."

The government reneged on treaty after treaty with the Utes.

"So far as our observation extends," wrote Samuel Bowles, "the greatest trouble with our Indian matters lies at Washington; the chief of the cheating and stupidity gathers there . . ."

Public opinion against the Ute gained momentum. And white buffalo harvesters reduced to near extinction the animal that provided a drygoods store of needs for Ute daily life. With buffalo, game and fish depleted, and mining towns sprouting like wildflowers all over their mountain homeland, the White River Utes reluctantly agreed to leave Colorado for the much-touted Uintah Reservation.

Treaties in March, 1868, April, 1874 and March, 1880, ceded to the U.S. Government all of their ancestral Ute homeland, except for a small reservation in the southwestern part of the state. The Montezuma *Millrun* like other Colorado newspapers, announced that all land of the Ute reservation, "lately occupied by the Uncompahgre and White River Utes" was "declared to be public land", by a July 28, 1882 act of Congress.

And so, in 1881, 22 years after the first white prospector discovered the rich Blue River gold fields, the centuries-old White River Utes left Nah-oon-kara, never to return.

Breckenridge:
Colorado's First Western Slope Community

"Gold!"

Ruben J. Spalding's cry rang out against the mountains rimming the Blue River Valley that August 10 afternoon of 1859 — and reverberated across America. His discovery: Breckenridge gold, glittering in creekbeds, seaming rugged gulches, lacing hillsides, rich enough to rock the nation. Breckenridge gold, world-famous wire and leaf, stunning in its unparalleled beauty. Breckenridge gold, a chance for those who came to the little alpine placer digs to escape a depressed 1850's economy and grab at the American dream.

Spalding's party, under the leadership of General George E. Spencer, future U.S. Senator from Alabama, started from Denver on August 2, 1859, the year of the Pikes Peak Gold Rush. Twenty-nine men and one woman penetrated South Park. The party split and 14 continued on to Fairplay. They scaled Hoosier Pass and descended into the Blue River Valley, the first white prospectors to cross the Divide to Colorado's western slope.

By 1889, Breckenridge had grown rich on its 1859 gold strike. Miner Felix Poznansky chose this site in 1860, but rival Geo. Spencer maneuvered to gain townsite rights.

34

The men sank a hole three feet into a bar on the Blue River, one-fourth mile below today's Breckenridge. Ruben Spalding, an experienced miner who had gained expertise in the California gold rush, was selected to pan the first "dirt". His yield: 13 cents worth of placer gold, including a large grain about the size and shape of a flax seed. The next pan yielded 24 cents in gold.

Today, the Little B Trailer Court near the Valley Brook Cemetery marks the area of Spalding's 1859 strike.

Everything began popping.

Spalding received the discovery claim, 200 feet along the river and across it, including both banks. The others proceeded to stake standard 100 foot claims along the Blue. William H. Iliff immediately discovered gold, $2 to the pan, on the Blue's east bank across from the Spalding discovery. This 40 square-foot claim later yielded $7,000 in gold.

Spalding built the first log cabin. But General Spencer entertained much bigger thoughts: He began to organize a townsite near the discovery diggings. His town would be Breckenridge, the first permanent town on the Colorado western slope.

This version of Blue River Diggings "discovery", documented by historian Frank Hall in his 1895 book, *History of the State of Colorado*, best fits known facts. But interested readers will discover varying versions in almost every Colorado history book they pick up.

Historian Orvando J. Hollister asserts that 100 men crossed Georgia Pass to prospect for Blue Valley gold, but beat a hasty retreat due to a Ute Indian scare. "Not having found the fabled 'pound diggings', the prospectors were glad of a pretext for a general stampede back," wrote Hollister. Later miners persevered in prospecting and struck success. Hollister's 1867 account persists in many of the discovery stories.

Colorado ghost town historian, Robert L. Brown retells the story this way: 59'er General George Spencer led a party of 100 across Georgia Pass in spring, 1860. They heard rumors of Ute murders and scurried back over the Range. But later more miners came and proceeded to settle what is now French Gulch.

Frank Hall's version, the one restated here, is based on the personal memories of Ruben J. Spalding, key participant in the history-making events.

From here on, historians usually relate the facts the same way. Fearing native Ute Indians, the prospectors erected a green log fort and dubbed the little blockade "Fort Mary B" (also called Fort Meribeh, Fort Marbery) in honor of Mary Bigelow, the first woman to cross the range to the Blue Valley. The fort, just north of today's Breckenridge, consisted of earthen-roof block houses, homes for those who decided to winter in the isolated valley. The dwellings, arranged to face inward on a hollow square, joined to make the fort. Two entrances to the court could be easily defended if necessary.

Three mining districts soon divided the Blue River Diggings. Pollard (Pollack) at the south end of today's Breckenridge; Spalding at the north end; and Independent between the two.

The group settled in for a high country winter. Abundant wild game — deer, antelope, elk, bear and fish — prevented starvation, but the new settlers yearned for luxuries like bacon, coffee, tea, tobacco and flour. One thing they had plenty of: Snow. Twelve feet, ten inches by one pioneer's gauge. The much-feared Indian attack never came. In fact, the Utes proved downright friendly.

Miners had busied themselves all fall with the herculean task of turning the Blue River's course. They dug a large canal to reroute it, hoping to placer mine the river bed. When the canal was complete, Ruben Spalding immediately began sluicing. Some newcomers arrived with whipsawed lumber for sale. Spalding remembered: "With the lumber I made three 'toms' (a kind of miners' sluice box) and went to mining in water ankle deep, and having nothing better to wear on my feet I roped them with pieces of a saddle blanket . . . The first day's work netted me $10 and a bad cold." (Of course, $10 was nothing to sneeze at in 1859.)

Gold in the Gulches

If his first day of placer mining went poorly, at least Ruben Spalding couldn't complain about his first prospecting jaunt down the Blue. ". . . we mounted our snow shoes (miners' skis), taking blankets, tools and provisions and went down the Blue River about six miles, where we built a cabin of small pine logs and claimed a town site, calling it Eldorado West . . . Mr. Balce Weaver went prospecting and discovered Gold Run diggings beneath snow eight feet deep."

Gold Run proved fabulously rich. Fifty men from Tarryall, across the Range in South Park, heard about dazzling Gold Run and puffed over the Divide on heavy homemade skis to stake claims. One of them, William A. Smith, whose urbane letters from the Blue River Diggings appear in *Blasted, Beloved Breckenridge*, said he found 20 men, one woman (probably Mary Bigelow) and four children wintering in the valley. But the Tarryall miners made no big strikes. Despite their efforts to build bonfires to thaw the ground, the snow proved a real deterrent to prospecting.

March winds blew warm and the sound of chopping and whipsawing board for sluices and buildings filled the formerly tranquil Blue Valley. Town construction would begin as soon as heavy winter snow disappeared. In April, the few dozen miners working took out $10 to $40 per day per man. (In todays dollars, that amount translates to $70 to $280 per man.)

Blue River Diggings remained remote and small. But as melting snow continued its forever drip-drip-drip from Fort Mary B's sod roofs, a great horde of excited prospectors gathered in Denver and the South Park towns, awaiting the great thaw, when the "Snowy Range" would finally permit their crossing.

Ruben Spalding's strike had ignited a fuse that sizzled slowly through the long 1859-60 winter. Consuming itself, the shortening fuse inched toward its charge. In May, 1860, the bomb blew: People, pack trains and wagons streamed over Hoosier, Boreas, Georgia and French Passes to unearth Blue Valley gold in incredible amounts. The placer boom began.

One to two hundred prospectors arrived daily. Discoveries popped like July 4 firecrackers. French Pete discovered French Gulch gold. A group of Georgia miners penetrated a gulch they named Georgia and their Mr. Highfield discovered bonanza Georgia Gulch gold, yielding $12 to the pan. "The richness of Georgia Gulch is almost fabulous," William A. Smith reported on July 1. Georgia, and the new Humbug Gulch placers, averaged returns of $20 a day per man.

Claims began to sell for $1,000 to $7,000. During the summer, prospectors continued to make dizzying discoveries at Galena, Brown's, American, Georgia and Humbug Gulches, plus Nigger Hill and Illinois Gulch. Quantities were "almost unreasonable". Excitement blazed in the camps. Enthusiasm reached the frenzy stage. Breckenridge, hub of the Blue River Diggings, sprang into life.

How did the town get its start? General George E. Spencer, intent on capturing ownership of the Blue River townsite, had planned to locate his community near Fort Mary B, according to Breckenridge historian Mark Fiester. A miner named Felix Poznansky had organized a group to lay out a town called Independence one mile south of the Fort. When spring came, Spencer discovered his Fort Mary B townsite already claimed. He decided to use Poznansky's site. Naturally, conflict arose. The two had a confrontation in late spring at Tarryall. Spencer vowed to Poznansky that he would gain the townsite by "first improvement". (Congress' townsite law awarded townsite rights to the claimant who built the first eight-log high structure.) Poznansky refused to be outdone. He penned a message to his son at Independence: "Get help and begin building a cabin." A messenger carried the note during the night to the younger Poznansky. When Spencer arrived to seize his townsite, he encountered an eight-log cabin perched atop the winter snowpack. Poznansky had won!

But General Spencer was no man to hoodwink. He persuaded the Independence miners to let him survey the town (warming them up with an offer of 12

Prospectors in 1859 never dreamed that a prosperous Breckenridge, 50 years later, with stately courthouse and bustling railroad, would face devouring gold dredges.

choice lots, one for each, except the blackguard Poznansky). Spencer wanted only to own the leftover land and the right to name the town. The prospectors agreed.

The General proved himself a politician. He knew his new town would need a postoffice. And he learned just how to get one. He chose the name "Breckinridge" (with an "i" where the "e" is today), after U.S. Vice President John Cabell Breckinridge, who then served in President Buchanan's administration. Spencer's bait snared the political fish. On January 18, 1860, Breckinridge obtained a postoffice and General Spencer got a new job: Postmaster, Breckinridge, Utah Territory. (Until February 28, 1861, when Colorado Territory was formed, the Western Slope was designated Utah Territory and the Eastern Slope, Kansas Territory.)

By May, pack trains bearing supplies poured into Breckinridge. "Large numbers of wagons are arriving daily from Denver and the States," William A. Smith wrote. The town of Colorado Springs emerged as a supply center for the Blue River Diggings.

Four new stores were under construction. One report estimates an 8,000 Blue River population in June, 1860. There was one woman in Breckinridge and another in Gold Run. By June, canvas-covered wagons and tents dotted the landscape white for 12 miles down the Blue. Stores, dwellings, shops and saloons blossomed in Breckinridge.

"We can now buy anything in the line of provisions or clothing . . .", Smith gloated. Iddings and Company operated a Fort Mary B store and Schollkaph, Whittemore and Company debuted a well-outfitted store in Breckinridge. (The pioneering Silverthorn family would soon take over the store building for use as the Silverthorn Hotel.) South Park prospectors H. Solomon and George Wing left mining to launch a lucrative freight business over Georgia Pass to Georgia Gulch's booming new town, Parkville.

Civil War spirit reached its long, controversial arm to Breckinridge. Lincoln captured the vote in the 1860 elections. A deposed Vice President John Cabell Breckinridge won a Senate seat. But the Rebel politician balked at Lincoln's war. He resigned his Senate seat to join the South's Confederate Army. Breckinridge residents saw red. The irate townsfolk yanked the "i" from the Rebel's namesake, replacing it with an "e" for Breckenridge.

(An early edition of the Summit County *Journal* traced the town's name to Thomas E. Breckenridge, allegedly a member of the original party. Thomas E. Breckenridge also reportedly accompanied Colonel John C. Fremont in his 1848 Colorado expedition. He turned up later in Durango, Colorado.)

Prospector Influx

The Cincinnati *Commercial's* Henry Villard visited Colorado during the rush and wrote his book, *The Past and Present of the Pike's Peak Gold Region*, published in 1860. Villard estimated that 100,000 Americans joined the Pikes Peak gold rush. Only 50,000 reached Colorado. And at least 25,000 returned home to "the States" after a brief stay, damning Colorado gold with the 1800's putdown of "Humbug". Villard's figures are easy to believe. In the gulches near Breckenridge, life revolved around hard work. Beans, side pork and tea made miners dream of home cooking. The men formed a motley society of strangers. "Young America" ran into the hard face of reality in these rough placer camps and the hopes of many a youthful Argonaut were dashed.

Young Daniel Ellis Conner arrived in Breckenridge (which he calls "Miners District") in May, 1860. His account of the summer rush in *A Confederate in the Colorado Gold Fields* details the annoying reality of "claim-jumping":

> Immigration now began to crowd Miners' District with an unruly population, the individual number of which were nearly all unacquainted with each other; and in truth, there were but very few acquaintances there, because of the continuous influx of strangers, who immediately became savage on the question of the ownership of mining claims. A miner could hardly leave his pit long enough to get his dinner without finding someone in it at work with all the tools left there when he returned. This was called jumping claims. The result of this sort of conduct was that neighboring claim holders united their protests on such occasions by visiting the "jumped" claim in an armed body, and invited the intruder to leave without standing upon the manner of going. This gradually got up a fashion of prepared resistance, again resulting unfavorable to mine owners. Lives were lost and conflicts inaugurated without limit. A body of tramps would unite and "jump" the whole district, drive out the original owners and pass new laws, and work until they would be served the same way. But somebody always had possession.

Young John Hall, a Breckenridge placer miner, wrote a letter from "Breckinridge, Utah Territory", on September 9, 1860. The letter, postmarked in October, 1860, communicates the author's yearning for home, for the pretty girls he knew there, and for a lot of distance between him and the isolated placer camps of Breckenridge. His letter, like all 1860 Breckenridge mail, traveled by private express until later in fall, 1860, when the first government mail under U.S. contract began arriving. The envelope bears the address: William L. Thompson, Mapleton, Niagra (sic) County, New York.

> Col Thompson Dear Sir:
> I wished you was here for one week to take a view of things. 'All is not Gold that glitters' is an old saying and every man who comes here does not go home rich is just as true. The most of the miners will be gone or going home in three weeks and not more than one in fifty will take home any more after all expenses are paid than they could have made at home. Yet forty nine out of every fifty now here will return another year to try it again and most of them will doubtless do well. There are a good many reasons why they have not made much this year and why they will do better next year. Nearly all who came up here never had any experience in mining or traveling the Plains and as a natural consequence made a great many blunders, bad bargains and with a little bad management it is to be wondered at that so many come out of the little end of the horn the first year. On the other hand they found their hopes of success another year on their experience and by bringing their own provisions, tools, and by securing good claims this fall for another year. . . . the winter here is long and dreary and as there is no work to do it is no use to stay here and do nothing and live on provisions at 22 cents per pound for Flour, 35 cents for Bacon and everything else in proportion. Mining here will with but a few

exceptions (end) by the first of October and will not be resumed until the first of June. You plainly see that the season here is very short as there is only one kind of timber grows here, scrubby Pine which grows on the highest elavation (sic) of land . . . and it is but a short walk to the Bald Mountains where nothing grows but weeds and where snow is found all the year round. We can go back to the river for a little nothing and we can work all Winter and make some money and see the country and then come out early in the spring. I have not received a letter from you since I left Mich yet have sent a good many to you . . . . What is Gen Brun Thayer doing this summer how are crops on Rankins Farm this year(?) Give my love to Miss Crosby if you please.

Yours in haste John N. Hall

P.S. If you have any friend at home who thinks of coming out here and you have any feelings for them tell them to stay at home if they can get a living. I never want any of my friends to go to Gold Country to get fortune. The hardest, slowest, most uncertain way of making cash that ever was known is in a Gold Region . . . Give my love to all my friends, Miss Augusta in particular.

By 1862, the homesick boys in the gulches began returning to the haven of hometown life, because Breckenridge placer gold was running out. Free gold, washed into stream beds by nature's relentless erosion, had disappeared into the bulging gold pouches of the pick and pan prospectors. A handful attempted hydraulic mining, with great hoses washing out hillsides to mine their hidden store of placer gold. (Villard, in his 1860 book, discussed hydraulic mining.) But most knew nothing of hydraulic potential or the next step, lode mining. So they scrambled back over the high passes, leaving the Blue Valley to a few hangers-on.

Breckenridge Becomes County Seat

Parkville, seat of a huge Summit County that encompassed the entire northwest corner of Colorado began its decline. A burgeoning Breckenridge, envious of Parkville's county seat status, carried out a moonlight requisition of the county records in 1862. Perpetrators of this legendary heist hid the county documents in an isolated log cabin until outraged Parkville citizens regained some measure of calm. Then Breckenridge assumed its new role as government headquarters of a large area, spreading to the Utah and Wyoming borders. The Silverthorn Hotel temporarily housed the county records. First official Summit County Clerk and Recorder office was William P. Pollack's house, built in 1862 and still standing at its original location, 115 North Main Street.

"I had the interesting experience of seeing the first records of mining," wrote Agnes Miner quoting her mother in "The Founding and Early History of Breckenridge, Colorado." "These were written in 1859 and are just as plain as though written yesterday. One book had a bullet hole through it . . . and it speaks of the men as 'Gents'."

As Breckenridge mushroomed in spring 1860 and the few years following, Fort Mary B, the original settlement, faded. The fort was deserted by 1861. By 1863, the stockade stood empty, its sod roof caved in. In later years, the Wilson smelter occupied the Fort Mary B site. But the dredges, spewing out rocky tailings, demolished the smelter's smokestack, obliterating the last remnants of the site. Dredge men like Johnny Johnson decades later reported finding 50-caliber bullets in the Fort Mary B dredge tailings.

South Park historian Virginia McConnell states that Mrs. Hiram Turner gave birth to the first white baby born in Summit County (and probably on the Western Slope) in the early days of the Blue River Diggings. Other early Breckenridge residents included Judge Marshall Silverthorn and his family, J. D. Roby, a grocer who was the Judge's mining partner, famous naturalist Edwin Carter, blacksmith George Bressler, Judge A. L. Shock, D. Shock, J. Shock, George Jones, Clerk and Recorder W. Pollack, Hotelkeeper J. E. Rankin and William H. Iliff.

Early Visitors Report

In July, 1861, *Rocky Mountain News* editor William Byers described Breckenridge:

> Breckenridge is the first point of importance, reached by the traveler over this road, and until recently the most town-like of any settlement in the Blue River country. The population is probably between seventy-five and one hundred persons — embracing quite a number of families. There are several stores, hotels, meat markets, saloons and a U.S. Post Office — the only one west of the Range.

Author-lecturer Bayard Taylor also penned his 1866 impressions of Breckenridge in his book, *Colorado: A Summer Trip*:

> Finally, the wood came to an end and green meadows and snowy peaks refreshed our eyes. Over ditches, heaps of stone and gravel, and all the usual debris of gulch mining, we rode toward some cabins which beckoned to us through scattered clumps of pine . . . canvas covered wagons in the shade; a long street of log houses; signs of "Boarding", "Miner's Home", and "Saloon", and a motley group of rough individuals . . .

> The place dated from 1860 — yet, of the five thousand miners who flocked to this part of the Middle Park in that year, probably not more than five hundred remain.

Taylor saw evidence of new life in Breckenridge — lots were staked out and signs displayed "preempted by _____".

Byers later reported that these homes had been built and Breckenridge looked "quite prosperous".

Three years later, in 1869, author Samuel Bowles visited a dwindling Breckenridge of 20 to 30 homes. In his *Colorado: Its Parks and Mountains*, he commented:

> At Breckenridge, we got above the washings and the river was clear again. This is the center of these upper mining interests, but a village of only twenty or thirty cabins, located ten thousand feet high, and scarcely habitable in winter, though many of the miners do hibernate here . . .

Following Bowles' footsteps came geologist William H. Brewer. In his 1869 *Rocky Mountain Letters*, Brewer wrote:

> We found the mining town of Breckenridge . . . its single street of one-story cabins, most of which, like so many in the country are covered with dirt instead of shingles.

41

Brewer stayed in Rankin's Hotel and slept in a bed for the first time during his mountain sojourn.

Princeton Scientific Expedition members, undergraduates on a scientific romp through the Colorado mountains, reeled in disgust over Breckenridge's raw society:

> We have spent some very queer days out her, but this beats them all. To get out of the reach of the noise was impossible, and you might think that there was a den of wild animals being fed, or something worse. We heartily recommend Breckenridge as being the most fiendish place we ever wish to see. We were forced to spend the morning and afternoon in the company of men whose language was vile, and whose actions were tinged with a shade of crime that shocked and hurt our senses; never did anything so bestial and so unworthy even a mention by manly lips happen before our eyes.

Despite the presence of Judge Silverthorn, early Breckenridge often settled its disputes with the traditional arbitrator of the 1800's: The duel. In 1864, according to Alice Polk Hill, writing later in the 1880's, a melodramatic confrontation had occurred:

> About twenty years ago two gentlemen, who were in every respect valuable citizens, quarreled about some trifle — I've forgotten what, but it resulted in a challenge to mortal combat. We were all greatly distressed, for they were good fellows, and we made every effort to pacify them, but without effect. They agreed to fight with hatchets, thirty paces apart. Mr. Bressler, that handsome blacksmith across the way, sharpened the hatchets and the work was well done; they were as keen-edged as razors. The gentlemen practised so earnestly that almost every tree around the town received a scar from their weapons. The evening before the fight was to come off, one of them received a letter from his mother, in which she informed him that his antagonist was the son of her dearest friend, and she hoped the boys would love each other like brothers. This letter brought about a reconciliation, and they are still living, both filling prominent positions in other States.

Another Alice Polk Hill adventure in justice turned out this way:

> Two fellows were mining over here in Galena Gulch and they had a dispute about a girl, which resulted in a challenge. It was left to a meeting of the Miners' court to determine the manner of fighting. The miners had no confidence in their courage, and it was decided that they should stand back to back, walk off fifteen paces, then right about face and forward march, shooting and continuing to shoot until one was killed, or their revolvers emptied.

> At the appointed time they met and were placed back to back in the presence of the entire population of the gulch. When the order was given to walk fifteen paces, they started off bravely. Upon reaching the line, instead of turning to face each other, they both walked on as fast as their legs could carry them, clear out of the country, probably thinking:

> "He who fights and runs away
> Will live to fight another day."

Bayard Taylor noted Judge Silverthorn's 1866 log courthouse with faded U.S. flag.

When Bayard Taylor first arrived in Breckenridge, he noticed an American flag, faded completely white, flying at half-mast. Taylor, fearing news of national tragedy, inquired about the "white flag". He learned the flag mournfully acknowledged that the bully of Buffalo Flats had whomped Breckenridge's best bully, a stout German grocer, a day earlier.

Raging fires menaced life in early Colorado mineral camps. Breckenridge would undergo devastating fires in later years. As early as June, 1860, a forest fire broke out near Breckenridge to engulf rich timber forests and cause severe personal injury and property damage to area gulch miners. Flames towering 150 to 200 feet high roared from an area near the mouth of French Gulch at the Blue River, up French Gulch's south side and over to Nigger Gulch. Miner William A. Smith and friends escaped by jumping into a deep sluice hole, rolling over and over in the flowing water there to prevent their clothes from burning. One man suffered severe burn injuries. Tents, cabins, animals, wagons, sluice boxes and more were destroyed. Miners believed the fire was purposely set.

Early Breckenridge visitors described the desolation of charred black timber forests along the Blue River trail to the town.

Sleepy Breckenridge dozed through the late 1860's and the '70's with little excitement to disturb its unruffled slumber. A late 1870's *Colorado Business Directory* omitted listing the town. Like Rip Van Winkle, Breckenridge would waken.

Breckenridge paused before its second boom, an explosive rebirth sparked by the discovery of lode mining. Crofutt's 1885 *Gripsack Guide* pinpointed the cause of Colorado second rush:

> From the time of the rich mineral discoveries at Leadville, of 1878-9, dates a new era in the mining industry of Colorado. It filled the whole mountain region of the state with prospectors, and the hunt for rich quartz lodes commenced, and with what success, the cities of Breckenridge . . . and many others stand forth as monuments endorsed by millions in gold, silver, copper and lead, added to the wealth of the country.

A *Rocky Mountain News* reporter writing in the 1880's looked backward to describe Breckenridge in October, 1877, just before the boom:

> The town consisted principally of Judge Silverthorn's Hotel, J. D. Roby's store, the offices of Judges Pollack and Bartlett, the clerk and recorder's office, the blacksmith establishment of George H. Bressler, and Carter's museum. Every man you meet will draw from his pocket specimens of gold or silver.

But, the newspaper observer pointed out in his June 16, 1880 report, "Things have changed in Breckenridge".

Will Iliff, 1859 discovery party pioneer, returned to Breckenridge in 1878 to strike Shock Hill's rich Blue Danube quartz lode. Slumbering Breckenridge awoke to another frenzied mineral rush. One hundred mining companies formed, 6,190 location certificates were filed, population jumped from 250 to 2,000 and $25 lots jumped in price to $1,500. One hundred buildings under construction filled the town with joyful racket. Six more fissure and vein strikes by April 15, 1880, added to the excitement.

"Carpenters' hammers never stopped day or night . . ." wrote Agnes Miner, grand-daughter of old Judge Silverthorn. In 1879, during the rush, Summit County had a 6,000 population. Next year, according to Mrs. Miner's estimate, county population jumped to 8,000, and prospectors continued to pour in.

Wild and Wooly Town

The influx blew Breckenridge wide open. "The place was wild then," remembered Dr. Arthur V. Garretson who visited Breckenridge as a wide-eyed 10-year old in the early '80's. There was "a saloon or gambling house at every other door".

Garretson was right. Raucous Breckenridge had three dance halls and an eye-popping total of 18 saloons in 1880. (After the dance hall girls abandoned one rip-roaring establishment at French and Lincoln Streets, another set of ladies, the prim sisters of the Benedictine Convent, moved in!)

A second dance hall stood on a site that later became "hallowed ground" — the home of the Summit County *Journal*'s crusading editor, Jonathan Cooper Fincher.

In April, 1880, according to historian Frank Hall, Breckenridge residents organized a town government and elected town trustees. They were William H. Iliff, James Whetstone, J. Roby, George H. Bressler, Samuel De Matte and Peter Engle.

In 1880, Breckenridge boasted:

12 attorneys	2 dentists	1 meat market
6 bakeries	10 laundries	3 dance halls
5 boarding houses	4 lumber dealers	18 saloons
3 sawmills	3 jewelers	4 assayers
1 smelter	4 blacksmith shops	10 restaurants
6 mining exchanges	9 physicians	

Methodist minister John Lewis Dyer characterized the 1880 boom according to his own lights. He recalled that a report was spread that Breckenridge held immense bodies of gold "three feet deep".

> People of all classes came across the range, and, of course, the inevitable dance house, with degraded women, fiddles, bugles and many sorts of music came too. There was a general hubbub from dark to daylight. The weary could hardly rest.

All this glorious hubbub demanded a needed face-lift for the rough 20-year old camp. Stump-pulling squads attacked Lincoln Avenue. Work teams cleared Main Street of boulders and filled in "cellar size" holes. Ragged tents, shanties and structural skeletons were scourged from Ridge Street, which would become the showiest street in 1880's Breckenridge.

Shepherding the changes was Breckenridge's first newspaper, the historic Breckenridge *Daily Journal*, launched July 22, 1880. Its publisher soon spearheaded the *Daily Journal*'s successor, the weekly Summit County *Journal*, on August 4, 1883. The newspaper soon celebrates its centennial. The *Journal* yipped at the heels of Breckenridge town fathers, pushing the progress Breckenridge needed.

The Denver, South Park & Pacific Railroad penetrated pastoral South Park, and 1880's rumor mills ground out stories of the railway coming to Breckenridge!

In the meantime, 1880 travel to Breckenridge from Denver meant a long ride,

Fever-pitch excitement held Breckenridge in its grip at onset of 1880 lode mine boom. Miners slaked thirst, swapped tall tales in any of the town's 18 saloons.

45

traveling via D.S.P. & P train to Como, then the often hair-raising stagecoach ride over Boreas Pass.

In summertime, the trip proved delightful. A passenger reported to the *Rocky Mountain News* in June, 1880: At Como, "through the courtesy of Col. Bob Spottswood, I got aboard one of the splendid Concord coaches of the pioneer stage line and finished the journey to Breckenridge, a distance of 17 miles made in three and one-half hours over the Park Range. The beautiful scenery on both sides made the trip short and charming." (All this for only $11.80.)

The writer stayed at the Denver House in Breckenridge, which he termed "excellent . . . recently enlarged and newly furnished". Breckenridge in early 1880's could boast some fine hotels: The Arlington, the Grand Central and, until around 1883, Silverthorn's.

Breckenridge had awaited the railroad. Frieght costs on weighty, gold-bearing quartz ores crimped profits on lode mine operations. Freight from Denver on most goods ran $30 a ton in 1880. Cost of living, too, remained high. While average Breckenridge wages stayed at $2 to $3 per day, board, for example, ran $1 or more per day.

Hurrah for the Railroad

In August, 1882, the first D.S.P. & P. train steamed into Breckenridge, amid cries of joy from a welcoming crowd. Its arrival spelled relief for lode mine companies and for the town's isolated residents, who could then whisk themselves to Denver for a visit whenever the whim struck. A new influx of visitors traveled to Breckenridge. Visitor Alice Polk Hill described her 1883 rail descent from Boreas Pass this way:

> At Rocky Point, where we reach the acme of scenic glory on this line, the town of Breckenridge commences to play "Bo Peep" with the admiring tourist; first on this side and then on that, we see it — making another turn, a full view is obtained.

Mrs. Hill called 1880's Breckenridge a "pretty little frontier town".

Near the railroad station in West Breckenridge, across the Blue, lay the town's leafy "Central Park", with dancing, parlor skating and music to entertain a proud populace.

Who were the town's leading citizens?

"Back in the '80's in Breckenridge, George Bressler ran the livery stable, John Klinefelter was the assayer, Findings ran the hardware and Mr. Coyne was the grocer," remembered Dr. Garretson of his boyhood Breckenridge days.

Like many early visitors, Dr. Garretson left with some "very nice specimens of wire gold" from Farncomb Hill.

The *Colorado Business Directory* lists Will Iliff as Breckenridge Sheriff in the mid-80's; J. D. Roby, the grocer, also served as city treasurer. The Engle Brothers Billiard Saloon and the Keystone Lodging House appeared, as did H. N. Nichols & Company's Eureka Stamp Mill and a set of attorneys aptly named "Breeze & Breeze".

Some of Breckenridge's finest citizens and longtime resident families still in Summit County today arrived in Breckenridge during the 1880's boom. These stable citizens built a life in Breckenridge, became community servants, erected homes, planted flowers on mine-blackened hill sides and held permanent jobs. They transformed the rugged camp of Breckenridge into a charming and permanent mountain town.

Robert Foote, patriarch of Breckenridge's Theobald family of today, managed the Minnie mine, owned a Shock Hill mine property, and helped develop the fabulous Wellington Mine, building the first ore mill here. Robert Foote gained distinction as the genial owner/host of Breckenridge's prestigeous Denver Hotel.

The Formans contributed to Breckenridge life. Their exquisite home on High Street was a landmark. Mr. Forman served as Summit clerk and recorder for years. His home, built on Nickel Hill, was a showplace with fancy cornices, lattice work and a dainty iron fence.

People like the Formans and Miners, Footes, Kaisers, Engles, Fletchers and Gaymons clamored for schools, churches, hospitals, fire departments and public buildings for a growing Breckenridge — and they got them.

Academic "Burlesque"

Breckenridge boasted a 2,000-strong population in the early '80's, yet its children crowded into a tiny 20 by 25-foot one-room schoolhouse on North Main Street. Some young scholars were unable to attend due to walking distance. Summit County School District No. 1 came under fire beginning in 1881 for this "burlesque" upon academia. The 1881-82 school census counted 134 Breckenridge pupils. Early teachers, like Miss Mary Guyselman and Miss Ann S. Hamilton, had done their best to cram the "3 R's" into students attending two or three months sessions yearly, but a booming Breckenridge required better school facilities. A new two-story, four-room schoolhouse, completed October 5, 1882, pleased citizens with its fine pealing school bell, donated by contractor Elias Nashold. (Nashold would leave his mark on Breckenridge; many of the

Four-room, $4,000 school-house opened for "slate and switch" Oct. 5, 1882. School, under Prof. Arbagast, replaced cramped 1870 one-room facility at Main and Carter. Handsome new school, at Lincoln and Harris, served till 1909.

town's architectural gems reflect his design talent.)

The school served Breckenridge until 1909, when a $20,000 public investment underwrote a handsome new building. Summit schools had gone only as far as tenth grade, but a new 11th and 12th grade program enabled not only Breckenridge but all Summit students after 1909 to attain a full high school diploma.

The Summit County *Journal* trilled praise for the "wisdom, sagacious executive ability and keenness" of the schoolboard.

In 1920, another sagacious school board added an auditorium-gymnasium to the school complex. The school board also upgraded teachers' compensation, with ample discrimination by sex. Male teachers received $67.50 monthly; female: $49.50.

The Benedictine Sisters came to Breckenridge in 1886 to open St. Gertrude's Select School for boarders and day students. The academy operated on the northeast corner of Lincoln and French for four years.

If Breckenridge's first schools had earned the label of inadequate, so its first hospital eminently qualified for citizen censure. Grisly mine accidents, explosions and maimings occurred with sickening regularity. Frozen limbs were a common affliction. And epidemics of contagious disease swept through town. Yet hospital facilities were deplorable. The Miners Protective Association teamed up with the county to launch a new hospital. Their limping effort was rescued in 1886 by those capable Benedictine Sisters, whose competent service proved a boon to Breckenridge. But their hospital, crowded and inadequate, needed a new home. The Sisters had departed in 1890, and the tumbledown facility had not been upgraded. Finally, in 1906, the County Commissioners appropriated $2,500 to buy the old Sutton residence, on French Street between Adams and Jefferson, as a hospital. (The old hospital sold for $25!) The spacious new grounds and two-story house had belonged most recently to Masontown's Victoria Mine part-owner, A. E. Keables, who also served as business manager of the Summit County Mining Exchange. The Hospital today is a residence once more, the home of the Robert A. Theobalds.

Fire Forges Town Response

Breckenridge also formed its historic fire department in 1880 — again in answer to a crying need.

On June 11, 1880, a raging forest fire threatened Breckenridge's very existence. Two timber blazes traveled toward town from the south, and a third fire ate through the forest on the north. *The Rocky Mountain News* on Sunday, June 13, 1880, reported a "Destructive Conflagration in the Valley of the Blue". "The town of Breckenridge narrowly escaped destruction by fire on Friday night," the newspaper said. Exceedingly high winds fanned a fire in the timber a mile southwest of town. The fire "swept down the valley of the Blue with uncontrolled fury. It destroyed hundreds of acres of the splendid timber adjacent to the town."

On Saturday, a sharp wind inflamed embers. "The town was repeatedly fired by flying sparks," the *News* said. "A fire brigade of 100 men is at work."

Social pillars worked beside the grubbiest gulch miner to man the buckets against the fire. A merciful rain finally quenched the fearful blaze. But Breckenridge learned its lesson. "A meeting is called today for forming a permanent fire department . . ." the *News* announced. In the meantime, every citizen was asked to keep a fire bucket at hand at all hours, day and night, in case the fire rekindled.

This time Breckenridge didn't tarry over its public project. With unmatched speed, the town erected a $1,864 firehouse. Firemen conducted a meeting there on July 13, a month after the big blaze. Firemen's Hall, with its wonderful louvered belfry and peaked Victorian roofline, became a Breckenridge landmark. First erected on French Street, next door to Father Dyer's Church, the hall with its bell tempted the Methodist preacher. He rang it on Sunday mornings for

Tireless servant of the Lord, Rev. J. L. Dyer found no rest in raucous 1880's Breckenridge.

services, to the puzzlement of firemen who never knew if Father Dyer's special brand of brimstone, or an earthly blaze, summoned.

The Pioneer Hook & Ladder Company, the Independent Hose Company and the Blue River Hose Company proudly, and sometimes competitively, carried out their commitment to firefighting in an emerging Breckenridge. (One hundred years of service will culminate in a centennial celebration in June, 1980.)

Their commitment met its first crucial challenge in 1884 when fire raged on Ridge Street, the central business district. The blaze leapt from Washington Avenue to Lincoln and from Ridge Street to Main, destroying in its path an entire block. The large and elegant Grand Central Hotel, a grocery, hardware, clothing and dry goods stores disintegrated to cinders in the fire's path.

As Breckenridge cruised into the 1890's, and gold flowed freely from the area's rich lode mines, the social graces enjoyed a new surge of popularity. No more tin cups and newspaper-chinked log cabins for Breckenridge! Ladies in bustled gowns sipped tea from real china cups in carpeted and wallpapered parlors, and left calling cards for their hostess. Gentlemen created a cult around drinking whiskey together over the faro tables of popular retreats like Robert Foote's Denver Hotel, Johnny Dewers' Saloon at Lincoln and Main, and Knorr's Saloon.

Organizations like the Masons flourished. At 7:30 p.m. each Saturday following the full moon, Breckenridge Masons gathered in their temple for the monthly ritual. Every year, the Masons hosted a dance, with fresh flowers and formal gowns for the ladies, dark suits for the men. The annual Red Men's Lodge masked ball, a 50-year Breckenridge tradition, was a masquerade — but guests had to remove their masks in a private room before entering the hall, a measure designed to prevent local prostitutes from crashing.

Men of the cloth, like Reverend John L. Dyer and later Reverend Florida Passmore, turned purple beneath their clerical collars in holy anger over Breckenridge's balls. But dancing continued for years as Breckenridge's most popular social pastime.

Prostitution remained popular, too. Elizabeth Rice Roller, longtime Summit resident, remembered a time when the soiled doves had their day in old Breckenridge:

> . . . a group of residents from the red-light district invaded the town intent upon a high time. In flowing costumes, Merry Widow hats and feather (boas) they hired a fancy rig from the livery stable and went for a wild ride up and down the streets. They stopped at saloons for fresh inspiration and descended upon the stores whence respectable shoppers fled. They were finally routed and returned to their domain by the sheriff and some hardy aides.

Minnie Cowell, a well-known Breckenridge madam, operated an establishment on the much-traveled road to the Wellington Mine. Minnie mixed sin and saintliness in her colorful lifestyle. She used her earnings as a painted lady to purchase a new house for a destitute family, homeless with five or six children due to a tragic fire.

Despite Minnie's charity, Breckenridge held tight to rigid rules of social acceptability. "Celestials" (Chinese) were not even permitted to work in mines. Mormons were feared. "Niggers" were banished from "Nigger Hill", today called Barney Ford Hill after the famous Negro pioneer.

White glove affairs like lectures, lyceum, Chautauqua and concerts, plus card parties for whist, euchre, five hundred and poker created social cliques. Soon a social elite emerged, which Summit County *Journal* editor Fincher labeled "too excruciatingly exclusive".

Many social activities continued to revolve around church. Strawberry socials, oyster suppers, choir and musical programs, plus ladies aid societies, cemented Breckenridge's strong affiliation with church as a focal point in 1890's life.

Young people found high hilarity in sleigh rides, hay rides, sledding down east Lincoln Avenue, skating and skiing on long, heavy 1800's skis.

The "Warm Stove Mine"

While the matrons indulged in parlor gossip, their men beat a path to George B. Watson's Store on Main Street, where thrilling exploits of solid gold strikes and daring wild game hunts took place at the famous "Warm Stove Mine". This mining crew utilized a vivid group imagination in lieu of pick axe and ore bucket. Large amounts of valuable gold emerged from the efforts of the Warm Stove group to be shipped to "Fairyland" where it underwent treatment in the "Hot Air Smelter". Judge William Guyselman headed a Warm Stove contingent of brilliant hunters who related tales of narrow escape and eventual triumph over dangerous grizzlies, tigers and lions. O. K. Gaymon, late 1890's Summit County *Journal* editor, printed these adventure stories. Ed Collingwood; Judge

G. B. Watson, Clothing and Gents' Furnishings,
BRECKENRIDGE, COLO.

D. W. Fall, Breckenridge assayer; Dr. J. F. Condon; Colonel C. L. Westerman; Jake Conrad; and A. W. Phillips kept the hot air circulating under the direction of Warm Stove Mine superintendent George B. Watson. The group's prominent Dr. Condon who lived in Barney Ford's elegant Washington Avenue home, later shot and killed Breckenridge's well-known saloon keeper Johnny Dewers in an August 4, 1898 street gunfight outside the Warm Stove Mine. Improper attention to a wife caused the tragic falling out.

Tempers flared frequently enough to scratch a thin veneer of social elegance and reveal Breckenridge as the western frontier town it was. When Florida Passmore, the Methodist minster after Fr. Dyer's day, crusaded for Sunday closure of Breckenridge's saloons, the town rose up in anger to smite the errant pastor. They ended up by dynamiting his church bell!

A Colorado Saloon Law, enacted April 7, 1891, required that saloons close at midnight on weekdays and all day Sunday. This law was a blessing direct from the Lord for Rev. Passmore, who immediately began to kick up a terrible fuss over saloon closure in Breckenridge. He demanded that Breckenridge's reluctant sheriff F. F. Brown enforce the new law.

Irate residents, like *Journal* editor Fincher, labeled Passmore "unreasonable and unChristlike". The Dillon *Enterprise* went further: "We think the fellow ought to be hung." Finally, on August 17, 1891, anger reached the tempest stage. A crew of miscreants dynamited Passmore's church bell, blowing off the whole belfry as well.

Passmore, undaunted, dredged up an old 1866 Gambling Law and insisted on closing down Breckenridge's popular faro and poker tables. This struck at the very core of personal freedom for the men of Breckenridge.

They hung Passmore in effigy.

Passmore pressed legal charges against saloon-keeper Johnny Dewers in violation of the saloon closing laws. Fincher scored the tax-exempt, Sunday-working preacher in his editorial columns:

> A burlesque of a trial for shaking dice came off before Judge Davis on Thursday last, at which a non-taxpaying gentleman arrayed in sacerdotal robes played the role of prosecuting attorney. The taxpayers footed the bill.

Though Breckenridge saloons temporarily obeyed the closing law, Passmore eventually lost his crusade. He ended up a double loser, for the Methodist Church later tried him in church court for insubordination. The unpredictable Fincher who had lashed Passmore unmercifully with the editorial pen, traveled to Denver to appear as a witness in Passmore's defense!

Breckenridge emerged unscathed from the Passmore crisis. Life proceeded with relative calm until 1896, when a tragic fire raged out of control on upper Main Street, devastating both sides of the street between Washington and Adams. A town water works, completed in 1899, was built by a community fearful of another 1896-style conflagration.

In 1898-99, a new crisis challenged Breckenridge's mettle: The winter of the Big Snow.

Snowbound

Despite the annual autumnal prayers of today's ski area operators for early winter snows, Summit County rarely gets its big dumps much before Christmas. Fall, 1898 followed this pattern. A balmy autumn stretched lazily till Thanksgiving time. Then on November 27, flakes began to tumble from a cloudy sky.

Mrs. Gertrude Engle (left) and friends peer into 1899 snow tunnel.

53

Snow fell in sheets throughout the night and surprised Summit residents awoke to a full five feet of snow by 9 a.m. November 28! But this was just the opening number of a snowstorm extravaganza unparalleled in known Summit history. Snow poured from the skies every day from November 27 to February 20. Snow depth rose to rooftop level. Snow tunnels provided pedestrian access to Breckenridge business places. One burrowed from Finding's Hardware across Main Street to the popular Denver Hotel. People dug out from their homes by cutting steps in the snow to reach surface level. Anything not maintained by constant shoveling was lost — cabins, wagons, railroad freight cars. Atop Boreas Pass, only a bit of exposed chimney pipe emitting smoke signalled the existence of the rail buildings buried below. A 20-foot snow tunnel served as the station entrance.

Denver, South Park & Pacific trains tried valiantly to surmount snow-choked Boreas Pass. The trains encountered 40 to 50-foot drifts in South Park, then with the help of a rotary snowplow, pushed by seven locomotives, attacked the wall of snow that inundated Boreas Pass. Right behind them, the angry Storm King Boreas blew his blustery breath, re-covering the freed track with huge drifts of windblown snow.

Trains stalled with regularity. Ed Auge told the story in a 1935 Summit County *Journal* reminiscence: "On February 4, 1899, a train arrived, being about the first one in a week, but could get no further than Breckenridge. This train departed February 5 and no train was seen again for a period of 80 days." The blockade cut off Breckenridge (and other Summit communities) from rail service, normal mail deliveries, sufficient fresh food stocks and all other supplies until April 24, 1899. (Wagons began to transport limited supplies after March 1.)

Everyone ran short of everything. The *Journal* ran low on paper. Animal owners ran out of feed and sometimes butchered the skinny livestock for food. Butter, eggs, milk, fresh fruits and vegetables and cream became subjects of fantasy. But basic food supplies lasted, and though waistlines grew trim, no one in Breckenridge starved.

Miners attempting travel encountered some hairy moments. S. T. Richards carrying gold, mail and supplies on snowshoes across Boreas Pass, plunged into a 40-foot drift with his heavy load. Ed Auge relates the tale of three miners walking from Breckenridge to the Minnie Mine daily who often had to break trail both ways. The tops of telephone poles for a private line from Wapiti Mine offices to town stood below their trail.

Jess Oakley volunteered to cross Boreas on cumbersome showshoes to fetch the Breckenridge mail. According to Breckenridge writer Helen Rich, Oakley

> . . . slung 45 pounds of first class mail on his back and took off for Como, 19 miles away across Boreas Pass. When he got to the top of the Pass, he wanted nothing so much as a cup of strong hot coffee, but he couldn't locate the railroad station house. He finally saw smoke . . . from a chimney six inches below the snow. He found steps dug from the snow leading down to the house 20 feet below. He had his coffee, got to Como and brought back newspapers to sell for $1 each.

After Oakley's several trips, a pair named Shaw and Utes took over with a contract to carry the mail on skis.

Fed up with nearly three weeks of isolation, Henry C. Foote and his friend, H. W. Mott decided to hazard the wind-whipped Pass to reach Como and the railroad to Denver. As they started up the Pass, a blizzard swirled around them, with white-outs that obscured vision and disoriented the men. They had begun at 8 a.m. and arrived in Como at 6 p.m. that evening. "Each one carried over 30 pounds of baggage . . . ", a February 22, 1899 Denver newspaper reported.

> "The snow in the vicinity of Breckenridge is from four to forty feet deep," says Mr. Foote, "and the wind is frightful, blowing continually at the rate of fifty miles an hour over the ranges. There hasn't been a train into Breckenridge since two weeks ago last Sunday. We have not had any mail up there at all. Why, you may not believe it, but we haven't even had a newspaper to tell us what is going on in the outside world.
> "Provisions are running low! The merchants are completely out of butter, eggs and ham, and when a miner can't have a little ham or eggs, it's mighty hard to get along. At the present time, there is scarcely any feed for the live stock, and unless the railroads succeed in getting in within the next few days, the stock stands a very good chance of perishing from starvation."

Despite heavy snows and relentless hard winds, Summit mines continued to operate. Tucked away in their burrows, the miners produced ore and let it pile up, awaiting the snowmelt and transportation to a working railroad.

Finally, Breckenridge regained access to the outside world. Ed Auge wrote:

> About March 1, all able-bodied men both young and old, volunteered to shovel out the wagon road over Boreas to Como. All the men and all the horses in town completed the job in about ten days, and all the mail and necessities were freighted by team over Boreas until the train arrived.

Righteous indignation arose from some when cheering townspeople greeted the first freight wagon, only to discover it carried a load of whiskey!

The trains remained stuck.

A plucky party of twelve said good-bye to snowbound Breckenridge in early March and laced on their snowshoes for a trip to Denver. Among those scaling blustery Boreas Pass were Charles A. Finding and his two daughters, Agnes and Tonnie. A March 8 Denver *Times* report lauded the group with a story headlined, "Dozen People Escape from Snow-Beleaguered Town". Tonnie did not travel on her own skis: "The younger Miss Finding and her father came through on one pair of skis, going as the mountain men called it 'in tandem'. She stood on the skis just a little behind her father and he, being an expert, carried her through without mishap." Agnes "kept up without difficulty".

The travelers arrived in Denver very sunburned.

Mrs. Kaiser's Cow

Meanwhile, Breckenridge made merry: A constant round of dances and parties (sorry, no refreshments), five-hundred parties and chatty soirees created warmth and fun during the bleak blockade days. The only Breckenridge housewife who wasn't smiling was Mrs. Christ Kaiser, who went to her barn to milk her cow one morning. She found it strung up and butchered. Her grocer husband claimed the act "was done in the name of necessity".

On April 24, the first train to break the blockade arrived to be greeted by a jubilant crowd. The fire bell, church bells and school bell pealed out a glad welcome. The blockade ended, but snow remained in the mountains through the summer. The Leadville road finally re-opened in June and the first stage to Swandyke broke through July 4. Special excursion trains brought summer tourists up to "ooh" and "aah" over the vast snowfields remaining on Boreas Pass.

Prosperous Breckenridge, now a cosmopolitan mountain community, stood ready to enter the 20th century. The town boasted some trappings of modernity: In 1892, electricity came on the Breckenridge scene, but power operated only at night. As early as 1879, telephone lines had crossed Summit County enroute to Leadville, where silver magnate H.A.W. Tabor had built a telephone exchange. The toll lines mounted Loveland and Mosquito Passes, the highest telephone lines in the world. They were purchased by the Colorado Telephone Company in 1889. But storms smashed the lines and they finally were buried. In 1899, permanent telephone lines were installed. Breckenridge received telephone service in 1899 for the same reason the town had obtained rail service in 1882: It was on its way to silver-rich Leadville.

Breckenridge mining man A. E. Keables described turn-of-the-century Breckenridge in his booklet "Goldfields of Summit County, Colorado":

> (Breckenridge) has well appointed and comfortable hotels, stores of all descriptions, livery stables, well filled with good vehicles and stock, a bank, churches, good schools, two weekly newspapers, and a mining exchange. It is lit up by electric light and has a local and long-distance telephone system . . . The water works system is a fine one and the local firefighting organization is efficient and energetic. The Breckenridge Branch of the Denver Smelting and Refining Company has a complete assay and sampling plant and affords a good local market for smelting ores.
>
> The Gold Pan Engineering and Mine Supply Company has extensive and well-appointed engineering and fitting shops for the manufacture and repair of all kinds of mining machinery.

Breckenridge population numbered 2,000 in 1900, according to the *Colorado Business Directory* for that year. The Breckenridge *Bulletin* competed with the *Journal* for newspaper supremacy. Maude Evans McLean served as postmistress, and W. F. Forman was county clerk and recorder. Four churches provided worship opportunities, while at least six saloons offered revelry and spirituous drink. Son Lee ran the Chinese laundry. Breckenridge had a telegraph office, and a train depot. The *Directory* failed to list the town's several licensed houses of prostitution and its single pest house.

Affluence ushered in new elegance. Hotels offered Blue Point oysters and Mumm's Extra Dry Champagne. Breckenridge's best 1900 hotels were the Arlington, with its colonaded porch and ornate cornices, the Denver Hotel, located on the site of today's Breckenridge Ski Shop, the Colorado House and the Occidental House, run by Mrs. F. E. Braddock.

(For readers who want more details, Ed Auge in his 1935 Summit County *Journal* series names all the turn-of-the-century businesses, their owners and street locations.)

An entire town's pride focused on Breckenridge's stately new courthouse, built in 1909 and dedicated March 17, 1910. When the courthouse cornerstone was laid, Saturday, July 31, 1909, a town resplendent with banners and streamers celebrated with a grand parade. Masons, 75 strong, in full regalia, Breckenridge firemen with polished brass buttons, a dandy brass band and chorus marked an unforgettable day.

Life was rarely dull in old Breckenridge. Though many staunch, God-fearing Breckenridge families worked at serving their Creator, the devil also had his day. His handiwork appears in this tale:

"I'll Take You, Katie!"

One August night in 1912, a drunken vagrant lurched his way up toward Curtin Hill (today's Wellington Hill) intending to call upon the ladies of the night. Their establishment had recently moved to the hill from the red light district on the Blue River's west bank. As the drunk stumbled in the wrong direction up the hill, the Daughters of St. John, an Episcopal club for girls and young women, sat primly in Mr. and Mrs. Robert Gore's parlor. They sewed as Miss Agnes Finding read aloud from an inspirational work. Mrs. Mabel Gore sat in the kitchen, absorbed in conversation with a friend. Young Zoe Gore had trouble concentrating on her stitchery. She was listening for her father, Breckenridge's beloved Robert Gore, to return from another long day as dredgemaster of the Reliance gold boat. The dredge had struck bedrock; she knew her father was exhausted.

Our confused vagrant finally found the brightly-lit house he'd been hunting. He fumbled at the door. Inside young Zoe heard the noise, jumped up and hurried to let her father in.

She opened the door: The inebriate, exuding whiskey fumes, took one look at the fresh young miss. His bleary eyes brightened. He lunged at Zoe, bellowing, "I'll take you, Katie!"

The ladies in the parlor all but fainted in terror. Mabel Gore, hearing the commotion, armed herself with a rolled-up copy of her 1900's fashion magazine, the "Delineator", charged into the entry way and proceeded to pommel the unsavory intruder with all the force that an enraged 100-pound mother can muster. (In this case, plenty!) She drove the drunk out and turned her efforts toward calming the shaken young ladies with cookies and hot chocolate.

Sheriff Jerry Detweiler later arrested the drunk and discovered he was armed.

Tiny, five-foot Mabel Gore could summon up the ire of a mother lion when danger threatened. Shepherding her children and blind mother on an 1898 rail-coach to San Francisco, she watched a pistol-toting drunk spewing profanities, confront a conductor with his gun. The conductor froze. Mabel jumped up on a seat behind the troublemaker, grabbed his neck, and drove her fingers neatly into his windpipe. She maintained this painful hold till help arrived.

Early 1900's transportation remained less than dependable. Motor cars had appeared in Breckenridge just after the turn of the century. "Birdie" Evans, wife of the Gold Pan Shops' George Evans, owned a fashionable electric car, but Breckenridge's rock-strewn streets threatened to destroy the machine. In winter, the snow closed roads, so Breckenridge's few autos went up on blocks in September. Sleighs carried merry groups to Frisco and other destinations. Delivery sleds made their way through town throughfares. The Kaiser Market sled frequently caused local chaos when its mules ran away with groceries bouncing and scattering behind. And the railroad, now under the name Colorado & Southern (C & S), transported travelers to Denver, until its 1937 shutdown. The train, scheduled its departure at 11 a.m., with arrival in Denver at 6 p.m. Old-timers report it was "never on time".

Conductor George "Fatty" Patton moved his bulky frame through the narrow rail car aisles, laughing and joking with passengers as they relaxed on the rich red-plush seats. Fatty's diamond studs, almost dime-sized, caused much comment until they were stolen by rail bandits.

Jolly times and good fun punctuated 1900's life in Breckenridge. Gay Loomis, grand-daughter of Chancey Carlisle Warren, who operated the Warren's Station stage stop on Loveland Pass in 1879, remembers the good times:

> The old bakery in Breckenridge was one of our favorite stops when we'd go up there on Saturdays. They say things taste better when you're a kid, and maybe they do, because those buns we got from Breckenridge bakery — it was on Lincoln Street — were awfully good. One day my sister and I went up there to go to a show, and we found the only show with tickets left — it was *The Face on the Barroom Floor*. My mother wasn't too pleased when she heard that's what we were going to see (we were still little girls), but she let us go after all. And when the show was over, we went and bought big creampuffs at the wonderful bakery.
> Vaudeville shows would come through from time to time on the train, one of them the Rio Grande; it came from Denver through Frisco and went on sometimes to Leadville.

Breckenridge could boast some outstanding citizens during its heyday years. Chapter 17 details the contributions of the Silverthorn-Finding family and dredge king, Ben Stanley Revett. But there are others who deserve remembering.

(Certainly, no one can forget the patriotic ladies of Breckenridge who invited Colorado Governor Edwin C. Johnson to town to induct Breckenridge into the legal confines of the United States of America. These women had discovered that Breckenridge and its environs ranked as a "No Man's Land", land never formally annexed by the U.S. Despite last minute assurances by respected Colorado historian Leroy Hafen that the Treaty of 1819 solved the town's problems, the ladies went ahead with their annexation ceremony. The Kingdom of Breckenridge reclaims its "No Man's Land" status for a three-day celebration every August.)

The lives of a few families and individuals important to Breckenridge are capsuled here.

The George Engle Family

Around 1888, the Breckenridge bank floundered, making miners uneasy about depositing their gold in its coffers. Peter and George Engle had a vault in their billiard saloon, located where the courthouse now stands, and the miners entrusted their gold to the saloon safe. Finally, George and Peter Engle launched their own banking business, the Engle Brothers Exchange Bank, in today's Exchange Building. Their efforts earned success. Banker George Engle, Swiss-born and reared in France, became one of Breckenridge's leaders. In 1893, he married Gertrude Susan Briggle, an Ohio girl who came west to teach in Summit's Montezuma school. She also taught at old Kokomo, Lincoln and Breckenridge.

Gertrude plunged into Breckenridge life as a meticulous homemaker, bank vice-president, Women's Christian Temperance Union booster and Sunday school teacher.

The Engles lived above the bank, barricaded against the common threat of bank robbery. (Once a mentally-deranged bank loan reject threw a bomb into the Engle's bedroom to gain revenge.)

A daughter, Elizabeth, blessed the Engles in July, 1903. She attended Summit schools, belonged to Sister's Mustard Seeds, a charitable group, helped launch the Home Demonstation Club, taught elementary students and served for 12 years on the Summit school board. Elizabeth married H. G. Culbreath. Their children remain as well-known Summit local residents.

The Guyselman-Knorr Family

William Guyselman came West from Missouri in 1879, stopping at Leadville, then settling at Breckenridge. As an attorney, he served as district attorney and also as a Summit County judge. In 1881, Judge Guyselman bought a ranch at Lakeside, on the lower Blue River.

In 1899, German-born William ("Billy") Knorr bought the ranch. But he quickly reunited the property with the Guyselman fold by marrying pretty Corrine Guyselman in 1900. Billy and his brother ran Breckenridge's popular Knorr Brothers Pioneer Saloon. But soon he and Corrine moved to the ranch and began raising a family. The Knorrs played a vital role in the lively events to follow at Lakeside, a place fondly remembered by Summit old-timers.

The Fletcher Family

Eli Fletcher grew up in the rough and tumble, log and shanty, placer camp of early Breckenridge. He married Emma Nauman there in 1881, with Father Dyer officiating. The Fletchers honeymooned at Braddocks, then headed for a challenging winter working atop Boreas Pass. Eli later became a Breckenridge butcher. He spent his spare time hand-crafting skis for local winter-sport enthusiasts. The Fletchers had eight children. Family members have long contributed to Summit County life. Son Ted Fletcher served as Breckenridge mayor and town council member. His wife, Helen, became county assessor. Fletcher family descendants still live in Summit County.

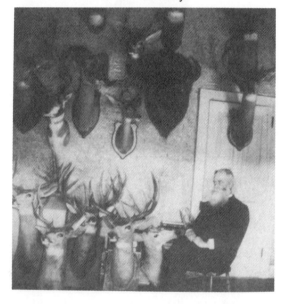

Edwin Carter

A Summit County pioneer who participated in the 1859 Colorado gold rush, Edwin Carter left a legacy to Colorado. A brilliant naturalist, he assembled the unrivalled Rocky Mountain bird and animal collection that spearheaded Denver's Museum of Natural History. Carter's collection today has been viewed by well over 30 million visitors.

The "log cabin naturalist" worked for decades in a tiny cabin at 111 North Ridge Street in Breckenridge. Carter studied taxidermy as a furrier's apprentice in Black Hawk (or possibly Georgetown; details remain obscure). He set himself an ambitious goal: To create a complete collection including specimens of every Rocky Mountain bird and animal. Carter constantly walked the hills, studying wildlife habits. He snared and stuffed buffalo and bobcats, grizzlies and grouse, along with rare birds, which he presented in their nests filled with delicate colored eggs. Tens of thousands of specimens resulted from his life work, including American and Golden Eagle specimens. What Carter failed to find himself, he purchased from other taxidermists, using funds derived from the sale of his duplicate specimens. The naturalist refused to sell, at any price, items that he could not replace.

Eminent visitors and scientists traveled to Breckenridge to view Carter's collection. He began negotiations for the transfer of his life work. But he died in 1900 before the transfer could be completed. Carter succumbed to arsenic poisoning, long absorbed into his system during specimen preparation. The $10,000 sale proceeds went to Carter's heirs, after much negotiation by estate executor George Engle and Breckenridge mines owner John F. Campion, the prime mover in the effort to create a Denver natural history museum with Carter's work as its nucleus.

The humble naturalist contributed more than his taxidermy talents to early Summit County. In 1860, he helped organize the first Masonic Lodge west of the Continental Divide in Georgia Gulch's Parkville and became a charter member of this lodge, Summit County Lodge No 2, A. F. & M. A longtime member of Breckenridge's Masonic Lodge, Carter assembled a large personal library of Masonic books.

Carter prospected in Leadville's famous California Gulch, then at Salt Lick near Dillon, the Swan Valley, Humbug and American Gulches. But soon taxidermy took all his time. He worked in a small cabin behind the now-extinct Carter Museum in Breckenridge. He added a larger building in 1875.

Carter's grave rests in Breckenridge's Valley Brook Cemetery, marked by a tombstone that the famed and gentle naturalist almost didn't get. Heirs, reluctant to part with even a bit of their new-found wealth to buy a grave a marker, implored Engle: "Please do not set apart a large amount, we beg you . . . Would not $50 be sufficient? . . . Let Breckenridge honor him in his death."

A determined Engle went ahead and spent $250 for a proper monument to Breckenridge's famous son.

Father John Lewis Dyer

A Colorado pioneer honored in a Colorado State Capitol stained glass portrait, Father John Lewis Dyer preached God's word to the raw gold and silver camps of 1860's Summit County and its neighbors.

And raw they were. The Princeton Scientific Expedition, visiting Breckenridge in 1877, described the "world" that Fr. Dyer attempted to save: "Sunday is a day for general dissipation, and is spent by the miners in the wildest sorts of vice.

Churches are unknown and there is nothing to remind anyone that it is not a weekday."

Dispite his advanced age, Fr. Dyer traveled on snowshoes, the cumbersome miners' skis, to humbly serve these bawdy settlements. The penniless preacher carried the mails, in heavy canvas sacks, over perilous snow-packed high mountain passes, to earn enough money to continue his missionary work. The task proved exhausting to an old man, but Fr. Dyer's spirit pushed him onward.

The Methodist minister built Breckenridge's first church, today's Father Dyer Methodist Church on French Street. He discovered the Warrior's Mark Mine near Boreas Pass and in 1880 spearheaded Dyersville, an Indian Gulch town close to the mine. He once lived in a rude cabin in early Lincoln.

Many lively stories about Fr. Dyer's sojourns in Summit County exist, but others have told them well. In his autobiography, *Snowshoe Itinerant*, Fr. Dyer chronicles his joys, sorrows, achievements — and his skirmishes with death.

Barney Ford

Phoebe, a black, illiterate slave in 1840's North Carolina, stole the dictionary from the master's house. That night, she set a tallow candle in her dirt floor, opened the book and forced her blue-hazel eyed, olive-skinned mulatto son to hunker down before it. She bade him to read.

When the boy failed to decipher the mysterious markings, she switched him till his legs raised red welts. Then she cradled her son, sobbing, "My poor little Barney boy. Mama want to help him, but she don't know how."

Barney Ford never forgot those words.

He learned to read. He escaped the plantation, found his way to Denver, and eventually to 1860's Breckenridge.

A black could hold no legal title to mining property, so a kindly Denver lawyer suggested that young Ford file any possible discovery in the attorney's name. They would split the gold profits, 80-20.

Ford prospected a little fork off French Gulch and found good "color". He filed a claim in the Denver attorney's name. The contents of his little placer gold dust bottle grew each day.

That was until the sheriff showed up. He ran Barney off the claim. The lawyer had sworn out legal papers to eject Ford. Their agreement had been verbal.

Ford fled Breckenridge. But back in town, the rumor mill churned full speed, grinding out a tale of riches hastily buried on a mountainside by fleeing Negroes. Greedy fortune hunters (and 1860's Breckenridge had plenty of these) swarmed over Barney's hillside home, searching for buried treasure. They began to call the site "Nigger Hill".

Ford engaged in various job activities in Denver. When Breckenridge boomed again, with Will Iliff's 1878 Blue Danube strike, Ford returned. He rented a one-story frame building and opened a restaurant.

Ford's Chop House caught on, becoming a popular Breckenridge gathering spot. In a year, Ford bought the building. He built a home at the corner of Washington and Main Street, a gem Victorian structure that still stands proudly today as a private residence. The Summit County *Journal* remarked that Ford's luxurious home "deprives us of the power to realize that we are in the land of log cabins and tented homes".

Barney Ford invested with others, including hotelkeeper Tom Brown (his hotel is today's Ore Bucket), in ownership of the Oro Mine. A dazzling yield from his small investment made Ford a rich man. His career steamed forward like an 1880's locomotive. He helped create Colorado history, influenced gubernatorial and senatorial elections. They called him "president-maker".

But Barney Ford's crowning moment came in 1882, when he was invested in the Colorado Association of Pioneers, an honor long withheld because Ford was black.

Mrs. Julia Ford later earned a listing in the Denver Social Register, the first time that exclusive society admitted a Negro.

In 1964, the Board of Geographic Names officially changed Nigger Hill's name to Barney Ford Hill.

Otto Westerman

Little is known about photographer Otto Westerman, but one fact is certain: Westerman made an invaluable contribution to Breckenridge history by faithfully recording its lives and times on primitive photographic film. Undaunted by his game leg, the crippled camera buff scrambled up hillsides, ran before parades and hung off high balconies to capture every facet of Breckenridge life. Westerman ran his photography business in Breckenridge from 1889 until somewhere around 1917. His sense of history gave us a legacy of pictures that say more than the proverbial 1,000 words could ever relate.

Montezuma:

One Hundred and Fifteen Rollicking Years

The group of prospectors had clawed their way over a craggy Continental Divide to scout the Snake River mountains for silver. John Coley had in 1863 smelted silver ingots from Colorado's first silver strike on nearby Glacier Mountain. Word of peaks seamed with silver had traveled on the wind. The year: 1865. The men: Henry M. Teller, who later became a U.S. Senator from Colorado; D. C. Collier, former senior editor of the Central City *Register*; Maurice O. Wolf; J. T. Lynch, who later discovered the rich Sukey lode; Oliver Milner, who later located the Don Pedro and Aladdin's Lamp mines; and D. Wiley, later one of the discoverers of the Tiger and Tiger Extension lodes. These men, camping in a beautiful 10,200-foot mountain-rimmed valley bisected by the Snake's tumbling South Fork, decided to name their tent commune. D. C. Collier blazed the name "Montezuma" on a tree. The name of Mexico's last Aztec emperor, famous for the golden treasures that dazzled his Spanish conqueror, Cortez, signified waiting riches. The town, Montezuma, was born.

In 1868, when a rough route over Loveland Pass opened, miners with pack trains began to pour over the Divide from Georgetown. M. P. Felch and George Turnbull put up Montezuma's first hotel in 1868 to house the horde. R. O. Jones built the Preston House in 1869. This hotel, later renamed the Summit House, would remain to serve a host of visitors over many decades.

When William Brewer visited Montezuma during his 1868 sojourn through Summit County, he described Montezuma:

> At last, the road turns up a side stream, growing steeper, and the forests denser than any we have seen before. At last we came to the mining town of Montezuma, whose newly shingled roofs gleamed through the trees. It looks thriving for it is a new place — a town with new silver mines of supposed great richness, so the town has its share of expectations for the future. New houses are going up — it is thriving — although above where all grains will grow — even potatoes — for it lies at perhaps 10,000 feet, possibly more.

He rated Montezuma's sole lodging facility with this comment:

> We stopped at the only hotel, kept by a smart Vermont Yankee, his wife a smarter Yankee, Vermont woman. . . It had three rooms downstairs — the outside or sitting room, dining room, and kitchen. The overworked woman had no female help, but the table was well-served, notwithstanding the influx of eight hungry travellers in addition to the already large family. Her husband had gone to his ranch (nearly a hundred miles distant) for vegetables to supply his table. He returned while we were there, the coveted "grub" packed on donkeys or mules. Such is life here in the mountains. We slept in the common garret, with perhaps eight or ten others, hardy, tired miners and prospectors, some of whom snored loud enough to wake the dead.

Another visitor stopped at youthful Montezuma in 1868 — Colorado Governor John Evans, on a tour of the state's blossoming mine camps. Evans later developed the mountain railroad that alleviated Montezuma's 20-year ore freight problems.

By 1871, Montezuma had an ore reduction works built for the Sukey Mine and St. Lawrence Mining Company. The town's steam sawmill was owned by the Webster brothers, developers of Webster Pass. The town's first livery stable opened for business in 1875 and its first tin shop in 1876. Montezuma had 30 houses in 1875.

The 1877 Princeton Scientific Expedition, that somewhat snobbish group of

Late 1870's Montezuma had Rocky Mountain House (left), built before 1877; Miner's Resort (right rear, "saloon" sign); Summit House (sign); and Town Hall.

undergraduates touring the high Rockies, had registered vehement dislike for Breckenridge. But Montezuma proved more to diary-keeper William Libby's liking. He wrote:

> When we came to the Snake Valley, we rode up that stream ten more miles, through a most glorious piece of woodland scenery. We found we were in the neighborhood of Montezuma, and halted at the hotel for our dinner, which turned out to be a regular New York feast — mock-turtle soup, steak with mushrooms, etc. This fact, as well as the presence of New York papers, *Harper's Weekly* and *Monthly*, and the genteel appearance of our host, led us to make inquiries, whereupon he was recognized by two of us as one of those voluntary exiles from society, where he once moved with honor.

Which hotel entertained the Princeton men in such lavishness is a mystery. The Rocky Mountain House had joined a growing roster of Montezuma hotels by the time the group visited.

An 1879 *Colorado Business Directory* listed J. H. Yonley's assay office (Yonley was appointed Territorial Assayer in 1872); the Montezuma House; the Summit Hotel, (J. D. Perry, proprietor); Maurice Wolf's general store; the Boston Silver Mining Company; and the Sukey, Yonley and St. Lawrence silver ore mills. Yonley built his pioneering Sisapo Smelter and Sampling Works in south Montezuma around fall, 1880.

The bustling Sts. John silver mine, just two miles above Montezuma, on Glacier Mountain, helped the valley town to grow. But when the Sts. John Mine, the town's lifeline, had closed down in 1878, empty cabins left by its workers made Montezuma look like a ghost town. The valley community would, however, survive without Sts. John. Montezuma mines, discovered but formerly undeveloped, began to blossom. In 1880, Montezuma stood poised on the brink of becoming a real town.

Even Montezuma's competitor, Chihuahua, had to sit up and take notice. The *Colorado Miner* on July 3, 1880 intoned:

> Montezuma has thrown off its wintry covering and is blooming with the pilgrim and the tenderfoot. The festive saloon keeper is driving a flourishing trade; boarding houses have "standing room only", and all things being equal, Montezuma is having a quiet little boom of its own. Some say that Montezuma is dependent upon the crumbs which, metaphorically speaking, fall from Chihuahua's table, but the fact is the Chihuahuaites have to come to Montezuma to invest, as the Bell and Blanche lodes are now owned and being worked by representative from that town.

Along with its ore transport hassle, isolated Montezuma faced the challenge of mail delivery. No stage lines or trains served the 1860's mountain camps. Hardy pioneer Oliver Milner volunteered to pack 1869 mails from Montezuma to Breckenridge for round-trip private subscription pay of $15. Rain, snow and dark of night, plus other inclement alpine weather hazards, all contrived to prevent the mail from getting through, but Oliver Milner conquered them all. The only thing that threatened to beat Oliver were his skis, heavy eight-foot long boards used for winter travel.

John Irving Hastings, who lived at St. John in 1872, remembered the mail's arrival one March day:

> The carrier, with his pack of mail, could be seen for miles away on the mountainside before reaching camp. Then the crowd assembled on the boardinghouse porch to watch his progress into camp. They tell of one time when he came down the mountain with almost incredible speed and trailed with a cloud of flying snow behind him, only to break a ski as he struck a snow bank in front of them all and suffered a bad fall.

Normally, Milner blew a long tin horn to announce mail call, but his spectacular arrival that day needed no further introduction. The dauntless mailman, bruised and somewhat shaken, continued on to Montezuma.

Hastings' diary comments:

> Let us all forget about this catalogue and circular age that we live in. Possibly there were two or three newspapers in the mail and they would be read to shreds. The mail consisted of mostly letters. The mail carriers used the Norwegian ski. I never saw a man on a French Canadian snowshoe or racket.

The Montezuma *Millrun's* first issue in June, 1882, capsuled the area's history. The paper explained the early mail carrier's route: "Over the pass at the head of Bear Creek" (today called Sts. John Creek) "then along the Swan river to Breckenridge".

Another early day miner-mailman, W. L. Mitchell, carried mail between Montezuma and Decatur, high in the Peru Creek Valley near the Argentine Pass base. Mitchell's wife, Fanny, never spoke to her husband, although she was a very verbal lady, the author of magazine and newspaper articles. The pair mined their lode claim in stony silence, living in separate cabins halfway between the Peru Valley towns of Decatur and Chihuahua.

If moving the mails proved problematic, obtaining foods also presented a challenge. Beans, potatoes, onions, rutabegas, carrots and parsnips provided daily winter vegetable fare, according to one-time Montezuma resident Elizabeth Rice Roller in an August, 1964 *Westerners Brand Book* article. Cooked steel-cut oats made a daily breakfast. In harvest season, ranches on the lower Blue supplied fresh green edibles. "I used to accompany my father on his produce wagon from which he sold beef, vegetables and fruits to the scattered residents of the valley," Mrs. Roller wrote. A Rice family neighbor, the Clancy family, lived nearby during their years in Chihuahua, and also had a dairy ranch. Sometimes their delicious fresh cream replaced Eagle brand condensed milk in the Rice family diet. Fresh milk and butter were special treats, too. (Infant graves of two lost Clancy daughters still remain off the Peru Creek Road to remind passersby of the hard days a century ago.)

Stephen Decatur, 1860's Decatur founder, took a regular Sunday horseback jaunt to a dairy ranch for a Sabbath indulgence in fresh, sweet cream. This dairy ranch about 12 miles from Decatur was probably the dairy farm that occupied the site of today's Keystone Ranch golf club over 100 years ago.

Montezuma flourished when the Webster Pass Road opened in 1878, providing a vital link to South Park and Denver. Ores traveled this new wagon road to market, stage lines delivered mail, and food supplies arrived via ox wagon. In September, 1881, a mushrooming Montezuma became an incorporated town. Townspeople, now almost 800-strong, elected trustees in April, 1882.

New town trustees came down hard on Montezuma's sporting element. The flag of decency waved in new Montezuma. Drunks were fined a steep $5 to $25, depending on degree of dissipation. Gamblers paid $5 to $20 for offenses against new laws that forbade popular pastimes such as faro, keno, shuffleboard, bagatelle or playing cards with intent to gamble. What's more, ladies of the night

Saloons like Tim Looney's dispensed spirits to prospectors and townsmen, but card sharks had to find another watering hole when 1882 town law forbade gambling.

had to scurry for cover as the law's glaring gaze focused upon them. Verna Sharp quoted Montezuma's law in her 1962 *Colorado Magazine* article, "Law and Order Come to Montezuma": "No bawdy house, disorderly house, house of ill-fame or assignation, or place known as a dance house shall be kept or maintained within the limits of Montezuma . . ." Inmates of such a house would be fined from $5 up to a whopping $50.

(Compare this to bawdy old Breckenridge with hurdy-gurdy dance hall music filling the street and licensed houses of prostitution!)

All this legal flim-flam failed to daunt Montezuma's resident red-light lady, "Dixie", who kept a neat white cottage back from Main Street. (Her home, now painted gray, still stands on the right as you enter Montezuma.) Dixie employed two or three inmates during prosperous mining periods and winged it alone during hard times.

"Dixie", (real name Ada Smith) loved gaudy colors, gauzy scarves, and big picture hats, according to Elizabeth Rice Roller. No fly-by-night shady lady, she maintained residence in Montezuma for many years. Because she carefully avoided ill-will, Dixie became an accepted community member. Mrs. Roller remembered:

> She bought groceries at our store. At first my father took her orders but later any other member of the family waited on her and she was always proper and business-like. She was very fond of coupon deals — (yes, we had 'em in those days, too). She bought Columbine milk by the case and fed it generously to the cats and dogs in town to obtain more labels.

Dixie loved baseball (So did Montezuma!) and appeared at the ball games in flagrant finery, catching stares as she hollered for the home team.

Montezuma's favorite soiled dove lasted through the town's boom and bust cycles. When times grew bad, she refused to forget her local clients. Mrs. Roller remembered: "As the old prospectors grew feeble, she was concerned for them, carrying soup and delicacies to their cabins and caring for them in an illness." Dixie and her girls also cared for Montezuma bachelors during the disasterous 1918 flu epedemic. Many gravestones in Montezuma's shady hillside cemetery mark this sad event.

Buckskin Joe had its beautiful and mysterious "Silverheels", who nursed miners through a deadly smallpox epidemic, then disappeared. But though Dixie created her own legend, she was no beauty. Tiny and thin, her wrinkled face reminded Elizabeth Roller of a dried apple.

Other businesses besides Dixie's flourished in 1880's Montezuma. *Colorado Business Directories* listed these mid-80's commercial enterprises: George Frey's Rocky Mountain Hotel; Mrs. L. J. Myers' Summit House; Matt Williams' grocery store; Maurice Wolf's general store; Mary Winart's periodicals and confectionery shop; Mary Randolph's restaurant; Domedion's Saloon; W. J. Lusher's livery and feed stable; Gill and Morrell's Hardware; J. King's blacksmith shop; and Alan & Markey's meat packing company. James Oliver published the Montezuma *Millrun*. The Silver King and Sts. Johns Mines had Montezuma offices. A bank opened to serve these brisk business operations.

J. W. Swisher was the town lawyer. Ed McHall wore the marshall's badge. And J. C. Davis served as justice of the peace.

Montezuma school children had hiked up to the Halfway School, between Montezuma and Sts. John from the time the Summit School District formed in 1876 until 1880. Then Montezuma's first school opened and the Sts. John children began walking the two miles down Glacier Mountain to attend. (Some carried their shoes until they reached town to save on shoe leather. How that rocky road must have hurt bare young feet!).

Montezuma children soon crowded the 1880 school. The town built its present schoolhouse and later added the entry hall, belfry and school bell. Box supper socials raised money to purchase the school's first organ. Teachers included Octavia Newman, 1884; Gertrude Briggle, 1885; Miss Loecher, early 1890's; and Ruby Carle, 1899.

Schoolmarm Gertrude Briggle became Mrs. George Engle, matriarch of an outstanding Breckenridge family. Though the Briggle family followed Gertrude from Ohio later and launched a business in old Breckenridge, Gertrude made her first trip to faraway Montezuma all alone. She lurched through the long train trip to Denver, then boarded the narrow-gauge Denver, South Park & Pacific for her eight and one-half hour mountain rail journey to Dillon. From there she bumped on a horse-drawn wagon over rough, rock-strewn roads to remote Montezuma — beyond the edge of civilization! Miss Briggle was the only female lodger at her Montezuma boardinghouse. She tramped through deep snows and toted wood to start an early morning winter fire in her schoolroom for 16 students in eight grades.

Teacher Ruby Carle, who grew up in Chihuahua, was the sister of Mabel Carle Rice, part of the Carle-Rice family that pioneered in Montezuma, and in the Peru Creek Valley.

According to a taped lecture by former Summit school adminstrator Ruby Lowe, Montezuma had 21 students in the 1882 school census. By then, nearby towns of Chihuahua and Decatur had their own school. The quaint, white, one-room schoolhouse, remaining in the grassy meadow at Montezuma's east edge with desks intact today, served Montezuma until 1958.

Protestants held services in the old schoolhouse, but Catholics had their own 1880's church in Montezuma. Reverend C. M. Alger, 1892 itinerant priest, took a long train trip, then a stage ride from Breckenridge to serve Montezuma Catholics. (Or, he traveled on horseback when the Catholic liveryman at Breckenridge gave him a free horse.) In 1892, when silver values plunged, Fr. Alger had only three church-going families at Montezuma, because the Sts. John Mine had closed down in response to depressed silver prices.

But Colorado's skiing preacher, Fr. John Lewis Dyer, had drummed up impromtu Methodist congregations every time he visited the sequestered Snake River Valley. Fr. Dyer, who held his first services at a fledgling Montezuma in 1865, traveled from camp to camp bringing the Lord's word. "The call to worship was given by pounding on a circular saw with a piece of iron," reminisced an

Mid-1880's schoolhouse still stands, transformed by white-painted siding, entry hall, belfry. Town's second school replaced crowded 1880 structure.

71

1885 Montezuma *Millrun*. Since Fr. Dyer preached his 1865 campfire service on Independence Day, the group sang the "Star Spangled Banner" under the leadership of Commodore Decatur.

The *Millrun*, Montezuma's pungent news publication, continued under publisher James Oliver, its chatty and informative reporting from June, 1882 until 1887. Then, in September, 1887, J. W. Swisher took the editorial chair until the newspaper's demise in 1888.

Later, on April 14, 1906, another newspaper appeared on Montezuma streets, the Montezuma *Prospector*. Owned by L. D. Hart, the *Prospector* flourished under the editorial hand of Colonel James Myers who had his talented hand into so many early-1900's Summit enterprises. Myers spearheaded the big Lenawee Tunnel and Lenawee Mill near Montezuma and supervised a bulging portfolio of mines. Small, bearded and energetic, Colonel Myers busied himself as Montezuma mining's chief promoter.

Despite its promoters' best efforts, Montezuma could never have mushroomed into a mining hub had road builders not hacked out wagon routes over the cloud-scraping Continental Divide mountains that barricaded the town. In 1869, Stephen Decatur and others built a wagon road over 13,132-foot Argentine Pass, Summit's most challenging mountain-scaling route. In 1878, William and Emerson Webster, with the Montezuma Silver Mining Company, cut the wagon road that made Montezuma's future. Post Road No. 40 from Montezuma over Webster Pass to Hall Valley through Harndcart Gulch linked the struggling mine camp with Denver ore markets. In 1879, the Loveland Pass Road from Georgetown opened, a boon to Montezuma, which then lay close to daily stagecoach service and wagon freight lines. The Denver, South Park & Pacific railroad built a branch to old Keystone in 1883. Then ore pack trains, descending from steep Montezuma gulches, could haul ore to the freighting station at today's Ski Tip Ranch. Ore then traveled in wagons to the Keystone railhead.

Ski Tip, known as Elwood's in the old days, also served as a social center for not only Montezuma, but all of Summit County. Old-timers fondly recall the big summer pot-luck picnics, with people from Breckenridge, Kokomo, Frisco and Dillon, as well as Montezuma, gathering for lively fun and delicious food.

Prospector Elwood had built the first cabin there in 1869 (the walls were stuffed with 1869 London newspapers). Thomas Black and his family, well-known Montezuma residents, homesteaded the ranch after 1915. Max and Edna Dercum, well-loved Summit residents, arrived in the 1940's to transform historic Ski Tip into a lodge that attracted skiing celebrities and movie stars.

Other favorite picnic spots included the soda springs north of Montezuma, the Rock Soda Spring near Chihuahua (the nose-tickling soda water made "fizzy" lemonade) and the elegant Franklyn House, on the Snake River south of Montezuma.

But Montezuma residents didn't satisfy their social needs with picnics alone. The remote 1880's camp, often imprisoned by deep winter snows, hosted some fancy dress balls that made those snooty Easterners show some respect. Pastel silks, black brocade satin, lace, diamonds, cameos, and pearls, and feather boas

strutted out to the strains of violin music on a polished dance floor. Hall Valley residents, from the eastern side of Webster Pass, turned out for these balls, which featured an elegant midnight supper and a sleepy return home lit by the early rays of the sunrise.

Montezuma needed its bright hours, for grim days would come. As the silver community entered the 1890's', silver prices began to plummet. The government's devaluation of silver and return to the gold standard, prompting the Panic of 1893, struck hard at the Montezuma district, one of the nation's biggest silver producers.

Elizabeth Rice Roller remembered the bleak days following devaluation:

> But in 1893 came the panic and panic is the word for it. Banks and businesses collapsed — the big bank in Denver that held Father's savings failed completely. All over the country people were penniless. There was no market for silver and therefore no ore to haul. The family moved to the ranch. It was a difficult year. In a letter written by my mother a month after my birth in March of 1894, she says, "We hope to get some hens from Mr. D. on what he owes, but if we cannot get them we'll get along without as we have been doing." I take it she meant get along without eggs. She told me that many times that winter she did not have stamps to send letters to her parents.

Still reeling from the silver crash, Montezuma sallied forth unwittingly into the phenomenal "Big Snow Winter" of 1898-99. Autumn lingered pleasant in the Snake River Valley that year, but when snows began to fall in late November they just didn't quit. Snow shoulder and chin high accumulating overnight during the first snowfall shocked Montezuma residents. By the New Year, snow reached the rooftops. Montezuma stood alone, cut off from supplies and facing the spectre of starvation.

But the town drew together, sharing meager supplies. Montezuma resident Isabella Graham Black reported no profiteering by those who had foodstuffs. When every last grain of sugar in Montezuma was long gone, Saloonkeeper Dolph Domedion discovered a sack of it in his back room. Domedion measured out the precious sugar, pound by pound, and distributed it free to Montezuma residents.

Several families endured silver panics, snows and mining's final demise to emerge as respected long-time Montezuma citizens. The Clinesmith-Sharp family is one. Roberta Clinesmith served as Sts. John librarian. She also taught in Argentine in 1902-03 where she met and married Thomas Sharp. She and her husband had two sons, Leland and William, who long mined Montezuma silver. Mrs. Verna Sharp, Leland's wife, wrote an excellent history of Montezuma and its neighboring towns. The Myers family, beginning with patriarch Colonel James H. Myers, local mining promoter, continued with the Colonel's son, James H. ("Dimp") and his wife, Lula, former Frisco schoolteacher. Lula Myers' cabin now stands as a historical display at Dillon's Summit Historical Society Museum. The Bianchi-Black family, pioneering miners, lived around Montezuma, with Mrs. Isabella Graham Black operating Montezuma's Montezuma Hotel for years. Chihuahua's Carle-Rice family lived in Chihuahua, Montezuma and the Soda Creek ranch. The Filgers were popular early residents. Isaac Filger discovered the Winning Card Mine. He died in Breckenridge in 1903. Many of these names appear on headstones in the rustic, pine-shaded Montezuma Cemetery.

Montezuma experienced a new surge after the turn of the century when silver prices rose and mining technology made processing low grade ores profitable. Around 1905, the town bustled with mining activity. The much-heralded Vidler Tunnel through Argentine Pass would soon be complete. As late as January 3, 1920, the Summit County *Journal* quoted Montezuma's mining expert, E. W. Fairchild: "1920 will be a banner year," he predicted in a New Year forecast. The signs pointed to progress: The Sts. John concentrating mill had reopened and the St. Elmo Mining Company and Mark Twain Mine just above Montezuma on Glacier Mountain had launched development.

(Fairchild's beautiful Montezuma home, the "White House" later served as a 1940's lodge operated by Gladys Meadows. Visitors admired the home's antiques, ore samples and 100-year old painted china lamp.)

In the 1930's, Montezuma functioned as a hub for the big New York, Pennsylvania and Ida Belle Mines.

More threatening than silver's fluctuating values were the five fires that ravaged the insular, often snowbound, community. The 1889 forest fire that destroyed Chihuahua would have devastated Montezuma if hard work by miners and a sudden wind shift had not saved the town. But the fire cut the town off from the outside world for days.

Fire wiped out one side of an entire street in 1915. The fire started in the kitchen of Isabella Black's hotel and consumed the building. It leapt to Rice's barn, a building saved from Chihuahua's disastrous 1889 fire. The conflagration moved on, leaving a "blackened ruin" of Brines' Saloon, Kirts and Bernachey's Saloon, the Black, Waters, Howe, McElwain homes and many other buildings. The post office and telephone station, located in the Montezuma Hotel, burned and wiped out area communications. Loss in 1915 dollars totaled $30,000.

Franklyn House

In 1949, Montezuma's then-spare 80 residents couldn't control another blaze as it leapt from Noble's combination general store-pool hall-tavern. One of Montezuma's historic log cabins burned, as did the town's third oldest building, a barn structure. Damage reached $20,000.

Only nine years later, a December 17, 1958, fire destroyed 10 frame buildings, including the historic 1869 Summit House Hotel and the landmark town hall. The fire, with a $50,000 estimated loss, made a very sad Christmas for 75 Montezuma residents.

Fire consumed the 1870's Rocky Mountain House in a 1963 fire five years later.

Throughout Montezuma's colorful history, the town has never been boring, never lackluster. Montezuma always burst with energy, always provided the unexpected.

Big dreams characterized Montezuma's early residents. Illinois transplant Dr. McKenney envisioned a resort village on the Snake River two and one-half miles north of Montezuma near the present Denver Water Board shaft. The spa, dubbed "Adrian", would run excursion boats on the rough and tumble river and offer luxurious living in cabins the good Doctor had built. But Dr. McKenney died before his pleasure village became a reality. The few cabins were later torn down.

Another sybaritic Snake River retreat, Franklyn, arose at the confluence of the Snake and Deer Creek, one and one-half miles south of Montezuma. Spearheaded as a plush company headquarters for the Montezuma Silver Mining Company, Franklyn consisted of the company superintendent's impressive two-story frame home, a boardinghouse and sawmill. The lavish showplace home, according to Montezuma historian Verna Sharp, served as a beautifully-

75

Montezuma's boom-bust cycle fluctuated with silver prices. Businesses, like this 1905 barbershop, prospered when silver recovered. A town newspaper debuted in 1906.

furnished "executive" entertainment spot for well-heeled prospective mine investors. But the white-frame house proved the last realization of Franklyn, a dream town.

Crazy stories of bizarre happenings in old Montezuma abound. One popular tale focuses on Montezuma's early leaders and their serious dedication to the game of poker. A slick professional gambler sauntered into the Rocky Mountain House one afternoon. Montezuma, last town on his poker-playing circuit, looked like an easy take for a card shark dealing to local rubes. He carried a satchel full of cash, lured from the pockets of similar bumpkins.

The gambler, with oily ease, announced that he wouldn't turn down a friendly afternoon game. He discovered Montezuma's poker players dealt a mean game! Afternoon melted into evening, evening blurred to night, night gave way to dawn and the relentless game continued. Players dropped out till only the hustler and early Montezuma resident T. R. ("Theo") Newman remained. Finally, the gambler stood up, and pulled out empty pockets. Newman bought his breakfast, then sent him packing — on foot, for the gambler had no money left for Denver stagecoach fare.

Another true story concerns "high-grading", the miner's term for workers pocketing nuggets and dust from their employer's mine. A notorious high-

76

grader lived in the Montezuma area. One day, two deputy law officers appeared at the family home with a search warrant. Two innocent-looking children opened the door, saying their parents were away. Finally, the miner's wife, a huge, militant-looking woman in a stiff slat bonnet, came to the door and bellowed, "What's going on here?" The young deputies presented their search warrant.

"Go ahead and search," she retorted.

The inexperienced officers came across a box the woman insisted contained nothing but old clothes. When they persisted in examing it, the musclebound lady let loose from behind with a volley of blows from a heavy chain in one hand and a hammer in the other. Despite a severe beating, the officers managed to restrain their chain-swinging hostess and later retrieved a small fortune in looted ore.

Red Mike, an 1879 Webster Pass wagon freighter, played poker with his drinking crony fellow wagoneers at the evening camp on the pass. Mike got drunk and feisty. His companions, also sloshed, held a drunken kangaroo court. The verdict: Hang the disorderly ruffian Mike. They dragged a sodden Mike to a tree, looped a wagon rope around his thickly-muscled neck and tied him up. With justice dispatched, they resumed the poker game and later fell asleep, forgetting in alcoholic stupor their strung-up companion. In the morning, the men were shocked to find Mike dead, for they meant only to trick him, not to kill him.

The pair turned Mike's horses loose and agreed to declare Mike never accompanied them from Webster. When Red Mike's body was discovered, Montezuma presumed robbery and murder. The true facts emerged years later.

Mrs. Isabella Black related the story of her return move to Montezuma in the 1900's over little-used Argentine Pass. (Loveland had replaced Argentine as the route from Georgetown and the often-perilous Argentine road had soon fallen into disrepair).

Mrs. Black's irascible husband, Thomas, blew up when she insisted on bringing her milk cow from Idaho Springs back to Montezuma. Thomas left on the train in a huff, taking eight-year old Annie, and leaving Isabella to cope with a cow, a canary and her young sons. She led the cow over challenging 13,132-foot Argentine Pass with one hand, carried the canary cage with the other hand and attempted to herd her fatigued smaller child up the steep ascent. Phillip Bianchi, a relative, met them at the summit and fashioned a papoose sling from a woolen scarf to tote the younger boy while his older brother trudged manfully along. Windswept Argentine is the nation's highest Continental Divide road crossing. "And do you know," said Mrs. Black, "it must have been plenty cold on the pass. The next day, the end of the cow's tail dropped off — it had been frozen!"

Persevering pioneers like Isabella Black never found high country Montezuma life easy. Their courage helped an isolated silver camp nestled beneath soaring 12,000 and 13,000 foot peaks to survive its centennial and beyond. Today, new homes stand side by side with old log structures in Montezuma. Despite postoffice closure in 1972, the tenacious town's future holds nothing but promise.

Dillon:
Summit's Historic Crossroads

One hundred years ago, log cabins clustered around a trading post at the scenic confluence of three Summit County rivers — the Snake, Ten Mile and Blue. The tiny settlement "where the three rivers meet" had already become a key crossroads for Blue River Route wagon freighters and a new stagecoach line over Loveland Pass.

Later, in the early 1880's, two narrow-gauge mountain railways met and shared a depot at the three rivers crossroads. And in more recent decades, much-traveled U. S. Highway 6 and Colorado 9 intersected at Dillon.

Today the three rivers merge on the lake floor of Dillon Reservoir, completed in 1963. The area has gained a beautiful water recreation site, but has lost forever its historic status as the Summit County crossroads.

Dillon gents, including editor O. K. Gaymon on right bench, lounge on Main St.'s plank sidewalk outside Jim Ryan's saloon (today's "Mint", left) and Kremmling's store.

78

Even before the tiny log settlement of Dillon sprang up in the late 1870's and became a town in 1881, the three rivers locale served 1800s adventurers as a pleasant campsite. "La Bonte's Hole", the trapper's early rendezvous site, was probably at Dillon. And 1860's travelers, following the river routes to the gold camps, stopped regularly at the three rivers junction. Samuel Bowles, in his 1869 book, *Colorado: Its Parks and Mountains*, details Dillon's untouched natural beauty:

> This was at a still more picturesque spot, — a trinity of rivers, a triangle of mountains. The Blue and the Snake Rivers and Ten Mile Creek all meet and mingle here within a few rods; each a strong hearty stream, from its own independent circle of mountains; and while the waters unresisting swam together, the hills stood apart and away, frowning in dark forests and black rock, and cold with great snow-fields, overlooking the scene, which green meadows, and blue sky, and warm sun mellowed and brightened. A neck of land, holding abundant grass and fuel, between the three rivers at the point of junction, offered a magnificent camping ground. It is a spot to settle down upon and keep house at for a week. Ten Mile Creek overflows with trout; General Lord took ten pounds out of a single hole in a less number of minutes, — a single fish weighing about three pounds; and deer and game birds must be readily findable in the neighborhood. The Blue isn't blue, — its waters have been troubled by the miners, and it gives its name and mud color to the combined stream, which flows off through an open inviting valley to join the Grand, and thence to make up the grand Colorado of the West.
>
> We had come this way through a little obstinacy of our own, instead of taking the common and short cut over the hills, from the valley of the upper Snake to Breckenridge, — sure that the conjunction of the Blue, the Snake and Ten Mile must offer something worth seeing in the way of valley and mountain scenery; and so we were quite proud of our generous repayment, and desire all future travelers to make a note of our route, and follow it.

(Bowles' party took the "long route" via the Blue River to Breckenridge from Montezuma. The group ignored a quicker trail over a high mountain pass from Montezuma to the Swan Valley and nearby Breckenridge.)

Geologist William Brewer and crew enjoyed a scenic picnic at the "three rivers" site in 1868.

But author-traveler-lecturer Bayard Taylor failed to find the area so blithe. During the 1866 spring run-off, he and his traveling companions had already suffered some exciting mishaps attempting to ford Summit's rushing water-ways. Another ill-starred crossing took place at Dillon; with thrills (and chills) for *Rocky Mountain News* editor William Byers, and his friends McCandless, Sumner and White:

> Mr. McCandless plunged in, his mule breasting the impetuous current, and, after being carried down some yards, succeeded in getting out on the other bank. Mr. Byers followed, and then the pack-mule, Peter; but, on reaching the centre of the stream both were carried away. I was watching the horse, madly endeavoring to swim against the current, when there was a sudden call for help. The drift-timber had made a raft just below, the force of the stream set directly toward it, and horse and rider were being

> drawn, as it appeared, to inevitable destruction. Mr. Sumner sprang into the water and caught Mr. Byers' hand; but the next moment he was out of his depth, and barely succeeded in swimming ashore.
>
> . . . White rushed into the water with a lariat, and the danger was over. Horse and rider got out separately, without much trouble, although the latter was already chilled to the bones and nearly benumbed. The pack-mule, with all our luggage, was completely submerged, and we should probably have lost everything, had not White grasped the mule's ear at the turn of the river, and thus assisted the beast to recover . . .

A local legend ties the name "Dillon" to young Tom Dillon, a greenhorn who set off to find Colorado mountain gold with a party of Golden City (today's Golden) prospectors. Tom, deciding to hunt gold on his own, disappeared from the group and prospected the hills. High country winter descended upon Tom's isolated environs with heavy snows and stinging wind. The boy survived the winter and somehow found his way back to Golden, physically depleted and half-crazed from hardship. He babbled stories of crossing a high mountain pass (thought to be 11,750-foot Ptarmigan in the Williams Fork mountains), encountering Indians and finally emerging in a valley where three rivers met. Early Dillon settlers named their trading post camp for the hapless Tom.

Wagon roads crisscrossed Summit County in the mid-1860's. Passenger service via wagon and stage followed. The South Park, Blue River and Middle Park Post Road, plus the Empire, New Pass (Berthoud) and Breckenridge Post Road probably passed today's Dillon. A group of enterprising settlers built a stage stop and trading post where the Blue, Snake and Ten Mile Rivers meet. According to local historian Elizabeth Rice Roller, four men, Sam Mishler, William Teller, Hal Sayre and Harper Orahood, organized the settlement as early as 1873. By 1879, the bustling Georgetown-Kokomo stage route over a newly-built Loveland Pass road beefed up Dillon station business. More cabins sprang up around the thriving trading post-stage stop. By October 24, 1879, Dillon had earned a post office. In 1880, the Denver & Rio Grande railroad had entered the Ten Mile Canyon, heading north toward Frisco, with plans to follow the Blue River north and eventually reach Salt Lake City. Its route would pass the three rivers junction. All this activity prompted development on the three rivers site.

On July 26, 1881, the Dillon Mining Company received a patent on a 320-acre townsite on the northeast side of Snake River. The Denver & Rio Grande (D. & R. G.) railroad arrived at Dillon in 1882 and its rival, Denver, South Park & Pacific (D.S.P. & P.) chugged into town in 1883. The new town now rated a place on 1880's maps. Incorporation came January 26, 1883 with John Jones as first mayor. The town was named Dillon, and like young Tom, would endure many hardships.

A Stroll Through Old Dillon

Anna Emore, daughter of "Tip" Ballif, an early and prominent Dillon pioneer, wrote an excellent history entitled, *Dillon, the Blue Valley Wonderland*. The booklet can be purchased at Dillon's Summit Historical Society Museum on La Bonte Street. In her history, Mrs. Emore details the three rivers community's layout:

The two main streets of old Dillon going north and south consisted of five blocks, with five streets going east and west. Nearly all the business houses were located on Main Street. However, Back Street had the Hamilton Hotel, the I.O.O.F. Hall, *The Blue Valley Times*, owned by John Louthold, the Town Hall, the church, and the school. The building that housed *The Blue Valley Times* was bought by Leon Allen, remodeled, and later was moved to the new town of Dillon.

On Main Street there were four saloons, one pool hall, two general stores, a butcher shop, a drug store, a barber shop, two blacksmith shops, two cafes, a telephone office, a doctor's office, two livery barns, two hotels, the post office and the other newspaper, called *The Dillon Enterprise* owned by Mr. O. K. Gaymon. Mr. Gaymon served as town clerk in 1882.

From 1882 to 1888 the town of Dillon suffered many disastrous fires and it was voted to sink a well in the business section of the town. In 1888 this well was drilled and was located on Main Street and Montezuma Avenue. Later another well was drilled which saved the town from having many fires get out of hand.

Also in 1888 the property owners on Main Street built a very substantial sidewalk in front of their respective properties, on the east side of Main Street from the Gaymon residence to the DeBeque house, and from the Stouffer residence to the Ballif blacksmith shop on the west side. In 1887, an ordinance was passed allowing the Marshall 50c for collecting a dog tax.

The Mint and the Antlers were popular Dillon watering holes. A. B. Tubbs & Son operated a meat and grocery store. Albers' old grocery stand gave way to a new City Market in the early 1900's. Saul Baron, an orthodox Jew who kept a strict Kosher diet in isolated Dillon, ran a local store. J. C. Strong dispensed remedies at the Dillon Drug Store.

Dillon boasted several hotels during the early decades. The Hamilton owned by Tom Hamilton, the big Oro Grande, J. G. Cox's New York Hotel and the Warren Hotel. Later, in 1909, fire destroyed the Warren and Oro Grande hotels.

In 1882, rail workers constructed a depot shared by the Denver & Rio Grande and the South Park lines.

Dillon petitioned for a school on April 10, 1882. Summit School District No. 8 was established and a fine new school house opened in 1884. Mrs. R. N. DeBecque was the first teacher. Dillon students, seven girls and six boys the first year, learned their "3 R's" in that white frame building until 1910, when a new and larger Dillon school replaced the 26-year old school house. The quaint school structure survived several moves during its stint as the Union Church building and later as the Dillon Community Church. In 1971, some years after a new Dillon Community Church had superceded the old 1880's structure, the Summit Historical Society restored the old original school house as a museum. Primary exhibit there today is the 1880's classroom, with wood and wrought iron desks from Frisco's old school; Montezuma's much-used "Acme Grant" pot bellied school room stove and an antique piano (from Montezuma School) once owned by a colorful pioneer named Mabel Gore. The school's original bell, moved to the modern Dillon Community Church, returned to its original location, the 1884 school house's belltower, through Anna Emore's efforts.

Children from all over the area walked to Dillon School. The Cluskey children, who lived in Dickey, near today's Farmers Korners, hiked daily to Dillon for school. At one time, Frisco became such a wild town that teachers there couldn't contain the rowdy students, and they were sent to Dillon for a more disciplined academic experience.

Sturdy characters peopled early Dillon. Several early residents ranked as outstanding contributors to the embryonic town's development, lively, hard-working, fun-loving and sometimes cantankerous personalities who deserve remembering.

O. K. GAYMON, Dillon's first clerk and recorder, founded the outspoken Dillon *Enterprise*, a newspaper that defended Dillon's honor against snide territorial attacks by arch rival Breckenridge's Jonathan Cooper Fincher in his Summit County *Journal*. The Dillon *Enterprise* was published from 1882 to 1889. All the printing equipment for this pioneering newspaper was hauled over Boreas Pass by wagon.

Gaymon promoted Dillon as the new county seat to replace Breckenridge in 1882. The crossfire between the *Enterprise* and Breckenridge's Summit County *Journal* grew heavy.

"As a business center, Breckenridge is far ahead of any town in the county", the *Journal* intoned. Gaymon fired back this salvo in an October 27, 1882, *Enterprise* article: "Yes, ahead as a business center of wind and expectation. What business, trade, manufacture or mine productivity?" queried Gaymon. "Dillon is a natural business center and she don't boast. The railroad connects here." Robinson, Kokomo, and the Snake River District supported Dillon as the new county seat, Gaymon insisted. And Denver's powerful *Rocky Mountain News* stood behind the town's county seat move in a July 20, 1882, article, stating "the railroad has made Dillon a center. The county seat will be moved this fall and as Dillon is the only place that can command a 2/3 vote, the vote will be solid for the one place." Gaymon battled valiantly, but lost his bid for the county seat. He accepted the Summit County *Journal* editor's post, replacing his spitfire rival, J. C. Fincher in the 1890's. The Gaymons left their Main Street, Dillon home and moved to Breckenridge, where the Gaymon family still resides.

CHAUNCEY CARLISLE WARREN trekked west from New York to Colorado around 1869. Warren settled first at Central City where he ran a large ore mill. In 1871, his wife, Mary Elizabeth followed him to gold rush territory and the two took up residence in Silver Plume, above Georgetown, where Mrs. Warren taught school to miners' children. When road builders hacked out the 11,992-foot Loveland Pass Road in 1879, C. C. Warren opened a popular stage stop for Concord Coach passengers on the burgeoning Georgetown to Leadville route.

Chauncey and Mary Elizabeth Warren moved to the fledgling town of Dillon in the 1880's. Their genial hospitality so successful at Warren's stage station, aided them in operating the Warren Hotel in Dillon. Itinerant Methodist preacher Fr. John Lewis Dyer stayed there during his last visit to Dillon. Dillon's 1909 fire brought disaster to the Warrens when their hotel succumbed to the blaze. The Warrens and their five children survived the loss through their second business, a Dillon stable.

Dillon's cemetery stands out as unusual because it was patented by President McKinley on June 30, 1901, under the Cemetery and Park Act. C. C. Warren spearheaded the successful drive to patent the 53½ acre cemetery during his stint as Dillon mayor. C. C. Warren's son, Brad, married Catherine Scott Cherryholmes around 1900. Their first child, a daughter, named Gaybriella, lived in old Dillon until Dam construction in 1960 forced her to move her long-time family home to Adams Street in Breckenridge. (Five generations lived in the old house.) Gay and her husband, Ray Loomis, raised a daughter, Martha, in Dillon, who lives in Breckenridge today.

Gaybriella Warren Loomis remembers the lively fun that animated life in old Dillon:

> What fun we always had around here! Everybody was always having dances, dinners, and all kinds of social things. The church was active and the Rebekahs had big dinners; you might say people were just more sociable then. For the Saturday night get-together, someone would bake up some cakes, someone would make some sandwiches, and we'd serve them right up on the stage at the town hall.

Dillon's picnic ground, remembered fondly by old-timers, was situated at the southwest edge of the old town. This fun spot had a dance pavilion, band stand and other facilities. The Denver & Rio Grande hosted a huge July 4 picnic there each year and party-goers from as far as Leadville traveled to the much-loved event.

Gay Loomis also remembers these high points:

> The Elks would put on a sort of little fair, and it was a big event for my sister and me. One day when I was five years old we went out there, all dressed up and having a lot of fun, and we came upon this fellow with a hot griddle, probably some sort of gas griddle. He was flipping pancakes. When we walked up, he flipped a cake off the griddle right quick and rolled it into a point, kind of like a funnel, and then filled it with vanilla ice cream. It was an ice cream cone! We had never seen such a thing before, and I certainly had never and have never since tasted anything that good; to this day I believe that ice cream cone was the most delicious thing I ever ate.

According to Gay Loomis, picnics turned into gala gatherings and Dillon's horse races became locally famous fun-time events:

> Once in a while the whole town would take a notion and we'd have a picnic at the foot of Loveland Pass or somewhere, and everyone would bring something. On the Fourth of July we had horseraces and bucking contests — we never called them "rodeos" — and the men would race in the streets. This was all right then because there were no cars to bother about. If you look at it now, I guess we didn't have much fancy to do — but we had a lot of fun anyway!

Brad Warren found the beautiful country around Dillon full of game. "In the fall of the year, my Dad always found a few ducks down at the Hamilton ponds below Dillon . . . since there was no refrigeration, it was a treat to have something fresh on the table."

Gay's mother, Mrs. Warren, found her own fun. When telephone lines were strung along the Blue in 1906, Mrs. Warren decided to tackle a new job as switchboard operator. The switchboard was installed in the Warren home. Soon all five children were scurrying hither and yon, delivering messages to townspeople who didn't have phones, running to bring people to the office to receive calls.

Today, the old Warren home site lies beneath the rippling waters of Lake Dillon. But memories of life in the old town, where the Snake, Blue and Ten Mile met, still endure.

RUDOLPH KREMMLING, high country pioneer whose name the Grand County town of Kremmling bears, came to Dillon as grading boss for a railroad construction gang. Mrs. Kremmling cooked for the grading crew. Rudolph Kremmling built Dillon's second structure, a general store which housed the post office. The Dillon *Enterprise*, on October 27, 1882, carried an advertisement for R. Kremmling's Dillon Market: "Coffee sold at five pounds for $1.00 and ham at 21 cents per pound." A November 17, 1883, Montezuma *Millrun* news story also mentions Mr. Kremmling's popular grocery/general store.

Kremmling still lived in Dillon in 1885-86, the years he served a term as town mayor. Marie Lindquist Marshall Rennick, Breckenridge-born Summit old-timer who lived for years on the lower Blue Valley's Marshall Ranch, knew Mr. Kremmling. Marie, a schoolgirl in 1907, remembered Dillon storekeeper, Rudolph Kremmling, as a large, imposing man who delighted Marie and other local children with rides on his beautiful red sled.

Kremmling's general store, a Dillon landmark, became the Dillon Drug and Department Store. When Dillon Reservoir construction forced a town move in 1960, the historic structure moved to Frisco where it continues to serve Summit customers as the Frisco Drug & Department Store.

Tip Ballif hand-operates drill press in his mid-1880's Dillon blacksmith and wagon shop. Dillon's Summit Historical Society displays his well-worn tools today.

ADOLPHUS "TIP" BALLIF drove 1879 stagecoaches over Loveland Pass on Silas W. Nott's Georgetown-Kokomo line, which connected to mushrooming Leadville. Nott's drivers had a reputation for care and safety despite the hazards of storm-buffeted high passes and crude roads. Tip Ballif, a veterinarian, quit the stage line to set up Frisco's first blacksmith shop (located next to the town hall and razed in 1976). When the railroad penetrated the county and an up-and-coming Dillon began to attract new businesses and residents, several Frisco establishments moved to the new crossroads, including Jim Ryan's saloon (today the Mint) and Graff's two-story hall. Tip Ballif moved his blacksmith shop to Dillon. A. Ballif, Blacksmith and Wheelwright, advertised in early 1900's issues of the *Blue Valley Times*. He had expanded his horseshoeing and wagon repair business to include a shop at Keystone.

Born in Bern, Switzerland, on July 15, 1851, Ballif had sailed to America in spring, 1870, and received American citizenship on September 29, 1876, at Coshocton, Ohio. Soon after, he came west to Colorado.

Adolphus Ballif married Miss Emma Benson on May 12, 1891. Emma had emigrated from Torup Hallan Slan, Sweden in 1886, worked as a servant in Des Moines, Iowa, then traveled to Colorado with a friend in 1890, living first in old Kokomo, then in Dillon. There, Emma Benson worked at Dillon's Hamilton Hotel.

The year he married, Tip Ballif also made a mineral strike on Chief Mountain on Ten Mile Creek about one mile west of Frisco, according to an August 15, 1891, Summit County *Journal*. "Tip Ballif has uncovered a fine body of lead and silver ore on Chief Mountain, the streak of solid ore which is from 20 to 40 inches wide. Ore will go from 50 percent to 70 percent lead and 50 to 70 ounces silver per ton; it is a dandy."

The Ballifs had three children, Anna, Hilda and a third daughter who died in infancy. The family lived on a 164-acre ranch one and one-half miles south of Dillon. Emma had received the property from a man who owed her $12. Unable to pay, the rancher gave Emma his homestead. Mrs. Ballif sold cream, butter and milk from her ranch to Dillon townsfolk.

Adolphus Ballif served as a Dillon town trustee from 1883 to 1898 and also as a sheriff's deputy for many years. Anna Emore reports that Ballif helped scour the country in the 1898 search for outlaw-murderer Pug Ryan. (See Chapter 17 for Ryan's story.)

After almost a half century of pioneering service to Summit County, Adolphus Ballif died in 1926.

The Ballif's eldest daughter, Anna, became a well-known Summit resident honored by Dillon's "Anna Emore Days".

Born in 1892, Anna Ballif Emore attended Dillon's first one-room schoolhouse (today's Summit Historical Society Museum), enjoyed lively dances and parties at Breckenridge, Slate Creek, Dillon and Frisco. She married Lansing Emore, who worked for the new Colorado Power Company, French Gulch's famous Wellington Mine and on a gold dredge, where he once suffered serious injury. The Emores homesteaded a beautiful ranch above Silverthorne, building a three-room cabin that "grew" as the years passed. This charming ranch later owned by the Roush family and recently sold to JMC Company for homesites, perches in clear view from Silverthorne on the hillside west of town.

The Emore family continued to remain active in Dillon life. (A 1912 *Blue Valley Times* sports story reported that "Emore saved the baseball game" between rival Dillon and Breckenridge.) Emore children, Henry and Viola, and families still reside in the Dillon area.

"Big Snow" Winter Buries Old Dillon

The winter of 1898-99, famous "Big Snow" year, buried old Dillon as well as Breckenridge and other Summit towns with snow high as two-story building rooftops. The Denver, South Park & Pacific valiantly battled huge drifts on Boreas Pass track before shutting down service in February. Denver & Rio Grande cars were buried beneath drifted snow and slides in the Ten Mile Canyon. Dillon's lifeline, the railroads, was cut off. Dillon merchants failed to stock heavily during the fall of 1898 because they felt secure with regular rail deliveries. But the town managed to survive. Flour, bacon, sugar and other necessities arrived from Kremmling grocer Tracy Tyler through the sometimes heroic efforts of stagecoach drivers on the Kremmling-Dillon stage line. According to a *Colorado* Magazine historical article, drivers had to split the 41-mile stage route to Dillon. Bill Kimball battled snow-clogged roads from Kremmling to Cow Camp, one and one-half miles east of today's Green Mountain Reservoir. Charlie Free drove the fresh horses over the Cow Camp to Dillon stretch, with a stop at Jacob's house on upper Knorr Place. Mails came to Dillon, a luxury other towns went without, via Berthoud Pass, Kremmling and the Blue River stage route.

Cattle Ranches and Placer Claims

Ranching dominated Dillon life. The town served as a hub for railroad hay and cattle shipments from the lower Blue Valley ranches. (Most ranches sprang up under the 1882 Homestead Act; Summit granted its first homestead in October, 1883.)

Those pioneering ranch families "down on the Blue" worked hard to tame the land. But their spirits remained high. Some of the county's best-remembered merriment occurred at Slate Creek and the ranches on the Lower Blue. Families like the Marshalls, the Mumfords, the Knorrs and the Hills added strength and resiliency to Summit's social fiber.

The Dillon area attracted some mining as well. The Oro Grande pit, digging with Evans hydraulic elevators, was operated by Britisher George Evans of Breckenridge's Gold Pan Mining Company. Nearby Ryan Gulch (bordering today's Wilderness subdivision) produced placer gold for Buffalo Placer Company's extensive hydraulic washing efforts. Lemuel Kingsbury managed Buffalo Placer at the company's headquarters in Dillon. Salt Lick attracted early placer miners (among them famous Breckenridge naturalist Edwin Carter and pioneer Judge Marshall Silverthorn). The Treasure Vault Mine operated atop Buffalo Mountain. A local newspaper in 1882, reported 24 mines on neighboring Red Peak. And today's Gore Wilderness, especially the Willow Lakes region, was peppered with prospect holes.

Dillon: A Movin' Town

Like the nomad Utes who first wandered the Blue Valley, Dillon residents packed up and moved their town with surprising regularity. While Breckenridge busied itself through the years with shifting buildings from one site to another, Dillonites transported their entire town to new locations — and they did it four times.

Dillon's first townsite perched on the Snake River's northeast bank below the old cemetery. This early site was east of its later locations. The town's first cemetery sat on a hill that is today mostly submerged and the town first spread out on 320 acres north of that hillside cemetery. (There is a narrows in Lake Dillon at the Old Dillon site. At this narrows, there is an easterly point covered with short, young trees, that juts into the lake. This is the site of Cemetery Hill.)

When the railroads arrived, Dillon residents decided to relocate near the rail track. The town moved west across the Blue to settle on the rail line. Shortly after they completed this relocation, restless Dillon residents caught the moving bug again. Dillon's third site nestled among the three rivers, the Snake, Blue and Ten Mile, at the western foot of Cemetery Hill. And there the town stayed for more than half a century.

But a final move was in the making. During Depression years, beginning about 1929, the Denver Water Board began buying up Dillon property from financially-strapped owners unable to raise tax money. The Water Board planned to fulfill a long-held ambition to dam the rushing Blue River and pipe needed water to a mushrooming Denver metropolis. By the 1940's, the Denver Water Board owned most of Dillon. In 1956, the Water Board dropped bombshell news on the struggling little community. Homeowners and businessmen must vacate the town by 1961. Survey crews crowded into town, and excavating teams launched the four-year effort to construct the 23-mile long Harold D. Roberts diversion tunnel through the Continental Divide mountains. Men and machines moved in to build the big Dillon Dam.

Dillon's role as a ranching hub had declined after rail service ended in 1937. From 1930 to 1976, farms on the Lower Blue dropped from 60 to 25. Cattle population declined from 8,670 head to less than 4,200.

Dillon in the 1950's was anything but a bustling burg. Many Coloradans remember the lonely gas station at the junction of U. S. Highway 6 and Colorado 9. Dillon, population 80, had eight licensed liquor establishments, one for each ten persons. And no one complained that this exceeded the needs of the neighborhood!

Dillon residents had attempted to quench their thirst with spiritous drink for decades. During prohibition, moonshiners brewed their own whiskey in stills they set up in old mines and sawmills around Dillon. The best spirits came from a Straight Creek sawmill (in the I-70 corridor-Dillon Valley area) and a Montezuma mine.

All that drinking made Saturday nights in Dillon rowdy and raucous. Aramando Trujillo, nicknamed "The Chief"' was around to witness the glorious barroom brawls:

> In the old town of Dillon all the sidewalks were boards and it was just like a western town. Oh, it was a lot of fun then. You know, in those days you get the people fighting and when they're through they go back drinking together. Everybody would go to the Dillon Inn and get drunk once a week, and nobody would bother you either. There wasn't no police, just a sheriff, and if they see somebody fighting they just keep on walking. It was a nice town. I used to like to go to the Dillon Inn cause you could see

the women fight. I don't care much about men fights, but women is just like a wild lion. I'd as soon step on a lion's tail as mess with a woman! But every Saturday night there'd be fights, and the next day you're friends.

Lege's General Store supplied the area with its sole source of clothing, auto parts and other necessities. Medical and dental care remained non-existent until Dr. Peterson, Dillon's first dentist in 45 years, opened an office in the 50's. No new houses had gone up from 1929 to 1944, according to the Carl Enyearts in a 1977 Summit County *Journal* interview.

Nevertheless, Dillon's 80 residents, many of them old-timers and also ranch families living nearby along the Blue were a close-knit society. The final Denver Water Board ultimatum, giving residents 90 days to move, catapulted the town into a state of anguish.

Low payments for homes and property, the taxing financial toll of replacing water, sewer and road systems for a new Dillon community, construction of a possible new school, town hall and other buildings threw Dillon into economic chaos. Moving at winter's onset proved a hardship, especially for the aged. Loss of community services, businesses that couldn't survive moving costs, left Dillon limping.

Local resident Maxine Collard wrote a letter to Denver's *Rocky Mountain News*, published September 7, 1960, which expresses the mountain community's unhappy plight:

Dillon's Plight

EDITOR: . . . We were among the first to receive our 90-day notice to vacate, which will be Nov. 17, this is indeed wintertime in our community. In order to salvage our home, we are forced to move it to the new town site where there are no roads, water or sewer systems or lights. We will board it up and hope to find a place to live for the winter. Does the Denver Water Board plan to offer the necessary policing to protect our homes this winter?

. . . An underpass is proposed for the school children from the Blue River trailer camp to travel to and from school. When settlement for our school is reached, it will still take more than a year to construct a new building.

Why should we permit our children to suffer the hazards of these huge earthfilled speeding Euclids? The noise and distraction will certainly not permit satisfactory teaching or learning. The dust is a health sanitation problem no matter how much they sprinkle.

. . . Our little general store is having a close-out sale. Can any businessman move into our new town and wait a year to resume his business? Homes and businesses are going in every direction, but not into our new town . . .

MAXINE COLLARD

Relocating Dillon's cemetery proved the move's most agonizing task. Rumors of bubonic plague, issuing forth from the disturbed gravesites, spooked workers. Anguished dispute marked the cemetery move. Reluctance to disrupt peaceful graves, loss of burial records, and a long effort to notify relatives of the deceased clouded the relocation work.

Thomas Hamilton's historic 1883 two-story hotel on Dillon's Back Street is visible beyond the Colorado & Southern rail tracks and bridge in this April 4, 1912 photo.

Gold-seekers, gamblers, Dillon pioneers and railroad laborers, ladies of the night and unidentified miners had, till 1960, rested in peace at the old cemetery. Three hundred and twenty-seven known bodies were moved to a new Dillon cemetery, including 37 infants, 19 children and 271 adults. The words "Sweet Baby Helen, born March 9, 1892, departed this life, May 10, 1892", mark one infant grave. The earliest headstone dates to 1879, with "Boche baby" as its cryptic identification.

Dillon survived. A new town rose on the old Fred Phillips Ranch, occupying a pine-forested hillside above the new Lake Dillon. The old townsite soon lay beneath the reservoir's lapping waters.

Residents managed to preserve some historic buildings. Former mayor John Bailey's much-moved home, constructed in Dillon No. 2 and moved to Dillon No. 3, now occupies a north-side, hilltop lot on the Tenderfoot Street rise. Jim Ryan's old 1880's saloon, later named the Mint, went to its present location in Silverthorne. The historic Kremmling General Store, later the Dillon Drug and Department Store, moved to its present location as the Frisco Drug and Department Store. Graff's 1880 two-story hall, today the Three Rivers Rebekah Lodge and D & L Printing, relocated in new Dillon.

Tom Hamilton's vintage 1883 hotel, built with $10,000 worth of materials hauled by wagon over Boreas Pass, became the Dillon Hotel before its 1961 move to Breckenridge. The 14-room antique structure succumbed to arson fire there in May, 1963.

Twentieth century buildings such as the Antlers Cafe and the Holiday House went to Frisco. Dillon's Arapahoe Cafe resurfaced in new Dillon as the Tappan

House. The Old Dillon Inn now serves Mexican food as a restaurant-bar in Silverthorne.

No matter how vigorously Dillon residents opposed Dillon Reservoir, its creation has boosted the century-old town to a new era of prosperity. Nestled among snow-capped peaks, Lake Dillon's shining blue waters draw sailing enthusiasts, fishermen and campers to Summit County. One hundred years after the first cabins went up, Summit's "newest old town" remains a comer.

Dillon had seen better days than this one in 1950 when survival seemed to depend on quenching the thirst of auto traveler and car with package liquor and gasoline.

Frisco:
Century-Old Silver Town

Frisco! The 1875 name rings with excitement: It echoes San Francisco's fever-pitch 1849 California gold craze, boom town expectations and hurdy-gurdy high times.

Despite the catchy sound, nobody till now really knew why Frisco got its name — or how. Colorado histories repeat the story:

Version One: In 1873, H. A. Recen, a Ten Mile Canyon 1870's pioneer who mined a lifetime around Kokomo, discovered the fabulous Queen of the West Mine and founded the town of Recen, arrived at the Frisco site. He cut aspens to build a cabin on Ten Mile Island at the confluence of the Ten Mile and North Ten Mile Creeks. (*True*)

Two years later in 1875 a mysterious government scout named Captain Leonard came along, and tacked the name "Frisco City" over the cabin door, and then disappeared. And that's how Frisco got its name. (*Partially True*)

Version Two: Other twists to the story indicate that Captain Leonard built the cabin himself and named it. Example: Perry Eberhart in *Guide to the Colorado Ghost Towns and Mining Camps*. (*Untrue*)

Version Three: Frisco promoters put out an undated historical tour pamphlet some years before the Dillon Reservoir was built. Their lively story of Frisco's naming maintains that the mischievous Captain Leonard nailed the name "Frisco House" over Recen's door as a joke — a Leadville bawdy house also bore the notorious name "Frisco House." (*Untrue*)

Version Four: (*Authenticated by the author's research.*) Family member Henry Recen offered his more reliable story to the Colorado State Historical Society in a March 2, 1965 interview. He maintained that his father, H. A. Recen, built the first cabin in Frisco in 1873. A former government Indian scout later hewed off a log over the cabin door and wrote "Frisco City" on the rough surface. Later, this same "Captain Leonard" and his wife Hetty had the postoffice and candy store at Frisco, according to Recen.

Information in early *Colorado Business Directories*, then verified that "Captain Leonard" was really Captain Henry Learned, a prominent Frisco community leader whose wife ran a general store as late as 1900. A misspelling in his name has long obscured this fact. Captain Learned served in 1885 as Frisco mayor, school board member, notary public, justice of the peace, postmaster and grocery-notions store proprietor.

The tireless gentleman also managed the local Kitty Innes Mining Syndicate, according to the 1885 *Colorado Business Directory*.

Learned definitely not only named Frisco but also selected the townsite and boosted the town's beginnings. In 1879 newspapers announced that Learned and backers had spearheaded a new town "Frisco City", located in a "splendid" two-mile square valley. These men had inside knowledge on the railroad's plan to come through the Frisco site. The Denver *Daily Tribune* on April 5, 1879, reported:

> Mr. W. A. Rand, agent for Denver, Boulder and Leadville parties, has secured a large tract of land at Frisco for this company. Captain Henry Learned agent for Laurence, Kansas men, selected the site. Captain Reed of Boulder is putting in a sawmill soon. Buildings are under construction for a hotel, saloon, store, feed stable and corral.

Frisco, like its California namesake, boomed, but in a smaller way. The next year, 1880, the citizens voted to incorporate the town. Frisco applied for a town patent on September 9, 1880. The patent, signed by President Chester Arthur, was recently discovered in a Frisco attic. On December 4, 1880, the Denver *Tribune* reported Frisco had filed incorporation papers with the Colorado Secretary of State on December 3. Forty-nine Frisco residents voted unanimously for incorporation. Frisco had formed a town board of trustees in October, 1880. J. S. Scott, John Garrison, John Doble and C. F. Shedd are listed as trustees in Frisco's beautifully-scripted town records, kept by Frisco recorder, David Crowell. B. B. Babcock, then served as mayor.

Frisco had obtained its postoffice by at least April 1, 1880, according to historian Frank Fosset. By 1881, Crofutt's *Guide*, Volume I, listed Frisco, population 150, as a timber-rich town at the mouth of the Ten Mile Canyon, with two stores, two hotels (the Frisco House and the Leyner), one sawmill and "a score of other buildings". Some of these buildings, according to an 1881 Denver *Tribune* report, housed a blacksmith and wagon shop (belonging to Dillon pioneer Adolphus Ballif who came to Frisco in 1879) and grocery, hardware, clothing and carpenter shops.

Frisco's population jumped to 250 after the narrow-gauge railroads (two of them) arrived in 1882. Frisco had two railroad stations in the early '80's, to house the mountain-scaling Denver, South Park & Pacific and its arch-rival, the Denver & Rio Grande.

A flood of visitors scrambled off passenger cars at Frisco in a rush to find gold nuggets scattered about on the ground. (Passengers on the early Concord coach stage lines that stopped at the town did the same.) Frisco was called "Halfway Stop", because it was 32 miles to Georgetown and 32 miles to Leadville, the stage route destination. Frisco, a natural stop at the Ten Mile Canyon's terminus, also served as a favorite campsite for nomad Ute Indians.

In 1885, Frisco had the Coyne and Britton Saloon (Coyne was also the name of Breckenridge's grocer; Harry Britton was a longtime Frisco businessman); the Leyner Hotel (N. J. Coyne, prop.); a livery-feed stable; Learned's grocery and notions store; plus two lumber mills, one owned by Scott & Officer, the other by C. F. Shedd.

Adolphus "Tip" Ballif sidelined his blacksmith work with service as Frisco's 1885 constable. A. C. Graff ran a cattle dealership. G. E. Kearney worked as a contractor and also ran his lumber mill. A number of mining companies headquartered in 1886 Frisco. They were: Chief Mountain Mining Company (Frank Reandon, manager); Federal Mining Company (C. C. Royce, manager); Keifer Mountain Mining Company (C. C. Warren, manager. Chauncey Carlisle Warren was a Summit pioneer, arriving in the 1870's, who had an early stage station and later a Dillon hotel); the Kitty Innes Mining Syndicate (Henry Learned, manager); Little Mary Mining Syndicate; the Monroe Mine Company (S. H. Bushnell, manager); and the Tornado Peaks Mining Syndicate.

Another 1880's saloon, not listed in the 1885 *Business Directory*, was J. J. Clinton's Posy Saloon. In 1882, Clinton advertised in the Dillon *Enterprise* for help: "Wanted: 500 able-bodied men to unload schooners at the Posy Saloon, Frisco, Colorado." The Clintons kept Frisco lively, according to a Summit County *Journal* March 1, 1882 report: "Frisky Friscoans fling fluttering feminity fast and furious tonight at the dance at the Clintons."

The Dillon *Enterprise* ran announcements of Frisco's 1880's theatrical productions at the Graff Opera Hall. The Frisco Dramatic Society will "bring before the public in regal style the play on 'Conscience' on May 3, 1882," a news report stated. The *Enterprise* on October 27, 1882 promoted an October 30 Dramatic Association production, "All That Glitters Is Not Gold", a comic drama in two acts.

(Graff, the opera hall owner, was probably the same musical maestro who led Kokomo's 1879 brass band.)

Newspapers also lauded Frisco's up-and-coming new town look. "Frisco begins to look lively, bright and neat, with new buildings under completion", a news article stated. Crawford and Company had completed a "magnificent store" and V. J. Coyne worked to redo the Leyner Hotel, "adding new rooms, new bedding and papering".

The same 1882 newspaper announced "a new school district is being organized". Frisco, Summit School District No. 10, got its school in October, 1882. Mrs. Mann taught nine boys and eight girls that year. But student population soon plummeted when Mrs. Mann complained to the school board about an unruly mischief-maker named George Reynolds. George's father, Jasper Reynolds served on Frisco's first school board with Henry Learned and William H. Evans. An indignant Mr. Reynolds immediately yanked young George, and also his two daughters, from Mrs. Mann's school. The school teacher must have shared Reynold's disgust, for she, too, quit. Her 1883 replacements were Birdie Fincher and A. E. Jones. Each taught for a two months span, at a monthly salary of $50.

Mrs. Lillian Wise, the teacher in the 1890's, watched with apprehension as a big saloon building went up almost next door to the school. The building featured a fine, rock-lined wine cellar. But saloon construction came to a grinding halt. (Possibly a result of 1893's silver panic which hit hard in the silver-rich Ten Mile Mining District.) The saloon became Mrs. Wise's handsome new school and still stands on Main Street today as the Summit Schools' administration building. Around 1959, someone painted the historic, hand-hewn logs a vivid yellow. Today, the old schoolhouse has a more dignified coat of brown paint.

Lower Ten Mile Canyon silver mining would soon play out, but this 1909 Frisco school group, gathered outside the log building that began as a saloon, looked unconcerned.

95

Frisco old-timers fondly remember skiing on a hill behind the schoolhouse and warming up by the big pot-bellied stove in the schoolroom. They reminisce over frequent trips to the water cooler in the corner with its generous long-handled dipper. They also remember the stern eyes staring from a portrait of George Washington. Those eyes seemed to follow Ann Giberson Dale on each foray for a cool drink.

Charlotte McDonald, who grew up in early Robinson, in the Ten Mile Canyon, served as one of the Frisco school's 1890's teachers. Lula Myers, the winsome "schoolmarm" for whom Keystone named a long, meandering ski run, ran smack into Frisco politics in 1897 when she taught at the log school house.

Lula had fallen in love with a handsome young miner, James H. Myers, Jr., or "Dimp" as his friends called him. Dimp was the son of Colonel James H. Myers, King Solomon Mining Syndicate director.

Miners ranked as second-class citizens in Frisco in the post-Silver Panic 1890's, according to Marie Linquist Rennick, one of Lula's pupils. The Frisco school board then had three bachelor members. Two of them resented Lula's romance with Dimp Myers, Mrs. Rennick remembers. (Perhaps they had taken a shine to sweet Lula themselves.) When Lula returned to her school in the fall, she found the door barricaded with nailed-on boards. The school board had barred the young teacher from her classroom. But the men later relented. Lula taught the year through and married Dimp when she finished.

Lucy Osburn, Lula's sister, took the teaching post in 1907. At one point, rowdy students grew so disruptive that Frisco pupils were transferred to Dillon. Then a brawny male teacher, who towered over the big boys, according to Mrs. Rennick, arrived to solve Frisco's classroom discipline problem.

Elder Frisco residents sometimes behaved as badly as the students. Mrs. Rennick's family, the Linquists, had moved from Breckenridge to open a Frisco hotel. ("There were saloons everywhere, including one next door.") On the other side of the saloon, a diminutive but very determined lady, Mrs. Jane Thomas, ran a second hotel. When fights erupted in the saloon, who broke them up? Tiny Mrs. Thomas. Marie Rennick remembered one rowdy brawl where a scrapper pulled a knife and began to cut up an opponent. Bystanders, fearing for the victim's life, made futile attempts to stop the fray. Then the tenacious Mrs. Thomas intervened and stopped the fight.

Longtime Frisco resident Howard Giberson remembered tiny Jane Thomas in a Summit Historical Society taped lecture: "I could hold my arm out, like that, and she could walk under it and never touch it." Mrs. Thomas and Giberson shared their birthdate. "When I was 21, she was 80," he recalled. Saloons flanked the Thomas Hotel on each side, Giberson remarked, and Mrs. Thomas stopped brawls in both. "It didn't matter how gruff they were or how tough they were . . ." he laughed.

Mrs. Thomas also once waded through deep snows during a dark winter night to climb the steep trail to Mount Royal's Masontown when a doctor couldn't be found to aid a woman in labor. Mrs. Thomas single-handedly delivered twins that cold night in Masontown.

Main St.'s north side (above) had plenty of saloons and at least two of Frisco's six hotels—the Frisco Hotel and the Thomas, where stage stopped. Chief and Wichita Mts. guard town. Billy Nanetta's wagon pulled up for grocery stop at Frisco market (left) while a Sunday group gathered at much-mined Mt. Royal (below).

The Thomas Hotel, one of six in 1890's Frisco, stood two stories high, with first and second story porches. Early stage coaches stopped there. The hotel occupied the site of today's service station west of the Frisco Motor Lodge.

The Frisco Motor Lodge is an old building too, site of the 1880's Frisco Hotel. A fancy covered porch marked this Main Street hotel. A boardinghouse at one time, the Frisco Hotel became the Wortman Hotel, owned by Lillian Wortman until 1946, when Virgil Landis bought the old structure. Today the Frisco Motor Lodge is owned by the Charles Andersons, who have operated it for nearly 20 years.

Frisco's population dipped to 175 by 1900, due to a temporary mining slow-down, but the town still boasted many businesses, among them Ed Hunter's grocery store, Hattie Learned's general store, Harry Britton's saloon, Thomas' Hotel plus livery stable and A. D. Searles (the Ten Mile Canyon's Searles' Gulch is named after him) office, headquartering the Uneva Lake and Fish Hatcheries Company.

Peter Prestrud (the family still lives in Summit County) also had a general merchandise store in early 1900's Frisco. He advertised regularly in Dillon's *Blue Valley Times*.

Frisco area mining rebounded from the 1893 silver crash around 1904. Excitement reigned again, as the powerful King Solomon Mining Syndicate launched its ambitious tunnel project just a half mile from town in the Ten Mile Canyon. The Mint, Excelsior, Monroe, Wonderland, Admiral and other mining companies began pouring investor dollars into local glory holes.

When mining enjoyed a new heyday, Frisco's "frisky" social life resurged as well. Dances, picnics, hikes and other fun always included the whole town.

Longtime Summit resident Lura Belle Giberson, writing about her mother-in-law, Elizabeth Ann McDonald Giberson (fondly called "Mollie") recalled Frisco's old-time parties as family affairs. *In Women As Tall As Our Mountains* she wrote:

> Company and dances were the main entertainment in those days. A dance in Frisco was a big event. Mollie would see that each one had his turn in the old wash tub in front of the wood heater in the living room if it was Saturday night. She would heat rocks in the oven and loaded with rocks, blankets and a fur lap robe, the entire family would pile in the sleigh and go to the dance. The children would play until they were tired, then Mollie would make beds on the chairs in the dance hall where they would sleep while the grown-ups danced. If no dance had been pre-arranged, several would go over to Ike Rouse's maybe late in the evening and throw rocks at his upstairs window and tell him that they wanted to dance. He would dress and come over to the hall.

While Ike played the fiddle, Ben Staley or Ike's wife, Mary, would chord on the piano. Sometimes Ben called for the dancers' favorite, a quadrille.

Mary Ruth, born in Breckenridge in 1902, lived in Dillon and Frisco. She rode with family and friends to the gay Frisco dances in a hay wagon. "We dolled up fit to kill," she recalled. "Mama made my clothes . . . we wouldn't think of going to a dance not dressed up."

Friscoans didn't just party at home. They traveled to Summit County picnics at Elwood's near Montezuma, invited Breckenridge for balls and kicked up their heels in old Kokomo, as Edna Dercum recalled writing Lula Myer's story in *Women As Tall As Our Mountains*. Mrs. Dercum, a longtime Montezuma area resident, listened to Lula recall taking the railroad handcars up the track to Kokomo, where a dance at the hilltop schoolhouse was planned. A spirited group danced Saturday night away and remained to enjoy a sunny Sunday picnic before boarding the rail handcar for the return trip to Frisco.

> One can picture the women in their big hats with feathered ostrich plumes, long skirts and lacy blouses, and the men in patent leather dancing shoes, their Sunday best clothes and top hats. All were in great holiday mood, singing and coasting down the beautiful canyon. "Soon," Lula said, "we were really coasting! We found there were no brakes on the hand car and it literally started to fly down the canyon. The ladies hung on to their hats with the plumes flying while the men reached out to try to drag their feet to help slow down the flat car. It did help some because we made it into Frisco without crashing or turning over into the Ten Mile Creek. But, Lula continued, "their lovely dancing shoes were wrecked with the soles all gone!"

Hair-raising events became commonplace in old Frisco. Marie Lindquist Rennick related details of a picnic outing she will never forget. Five Frisco girls hiked the Mount Royal trail to picnic at the summit. They decided to take the shortcut home — down Royal's rock face. The girls discovered they had made a life-threatening mistake as they clung in panic to the sheer wall, wondering where to attempt their next downward step. One of the Recen nephews emerged from the family cabin at Mount Royal's base and saw the stranded yound ladies. He caught their attention by waving a red handkerchief, and with it, signalled to them the direction toward their safest route down.

Frisco's "suburbs" abound with fascinating historical sites. The charcoal kilns south of Frisco produced coke for ore smelters all over Colorado. Joe Lampkin and John Hathaway once owned and operated almost 50 of those ovens. A series of three or four of these kilns still stand near the old D.S.P. & P. railroad grade in the Ophir Mountain area.

Nearby is Rainbow Lake. There's an interesting tale about this popular camping and fishing retreat's origin. Frisco old-timers tell of prospectors up Miner's Creek who wanted to dam the stream for mining use. They snared a few beavers down at the Frisco beaver ponds and deposited them at the creek. The transplanted beavers cooperated, dammed the creek and created Rainbow Lake!

Historic Bill's Ranch nearby was a popular spot for visitors. Bill Thomas, owner, was the son of J. W. and Janie Thomas, proprietors of Frisco's Thomas Hotel. The family came from Georgetown in 1889, according to a Frisco historical brochure, and built the hotel. Children were Walter, Bill and Nell. Bill's Ranch served as the site of early 1900's Summit ski parties, for Bill's wife, Minnie Dusing Thomas, loved the sport.

Bill had dairy cows on the ranch and sold milk. Breckenridge-born Elizabeth Culbreath remembers the time he advertised a group of free ranch lots in a sales letter to Denverites. The lots were snapped up. Bill's reason for the bonanza offer: He wanted to create a built-in market for his milk.

Dickey, near today's Farmers Korners, functioned as a railroad coaling station with depot-section house, water tank and coal chutes. Today, the site south of Frisco is mostly submerged by Lake Dillon.

Masontown, an old Mount Royal mining town, anchored itself on Royal's eastern slope just a half-mile by trail from Frisco. A scar remaining on Mount Royal's flank, visible from Highway 9, marks the path of a snowslide that smashed old Masontown to toothpick splinters.

On the other side of Frisco, one can look up 10,880-foot Chief Mountain and see the Buffalo Placer Flume, a costly and futile project planned to bring water to the Buffalo gold placers in Salt Lick Gulch. After the company spent $60,000 on the flume, Lower Blue Valley ranches protested that the water rights belonged to them. Buffalo Placers Company had no legal water rights. (You can steal a rancher's wife, but never lay a hand on his water.)

Three miles up North Ten Mile Creek, the Square Deal Mine and Mill bustled with a small community as late as 1910. Colonel James Myers charged the Square Deal company with bilking investors, labeling the operation the "Crooked Deal" mine.

Square nails, used until the 1880's, kept Frisco jail, in alley south of Main St., sturdy for a century.

Beautiful Uneva Lake, old-time Frisco's favorite fishing and camping spot (the trout were voracious) was patented by its discoverer. An 1890's fish hatchery operated there. And the two railroads cooperated in plans to build a blissful summer resort by the shores of beautiful Uneva.

Pioneer Frisco residents Wilbert and Elizabeth Giberson honeymooned at Wilbert Giberson's Uneva Lake cabin in 1904. The Gibersons lived through history-making days in Summit County, living at the Ten Mile Canyon towns of Excelsior and Curtin. Web Giberson arrived in nearby Kokomo to work at the Colonel Sellars Mine at age 17. Mrs. Giberson had been born in old Robinson in 1883. The pair later moved to a 160-acre ranch two miles south of Frisco. The ranch grew to 720 acres, only to be swallowed up by Dillon Reservoir in the early 1960's and later bisected by U. S. Interstate Highway 70. Giberson family members Howard and Lura Belle still maintain a smaller portion of the ranch above Lake Dillon today. Sue Chamberlain, another Giberson family member, is a longtime Frisco resident.

Every town has its legends. Frisco's legend focuses on rich, gleaming wire gold, precious tangled mesh hidden high in the nearby Gore Mountains. An Australian allegedly discovered the wire gold patch, but was lost at sea on his return home, his secret sealed. A Frisco miner stumbled upon the gleaming masses of gold too, the legend says. But he stopped to help some men to build a bridge enroute down to Frisco, and fell. He struck his head on a stone and died. Again, the mystery of Gore Range wire gold remained intact!

Visitors admired the beauty surrounding Frisco a century ago and still enjoy it today. Early traveler Bayard Taylor remarked in 1866 on "the ripe green of the timber along the river . . . the forests dark, the glens and gorges filled with shadow, the rocks touched with lines of light . . . "

Those who stop at the I-70 Lake Dillon overlook near Frisco view one of Summit's most spectacular mountain panoramas, as awesome today as in Bayard Taylor's view yesterday.

Mining: The Pick, Pan and Blasting Powder Route to Riches

"I shall never forget those dear old mountains," sighed pioneer mother Mrs. Daniel Witter, sister of U.S. Vice President Schuyler Colfax, as she trekked across the plains during the 1859 Colorado Gold Rush.

"The first sight we had of them 75 miles out, they looked like silver and gold piled up in the sunlight, and I thought, 'Well, we can dig most any place and get the gold', but, oh, how disappointing these thoughts!"

One hundred thousand gold-seekers made the arduous journey across those dusty plains by horseback, mule train, ox wagon, wind wagon or on foot, some bearing heavy packs, pushing wheelbarrows or pulling hand carts. Impoverished by the financial panic of 1857 when banks failed and bankruptcies proliferated, these greenhorns dreamed of stuffing gunnysacks with gold nuggets and a blissful end to economic hardship. Urged on by William Green Russell's July, 1858 gold discovery at Dry Creek, (in today's Englewood, a Denver suburb), they pushed across the arid grasslands to Denver.

When the gold-seekers arrived, they found the early placers played out, every available inch of ground staked, and Denver a bedlam of tens of thousands of restless gold-hunters, many of them already crying "Humbug!" and preparing for a return to the States. The trail back lay strewn with discarded mining equipment, purchased at high prices in Missouri and Kansas outfitting towns, now too worthless to merit hauling.

But many persisted, among them the Georgians who first discovered gold in the United States. They took their skills to California in 1849 and again to Colorado in 1859. These men, and others like them, pushed their way into the gulches and over the Continental Divide to discover and develop Colorado gold. Georgians made the first big strike at Summit's fabled Georgia Gulch in Summer, 1860. The Georgians, and other miners experienced in the California rush, knew how to find "free" gold — nuggets, scale, shot, wire, grains, flour and dust. They shared their placer mining expertise with amateur prospectors.

Placer Mining

"Free" gold, eroded over eons by sandpapering glaciers, water and weather, provided the prospector with instant wealth. Placer mining, the separation of

102

free gold from the dirt, sand, mud or gravel in which it lay, required only determination and hard work. The simplest mining technique, placer mining could be accomplished by a single man with almost no financial investment. Called "poor man's diggings", placer mining was described this way by a gold rush guidebook: "No capital is required to obtain this gold as the laboring man wants nothing but his pick and shovel and tin pan, with which to dig and wash the gravel."

Gold is heavy, 19.7 times heavier than water and seven times heavier than the rock where it resides. Because of its weight, gold sinks to the bottom of a gold pan, rocker or sluice box. It works its way down through stream bed gravels to settle in bedrock cracks and crevices. Panning stream sand for gold involves swirling the sand with water in a wide, shallow sheet-iron pan with sloping sides and, perhaps, a copper bottom. The prospector agitates the pan, swirls out and over the edge lighter sand and rock materials. Hopefully, he discovers at the end of this process tiny grains or flecks of gold which settled at the bottom.

The prospector recovered these particles with tweezers, or by using mercury. Mercury has an uncommon affinity for gold; together they amalgamate. By heating the merged gold and mercury, the miner could vaporize the mercury and condense it for re-use. Even a large iron spoon, containing gold and mercury, could be held over a fire to achieve gold retrieval. This process proved expensive, because costly mercury evaporated. And it was dangerous. But free

Blue River Diggings led Colorado in placer gold production in the early 1860's. Sluicing, shown here, filtered off rocks, swept away sand and mud, caught free gold.

103

gold remained as the process' residue. At day's end, the gold-panning prospector always knew how much he had earned.

But early miners found gold-panning to be slow, hard work. Yankee impatience immediately demanded a more efficient, large-scale gold-washing operation. They first expanded the gold pan technique by using the rocker or cradle, which resembled a baby's cradle in size and shape. The precious "baby" to be rocked was gold-bearing gravel. Stream water rushed through the cradle as one man shoveled in dirt and another kept it rocking. A screen at the cradle's upper end filtered off larger rocks while sand and mud washed through. A series of riffles or cleats, crosspieces nailed to the cradle bottom, caught the gold.

Miners quickly innovated a more efficient placer mining device, the sluice. Simplest sluices were long ditches with rocks at the bottom as riffles. But wooden sluices, called Long Toms, appeared most often. Twenty feet long and one and one-half foot deep, the Long Toms, equipped with wooden riffles, featured one tapered end so that many could link together for more effective washing. Sometimes several dozen men operated two or three hundred-foot Long Toms.

Miners poured mercury behind each riffle. After washing, the gold-mercury amalgam went into an iron retort furnace to vaporize the mercury and retrieve the gold.

Sluicing required water, plenty of water. Some rich placer claims had no stream nearby. To supply placer miners with needed water, ditches and flumes were built to divert water from rushing streams to placer operations. Reports indicate more than 100 miles of ditch and flume in Summit County by 1870.

Samuel Bowles described Summit's extensive water channeling efforts in his 1869 book, *Colorado: Its Parks and Mountains*:

> In the valley of the Blue and its tributaries more extensive works for gulch-mining exist than in any other district; there, not less than eighty-four miles of ditches bring water to wash out the gold . . . and the amount of water they carry in the aggregate is eight thousand seven hundred and fifty inches. One of these ditches is eleven miles long; two others seven miles each; another five, and so on; and they cost from one thousand to twelve hundred dollars a mile.

The gulches around early Breckenridge crawled with miners panning, rocking and sluicing. Some prospectors, like Ruben Spalding's 1859 Breckenridge discovery party, were damming rivers or creeks, digging new channels, and washing the old stream bed for gold. (Spalding actually dug a channel and turned the rushing Blue himself; for the story of his party's historic 1859 discovery of Blue River gold, see Chapter 4 on Breckenridge.) Other prospectors dug shafts to stream bedrock using a primitive hand winch to draw up rich streambed gravels in an operation called "coyoting".

All this placer mining activity occurred during a tenuous time in U.S. economic history. The Panic of '57 became a thing of the past when Civil War broke out. Inflation sent the dollar spiraling. Americans doubted whether shaky Union and Confederate governments could stand behind their paper money. Gold, solid and stable, a reliable currency, became "the" investment. Eastern companies bought into or bought out Colorado placer operations. These moves came at a time when early discoveries began to play out. Only so much high grade free gold existed. The rewards had been great: Summit County led all of Colorado in placer gold production, with a $5 million yield from 1861 to 1863. (Today's value: $35 million.) Miners began to look at medium and low grade deposits. If large volumes of dirt could be washed quickly, these secondary diggings might yield handsomely. Summit miners transplanted California's most dramatic — and most destructive — placer innovation: Hydraulic mining. Eastern investors helped them launch massive new hydraulic operations. Hydraulic miners turned high-pressure hoses against the hillsides to flush out gold-bearing dirt. Naturally, the hillsides themselves washed away. Extensive flume systems, like the Fuller Placer Company's 25 miles of ditch and flume for Georgia Gulch hydraulic mining, brought water from the upper reaches of streams and rivers. The water fell with great speed through the flume and into a giant nozzle, called a "monitor", to create a huge spurt that gouged the hillside.

(A "giant", a type of hydraulic nozzle that could shoot a 250-foot stream of water, today stands on Breckenridge's courthouse lawn.)

Acres of mud washed down by the hoses passed through sluices thousands of feet long to catch the free gold. Sludge ("slickens") remained for miners to channel into a nearby stream or creek. (The Blue River didn't stay blue very long; it flowed muddy and brown for miles as a result of hydraulic washing.) ". . . gold-washing leaves a terrible waste in its track," moaned Samuel Bowles on viewing the destruction of the mountain valleys he had learned to love.

For those without the cash resources to build flumes for hydraulic mining, a simpler gulch-washing method existed. Called "booming", this technique involved damming a stream to create a small lake. When enough water accumulated, miners opened the dam gates and — Boom! — a great burst of water rushed down to wash out a gulch wall or small hillside.

Hydraulic mining created many of the scars that blemish Summit mountainsides today. Mounting Silverthorne Hill toward Frisco on I-70, just past the Dillon-Keystone exit, one can look to the right to view the red-earth scars created nearly a century ago by hydraulic mining at the Buffalo Placers claim.

Hydraulic mining loomed large in later years. Biggest hydraulic operations at the century's close were the Gold Pan Company at Breckenridge with its giant pit (today the Maggie Pond near the Four Seasons Center), the Gold Run Placer Company, the Washington, the Mecca Pit, Salt Lick, Banner, Buffalo Placers and the Iowa.

Placer mining's final form arrived soon after the turn of the century when 1900's gold dredges clanged their way onto the Breckenridge-area scene.

The Gold Dredges

Decades of dredging the Swan Valley, French Gulch and up and down the Blue River helped Breckenridge survive in the twentieth century. Gold Dredge King Ben Stanley Revett's tenacious struggle to launch gold dredging appears in Chapter 17. His long years of failure with four costly experimental dredges, ended in 1905 with the debut of a fifth, the successful Reliance dredge in French Gulch. The Reliance netted $50,000 in its first full season.

Mining the gold-rich glacial gravels that ran as deep as 90 feet at Breckenridge's Gold Pan Pit and 40 to 50 feet at the Swan Valley's mouth proved a valid concept. In April, 1912, the *Blue Valley Times* gloated over a "very rich portion of bedrock deposits in the Swan Valley", predicting "three-fourths of a million

Experimental Risdon Dredge No. 2, shown during 1898 construction, was assembled with machinery from San Francisco's Ridson Iron Works and wood hull built on-site.

dollars in gold this season". The newspaper also reported a Reliance dredge cleanup that yielded a $7,000 gold brick "just shipped out".

While a total of nine dredges scoured bedrock gold in the Blue River area, only five worked at one time, during 1917 and 1918. The powerful Tonopah Placers Company dominated area dredging at that time. The Tonopah dredge on French Creek once ran into a cliff of solid rock above the Wellington Mine that turned out to be ancient river bedrock. The strike yielded a neat $40,000 worth of gold. The Tonopah dredge could proceed no farther on the creek, however, and was forced to turn around there.

The dredge floated in its own self-made pond. Buckets on a revolving chain scooped up rock and gravel from the riverbed in front of the boat. After processing to retrieve the gold, these rocks tumbled from a conveyor belt off a chute behind the boat. Excavating in front and filling in behind caused the pond to "move" along the waterway.

On board the dredge a screen separated large rocks from gravel material. Screened gravel went through an advanced "sluice box" device, which washed the gravel and allowed heavy gold to collect in riffles below, while lighter sand and gravel were carried away.

Conveyor belts picked up the gravel tailings, transported them to an elevator assembly which dumped them via the stern chutes, to the rear. The dredge, secured to the shore by four cables, and to the river bottom by a mammoth spud driven into the riverbed, pivoted on the spud, swinging a slow arc across the pond. That is why the tailings took on a wormlike configuration, especially discernable when viewed from the air. (Often, just one swing across the pond took an eight-hour work shift.)

The Blue River Dredge Company's No. 1 dredge provides a good example of later gold boat function. (Misadventure marked the glorious days of gold dredging, to be sure.) Like all dredges, No. 1 leaked water. Pumps operated to rid the boat of this excess baggage. If the pump failed, water would come in one side of the boat and slowly capsize it — which is just what happened to Blue River No. 1. Also, boulders smashed through wooden hulls, causing the boat to flood — more hilarity.

Old No. 1 was a "nine foot boat", meaning each bucket held nine cubic feet of rock and gravel.

Pumps, used to drain the dredge boats, were fitted with huge hoses. The old Triflex pump had tremendous power, so much that it took a powerful man's entire strength just to hold onto the hose when the valve was turned on "Full". "If you let go, it would beat you to death," said a dredge man. A favorite dredge prank was to sneak up on a man holding the hose and switch the valve to "Full". The hapless hoseman had to hold on indefinitely, because he dared not let go to turn off the valve.

Dredge spuds in later years measured 80 to 85 feet long (that's how deep some of the advanced dredges were digging), and weighed 80 to 90 tons. Dredge man Johnny Johnson once hoodwinked a greenhorn shoreman by convincing him that the spud was "hanging too tight" and causing the boat to list. Johnson sent the greenhorn to balance with one foot on an electrical cable and one foot on the boat and pound on the 85-foot 90-ton solid steel spud with a 12-pound sledge hammer. The greenhorn slammed away for an hour, then looked up, exhausted, to see if the boat had stopped listing. "Do you think that's enough?", he asked Johnson. "No, better go a little more," came the reply. Finally, the dredgemaster heard Johnny's guffaws, came on deck to share the joke and told the greenhorn, "I think that's deep enough. You can come down now."

Only three men ran a dredge boat in later years, communicating over the clanging racket with signal bells. But everyone worked a long shift on Friday, "clean up day", when dredge gold was retrieved from processing equipment. Molten gold later was poured into molds to form gold bricks. Dredge cleanup averaged $20,000 weekly.

Though the dredges provided jobs for Breckenridge men when they dredged the Blue River through town, residents had a hard time living with the gold boats. "The noise was incredible," remembers Breckenridge's Frank Brown. "The dredge boats used to squeak and creak and the sound of rocks falling was like thunder." Residents became so used to sleeping through the racket, they would wake up if the dredge broke down.

The dredges ceased their raucous clatter on October 15, 1942 when a World War II war board order ended their operation. At their peak, Summit's dredges had gobbled up about $20,000 per week in riverbed placer gold. Colorado historian Phyllis Dorset claimed the Breckenridge area dredges unearthed a staggering $32 million from "played out" placer streams. In today's dollars, that amount translated to about $224 million.

Placer mining, by pan, sluice, hose or dredge, usually came to a grinding halt in November when vital water sources froze up. (After 1909, some dredge boats worked through the winter.) But another kind of mining would emerge when the placers gave out. Burrowing like earthworms into Summit mountainsides, the lode miners needed neither water nor warm weather— they moiled for gold year-round in their snug glory holes.

Lode Mining and Milling

Summit's second boom came with the lode mining explosion that rocked Colorado after the 1878 Leadville silver lode discoveries. Summit '59er Will Iliff struck gold at his Blue Danube Mine on Breckenridge's Shock Hill, and launched a second rush over the craggy Continental Divide into Summit County. Lincoln's Old Reliable and Illinois Gulch's Laurium silver veins numbered among Breckenridge's early (late 1860's) hard-rock strikes. Ten Mile Canyon prospectors stumbled on the stunning Justice Lode in 1861. And, of course, the Sts. John Mine, above Montezuma in the Snake River region, had plumbed its Comstock Lode for years. Sts. John built Summit's first stamp mill in 1872 to crush silver ores from the Comstock.

Prospectors again swarmed the Summit. Some relied on hot tips and luck to find ores; some followed the frenzied crowd, "rushing" here or there to

The Mining District

The Mining District, a legal organization, solved squabbles over claim ownership and evolved as the mine camp's first form of government. Miners wrote district constitutions providing a name, boundaries and officer-election rules for their mining districts. They established claim size (usually, placer claims measured 100 feet, bank to bank, and lode claims 100 feet by 50 feet), rules for staking, deadlines for recording claims, working requirements and water use regulations. They also devised a means of settling claim disputes through the Miners Court. Judge Marshall Silverthorn dispensed stern frontier justice as the colorful arbiter of Breckenridge's Miners Court. Summit County sprouted more than two dozen mining districts a century ago.

pockmark a hill with prospect holes; others, more experienced, studied the color of the earth and rock. Color change could signal mineral wealth.

"A mine is a hole in the ground owned by a liar," Mark Twain once said. Just getting that "hole in the ground" proved a challenge to hard-rock miners. Summit's Pre-Cambrian granite and gneiss rock encased much of the gold-bearing quartz and silver-bearing galena ores—"hard-rock" to be sure!

Miners and their equipment reached their mineral veins by openings, such as the horizontal tunnel or adit, and the vertical shaft. Andrew S. Hallide, who dreamed up San Francisco's hill-defying cable cars, invented its twisted steel-wire cable. This Hallide cable, run by a hoist engine, also hauled incredible loads from shafts in countless Western mines.

Within the mine, a network of passages, usually well-timbered for safety, provided access. "Drifts" were tunnels burrowed from the main tunnel or shaft that followed the "drift" or path of the vein. When a vein expanded to show good surface area, the large mass of ore removed from it created a chamber called a "stope". "Crosscuts" tunneled between major workings, connecting them for ventilation, communication and also exploration. Dead-end vertical shafts were called "winzes". (See end of chapter for a glossary of mining terms.)

Surface headworks for the mine included a headframe (sometimes enclosed in a shaft house), hoist house, pump house, offices, storage yard, boardinghouse, mess hall and changing rooms (miners had to watch out for wet, chilling clothing and mine owners had to be wary of disappearing gold, an all-too-frequent phenomenon called "high-grading").

Along with brute labor using sledge hammer and pick axe came gunpowder, which blasted rock to smithereens when used properly. (When used improperly, gunpowder and later, dynamite blew up miners as well.)

Miners usually drove in seven 24 to 36-inch deep holes to hold their blasting material. Before 1875, when compressed air drills became available, four-pound sledge hammers, wielded by brawny miners, drove a rod into the rock wall to create the gunpowder hot hole. This was "single-jacking". Double-jacking involved two or three men. One held and turned the rod; the others took turns slamming it with eight-pound sledges, rhythmically striking about 50 blows per minute.

Rare photo shows visitors in a large Chautauqua Mine stope or chamber. A silver mine on Glacier Mountain discovered in 1866, the Chautauqua relied on crude early lode mining equipment. Exterior shot depicts primitive ore car. By 1870, miners had hacked 100 tons of rich silver ore from the pioneering lode. Lower workings are visible 400' above Deer Creek Rd.

Blasters rammed powder cartridges into the holes and began lighting the rat-tail fuses. A cry of "Fire in the Hole" preceded the deafening crash that released ore to be sorted and hauled away by mule-drawn ore cars after the dust settled. The ores would undergo crushing in a mill. Then the concentrate extracted at the mill traveled to a smelter for refining. A ton of ore could yield a pound of precious metal.

The milling process demanded huge outlays in capital investment. The lone prospector, with homemade Long Tom and battered shovel, no longer played in this mining game, where the stakes had become high. Claims grouped under the corporate umbrella; stock sold readily to moneyed Eastern and European (especially British) investors.

(Boston money financed many Summit mining ventures. For example, the big 40-stamp mill, constructed at Sts. John in 1872, was financed by Bostonian investors. And Ben Stanley Revett knocked successfully on Boston bankers' doors to launch his gold-dredging scheme.

Gold milling, in its simplest terms, involves crushing auriferous (gold-bearing) quartz ore to begin recovery of the locked-in gold. Crude stone mortars

110

functioned as early, primitive pulverizing devices. Later, the Spanish invented the *arrastre*. Oxen or other animals provided power to run the *arrastre*. It consisted of two large stones, the lower one flat, the upper one attached to a pole so oxen could make it revolve. Gold ore was crushed between the two stone surfaces. Miners profited from arrastre milling only if the ore pulverized proved very high grade. A rapid crushing device, to handle lower quality ores in high volume, became a vital need.

The stamp mill answered this need. In stamp milling, heavy weights, raised by machinery, fall with thunderous force on quartz ores. Horses worked Colorado's first, cumbersome stamp mills. Then steam engines arrived and mill efficiency soared. In 1859, only one Colorado stamp mill operated near Nevada City. By 1860, 150 mills sprouted on hillsides and in gulches across the state's 240-mile mineral belt.

The Jessie Mill, still standing precariously in Gold Run Gulch, is a typical stamp mill. The Jessie, with 40 stamps in 1903, used gravity to move its ores. The mill had ore chutes, a two-car gravity tramway and Wilfley tables for shaking ore from crushed rock. In May, 1905, the mill worked round the clock, processing 80 tons of ore daily. Later, in 1907, a 300-ton cyanide plant to treat ores increased Jessie Mill production.

Ball mills, iron cylinders spinning like a modern clothes dryer, contained heavy metal pellets. These "balls" crushed ores as the mill revolved.

Both milling processes yielded a crushed ore that still required treatment by water and mercury. Some mining companies dug their own wells for this process, rather than rely on muddy and uncertain stream flows.

At Gibson Hill's big Jumbo Mine, like many others, a shaker table stood beside the ball mill. This mining innovation dramatically increased gold yield from crushed ore. Also seen at the Jumbo is a jaw-breaker, which crushed large rocks. Nearby the Jumbo, also on Gibson Hill, is the Extension Mine, where an Oliver Filter still remains. The Oliver Filter, a rotating cylinder-shaped drum, used suction to filter excess water from gold-bearing mud or sludge, which had caked onto heavy cloth covering the drum.

The milling process yielded concentrate, which mining companies then shipped to a smelter for final processing. From Sts. John, silver concentrate traveled all the way to Swansea, Wales for refining. This costly effort ended when the Boston Mining Company built its fine brick smelter at Sts. John around 1872.

Montezuma got its first smelter, the Sisapo, in 1880. Breckenridge boasted several smelters during the lode mining era as did smaller towns like Lincoln City (with a smelter as early as 1874), Kokomo and Robinson.

Summit's three mineral booms each offered the miner ripe potential for personal disaster. Placer miners narrowly escaped rampaging grizzlies and pouncing mountain lions. Early prospectors faced constant forest fire danger and frequently suffered frozen limbs. But the grisly mining accidents came with the lode era. Mangled by misused explosives, suffocated by bad air, crushed by falling rock and cave-ins, lode miners faced constant threat. On the dredges, drownings took lives, but the gold-boats biggest killer was electricity. Miners knew little about its hazards; electrocution killed many.

Breckenridge writer Belle Turnbull said it best in *Far Side of the Hill:*

> . . ."I think about my mother. In that window, she would set, that window over there. Day after day she set there patching, when her housework would be done . . . keeping an eye out in case a stretcher would come down the trail . . . A miner will come home all blowed to pieces . . . or if not, he will die of the puff."

Summit mining concentrated geographically in three main areas: Breckenridge, the Ten Mile Canyon and the Snake River district. A close-up look at each follows.

MINING TERMS

ADIT: A nearly horizontal passage from the surface used to enter a mine and provide water drainage.

AMALGAM: An alloy of mercury (quicksilver) with one or more other metals.

ARGENTIFEROUS: Rock or ore bearing silver.

ARRASTRE: Spanish milling device used to crush ores. The circular trough holds ore, while heavy stones dragged by horse or mule grinds it.

AURIFEROUS: Rock or ore that bears gold.

BALL MILL: A short tube mill which grinds using steel balls.

BAR: Streambank gravels worked by miners for gold.

BEDROCK: Solid rock underlying auriferous gravel, sand, clay etc. upon which alluvial gold rests.

BLANKET VEIN: A horizontal vein or deposit.

CARBONATES: Ores containing a considerable proportion of carbonate of lead.

CLAIM: The boundaries encompassing ownership of ground presumed to contain a lode or placer.

CONCENTRATE: Ore reduced to a state nearing purity by removing foreign matter.

CRADLE: Also called a rocker. Early placer miners shoveled pay dirt into the cradle while funneling water into it. The "rocking" helped gold to settle in riffles at bottom.

CROSS CUT: A short lateral tunnel at right angles to a main tunnel or shaft bottom used in a deep mine to explore, ventilate or communicate.

CYANIDE PROCESS: A method of recovering gold from slimes or tailings by dissolving the gold in potassium cyanide and precipitating it on zinc plates.

DOUBLE-JACKING: Hand drilling for blast holes when two men cooperate, one holding the drill rod, turning it after each blow from a heavy sledge; the other hammering it with steady rhythm. Single-jacking was a one-man job.

DREDGE: A barge used for placer mining the creeks using a series of buckets to dig to bedrock. Gravels were washed on the dredge and wastes dumped behind.

DRIFT: A deep horizontal mining tunnel that "drifts" to follow the vein. (A crosscut, in contrast, intersects a vein.)

DUMP: Low-grade ore and debris taken from mines; or the discarded ore tailings pile from mill or smelter.

FAULT: A break in the continuity of a body of rock causing a separation.

FISSURE VEIN: A cleft or crack in the rock material of the earth's crust filled with mineral matter different from the walls.

FLUME: A wooden trough (sometimes pipe) used to carry water, often great distances.

FREE GOLD: Metallic gold easily separated from its quartz ore or dirt — scale, dust, leaf, shot, flake, wire and nugget gold.

GALENA: A principle ore of lead, often containing silver.

GOLD PAN: Twelve to eighteen-inch flat-bottomed steel or copper pan used in placer mining.

GRUBSTAKE: To outfit a prospector with tools, food and supplies in return for a share of his find.

HEADWORKS: Buildings near mine entrance — shaft house, hoist house, tipple, pump house, offices and blacksmith shop.

HIGH GRADING: Stealing ore from a mine or dredge.

HYDRAULIC MINING: Placer mining with large-nozzle hoses using water under high pressure to wash gravel from hillsides into sluice boxes.

INCLINE: A slanted shaft.

LEVEL: One of the stories of a deep mine, providing access from the shaft to drifts and stopes.

LODE: An ore body, usually horizontal, occurring in hard rock. Also vein.

LONG TOM: A wooden sluice used in placer mining, usually about 20 feet long and 18 inches deep. Riffles (cleats) caught the gold at the bottom of the long tom. A tapered end allowed Long Toms to fit together in a series.

MILL: Site for crushing ore by several processes, possibly including a ball mill, and stamp mill. Ore then traveled to a smelter as concentrate ready for final processing and later emerged as "bullion", or lead, or zinc.

MINING DISTRICT: A section of land usually named and confined by certain natural boundaries where gold, silver or other minerals occur.

MINE: A mine includes surface headworks and machinery plus tunnels, shafts, levels, stopes or winzes below. Several mines can work a single lode.

PATCH: Small placer claim.

RIFFLE: Series of cleats in the bottom of a rocker, sluice or shaker table designed to catch free gold, frequently aided by mercury.

RUBY SILVER: A silver-arsenic sulfide mineral.

SAMPLING WORKS: A plant and its equipment for sampling and determining value of ores.

SHAFT: Mine opening either on an incline or vertically.

SHAKER TABLE: General term for mechanized table which vibrates to shake gold from silt and fine gravel and catch the gold in riffles. The Wilfley Table separates light and heavy grains and throws the heavy grains toward the

table's head, while the light grains wash away into a tailings box.

SLUICE: Boxes or troughs used to wash gold-bearing gravel in placer mining.

SMELTING: Process of reducing metals from their ore in furnaces.

STAMP MILL: Machinery to crush ore and separate minerals by a series of pestles or stamps, raised and lowered by a camshaft.

TAILINGS: The worthless slimes left behind after the valuable portion of the ore has been separated by dressing or concentration.

TIPPLE: Building over the shaft housing the hoisting apparatus, a tall and narrow structure.

TRAMWAY: An aerial cable system that transports ore cars to and from the mill. Miners sometimes caught a ride as well.

TROY WEIGHT: Weight system used for minerals:

24 grains = 1 DWT (pennyweight)

20 DWT = 1 ounce

12 ounces = 1 pound

TUNNEL: A horizontal opening to a mine, used to reach lode or vein.

WINZE: An underground shaft, either vertical or horizontal, which has no direct connection with the surface; frequently a connection between two levels.

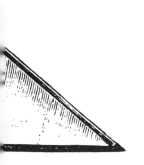

Gulches of Gold

Breckenridge Mining:

Incredible riches streamed from Breckenridge placers during the post-1859 rush. Though this free gold ran out quickly, and most of the prospector influx departed by 1863-64, Summit County managed to produce a hefty $6.3 million in gold before 1878 and the ensuing lode mining boom. Most of the gold came from the Croesus-rich Breckenridge district.

R. Widmar, in his "Blue River Gold Fields and Metal Mines", asserted around 1900 that Blue River placer gold production had reached an impressive "$35

Cashier Mine, dominating Brown's Gulch in Swan Valley, became part of big Tiger Mine.

116

million since 1859-60". No other Colorado placer mining area could match Breckenridge's phenomenal output.

A capsule mining tour of Blue River mines begins with the Swan River Valley. But, before you embark on this or any of the tours which follow, please observe these good-sense suggestions:

1. Bring a good topographical map, such as a U. S. Geological Survey map or an X-Y-Z Company map. The Breckenridge area tours, plus the Ten Mile and Montezuma tours that follow, require map use.

2. Take an altimeter, compass, binoculars (for viewing off-road mines) and good hiking shoes.

3. Drive the family car on main roads only. Many Summit back roads are fit only for jeepers, hikers or (in winter) cross-country skiers.

4. *Take no more than a photograph.* Souvenir-seekers are quickly destroying the last remnants of Summit's century-old mining era.

Sled train hauled $40,000 in Wellington ore down 1920 Breckenridge's wide Main St.

Swan Valley

A jeeper's Blue River mining tour, leading back through the decades to an exciting era of bonanza gold, might best begin at the entrance to the gold-rich Swan Valley. Start at the intersection of Colorado Highway 9 and the Tiger Road three miles north of Breckenridge. Across the modern highway, on the west side, lies the site of Braddocks, "Broncho Dave" Braddocks' 1880 rail stop. Ores from Swan Valley mines arrived here by ox wagon to be loaded onto railroad freight cars when rails arrived in 1882. Proceed east on the Tiger Road. This level plain was once Buffalo Flats, early placer mining site once dotted with tents and shanties. "Buffalo Flats is in the same district (Union Mining District) as Gold

117

Run; its production of gold is larger," said mining observer Orvando J. Hollister in 1867. Water shortages emerged as the area's biggest placer mining problem. An early solution: "Water (for sluicing) is brought by two ditches from French Gulch," said Hollister. Even when the placer boom fizzled, after 1863, Buffalo Flats managed to produce a half-million dollars in gold from 1867-77, according to the *Colorado Business Directory*.

Delaware Flats, another placer camp just beyond, was discovered during the summer 1860 rush to Gold Run. "Delaware Flats are just now the most noted of mines," said the Tarryall *Miners Record* in 1861. Several claims averaged $75 to $100 per day, big money in the 1860's. A town sprouted around the placer claims, and Delaware Flats population quadrupled in four weeks during summer, 1861.

The Swan River, inundated by dredge tailings, forms a pond nearby. Hidden behind gravel mounds in this pond, just off the road on the right, is the skeleton of an old dredge, manufactured for Ben Stanley Revett by Milwaukee's Bucyrus Company, and assembled on the Swan River. The gold boat operated from 1900 to 1904.

Galena Gulch, farther along the Tiger Road on the right, opens to the south. Early 1860's placer miners exploited this gulch's abundant free gold. Swan Valley gold then averaged $17 per ounce in value. In the 1890's, dredge pioneer Revett drove his first experimental dredge prospect hole at Galena Gulch's mouth, hoping to hit Swan River bedrock. Revett's first dredges were assembled here in 1898 and his initial stab at scooping bedrock gold made. One gold boat retrieved a 29¼-ounce troy-weight gold nugget where Galena Gulch opens onto the Swan. The North American Gold Dredging Company ran a turn-of-the-century double hydraulic elevator plant here, gutting gravels down to bedrock to mine settled gold.

The next gulch, Summit, boasted the Hamilton Mine, a silver-gold producer about one mile in from the Swan, with a 10-stamp mill that ran 24 hours per day and processed 70 to 80 tons of ore monthly. The Hamilton Group consisted of 12 claims owned in 1899 by E. W. Dee. By 1902, the Hamilton had a tramway, flumes and its own reservoir. By 1909, the mine, though poorly managed, grossed $400,000. The Hamilton operated from 1887 until at least 1910.

A little farther along, at the mouth of Brown's Gulch stood Swan City, its site now obliterated by dredge tailings. Offices for the Eddy Mining Company, IXL Mine, New York and Summit Mines headquartered here in a 300-population town with a sawmill for flume lumber and a concentrator owned by C. A. Weeks. (See Chapter 12 for details on Swan City.)

The Cashier Mine, a heavy longtime producer of silver-gold ore, was located on the east side of Brown's Gulch. The Cashier had adits on three levels, some very large stopes (chambers) and a 40-stamp mill. The mine yielded some beautiful specimens of tangled wire gold, like that found on famous Farncomb Hill. Just past Swan City, the IXL Mine had its 40-ton concentrating mill on the valley's south side.

A lone log cabin, the old Tiger assay office, marks the site of Tiger, former company-town headquarters of the powerful Royal Tiger Mines Company. In

May, 1917, the company, under John Traylor, grouped area mines, including nearby Swan City's rich Cashier and substantial IXL (five large claims) under one corporate roof. The IXL soon connected with the Cashier via tunnel. A 500-ton mill went up. A complete company town arose to house workers. (See Chapter 12 for details.) In 1926, Traylor purchased the dredge and properties of the powerful Tonopah Placers Company. The Royal Tiger Mines Company worked from 1917 to 1934, provided vital tax and payroll dollars for a depressed Summit County. Then, in 1938, the company filed for bankruptcy. B & B Mines Company acquired its property in 1940. (B & B now owns many historic Breckenridge-area mines.)

Continue on beyond Tiger until the road forks. A sign there indicates that the left turn leads to the Swan's North Fork. Perched high in a meadow near timberline on the North Fork is old Rexford, another company town. One hundred yards above it is Rexford's mine, the rich Rochester King (later called the Arrastre King), discovered by Daniel Patrick in 1880. The mine grossed about $5,000 per month in 1881. Consisting of six claims, the Rochester shipped 500 tons of gold-silver ore by 1883. The Black Swan, White Swan, Sweet William, Santa Claus and Ben Franklin claims merged to form the mine. Although the Rexford post office closed in 1883, mining continued here. In 1889, a new mill went up, with a wooden tramway connecting to the mine. (Chapter 12 details Rexford's history.)

The road to Rexford, washed out in recent years, is best traveled by foot, or cross-country skis (but watch for snowslide danger).

Driving south along the Tiger Road another split appears. Here one can proceed along a jeep road that follows the Swan's Middle Fork to Swandyke. (The road becomes *very* bad as you progress toward the old townsite.) At Swandyke, the Brilent Mine, the Uncle Sam, at the head of Wise Mountain, Three Kings, Pompeii and Isabella operated despite the town's isolated, near-timberline location.

Swandyke blossomed in the late 1890's. Its postoffice opened in 1898 and a big iron sulfide strike caused a minor boom in 1899. The Carrie Mine installed a modern electro-cyanide mill and a Tyler five-stamp mill that year. Strikes, including those at the Pompeii and the Swandyke Gold Mining and Milling Company's 12 rich claims continued through the next decade. In 1899, Swandyke's Uncle Sam Lode made news. A March 22, 1899 Denver newspaper reported a strike with samples that averaged $780 in gold, "the highest running $2,933". By 1910, the postoffice closed and Swandyke population dipped to 15. (See Chapter 12 for more on Swandyke.)

This tour follows the Swan's South Fork to the Georgia Gulch site of old Parkville. A broken Masonic marker, vandalized in 1978, indicates the townsite, which was buried above its rooftops by mine tailings. (See Chapter 16 on Parkville.)

Pick 'n pan prospectors found mind-boggling fortunes in placer gold near Parkville. Individual placers produced as much as $10,000 in a single June to October season during Georgia Gulch's placer peak. "The gulch was exceeding all expectation in richness," Georgia Gulch miner Daniel Conner observed in his 1860 Journal, *A Confederate in the Colorado Gold Fields*. "It was common for three or four men to take out from $300 to $500 per day of good-quality gold dust." (That translates to $2,100 to $3,500 daily in current inflated-dollar values!)

Georgia Gulch was discovered by a small party of Georgia miners led by a Mr. Highfield, according to Conner. "It proved to be the richest diggings ever found in this section of the Rocky Mountains," he said.

Water shortages challenged early Georgia Gulch miners and caused work stoppage. "Georgia Gulch is idle," William Byers reported in 1861. But enterprising pioneers soon brought needed water via the six and one-half mile American Ditch. "The ditch would sometimes spring a leak somewhere in its course around a mountain and finally break and wash away the side of the

Wooden flume carries needed water to hydraulic site near Breckenridge. A "Giant" nozzle helps release placer gold deposited in former creekbeds by ancient streams.

mountain before it was discovered," Conner recalled.

Later, in the 1870's the Fuller Placer Company purchased acres of rich placer ground around Georgia Gulch. Under company president T. H. Fuller, mining superintendent M. J. Cole supervised placer work in 28 gulches and patches in the Georgia area as well as the company's 1,000 acres in the Nigger Hill area. The company invested in the American Ditch, Pollard Ditch, Stevens Flume and what early writers called the Mount Guyot Flume, or the "Great Flume", which diverted eastern slope water to the western slope via Georgia Pass — the only place in the U. S. where Atlantic waters were channeled over the Continental Divide to the Pacific drainage. (An eastern slope lake situated higher than 11,811-foot Georgia Pass provided the water.) The powerful Fuller Placer Company probably owned more placer ground than any company east of California, historian Frank Fosset asserted in 1879. The company controlled 3,000 acres of pay dirt and pre-empted another 3,000 acres through its water rights.

Farncomb Hill

A jeep road penetrates Georgia Gulch to its head where in 1879 the first lode discovery at Farncomb Hill's Ontario Mine set off a history-making rush to the incredibly-rich hill. The Ontario, Key West, Reveille and Boss mines there produced gold then valued at a rich $17 to $19 per ounce.

In 1881, Ontario Mine gold, a dazzling kaleidoscope of rich and varied wire gold specimens, snared first prize at the Colorado Industrial Exhibition. In 1882, miners took out a stunning 60 pounds of native wire gold for owners Timothy Murphy, Patrick McCarty and Henry J. Litton.

Ontario gold, on three 150 by 1,500 foot claims, ran in veins three to twenty feet thick. In 1889, miners still made valuable new strikes here.

All the Farncomb Hill mines made 1880's headlines. At the nearby Boss Mine, early owners took out $40,000 worth of gold from a pocket in a single week. Later, three men retrieved 134 ounces of coarse gold and nuggets in five and one-half days, then averaged 50 ounces weekly for months!

Continue along the road up to Wapiti, where an ancient structure stands amid thin pines at the left side of the road. The building, originally log, served as headquarters for John Campion's historic Wapiti Mining Company. (The Wapiti town postoffice occupied the building as well.) Wapiti began with the Victoria Mining Company. When John Campion took over, he hired British mining savant Ben Stanley Revett to manage the rich mines group in 1894. The old Fair Tunnel at Wapiti ran southwest for 1,000 feet into the hillside. An on-site mill and a water flume from the Middle Swan boosted production. Large quantities of ore were extracted annually. Among them ranked the stunning Farncomb Hill wire gold specimens that created the John Campion gold collection. Visitors to Denver's Museum of Natural History can view these amazing twisted wire nuggets on display there.

From Wapiti, there is a clear view across to the head of American Gulch, where the famous Gold Flake Mine is located. Tom's Baby, a 13-pound, seven-ounce troy-weight gold nugget made national news when the Gold Flake relinquished it in 1897. In 1894, Sol Barret and others took out 652 ounces of Gold Flake gold worth $12,000 in 40 days. (In July, 1979 prices, that gold would be worth over $200,000.) In the next 20 days, the mine yielded 334 ounces. The Gold Flake, stoped for a length of 300 feet and to a depth of 450 feet, stands as a leader in a group of fabulous mines. The Carpenter, Black, Groton, Wheeler, Silver and Bondholder, along with the neighboring Fountain Mine, all produced wealth that made Farncomb Hill justly famous. The Gold Flake and its notable neighbors produced $13,000,000 in coarse gold before around 1905, according to Breckenridge mine authority, A. E. Keables.

The Hill's fissures are narrow, rarely over one-half inch wide, but incredibly long. Wire gold proliferated in the veins west of American Gulch, while beautiful leaf gold abounded in mines east of American Gulch.

In 1885, 100 men worked on Farncomb Hill. Besides lode mining, extensive hydraulic washing, using flume water from the Middle Swan, exploited old dumps and surface material near Wapiti on the north side of Farncomb Hill. The Hill's blue-ribbon production declined in the 1890's, but its peerless crystallized nuggets still captured first prize at the 1893 Chicago World's Fair and the 1904 St. Louis World's Fair.

French Gulch

A jeep road tackles Farncomb's steep slope from beyond Wapiti down to the French Gulch and Lincoln area.

On the southwest side of Farncomb Hill lies the famous Wire Patch Mine, site of storied riches in crystallized wire gold first discovered by Harry Farncomb. Farncomb quietly purchased property on the gold-latticed hill until news of its magnificent mineral stores leaked out — and precipitated French Gulch's Ten Years War. (See Chapter 12 on Lincoln.) Farncomb's Wire Patch Group, launched with the Elephant, included lodes and placers of the Little Morgan, Queen of the Forest, Triangle, Emperor, Frederick and Great Lode Mines.

These were rich mines. Before extensive development, the Elephant had grossed more than $75,000 by 1886; the Emperor $15,000; Queen of the Forest, $8,000. By 1888, when new owners formed the Wire Patch Gold Mining and Milling Company, capitalized at $5 million, the Wire Patch had 20 employees and six Huntington Mills capable of processing 60 to 75 tons of ore daily. By 1896, the Wire Patch had built a gravity tramway with self-dumping ore cars and added Hartz jigs and sizing screens to its mills. In 1899, the 40-acre Wire Patch had recently produced $10,000 in gold, silver and copper from three tunnels (800, 400 and 300 feet long) and a 500-foot shaft.

At Lincoln City, one of Summit's earliest lode mines, the Old Reliable, operated as early as 1869 or before. (Orvando Hollister claims the Old Reliable had the western slope's first mill, a water-powered ore crushing operation as early as 1865.)

French Gulch ore then averaged $16 per ounce in value. Early star among French Gulch's famous mines was the Cincinnati, originally the Robley placer claim, where high grade lead ores yielded 16 ounces of silver per ton. Developed in the early '70's, the Cincinnati once stood as the biggest producer on Mineral Hill, later surpassed by the rich Lucky Mine. In 1878, G. K. Gooding erected a reverberatory furnace for the Lincoln City Silver Company to treat ores from the Cincinnati and other veins.

The Lucky, another lead-silver mine, ranked as the district's chief silver producer.

Up in Australia Gulch, barely visible through the trees, stands the well-preserved Sallie Barber Mine, where zinc was mined from a 365-foot shaft. The Little Sallie Barber had a shaft also, burrowing the earth to a 300-foot depth. Located by G. T. Metzger in May, 1882, the Sallie Barber still shipped regularly in 1909, when most Breckenridge area mines stood idle.

The old Reiling dredge rests in peace in a pond below Lincoln on French Gulch's south side. And remains of the pioneering Reliance gold dredge, Summit's first successful gold boat, launched in 1905 by Ben Stanley Revett, are beached in a meadow below.

The Reliance Dredge

French Gulch dredges regularly scooped up exquisite wire or leaf gold nuggets, often about three ounces each, and well-rounded by stream action.

Visible across the valley from the Reiling dredge is the Minnie Mine, a lead-silver producer with its own onsite mill. The Minnie shaft house tilted dangerously in 1978, ready to tumble down. Nearby in the trees stands the old Johannesburg Mill, painstakingly restored over ten years by Denver-based airline pilot Leslie Horlt. Horlt spent two years removing 30-foot deep tailings before building a unique contemporary home within the mill structure.

French Gulch's notable neighbors, the Country Boy on the south base of Barney Ford Hill, and the Wellington on the south side of Mineral Hill, both began their decades-long mining careers in 1887.

The Country Boy, later owned by the Phipps family of Denver Broncos fame, mined its high-grade zinc into the 1940's. The Wellington's mine manager once ambled across the street to view raw, unprocessed zinc ore at the Country Boy and commented, "That's as fine as the zinc coming out of our concentrator!"

Gustave Myers and E. A. Rubasso filed Country Boy patent papers on June 21, 1887. By 1889, 20 men mined Country Boy gold, lead, silver and zinc and processed the ore in a new 20-ton capacity Huntington-equipped mill. The historic mine progressed through decades, adding electric power in 1905, striking a two-foot 45 percent zinc vein in 1906, shipping regularly in 1912-13 when most Summit mines had shut down. The mine worked into the World War II era, using two main adits, the upper 1,700 feet long and the lower, 1,100 feet long.

The Wellington ranks as Breckenridge's outstanding long-time producer, mining lead, zinc, gold and silver (in that quantitative order) from 1887 discovery until 1973. Famous Colorado Negro pioneer Barney Ford, with partner Captain Ryan first owned the 20-acre Oro Mine, from which the Wellington took its beginnings. By 1889, the Oro had a big and sophisticated new mill, processing 70 tons daily, and owners had driven a three or four-hundred foot shaft. Later, the mine worked in a one-half mile long adit that connected with the Extenuate Tunnel, opening 2,000 feet above in French Gulch.

In 1892, investors (among them Breckenridge's prominent Robert Foote) patented the nearby Wellington Mine.

In 1901, local owners formed the Colorado and Wyoming Development Company. This group included longtime members of Breckenridge's beloved "Warm Stove Mine" — Denver Hotel owner Robert Foote, newspaper editor O. K. Gaymon, Gold Pan Mining Company manager George H. Evans and J. T. Hogan. These investors in 1902 added the 20-acre Oro Mine with its 80-ton concentrating mill, 8,000 feet of tunnel and crosscuts, and electric tramway to the Wellington holdings.

The reliable Wellington still shipped 30-35 tons of galena and sphalerite concentrates daily in 1909. During the next 20 years, the mine provided needed employment for Breckenridge's work force. Its temporary closure in 1929-30 stunned the town's weak Depression economy.

But the Wellington resumed work; in 1948, owners grossed $80,000. The mine shut down during 1958-61, then worked through 1973, when mill machinery was shipped to Utah for use there.

In 1962, a trash fire ignited and destroyed historic Oro Mine buildings. Fire again threatened the Wellington in spring, 1978, but some mine buildings remain intact for visitors to see.

Historian Phyliss Dorset, in her book *The New Eldorado*, credits the Wellington with a staggering total production of $32 million.

Near the Wellington Mine, marked by its wood cribbing, is Mineral Hill's Union Mine, a lead-silver producer. The big Union Mill, a 100-ton concentrating mill, had ten Wilfley tables and six Hartz jigs.

Gold Run Gulch

A second jeep sojourn will tour glittering Gold Run Gulch, first discovered by Balce Weaver and his brother in February, 1860. Legend says the Weavers went home with 96 pounds of gold!

The Weavers, camping on the Blue River below Breckenridge, with other members of the 1859 discovery party, struck gold in Gold Run after digging away six feet of snow! Prospectors never were a tight-mouthed bunch when gold was discovered, but the Weavers managed to keep Gold Run's secret until summer, 1860. Daniel Conner observed in his 1860 Journal:

> . . . a rich gulch had been discovered across the rugged country north, some eight miles distant. It had been secretly worked with rockers for some time before outsiders knew of it. It was called Gold Run and it did prove very rich. I stampeded to the object of this new excitement with the rest of the ambitious, and found the gulch looking like it had been worked for months!

Placer miners brought needed water into Gold Run Gulch as early as 1860, with the six mile Buffalo Flats Ditch carrying water from the Blue. In 1862, a second ditch, the eight and one-half mile Blue River Ditch, aided sluicing operations.

In 1864 the Independent Ditch brought water two and one-half miles from French Gulch. The Gold Run Ditch Company built a bedrock flume in 1863. In 1863-64, they mined $70,000 in gold dust, then valued at $18 per ounce, as a reward for their flume-building endeavor. In 1865, the Gold Run Flume Extension and Quartz Prospecting Company organized to build a 1,550-foot flume and realized $30,000 in gold dust for their efforts. Hollister, writing in 1867, noted 800 placer claims in Gold Run Gulch. The area proved rich — John Shock, a California miner, took $500,000 from his 1863-discovered Gold Run placer.

Beginning at the Tiger Road and Highway 9 again, drive the short distance to the mouth of Gold Run Gulch, beyond the Summit Motor Inn. A dirt road takes off to the right. Drive the auto road into the gulch until a large weathered wooden mill structure appears on a hillside at the road's left side. This proud relic, a 40-stamp mill held upright by its magnificent beams, stands as a remarkable remnant of the busy Jessie Mine. Many buildings have disappeared — a bunkhouse, boardinghouse and possibly a cookhouse. (A cook here once waved a butcher knife in the face of each of 100 complainers until each in turn acknowledged the food was good!)

The Jessie produced a low grade gold-silver ore, averaging $3 to $6 per ton. E. C. Moody originally discovered the Seminole Mine and the Bonanza in 1886; these and 42 other patented claims on 200 acres extending to Galena Gulch, became the Jessie Mine. Moody and his mining colleague, Irwin, built a 10-stamp mill for the Seminole here in 1886. The Jessie had four long adits. Through the years, owners and lessees earthwormed an amazing network of tunnels. Two of these plumbed the rocky hillside at 2,000 and 1,100 feet long. Crosscuts also latticed the property. The Jessie had so many openings that entrances were caved in for safety purposes in this century.

The Gold Run Mining Company operated the property until 1892, when the Jessie Gold Mining and Milling Company took over. The new owners launched mill construction and began processing Jessie ores in 1894. Perseverance proved a rare virtue in the mercurial mining era: The Jessie Company quit in 1897, leasing the mine to the Dania Mining Company in 1898. Mining entrepreneur Ben Stanley Revett leased the Jessie in 1899, remodeled the 40-stamp mill and added concentrating tables.

In 1900, the Jessie employed 60 men. Wagons transported ore to Braddocks where the railroad hauled it to Breckenridge's sampling mill, the Kilton Gold Reduction Company.

Another lessee, J. T. Hogan, worked the Jessie in 1906. A 300-ton cyanide plant opened there in 1907. By 1909, the mine had ceased operation, to be resumed intermittently in later years. Later owners, B & B Mines (Boston & Breckenridge) operated the mill till 1926. A lessee worked it in 1936.

Total Jessie Mine production is estimated variously between $80,000 and $1.5 million, according to geologist Leslie Ransome.

Gibson Hill

The auto road leads up the Gulch to fabled Gibson Hill. Swaying wooden structures, some capsized, mark the old town of Preston, Gibson Hill mining "metropolis". Gibson's gold proved as rich as Farncomb's, though its beauty failed to match that of Farncomb's prized nuggets. The lucky Mr. E. C. Moody, Jessie discoverer, struck Gibson Hill's first lode at his rich Jumbo Mine in summer, 1884. Preston sprang up around the mine. The Jumbo, together with the Extension and the Little Corporal, created mining history on Gibson Hill.

The first mine you encounter on reaching Gibson Hill is the Extension and its mill site. An Oliver Filter, cylinder-shaped drum for de-watering gold sludge, stands beside the auto road to mark the mill area. The Extension worked the same bounteous free gold vein as the nearby Jumbo. The vein, 35 inches wide at the Extension site, produced five to ten ounces of gold per ton. The mine's 20-stamp mill served a half-dozen area mines and processed Jumbo ore transported up the hill to the Extension Mill by mine railway. Robert Foote, Breckenridge hotel proprietor, invested in the Extension. The mine, originally the Fair property, developed after 1892.

"During the summer of 1884, much excitement was created in Breckenridge, Denver and other places by reports of rich discoveries on 'Gibson Hill', a few miles from the city," reported Crofutt's 1885 *Grip Sack Guide*. Object of all this joy was the Jumbo where E. C. Moody's 50-foot shaft completed August, 1884, uncovered an eight-foot wide ore vein! (The ore, classed as low-grade free gold, made up for its quality by its abundance.) Midas-like Mr. Moody, who discovered his Buffalo claim the same year, grew weary of so much gold and in 1885 sold his Gibson Hill claims for hard cash — $25,000 — to a miner named Nichols. Investing heavily in the unproved Jumbo, Nichols began building a 30-stamp mill, a good wagon road and sawmill for his new mine. Nichols' faith paid off. Already in 1885, the Jumbo produced 35 tons of ore daily. The Jumbo Mill couldn't handle all this ore. Some went by rail and wagon to the Eureka Mill at the mouth of Cucumber Gulch near Breckenridge.

By 1898, the Jumbo yield exceeded $300,000. In 1901, workers completed a shaft connecting the Jumbo to the Little Corporal. Twelve miners worked the enlarged mine. Felix Leavick (a town near Fairplay bears his name) ran the Jumbo Mill with a large crew in 1901. The Jumbo worked intermittently until at least the mid-1930's. Lessees mined it during summers in the 1960's. Visitors comment on the chalky white tailings and charred-looking vegetation below the Jumbo. Cyanide, a mining technology breakthrough years ago, dissolved gold. Miners used it to treat gold ore, but they also "treated" the nearby landscape to a bad case of total devastation.

Few details are available on the Little Corporal except that it was mined via a shaft. Higher up on Gibson Hill are the Eureka shaft, the Alicia A. Mine and a big 1880's producer, the Kellog. Over the hill's crest, on its western base are the Pronghorn Company's Sultana and the Fox Lake.

Shock Hill

Looking across the Blue Valley to Shock Hill, one might be able to see tailings from the Iron Mask Mine, a strong producer of lead-silver ore with an 1,800-foot adit into the hill. The Iron Mask yielded $50,000 before 1909. Shock Hill's Blue Danube Mine discovered by '59'er William H. Iliff and George Bressler, precipitated the 1880's Breckenridge lode 'boom.

The Finding shaft atop Shock Hill drove 300 feet in 1898 with hopes of reaching silver ores rumored to match Leadville's high quality silver. These hopes were dashed by stark reality. Not visible on the hill's west side are the Brooks-Snider workings with a 20-stamp mill. The Ohio Mine, just north of the Blue Danube, was discovered by Judge A. L. Shock and Daniel Shock.

Breckenridge

The tour continues to Breckenridge, itself the site of considerable mining endeavor (sometimes to the great annoyance of its citizens!). Breckenridge was the site of the Spalding party's 1859 gold discovery (See Chapter 4 on Breckenridge). In the 1880's, the town hosted a 20-stamp mill and three smelters. The Wilson smelter, built in 1880, operated at the base of Shock Hill on today's Ski Hill Road. A pad and bricks remain there in testimony. Gold-gobbling dredges ripped up the Blue River coursing through town. The clanging racket drove residents half-crazy, old-timers say. The Maggie Pond, today neighboring the Four Seasons Center, once stood as a gaping 90-foot deep pit excavated by the 1900's Gold Pan Mining Company in its attempt to mine glacier-deposited gravels enroute to bedrock gold.

The Gold Pan Mining Company, later purchased by the Tonopah Placers Company, played a dominant role in Breckenridge history. The Gold Pan Shops in Breckenridge, originally built to manufacture the company's own hydraulic mining pipe, emerged as the largest machine shop west of the Mississippi, able to produce anything from simple pipe to a railroad locomotive.

The Gold Pan Company had acquired 1,700 placer acres just south of Breckenridge. To mine it in accordance with their ambitious plans, the company required water. Lots of water. Water under pressure, because the company planned hydraulic mining, washing gold-bearing gravels with high pressure hoses.

Investigation of shipping costs convinced the company to build its own shops to produce the needed hydraulic pipe and equipment. Located on Breckenridge's South Ridge Street, on the site of today's Breckenridge Inn, the Gold Pan Shops grew into a minor miracle, famous in the area. The shops building, with nearby storehouse and two-story "showplace" guest house with offices, reached completion in 1900. Large vats were built as dipping tanks to submerge and coat pipe sections with rust preventative tar and asphaltum. These stone vats remain in ruins near the present Breckenridge Inn chalets.

The shops boasted elaborate and expensive conveniences. For example: The railroad ran 9,669 feet of track into the Gold Pan Shops main building, a listed station on the South Park line. And the Gold Pan constructed its own electric plant, with power enough left over to light the whole town of Breckenridge, at very low rates.

To mine its Gold Pan Pit, the company piped water from Indiana Creek through a ditch to neighboring Illinois Gulch (near the Rodeo Grounds). There, water flowed into a five-foot diameter pipe to the Gold Pan (Maggie) excavation. At the pit, Evans hydraulic elevators (invented by the Company's eminent manager George H. Evans) hoisted millions of tons of gravel from a great glory hole. Previous hydraulic washing had loosened and released the gravels. The Gold Pan Pit, mined to 90 feet bedrock, left tailings still visible around the Peak Nine base area, plus enough to surface Breckenridge parking lots.

In 1913, Tonopah Placers Company bought the Gold Pan operation. The company, a subsidiary of the famed Nevada-based Tonopah Mining Company, planned dredge mining, and would use the shops for dredge equipment manufacture and repair. Tonopah Placers purchased the Reliance Dredge and two Colorado Gold Dredging Company gold boats. Then, they proceeded to make money! Between 1914 and 1923, Tonopah dredged up a whopping 148,675 ounces of gold and 36,225 ounces of silver. They shipped bullion worth $3,099,854 gross value to the Denver Mint.

Tonopah's gravel-gobbling No. 1 Dredge had clawed its way up the Blue to the Breckenridge town limits. In 1922, the Summit County *Journal* rose up in arms. Townspeople squabbled about protecting their town versus padding their poc-

Breckenridge old-timers recall misadventures of "Old No. 1", shown sinking in 1937. Gold Run Gulch's Jessie Mine burrowed gold-rich hillside with amazing tunnel network.

ketbooks. The dredge, like a voracious dragon of old, wormed its way to north of Watson Avenue, leaving a trail of damaged eardrums and desolate tailings behind. The dredge finally ceased its river-ravaging because Tonopah determined its work unprofitable.

(The North American Dredging Company gloated that year over discovery of a $500 nugget among its gravels.)

Tonopah wanted to dredge right through Breckenridge's Main Street. The town fathers balked. In 1925, Tonopah books began showing losses. Disgusted with Breckenridge's refusal to grant a right of way and shocked by a financial downturn after 12 hugely successful years, Tonopah sold out. Public Service Company of Colorado bought the renowned Tonopah-Gold Pan Shops. Tiger's John A. Traylor in 1926 purchased Tonopah dredges and in 1929 transferred the gold boats to his Royal Tiger Mines Company.

Depression hung heavy over Breckenridge and the nation in 1932. Any promise of payroll dollars now tempted the town fathers. The Breckenridge Town Board allowed the Royal Tiger Mines Company to dredge south into Breckenridge beyond Watson Avenue.

Raucous dredge boats, screeching and clanking, ripped the Blue to bedrock. The environmental disaster came to a clattering halt on October 15, 1942, when the War Production Board's Order L-203 stopped all Colorado gold mining to divert manpower, metal and machinery for World War II use. The burial of once-proud West Breckenridge with its narrow-gauge rail depot and pretty park, ended when the dredge came to rest at Jefferson Avenue.

Breckenridge's sensitivity to environmental rape was dulled by economic need. "Industry is always to be preferred to scenic beauty," a 1923 newspaper letter-to-the-editor proclaimed.

Jessie Mill skeleton remains in Gold Run Gulch, where relics of a half-century of gold fever abound.

Gold Run has old mine cabins, rusty mine equipment, flumes, ditches and glory holes aplenty (watch out, hikers!). But dredges destroyed many mining history sites along Swan River. Towns like Swan City and Valdoro were buried. But Tiger Mine (right) still stands, just off Tiger Rd.

130

Boreas Pass

Another Breckenridge mine tour follows the Boreas Pass road beginning just south of Breckenridge. The road begins leading east toward Illinois Gulch, one of the big placer gulches in the 1860's rush. In the 1880's and '90's, the railroad diverted from today's county road to avoid a steep grade and entered the Wakefield mining area. There the train curved southward along the east flank of Little Mountain and made a loop to return north. The old Puzzle and Ouray veins, rich in silver, lead and gold, intersect nearby, a fact that a caused much litigation between the two mining companies. The Gold Dust Mine also operated here.

The Puzzle vein proved phenomenal. It ran from Little Mountain through Barney Ford Hill, penetrated the big Washington Mine property in Illinois Gulch (called the Puzzle Extension there) and produced $700,000 by 1901. The Puzzle, with its own concentrating mill, worked off and on until about 1918.

On Little Mountain, one small pocket near the Germania tunnel yielded $30,000. The Germania, a steady producer, sometimes received $10,000 from the contents of a single ore car.

Mill machinery at Gibson Hill's Jumbo Mine includes ball mill, jawbreaker, shaker table and tram.

On Barney Ford Hill's south slope, north of the Puzzle are three veins of the Dunkin Mining Company: The Juniata, with its Huntington Mill, the Dunkin and Maxwell veins. One tunnel on the Dunkin vein, called the Gallagher Tunnel yielded $65,000. Charles Gallagher, who worked the mine in the late 1890's, probably drove the tunnel. The Dunkin was no flash in the pan. In 1912, when dredge mining prevailed and lode mines closed, the Dunkin still shipped ore.

One of Summit County's outstanding mines, the Washington, worked veins on Barney Ford Hill's northwest slope in Illinois Gulch. Announcing the Washington's sale in 1882, to new owners Corning (former Colorado State Auditor), Watson and Boyle, the January 13, 1883 *Rocky Mountain News* said a sizeable investment had made the Washington "the most complete and extensive in the Blue River district".

The Washington, discovered in 1880, was one of six 150 by 1,500 foot claims owned by Watson, Corning and Company. The Washington group had five shafts and six main tunnels. The company also owned the 230-acre Berlin Placers with a 20-stamp mill, extending from Barney Ford Hill's summit to Illinois and Mayo gulches. In 1909, geologist Leslie Ransome reported the Washington group output at between $400,000 and $500,000. These Washington properties operated from 1880 to at least 1920, steadily producing for forty years.

The Mountain Pride, leading the Illinois district in 1898 production, had two 300-foot shafts and a 50-ton concentrating mill with two jigs and five Wilfley tables. Northeast from this mine were the Golden Edge and Gold Bell Mines.

High up in Illinois Gulch on Bald Mountain's slopes lay the Laurium Mine, one of Summit's pioneer lode mines, discovered in the late 1860's. The Laurium originally produced lead ore, but in 1909, according to Ransome, processed a gold-silver ore in its 60-ton mill.

The county road (which uses the old railbed as its route here) passes Rocky Point, popular old-time Breckenridge picnic spot, then mounts Boreas Pass toward the old mine settlement of Conger's Camp near Mount Argentine. Conger's, about five miles above Breckenridge in Indiana Gulch, hugged a hillside three-fourths mile from the rail line. The Diantha Lode, a silver "blanket" vein running just below grass roots caused an 1880's stir here and attracted Eastern investors. An experienced Colorado miner, S. P. Conger, discovered the Diantha and named it for his wife. The Diantha Lode never merited the excitement it created. Its discoverer, old Sam Conger, however, proved himself one of Colorado's outstanding silver pioneers.

Between Conger's Camp (later called Argentine for the nearby peak) and the Indiana Gulch area, the road passes an old placer flume.

From its 1879 discovery, the Warrior's Mark Mine in Indiana Gulch created a long and colorful history of fuss, furor and fabled wealth. The mine's beginnings were notable: Colorado pioneer Father John Lewis Dyer located the stunning silver lode at 11,095 feet altitude just a stone's throw from his new settlement, Dyersville, at the head of Indiana Gulch. (See Chapter 12 for more on Dyersville.)

Blanket veins, contact veins and ore pockets hiding just below ground surface proliferated in the Boreas Pass area. Ransome described uncovering the Warrior's Mark ore body in his 1909 geological survey report: " . . . very little work sufficed to uncover an extraordinarily rich mass of silver carrying both lead and copper".

A pack of scoundrels descended upon the saintly Fr. Dyer in a scramble to exploit Warrior's Mark ore potential. The Methodist preacher shared his claim with two down and out young prospectors, Thompson and Parkison. Greedy businessmen persuaded the pair to sell out for $1,000 and $500 respectively. Then the new owners turned around and unloaded the mine for a neat $300,000. "Swindle," cried Thompson and Parkison. Purchasers hired 50 men and took

Part of the fun of visiting or living in historic Summit County is exploring the area's old mines. Some clung to steep slopes above timberline. Some penetrated rocky mountain shoulders in tunnels thousands of feet long. Some supported rough mine camps that sprang up to house workers. All represent the struggle and dreams of their owners. Enjoy these reminders of mining's heyday, but beware rotten floorboards, unstable mine tunnels.

out nearly $80,000 in just six months. A dismayed Fr. Dyer had accepted only $10,000 in stock for his share, and he worried that the stock might prove worthless.

Despite Warrior's Mark bonanza ore quality (silver content ran as high as a staggering 6,000 ounces per ton, according to Summit Historical Society researcher, John Dougherty), the mine was plagued with mismanagement by local Breckenridge owners, and a barrage of lawsuits. In 1885, lessee James Fryer ran the mine $19,000 in debt, with $8,000 in unpaid wages, and attempted to skip town. Legal snits, initiated by a rankled Thompson and Parkison, a John M. Denison (he won $41,000), the German National Bank of Denver (winning $1,225) and others, drained Warrior's Mark Company assets and closed the mine several times.

But Warrior's Mark always resurfaced from these plunges into turmoil. Owners had money to build a sawmill in 1883, for mine lumber. Two shafts and a large open cut, 35 by 35 by 25 feet wide, produced ore that went to the Aetra concentrator and later the mine's own 5-stamp mill. By the end of 1883 the mine had produced $100,000 in precious metals.

In October, 1885, the *Rocky Mountain News* reported, "The Warrior's Mark has been running continuously . . . and reaping good returns." Despite constant threats to its survival, the Warrior's Mark operated until 1900 and then reopened in 1920 to produce a smashing $96,000 in silver.

The Snowdrift Mine bordered Indiana Creek, side by side with its neighbor the Warrior's Mark. Located in March, 1881, the Snowdrift produced 25 to 150 ounces of silver per ore ton.

Breckenridge residents A. S. Hall and J. L. Klinefelter owned the Snowdrift with Denver's G. J. Washburn. They drove six shafts from 60 to 165 feet and excavated two tunnels, 75 and 100 feet long. These investors also owned the adjoining Snowdrift Placer. Ore piled up as Snowdrift owners awaited the arrival of the railroad which pushed over Boreas Pass in 1882.

The tour continues to roadside ruins of the 7:40 Mine on Bald Mountain's south slope. Mine tram structures, visible at roadside and all the way up Baldy's flank to the mine opening, mark the site. Colorado pioneer W. H. Iliff owned the 7:40 in 1883 and built a large boarding house, shaft house and bunk house. A railway switch was located here. Despite Iliff's investment, the 7:40 yielded nearly nothing until 1893, when new discoveries spurted mining activity that lasted well into the twentieth century.

Nearby stood old Farnham, a bustling mine town with postal and railway stations. (See Chapter 12 for Farnham's history.) The Boreas Pass mining tour concludes here.

Ten Mile Mining:
Storied Silver Canyon

Tumbling Ten Mile Creek winds 17 miles through steep, glacier-carved Ten Mile Canyon, courses through Frisco and empties into modern Dillon Reservoir. The roiling creek once supplied mines in the silver-rich Ten Mile Consolidated Mining District with a wealth of water-power. Orvando J. Hollister, in his 1867 *Mines of Colorado*, commented: "The Ten Mile Creek has a heavy fall and sufficient volume to furnish unlimited power for mines. Ten Mile Mining District is very large, taking in all sections drained by the stream . . ."

Hollister was discussing Ten Mile Canyon lode mining potential. The early mine expert gloated over the canyon's sheer granite walls ("offering great advantages for mining by tunnels") and raved about its rich galena (silver) ores. "Galena is one of the most economical of silver ores, especially where the proportion of silver is so large . . ." Hollister rubbed his hands at the prospect of $50 to $100 per ton returns on Ten Mile Canyon ores.

The narrow, craggy canyon, its steep cliffs clefted by many gulches, stretches from Frisco all the way to Fremont Pass. Breckenridge miners scaled the soaring Ten Mile Range to drop into the canyon just below Fremont Pass and joined California Gulch miners to make the canyon's first mineral strikes in 1861 in stunningly-rich McNulty Gulch. They stumbled on an Eldorado there, plucking gold nuggets that weighed two ounces and more, gleaning $100 in gold from a single prospector's pan. McNulty placers produced the fulfillment of every miner's dream, the fabled "pound diggings" — one pound (troy weight) gold per day per man employed.

Miners also unearthed metallic silver nuggets at the Ten Mile Canyon's head, weighing anywhere from one ounce to a hefty one pound! But placer mining quickly gave up its "skin-deep" treasure, and the pick 'n pan prospectors scurried back over the hills to Breckenridge.

The Leadville silver lode boom that rocked all of Colorado in 1878 sent shock waves — and prospectors — into the tranquil Ten Mile Canyon. Suddenly, canyon walls reverberated with pick axe cacophony. Leadville merchant George Robinson grubstaked two prospectors, Charles Jones and John Sheddon, in autumn, 1877, instructing the miners to plumb the upper Ten Mile around old McNulty Gulch just over Fremont Pass from Leadville. In return for his supplies and provisions, the Jones and Sheddon team agreed to accord Robinson one-half their discoveries. The lucky pair struck it rich with a dazzling chain of ten mines by June, 1878 and launched a Ten Mile Canyon lode boom. The Robinson Group became the nucleus of the Ten Mile Consolidated Mining District. Robinson Mines total production would reach $7 million.

A history-buff's mining sojourn through the Ten Mile Canyon begins at Frisco.

Mining Around Frisco

The Mint Mining and Milling Company operated on Ophir Mountain one mile south of Frisco. James H. Myers, mining superintendent who had his hand in practically every Ten Mile and Montezuma venture around the turn of the century, reported in a 1903 prospectus that the 3,000-foot Ophir Tunnel, then under construction, would cut seven lode claims. A five-acre mill site was part of the Ophir property.

Above Frisco, on Mount Royal's eastern slope, sat the Masontown Mine camp. First called the Victoria, the Masontown Mine was located at 10,000 feet. The Victoria Group encompassed five claims, the Rosa, Golden Anne, Lebanon, Lebtoria and Victoria. The neighboring Eureka consisted of seven claims. Miners Creek provided water for a 20-stamp mill, equipped with a cyanide plant. The mill produced about 50 tons of ore daily in the early 1900's. A tunnel from the base of Mount Royal, begun around 1903, aimed to cut the Victoria Lode.

Heading west through Frisco toward the Ten Mile Canyon's mouth, you see Chief Mountain ahead and to the right. The old Buffalo Placer water flume ran across the face of 10,880-foot Chief enroute to the Buffalo Placers hydraulic operation at Salt Lick near today's Wildernest, above Silverthorne. Look for remains of the wooden flume.

At the west Frisco's I-70 interchange is the North Ten Mile Creek's mouth. About two miles in on this creek was the Square Deal Mine. Capitalized at $2 million, the Square Deal Company planned a 162-acre townsite near Frisco, three major tunnels to penetrate Chief Mountain and predicted "ore enough to last centuries". The mine, situated on the old J. D. Hynderliter Ranch, displayed much promotional activity, but little production. The Montezuma *Prospector* nicknamed it the "Crooked Deal Mine". One tunnel did burrow 2,090 feet into the mountainside by 1909, but centuries of riches never happened.

Mount Royal, guarding the entrance to the Canyon on your left, is a 10,250-foot anthill, riddled with glory holes.

Just inside the canyon, in a cleft on the right, one-tenth mile past Milepost 201, was the Excelsior Mine, which had its own power station up on North Ten Mile Creek. The power operated a large concentrating mill, processing ore from the Excelsior's tunnel and a later shaft. Mill structure remains are clearly visible

Hike the North Ten Mile Creek trail and view the lone cabin remaining from Square Deal mining and milling venture about three miles in. Upper Square Deal tunnel (right) penetrated Chief, once called "the mountain of lead". Square Deal promoted its corporate integrity, though some disputed their claim. "The boys" (below) outside development tunnel, socialized down in Frisco, where saloons abounded.

beside the old Excelsior dump here.

Frank Wiborg, a printing ink magnate, owned the Excelsior in the early 1900's when lower Ten Mile Canyon mines flourished. The Excelsior shipped three carloads of ore in 1906 that showed its mineral content — 20 ounces silver per ton, two and one-half ounces gold and 30 percent lead.

The well-heeled King Solomon Mining Syndicate tunneled the canyon wall about one-half mile south of Frisco's Milepost 201 sign, on the canyon's east side. Eastern capitalists owned the King Solomon Syndicate. Colonel Myers, longtime Syndicate leader, managed the group's extensive mining interests. Myers planned the tunnel to penetrate the mountain for 3,000 feet in length. How far it went is questionable. Excavators reached the 800-foot mark in spring, 1906, according to the Montezuma *Prospector*. They struck four "good, strong veins" along the way. Workers discovered a crevice full of "solid, pure metallic gold" there, along with stunning shot and wire gold nuggets. By 1909, according to the Breckenridge *Bulletin*'s July 31 Frisco edition, the King Solomon Tunnel had reached 3,000 feet and was still progressing by ten feet every 24 hours. Miners discovered "flour" gold along the way, created by sand and water abrasion on the ore. A Frisco promotional pamphlet, published in the 1950's, reported the King Solomon tunnel had driven 11,500 feet into the Mount Royal flank, with side cuts every 1,100 feet.

The King Solomon shipped its gold-silver-copper ores as late as 1910. The Colonel's son, James H. ("Dimp") Myers, Jr., served as mine Superintendent.

By 1904, the Syndicate owned every known east-wall Ten Mile vein from Frisco to the Wonderland properties several miles south.

Big tailings dump and ruined mill now mark Excelsior. Mine office became Frisco home.

Proceed south on Interstate 70, or for a better view, ski, hike or bike the bicycle path, depending on the season. One and one-half miles beyond Frisco, or one-half mile past the Milepost 200 marker, a gray and brown tailings dump to the left signals the site of the Mary Verna and nearby Kitty Innes Mines. The Mary Verna had a 1,621-foot tunnel in 1909 and, below this tunnel, a large power house built along the railroad track.

You will pass beaver ponds on the left as you continue into the Canyon.

Curtin, an old railroad ore shipping station about two miles south of Frisco, near Milepost 199, served area mines with its big steam-powered compressor, located between the rail track (bike path) and the creek. Huge chutes here handled coal for the compressor, which produced compressed air for mine machinery. Brick and mortar ruins of the compressor remain along the bike path. Scattered bricks, boards with old-time square nails and building sites mark the Curtin townsite just above the bike path.

Two-tenths mile beyond Curtin, steel-gray tailings indicate the North American Mine. Tailings came from its impressive tunnel, 2,557 feet long in 1909.

Across the highway from the Curtin area, on the canyon's west side, miners worked the Cloudy Pool and Shady Placers. Further into the canyon, still on the west side, near beautiful Uneva Lake, were the Uneva Placers and Lucky Boy Placer.

Zigzagging back to the east side, the Admiral Mining Company and, further along, the Wonderland Mining Company operated their lode mines. "The Admiral Tunnel will push another 1,000 feet into the Ten Mile Range this summer," a 1906 Montezuma *Prospector* predicted.

At Officers Gulch, but across from the gulch's mouth, on the east wall, stood a wooden tower with an ore trolley that served mines high in the gulch. A lone cabin remained there for years, a last relic of the Monroe Mine. Owned in 1897 by Warren and Belford, the Monroe ore was heavily iron sulfide, with gold and a small percentage of copper.

Wheeler Junction

Continue to Copper Mountain, where a resort village now occupies land at Wheeler Flats, a former homestead and 160-acre patented placer claim. Copper Mountain takes its name from an old low-yield copper mine situated on the mountain. Nearby Graveline Gulch once bustled with the area's main mining activity. The Reconstruction, with six claims, and Storm King here, produced lead, silver and zinc. Graveline Gulch mines also included the Mona Group (two claims), Osage Group (11 claims), Summit Group (19 claims) and Hard Luck Group (43 claims).

The Wheeler area, site of Judge John Wheeler's frisky 1880's town, and the stretch of canyon south of Wheeler, sprouted a rash of sawmills, which supplied local mines with lumber, and later, cut ties for the two railroads that penetrated the Ten Mile Canyon. (See Chapter 12 for Wheeler's history.)

Mining Around Kokomo-Robinson

The sizzling hotbed of Ten Mile mining excitement lies ahead. Here, history-making mineral veins awaited the eager miner's pick axe and blasting powder. Silver-seamed Jacque, Sheep and North Sheep, Elk, Fletcher and Bartlett Mountains flaunted their mineral stores with frequent outcroppings of surface ore to lure early prospectors. Sheep Mountain alone boasted 50 mines in the lode boom's first year, 1879. By 1881, Jacque Mountain had 200 mines. Upper Ten Mile mine output already reached $2 million in 1881. But world-renowned molybdenum ores on Bartlett Mountain remained unrecognized, except by a lone prospector named Charles Senter.

Upper Ten Mile ores drove mining experts into a state of ecstasy. Blow-outs, those veins exposed by erosion and visible to the naked eye, were the teasers. The real thing was even better. "Some of the veins yield true silver ores, among them the ruby and the gray," wrote Hollister. "They are generally strong and well-marked, often cropping out above the surface for a long distance or lining the bold faces of the mountains." Ten Mile miners soon discovered a happy rule of canyon mining: The deeper you dig, the richer the silver ore becomes.

Hollister detailed one of these surface veins:

> The Justice Lode, discovered in 1861 and rediscovered every year since, on the mountain between Gilpin and McNulty gulches, is one of these. It crops out on the southern exposure and well up on the hill for six hundred

Kokomo's historic Kimberly Mill, though burned in 1891, served mines past 1930's.

feet in length and seemingly one hundred and fifty in width. It is supposed to be what is called a "blow-out", which laps over the walls, and the lower edge having been worn down by the elements, that wall, against which some slight excavations have been made, was easy found. The ore is not rich on the surface, but grows better very fast as it comes from a greater depth. It is "claimed" four or five deep, and recorded as high as No. 100 — two miles! — each way.

Geologists believed that the same stunningly-rich silver belt that surfaced in the rich Snake River mining district outcropped again in the upper Ten Mile Canyon. Assayed values reached a record $27,000 per ton, but averaged a very profitable $100 per ton.

On Jacque Peak, southwest of Copper Mountain, lay a myriad of rich mines: The Queen of the West, Rising Sun, Recen (discovered by the Recen brothers, Henry and Daniel, who came to the canyon before the boom in the early 1870's built Frisco's first cabin and became early Kokomo residents), Selma Wintergreen, Silver Queen and Bledsoe. The Aborigine Mine, later called the Sherman, became the object of a shotgun-punctuated squabble. A local newspaper headlined its story on the ownership fight: "Shotgun Policy Indulged In, But Nobody Hurt".

Crofutt's 1885 *Grip Sack Guide to Colorado* described the rich veins on Elk Mountain: "The lode mines in the vicinity are principally fissure, yielding richer returns every foot you go down. The principal are: White Quail, Aftermath and Climax on Elk Mountain to the westward; they are carbonate ores and run from $80 to $400 per ton." The Breene, Colonel Sellars, Silver Chain and Uthoff also worked Elk Mountain veins. (The Uthoff resurged during World War I when its Michigan-Snowbank-Uthoff Tunnel Group produced more ores than any other Ten Mile mine.) Peter Breene, an 1885 Colorado Lieutenant Governor, squeezed several millions from his Delaware-Breene group here by 1907.

Follow your map closely as the new re-routed modern highway passes through the Kokomo area. Roads owned by the Climax Molybdenum Company were, in 1979, open for summer use. They can take you to the Kokomo site, marked today by the remaining circa-1950 red-brick schoolhouse. Climax is preparing the Kokomo site to receive molybdenum tailings.

Kokomo, another 1880's mining hub, clung to Sheep Mountain's eastern slope. The town reaped mining history from A. R. Wilfley's invention of the Wilfley table at Kokomo's Kimberly-Wilfley Mill in 1895. A big processing breakthrough, the Wilfley shaker table vibrated to retrieve more precious mineral in a shorter time than the mining industry had dreamed possible. Relics of the proud mill remain near the mouth of Searles Gulch today.

Kokomo had two smelters, the White Quail and the Greer, its big Kimberly-Wilfley Mill and, by 1881, rail service from the Denver & Rio Grande.

Biggest drawback to Ten Mile Canyon lode mining profitability had been lack of transportation. A rough, rutted wagon road provided the sole access to ore markets at Leadville. But the Denver & Rio Grande's arrival from Leadville in 1881 solved all these problems and allowed the Ten Mile Consolidated Mining District to become Summit's leading early '80's silver producer.

Above lofty Kokomo (10,618 feet) rises even loftier (12,648-foot) Sheep Mountain, with its cornucopia of rich mines. The Crown Point, Ruby and Silver Mines returned an amazing $1,500 per ton. Other mines included the Washington, International, Eldorado, Felicia Grace, New York, Black Dragon, Invicible, Big Horn, Baby, Little Fortune, Hidden Treasure, Gray Eagle, Tiptop (with assays of 300 to 700 ounces silver per ton), Idalie (owned by pioneer Robert Emmet in 1879 and delivering 311 ounces silver per ton), Ballarat, Annie Lisle and Silver Tip.

The Wheel of Fortune at Sheep Mountain's summit, discovered in summer, 1878 by Jacob Hecht, opened an immense body of rich ore.

On Gold Hill, southeast of Kokomo, rich lead, galena and carbonate ores came from the Little Carbonate, Wooster and Pauline Mines.

Robinson, founded by Leadville's George Robinson, spread out on a grassy meadow below Sheep Mountain and south of Kokomo. Crofutt rates Robinson's ore processing plant as "the largest smelting and milling works in the mountains". (The town once rivaled early Leadville in prominence.) After buying out prospectors Sheddon and Jones, George Robinson had knocked on New York investment bankers' doors to capitalize his powerful Robinson Consolidated Mining Company. The Robinson Mines produced a magic $7 million in five short years. The mines, located on Sheep Mountain, were the Seventy-Eight, G. B. Robinson, Smuggler, Undine, Grand Union, Pirate, Little Giant, Big Giant, Checkmate, Rhone and Ten Mil.

Robinson veins ran rich, as historian Frank Fosset reported in 1879:

> The Seventy-Eight, Undine and Smuggler all show the same large, high-grade body of mineral — there being one great incline vein, pitching thirty degrees below and nearly parallel with the surface of the mountainside. The thickness of this vein is from two to eight feet, and most of it is composed of ore from $100 to $250 a ton . . . last winter and spring, ore was transported over terrible roads, ten miles on runners and seven in wagons, to Leadville.

Richest ores laced Ten Mile Canyon mountains on the valley's west side. But the east side had its memorable mines. On Fletcher Mountain, across from Kokomo-Robinson, the Whitney and Whiting Company engaged in a most ambitious project. Company men, under the direction of A. A. Sawyer, Esq., were driving a tunnel under Fletcher's rocky ribs, intending to strike the Capitol Lode at 1,200 feet from the tunnel entrance, and 1,000 feet from the surface. This was in the mid-1860's when only the crudest implements existed. Gold and silver

142

frenzy inspired mining men to tackle almost anything. Working round the clock, teams laboring with primitive tools progressed two feet every 24 hours. "On January 1, (1867) this tunnel had reached a depth of 160 feet and was to be driven all winter and forever by eight hour shifts," reported mining observer Hollister.

The gulches on the canyon's east side, especially Clinton, Gilpin and McNulty, sprouted lode mines like June wildflowers. Clinton Gulch, south of Fletcher Mountain and its neighbor, Gilpin Gulch, averaged $100 per ton on argentiferous galena ores. Best known silver lodes in these rich gulches were the Ino, Incas, Atlas, Oro Fino, Augustine, Boulder, Olympic No. 2, Blackstone, Balahoo, Uno, Curious, Colorado, Esmeralda, Merrimac, Keyes, Hard Cash, Tribune, Polygon, St. Regis and more. The Merrimac and Polygon stand out because each had an 80-foot shaft in a district where most miners dug tunnels.

And beautiful Mayflower Gulch, also on the canyon's east side, boasted the rich Boston Mines Group. The *Blue Valley Times* in 1912 heralded a big strike there as "one of the largest strikes ever made in the Ten Mile Mining District. Rich as early Leadville ores." The little mine camp surrounding the Boston Mine and mill remains today. High on the headwall that rims the Mayflower Gulch cirque hangs the Gold Crest Mine, which operated as late as the 1930's.

McNulty Gulch, Ten Mile bonanza discovery site, had relinquished $3 million from its golden stores during 1860-62. The gulch frequently produced gold worth $10,000 to $20,000 from a 25-foot square placer pit in the early 1860's. Colonel James McNassar worked the gulch in 1878, long after the placer miners left, and earned $4,000 to $7,000 per summer.

When free gold ran out, the early prospectors scrambled back over the range to Breckenridge or Leadville. Only the diehard Brandon Brothers remained to mine McNulty Gulch. Early lode miners, arriving in 1878, found the Brandon cabin the area's sole evidence of human habitation.

Lode miners burrowed their way to success in McNulty Gulch, unearthing successful lode finds like the Brook Silver Mine at the head of the gulch. Then in 1898, the placer miners returned to McNulty for another go. A June 25, 1898 Summit County *Journal* article boasted: "The Marguerite Mining Company which owns the McNulty Placers above Robinson is working twelve men . . . washing gravel. These are the richest claims in the West." A nugget reportedly weighing in at two and one-half pounds came from the McNulty Placers.

Traveling south toward Fremont Pass, you view big Bartlett Mountain on your left, site of Climax, the world's largest molybdenum mine. Charles J. Senter discovered this "gray gold" in 1879 and staked Bartlett Mountain mineral claims. The main problem was that nobody knew what Senter had. Although experts everywhere studied the mysterious gray-streaked ore, no one could identify it. Finally, the Colorado School of Mines properly pronounced it molybdenum, 21 long years after discovery.

Senter spent decades pleading with mining authorities to recognize his find. Finally, in 1913, the Pingrey Mines and Ore Reduction Company purchased options on Bartlett Mountain molybdenum claims. Soon, Germany's Gelleschaft Corporation bought in.

World War I demonstrated the wisdom of these early "moly" investors. As a steel alloy, incredibly tough moly became crucial to defense. "Big Bertha", the rail-mounted German gun which could shell Paris from the German border, was a molybdenum steel gun.

In 1916, American Metals Company executive Max Schott, based in Denver, began to crusade for American development of Climax molybdenum. The Climax Molybdenum Company soon emerged from his effort.

During World War II, allied interests "liberated" remaining moly claims from Gelleschaft and Hitler's Germany.

The 22-million year old moly deposit, displaced eons ago by the Mosquito Fault, contains a lot of molybdenum. Geologists estimate the supply, another 495 million tons, will last 40 more years of intensive mining (47,000 tons daily at present).

A crucial 1918 decision realigned the county boundary, placing the Climax Mine mostly in the legal confines (and tax-revenue district) of Lake County.

The Climax Mine purchased and razed Robinson and Kokomo townsites for use as tailing ponds. Kokomo became extinct as recently as 1971.

Despite fits and starts during the years since 1893's crushing silver devaluation, Ten Mile mines continued to produce. Rising metal prices stimulated mining from 1903 to 1907, but decreased in 1908. Sporadic bursts of activity followed during World War I. By 1923, when the Uthoff group shut down, it looked like Ten Mile mining days had ceased.

But the area bounced back. The Uthoff Tunnel was reconstructed in 1935. That same year, a prospector made a big strike at Kokomo, hitting a six-foot wide vein. And Henry Recen discovered the vein crossed his St. Louis claim nearby. The Kimberly-Wilfley Mill chugged busily through the summer of 1935.

World War II stepped up base metal demand. The Lucky Strike, Wilfley and Kimberly re-opened in 1942-43 and the Lucky Strike produced until 1950. A big zinc discovery at the Wilfley in late 1948 made Denver *Post* headlines.

No overall mining output figures exist to document the rich Ten Mile Consolidated Mining District's total production, but historians estimate the area's dollar yield as a whopping $20 million. (Today's value: $140 million!)

Montezuma Mining:

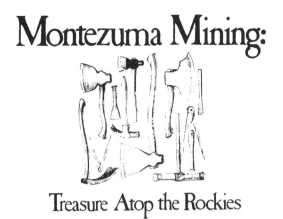

Treasure Atop the Rockies

Nowhere did cloud-scraping altitudes, severe weather, transportation difficulties and the vagaries of silver's value challenge mining more than in the steep canyons and stark mountaintops of the Montezuma mining area.

At Montezuma, most lode veins occurred at 11,000 to 13,000 feet altitude. There, more than half the district lies above 11,700-foot timberline. The glaciers ruthlessly carved Montezuma's topography. Geologist Thomas H. Lovering described it in 1935: "Most of the valleys have been severely glaciated in recent geologic time and are broad and U-shaped. Steep walled cirques are common at altitudes above 11,500 feet . . ." Gray's Peak soars to 14,274 feet here and other mountains towering along the Continental Divide rival it. Lovering spoke of the "rugged, broken character" of the area's mountains.

Snow falls early, late and heavy on this Snake River district. Snow depth closed the area in winter. Miners stockpiled supplies in autumn and traveled to their silver-seamed burrows on snowshoes (skis) once winter came. Colorado mine historian Frank Fosset wrote in 1879: "Securely housed in warm and comfortable quarters, the miners continue to tunnel, drift and blast, regardless of storms without." Avalanches rolled down steep mountainsides, destroying mine buildings, especially around old Decatur, until miners learned to construct snowslide-proof headquarters.

Georgetown's *Colorado Miner* on October 19, 1878, described the design:

> A space is excavated at the mouth of the tunnel, a house is built in the space, and the roof is built to correspond with the slope of the mountain, and as the snow comes down, it glides over the roof and lands in the valley below, leaving the miners safe in their cozy house.

Miners struck silver in the Montezuma area in the 1860's, but transportation of ores from the isolated mountain-ribbed valleys proved a stout challenge. Good wagon roads, over Argentine Pass to Georgetown in the '60's, and later Webster Pass to South Park in 1878 and Loveland Pass in 1879, eased the problem. But moving ore to mills and smelters continued to cut into the Montezuma mining profit picture. When the railroad puffed into Keystone in 1883, a "Hurrah!" rang against Montezuma canyon walls. But miners high in the Peru Creek Valley or the craggy mountains beyond Montezuma still faced a long and costly haul, via pack train to today's Ski Tip Ranch, then via wagon, to reach the Keystone rail head.

The 1893 Silver Panic hit hard at Montezuma area silver mines. When silver's value plummeted, many miners shut down and communities nearby withered. But silver's prices fluctuated. By 1899, a local newspaper had noted a resurge. On August 19, 1899, the newspaper commented: "After about six years of inactivity, this old camp is attracting much attention from investors outside Summit County. Before the Panic of 1893, Montezuma was one of the largest producers of silver in the country. While silver properties are receiving a lot of attention, those carrying zinc are equally sought."

Snake River District silver ores contained a large percentage of lead and zinc. During the early years, this lead-zinc content presented problems to primitive mills. When advanced ore processing equipment came on the scene, after the turn of the century, Snake River mines blossomed anew. "In the 1860's and 70's," a Montezuma mining broker said in the early 1900's, "miners sought only gold and silver. Only the richest mines could bear freight costs." But new mine machinery, improved ore reduction techniques, electric power and improved transportation re-opened Montezuma area mines. Even old tailings dumps yielded rich mineral wealth.

John Coley had launched Snake River mining in 1863 when he discovered Colorado's first silver lode at Sts. John. The Little Annie nearby (also called the Harrisburg) added to mining excitement as the first lode discovered after Coley's strike. Early miners W. P. Pollack, John Christian and their companion, Pratt, probably stood gaping at the Little Annie's outcrop on Glacier mountain's surface. The ore streaked across ground level for five to six hundred feet!

The Montezuma Canyon

For a Montezuma district mining tour, drive east on U. S. Highway 6 from Dillon toward Keystone and Loveland Pass. Until the tour reaches Montezuma, most of the mines are located at such imposing altitudes that seeing them requires a side trip by jeep or by foot.

As you pass Keystone, you will see the Keystone ski mountain at your right. On Keystone Mountain's southwest slope, at 12,000 feet altitude, is the Erickson Mine, reached by a jeep road up Keystone Gulch. Discovered by J. B. Erickson in July, 1880, the mine has a 250-foot shaft at Keystone Mountain's crest and three major adits, one of them 250 feet, penetrating the peak. The Erickson Mine produced in the mid-1880's, and delivered ore as recently as the 1930's. Mine buildings now cling precariously to their stark slope sagging, but hanging on. From the summit, you can look into Jones Gulch and see the Ida Belle, hugging a sheer mountainside.

Just past Keystone, turn right onto Colorado 294, the Montezuma Road. Keep left where the road forks, leading back to the ski area. Independence Mountain will loom to your right, on the south side. There on Independence Mountain's western slope, is the Copenhagen Mine, reached through Jones Gulch. Discovered at 11,500 feet by Hans Brandt in 1886, the Copenhagen was a small silver producer. The Ida Belle Mine, just 800 feet north of the Copenhagen at 11,450 feet in Jones Gulch, shipped silver steadily throughout the 1880's. The Ida Belle was discovered in 1880 and opened with three adits by 1883. During World War II, the Ida Belle aided national defense by re-opening to produce lead, copper and zinc.

On Independence Mountain's east slope are the Hunkidori and Don Pedro Mines. They are high up in Grizzly Gulch, a glacial basin which opens onto the Montezuma Road before the Peru Creek turnoff. The Don Pedro, discovered in 1874 by longtime Montezuma resident Oliver Milner and his friend Joseph McKenney, produced from 1880-87 and had four adits.

Bullion King, its aerial ore tram shown here in 1907, delivered a stunning 4,500 ounces silver that year. Tyler boys discovered this Collier Mt. mine, one mile past Montezuma, in 1870.

The nearby Hunkidori Mine, at 11,200 feet, dazzled miners with its 32-inch wide vein of silver that averaged a rich 157 ounces to the ton, with 40 percent lead, according to an 1883 Colorado Mining Directory. Prospectors Penry, Dougherty, Murphy and Keogh discovered the Hunkidori in July, 1880. (The Hunkidori Mine can be reached on cross-country skis or by hiking via the Sts. John road from Montezuma and then the road crossing the meadow past the Marlin Mine. The mine is a little over three miles from Montezuma.)

East of Ski Tip Ranch at your left on Lenawee Mountain are the ruins of the once-proud Lenawee Mill. Colonel James H. Myers, Summit County mining mogul, headed the Lenawee Reduction and Tunnel Company along with many other local mining ventures. Myers' mine tunnel produced zinc, lead and silver.

The big Lenawee Mill, located at the mouth of the Lenawee Tunnel near the confluence of Peru Creek and the Snake River, measured 85½ feet long, by 64 feet wide, by 40 feet high. John O'Neill served as mill superintendent. The Lenawee Mill held great promise for Montezuma area mines as a nearby ore processing plant. On July 7, 1906, the Montezuma *Prospector* reported on the mill nearing completion: "The Lenawee Mill, at the mouth of the Lenawee Tunnel, was planned to take advantage of rail extension from Keystone. Rockford, Illinois, investors plus $25,000 from treasury stock provided the capital needed to finance tunnel excavation."

Although the railroad never arrived here, the big Lenawee Mill processed a capacity 100-125 ore tons every 24 hours. The mill began with 20 stamps (planning to install 20 more later) crusher, roller, sizing screens, a roller mill for regrinding and an electric zinc separator. The modern structure also boasted electric lights. The mill ruins today stand on private property.

Up ahead, near where the Montezuma Road meets the Peru Creek turnoff, lies the Fisherman Mine at 10,040 feet. A high bridge once dominated the road scene near the Fisherman. Today you can identify the site because the road is bastioned by fill there. The Fisherman, discovered in the late '80's, produced little recorded ore until 1905, when the mine began shipping.

You have passed the Peru turnoff, and Tip Top Peak now rises at your left (east) as you proceed toward Montezuma. On Tip Top's southwest spur at 11,400 feet, lies old Bob Epsey's Lancaster Mine. Epsey, a local party-lover, once made a fabulous silver strike while reeling in recovery from a legendary drunk in Montezuma.

The Morgan Mine, on Tip Top's south slope, produced sporadically from the '80's until almost 1920. Just one-half mile east of Montezuma, the 11,000-foot high Morgan generated 401 ounces of silver in 1917.

Continue on toward Montezuma. One-fourth mile north of the old 1860's town lies the Toledo. Located on the old Montezuma to Chihuahua road (which takes off from Montezuma), the Toledo Tunnel had its portal at roadside at 10,300 feet. A large mill rose across the road, but was dismantled in later years. The tramway, also dismantled, was moved by wagon and rail to a Boreas Pass site. According to the July 18, 1908 Breckenridge *Bulletin*, the Toledo Mine tunnel worked 24-hour shifts on the ambitious 3,150-foot excavation, to cut the Tip Top

Mine on Collier Mountain over 1,500 feet deep. Today, the tunnel stands deep in water and the portal bears a sign reading "Danger, No Entry". You can see the Toledo's extensive dump at the Montezuma Road's left side before you enter the town. A short trip on the old road leads you to the site.

Old Montezuma truly qualified for the term "mine camp" — mines crowded the town's limits. Drive through Montezuma and look for signs of old tunnels — they abound. The Waterloo on Collier Mountain's west slope had its dump on the hamlet's southeast city line. Nearby the Waterloo on Collier, just outside Montezuma, stood the Old Settler Mine, discovered by Joseph Duffield in 1865. This mine, working the same vein as the Waterloo, produced intermittently in the '80's and '90's, and had a 260-foot tunnel, according to an 1870 mining report. The Old Settler's two foot-ore streak assayed at 20 to 100 ounces of silver per ton.

A road to the left leads uphill to the New York Mine. The rich New York Mine, just outside Montezuma, past the town's southeast edge, had a tunnel opening at 10,350 feet. You can easily explore around this mine. Geologist T. H. Lovering said in his 1935 Montezuma mining report: "The ore in the New York vein is the largest and most continuous body of ore which the writer has seen in the Montezuma quartz monzonite." Because the New York Mine's ore ran high in zinc and iron, it required a flotation mill for processing. Unfortunately, the area offered no such convenience for the New York and other mines high in zinc-iron.

The Aladdin's Lamp, its exotic name supplied by 1882 discoverer, Oliver Milner, was the New York's neighbor on Collier Mountain.

Famous mines sprouted like dandelions in Montezuma's rich back yard. The dazzling Sarsefield, high on Collier Mountain at 12,270 feet, boasted a recordbreaking silver vein. The single vertical ore shoot, three feet wide, cropped out on a shoulder of Collier Mountain to entice miners. "The richest part of this shoot was nearly pure galena ore three feet wide," wrote Lovering. Originally located in the 1870's as the Waterman, the mine took the Sarsefield name in 1881. After owners Cunningham and Taylor drove the mine's second adit in 1885, Sarsefield production took off: The mine yielded 16,121 ounces of silver in 1899.

The Atlantic, neighboring the Sarsefield at 12,000-12,500 feet, probably worked the same stunning silver vein. Located in 1873, the Atlantic produced for about 10 years. The Buena Vista, just 1,000 feet northwest of the Sarsefield at 12,000 feet produced in the late 1880's.

A steep jeep road leads from Montezuma up Collier Mountain to these mines. The Quail, on the old wagon road at 12,000 feet altitude, perches on a steep slope near the head of Morgan Gulch's south fork. Phillip Bianchi, longtime Snake River Valley resident (his grave rests in the Montezuma cemetery) discovered the Quail in the 1890's. Miners worked in two adits here.

At the head of Morgan Gulch at 12,500 feet was Isaac Ware's Washington Mine. Discovered in 1873, the Washington produced silver and copper intermittently during the 1870's and '80's. Ores assayed at a lucrative 100 to 200 ounces silver per ton and 20 percent copper.

149

Proceed south from Montezuma. On Collier Mountain near Montezuma was the Bolivar Tunnel, a much publicized venture in its day. A July 18, 1908, Breckenridge *Bulletin* reported two daily shifts hacking away at the Bolivar excavation.

On the right (west) side of the road about one-half mile south of Montezuma stood the Bolivar Mill. Just 200 yards away, the proud Silver King Mine on Glacier Mountain's east slope, produced ores from 1866 late into the 1920's, a half-century of achievement. Montezuma's J. T. Lynch discovered the old Sukey in 1866. He organized a silver mining company and built the Sukey Mill, working the property until 1869 when he lost the vein. An 1870 report listed the Sukey with two adits, 96 and 330 feet, and a 40-foot discovery shaft. Its vein ran a generous four to six feet wide.

In 1880, the property became the Silver King, owned by the Silver King Mining Company. The company also owned a five-stamp mill, roasting furnace and two amalgamating pans to treat Silver King ores, which averaged 50 to 100 ounces silver per ton and 55 percent lead. By 1882, the mine had a 10-stamp mill and processed Radical and Chautauqua ores along with its own. Historic Silver King claims merged with the neighboring Burke-Martin Mines in recent years.

Just a few hundred feet northwest of the old Silver King tram was an 1880's producer, the Cable Mine, located in 1881. Also in the area, on Glacier's northeast face, were the Jerry, Equity, Denver and Celtic Mines.

Burke-Martin Mines, with its buildings clearly visible on the right from the Montezuma Road, belonged to Montezuma old-timer John Burke. According to "Opinions", an early 1900's mining newsletter, Burke was then driving a "large tunnel" into Glacier Mountain. "The bore will open a half-dozen or more of the largest producing lodes in the district, at 1,000 feet below their present workings."

The Burke-Martin Mine rated front-page Denver *Post* headlines as late as 1956, when mine superintendent Tom Martin announced a smash silver strike, with ores valued at $2,000 per ton.

A little farther down the road, about one mile southeast of Montezuma, the Bullion Mine (also called the Bullion King) perched on Collier's west slope, at 11,800 feet, just about 1,500 feet above the Snake River basin. An electric aerial tramway, built in 1902, transported ores from the rich Bullion Mine to waiting ore wagons on the road below, but the tram was partially dismantled, with cables gone, by 1947.

The Bullion, discovered by the Tyler Brothers around 1870, merged with the Yellow Jacket lode. During the 1880's and '90's, a second owner, Colonel Williams, invested heavily in developing the mine. But production surged later with a third owner: 1907 Bullion yield totaled 200 tons of ore, with a smashing 4,500 ounces of silver and 141,176 ounces of lead, plus some gold. A final owner, the Golden Cycle Company, held the Bullion property into the 1930's.

The Clarion Mine, between the Bullion and the Silver Wave, at 12,200 feet, featured both silver and gold ores. A ton of Clarion ore yielded 40 to 100 ounces of silver and 30 ounces of gold. Located by William Howell in 1880, the mine operated until at least 1917.

Also nearby was the Hannibal Mine, along a steep trail that led past the Bullion to the Hannibal site at around 11,000 feet. The Hannibal was discovered in 1880.

Snake River To Webster Pass

The road forks, with a left hand branch following the tumbling Snake River and a right hand branch bordering Deer Creek.

Following the Snake River branch, one passes beneath towering 13,180-foot Santa Fe Peak on the left, or east side. Sullivan Mountain lies just beyond. Between the two mountains is the Lucky Baldwin Mine at 12,000 feet, and its impressive neighbor, the Silver Wave.

The Silver Wave Mine, located in a small gulch two miles southeast of Montezuma at 12,567 feet, yielded stores of rich silver from its 1882 discovery well into the 1900's. On November 18, 1885, the *Rocky Mountain News* said, " . . . the ore body in the Silver Wave is simply immense, being about three feet wide . . . ore to grass roots." The mine's No. 2 adit gave up ores that assayed at a creditable 160 ounces silver per ton. The Silver wave operated with six adits and a long aerial tramway that ran from the lowest adit, at 12,657 feet, some 1,650 feet to the wagon road in the Snake River Valley below.

Various owners worked the Silver Wave. The mine probably stood idle most of the years from 1890 until 1905, when the Silver Wave Mining Company took over. The Silver Princess Mining Company purchased the mine in 1909. In 1912, the mine shipped 8,714 ounces of silver.

The Blanche Mine, on Collier Mountain's southwest slope near the Silver Wave, worked the mountain's rich silver reserves from 11,000 to 12,250 feet. Located in 1874, the Blanche produced until 1890 with two adits and an 85-foot shaft. Blanche ores were low grade: 35 ounces silver per ton and 35 percent lead.

The road continues south, finally leading to an intersection with the Webster Pass Road, an historic route used by Snake River District miners since 1878 to haul ore out and vital supplies in to their isolated mining mecca.

Between the Silver Wave Mine area and the Webster Pass Road junction, Teller Mountain rises magnificently on the right, west of the road, its shoulders seamed with precious mineral ore. On Teller's northeast slope is the Mohawk Mine, discovered in 1880 by John Sondregger, a lively and persistent old miner who was still hacking away at the Mohawk ore body in 1928.

On Teller Mountain's north slope, the Iowa Mine, also discovered in 1880, produced small shipments between 1883 and 1885.

Pass the Webster Pass Road intersection and the road continues westerly toward the historic Cashier Mine high on Teller Mountain's southeast slope. The mine had four adits perched between 12,000 and 12,450 feet. The main vein cuts Teller's lofty crest. Silver miners snapped to attention when tales of the rich Cashier and neighboring Champion were told. "The Cashier is probably one of the best-paying mines in the county, if not the state," glowed the Montezuma *Millrun* in its debut edition, June 24, 1882. Rich ores from the Cashier and Champion, two mines that shared three parallel silver veins, assayed at 200

Cashier Mine, at lofty 12,450 feet, had three smashing silver veins that made it one of Summit's best-paying mines. At Teller Mt.'s crest, Cashier averaged $250 per ton.

ounces silver per ton. Frank Fosset, writing in the late 1870's, said the Cashier and Champion "have been producing from $15,000 to $30,000 per annum — the ore averaging $250 a ton". (That's $105,000 to $210,000 in today's equivalent dollars.)

Dickson Southworth discovered the Cashier in the early 1870's and worked its rich veins until 1880. The Cashier and Champion Mining Company, organized in 1883, developed the property for a decade under G. K. Sabin, mine superintendent. The company completed more than 2,000 feet in tunnels for access to the 20-inch wide veins. In 1889, the mines produced a staggering 1,599 ounces of precious silver.

After 1892, the mines probably stopped producing, because no mining records exist after that date. In 1977, the grandson of a Cashier mine worker began to seek his fortune on the west side of Teller Mountain, sinking a 150-foot shaft for the Vega Mine.

To continue the Montezuma area mining tour, return to the junction of the Snake River Road (which you have been travelling on) and the Deer Creek Road. Take the Deer Creek Road southwest to an area rich with mines.

Deer Creek

The first is the Bell Mine at 11,600 feet on Glacier Mountain's east slope. (This mine has a lower tunnel portal on the old Bolivar Mill road which takes off just south of Montezuma and can be reached via that route.) William Bell's 1866 discovery on the California property consolidated here with the Sunburst, Meteor and Silver Wing claims to form the strong, well-developed Bell Mine, a significant silver producer.

The Bell had six adits with 3,000 feet of drifts and crosscuts. By 1882, the Bell had shipped 1,000 tons of ore containing 25,000 ounces of silver and 900,000 pounds of lead. The mine operated for decades. As late as 1926, the Bell yielded 12,640 ounces of silver and 439,957 pounds of lead.

Proceeding farther along the Deer Creek Road, you may see evidence of the Chautauqua Mine's lower workings about 400 feet above the road. The Chautauqua, with its main workings at 11,000 feet on Glacier Mountain's southeast shoulder, was discovered in 1866 by M. M. Teller and Giol Ball. By 1870, these pioneering silver miners had hacked out 100 tons of silver ore with a whopping 363 ounces silver to the ton!

The Montezuma Silver Mining Company acquired the Chautauqua in 1879. The company, which owned a sawmill and ore concentrating mill, developed the mine, maintaining the Chautauqua's heavy production until 1892. Frank Fosset detailed development in 1879: "Two tunnels are being driven, with machine drills and air compressor, towards the Chautauqua lode." One of the new tunnels measured 550 feet and the other 1,000 feet. The Chautauqua discovery shaft burrowed 200 feet into tough, rocky Glacier Mountain.

On the other side of the Deer Creek Road, the southeast side, the fabulous Star of the West Mine clings to Teller Mountain at 11,800 feet. Its ores were latticed with valuable minerals, including free gold! Frank Fosset asserted that Star of the West silver amounted to "over $200 per ton and generally more gold than silver. Copper, iron and lead are also ingredients of the ore".

Everyone talked about the Star of the West.

When the Montezuma *Millrun* hit the streets with its premier issue, it said: "The Star of the West, owned by J. Harvat of Georgetown, is very prominent for its richness; assays as high as 22,000 ounces in silver and 70 ounces of gold per ton have been obtained . . ."

The Star of the West, discovered in 1874, sat just 1,200 feet north of another famous mine, the Radical, according to Fosset. Star of the West No. 2, discovered in 1880 by Montezuma's peripatetic mailman-miner, Oliver Milner, lay one-fourth mile west. No. 2, working two adits, had ore assayed at 75 to 125 ounces silver per ton and 40 percent lead.

The Radical Mines were located on Radical Hill, a western spur on Teller Mountain. The Montezuma Silver Mining Company, organized around 1878, included the Radical and Radical Junior in its hefty portfolio of mine properties. Radical ores, averaging 60 ounces silver per ton and 60 percent lead, were "dressed at the company's concentrating mill".

"General Craig is general manager and George Teal superintendent," wrote Frank Fosset in 1879. "The property is being opened as rapidly as possible and bids fair to be very productive."

Saints John Basin

Return to Montezuma's southern edge and take the marked Sts. John jeep road/hiking route/cross-country ski trail up Glacier Mountain to continue the mining tour.

The road forks one-half mile west of Montezuma. The left fork leads to the Mark Twain and St. Elmo Mines at 11,400 feet.

The 550-foot St. Elmo tunnel penetrates the northeast slope of Glacier Mountain and a 225-foot shaft plumbs its depths. Producing till 1892, the mine stood idle from then until 1918, when the St. Elmo Mining Company shored up the tunnel and resumed operations.

An 1883 mining report cited by geologist T. H. Lovering in his 1935 Montezuma mining study bemoaned the area's transportation problems. The Mark Twain, the report stated, stood ready to employ a 150-man work force, but shipping difficulties necessitated using only a 14-man team. The rich Mark Twain, with a 140 ounce per ton silver assay, had a 205-foot shaft to its eight-inch pay streak. Production ceased here in 1890.

In a sweet meadow about one mile up the Sts. John Road lie the ruins of the Marlin Mine (also called the Roberta)

Proceed uphill another one-half mile until you reach the bleached wood skeleton of old Sts. John, once a resplendent gem among mine towns. The historic Sts. John Mine, Colorado's first silver strike, remains dignified even in demise. The old tunnel into Glacier Mountain is visible on the left as you enter the town. Brick ruins of a once-proud smelter scatter across a nearby mound. Farther along, strewn planks and tumbled beams on the left mark the site of Sts. John's stamp mill, built in 1872.

The story of Sts. John town in Chapter 16 tells tales of the prim Bostonian mine camp in its cultivated heyday. The story of the mine, long, lively and detailed, can only be capsuled here.

The Boston Silver Mining Association, organized in 1866, packaged John Coley's history-making 1863 silver strike, the Coley Mine, with another rich vein, the 1865 Comstock. The company drove two tunnels and began taking out silver ore carrying 100 to 170 ounces silver per ton. By 1870, 3,000 tons of ore piled up in a mini-mountain at the 10,800 foot altitude tunnel mouth, ready for a 50-ton per day concentrating mill completed two years later. In 1875, the new mill opened its door to "custom ore", processing for other mines.

Mining savants looked with awe at the Sts. John Mine. They raved about its 1,500 foot tunnel, because it was unwaveringly true and flawlessly level. Frank Fosset termed it "splendid" and "the finest tunnel in the state". Colonel W. L. Candler (Chandler) who managed the mine and Captain Sampson Ware, superintendent, received high praise.

The mine company became the Boston Silver Mining Company in 1867 and hired Ware soon after. A newspaper stated "In '68 Captain Ware took charge of the works and now there is no more completely developed mine in the State . . . a master hand directed it." Stephen Decatur, in Georgetown's *Colorado Miner* called Ware "a chief among miner men. . ."

In the 1870's, nearly 100 men worked in the Sts. John Mine and its related activities — teaming, timber cutting, charcoal burning and construction.

But the mine encountered obstacles. Barite in the ore rendered processing in the new mill hopeless at times. Moreover, according to Fosset, the half million spent during the decade of operation was partially wasted due to "mismanagement, mistakes, experiments etc.," directed by Boston owners, who determined policy and made decisions.

These obstacles prevented the Sts. John Mine from steady production in the early '80's. The mine closed briefly when silver prices plunged in 1892 and shut down again from 1900 to 1913. Along with its stale years, the silver property experienced production years that sent stockholders heels a-clicking: In 1891, the Sts. John Mine yielded a stunning 32,274 ounces of silver! In 1924, a low year, 2,174. Even interrupted production from 1866 to the mid-1950's spreads Sts. John Mine activity over a 90-year period — a proud record.

Near the Sts. John Mine's main adit, just 500 feet away, stood the More Work Mine which shipped ores from 1910 to 1917. Just south of the Sts. John Mill stood Ed Guibor's 1863 discovery, the Potosi. (Guibor built Sts. Johns' first cabin.) His Potosi ores assayed at 150 ounces silver per ton.

The Harrison, at 11,200 feet, produced lead-silver ores from 1883, when it began shipping, until 1890. Discovered in the early 1870's, the Harrison ore was rated as "nearly solid galena" by geologist Lovering.

Above Sts. John, on Glacier's western slope, three miles from the tour's starting point, the rip-snorting Wild Irishman camp surrounded the silver-rich Wild Irishman Mine. The mine developed rapidly until 1883, then shipped high-grade ores steadily through 1886. Barite in the ore caused processing problems similar to those at Sts. John. "A small concentrating mill was built at the mine in 1884," reported Lovering, "but was unsuccessful in separating the barite from the sulphides and was soon abandoned." After 1900, the Wild Irishman was dispensing its rich ore again, with an impressive 5,726 ounces silver produced in 1901.

Wild Irishman ores ranked as unusual because they occurred in nearly vertical shoots ("chimneys") 40 to 100 feet long.

Terrence Connors, who managed the mine in 1906, organized the Miners Association of Montezuma, an alliance to protect investors from promoters peddling worthless mine stock. The colorful Mr. Connors' favorite adage became popular around Montezuma: "You never heard an ass bray when he had grass."

The mine dump and tunnel, plus several log cabins, remain to identify the Wild Irishman site.

The neighboring Silver Prince, at 11,300 feet, worked a continuation of the Wild Irishman vein. Nearby, the Altoona at 11,500 feet, produced small ore shipments beginning around 1881.

At Glacier Mountain's crest, the Tiger, Tiger Extension, St. Cloud and Windsor mines formed a group discovered before 1870. Among several shafts, the deepest drove 100 feet into Glacier. An 1870 report mentioned a rich six-inch vein assayed at 1,000 to 2,500 ounces silver per ton, but this vein proved a fluke. Owners sold ore to the Sts. John smelter before 1880.

Ed Guibor's Herman Mine, near the head of Sts. John Creek at 11,700 feet, kept 1880's pack trains busy on steep Sts. John Basin roads. Guibor located the Herman in 1875 and developed it in the early 1880's. A newspaper proclaimed the mine a "heavy shipper" of lead-silver ores in 1882-83. "This is probably the largest ore body in the district," an 1883 Colorado Mine Directory stated, "and with development will probably be one of the largest producers."

Peru Creek

To tour the mines located in beautiful Peru Creek Valley, return to Montezuma, travel through town and continue northerly to the Peru Creek turn-off Follow the Peru Creek Road through an archway of aspen trees. About one and one-half mile along the road, the Maid of Orleans Mine ruins appear at roadside on Peru Creek's north side at 10,300 feet. Discovered in 1882, the Maid of Orleans Mine produced silver worth about $60 per ton from 1885-88.

Massive Lenawee Mountain looms at left. Near Lenawee's crest stood Isaac Filger's Winning Card Mine at 12,500 feet. A large crew worked the mine and Filger dreamed up the idea of a skyscraping "city" to be built in the rarified atmosphere close to the Lenawee summit. Filger erected several cabins as a nucleus for his new resort city. But Filger City never became a reality.

However, Filger's mine, the Winning Card, boasted a dream-come-true vertical ore seam, continuous for 130 feet. A 50-foot shaft driven in 1885 paid off with a rich new strike. As late as 1906, the Winning Card shipped seven tons of ore to the Argo smelter and received in return a healthy $36,000 check.

Also perched near Lenawee's soaring crest was the American Eagle Mine (locally known as the Eliza Jane), just southwest of the Winning Card at 12,500 feet. Located in 1880, the mine "produced some very rich silver ore in the next few years", according to geology researcher T. H. Lovering. In 1881, four tons of gray copper ore returned $500 per ton, enough to make any miner toss his hat in joy.

Chihuahua, an 1880's silver camp, stood at the mouth of Chihuahua Gulch, about two miles in on the Peru road. On Peru Creek's north side, above old Chihuahua at 11,500 feet, the Congress Mine ran a wooden tram to the Peru Creek wagon road. The Congress' unusual pockets gleaming with lead, silver and gold (rarely found around Montezuma), created much miner's gossip over the day's end bucket of beer.

An old wagon road took off from Chihuahua and led to Montezuma, later replaced by the more modern county road. This historic roadway once served as part of the Argentine Pass toll road. On this road sat the Jumbo, located on Morgan Peak's north slope, just south of the Maid of Orleans. The Jumbo, clearly visible from today's Peru Creek Road, shipped about 100 tons of ore in 1888. In 1914, when the Philadelphia Mining Company operated the Jumbo along with its Toledo Mill (near the end of this old road), the mine began shipping heavily again. From 1914 to 1918, the Jumbo produced 6,798 tons of ore.

Beyond old Chihuahua, roughly across from Warden Gulch, on the road's left (north) side, Cooper Mountain rises. On its south slope the 1880-located Buda at 12,000 feet produced from 1886-89. The Buda worked a 25-foot shaft and 300-foot adit.

One thousand feet above the road, the old Tariff Mine on Cooper earned glowing praise from early mine chronicler, Frank Fosset: "The Tariff is considered one of the best lodes in this section . . . a rich vein of solid ore has been opened . . . ore assaying 3,400 ounces." The Tariff, by its wealth, managed to sidestep the profit hazards of ore transport costs and the mine's own isolation. The Tariff furnished the display of Colorado silver at the 1893 Chicago World's Fair, a ruby silver slab about the size of a car seat cushion, according to longtime Montezuma area resident, Max Dercum.

Proceed to the mouth of Warden Gulch on the right, where the Bond, Chrysolite and Orphan Boy Mines riddled Morgan Peak's east slope seeking precious minerals. (The Bond yielded both gold and silver.)

The Orphan Boy, at Warden Gulch's head was first the "Orfint Boy", located in 1875 by a semi-literate Pennsylvania miner long on mining savvy, but short on spelling skills. The mine worked three adits between 11,800 and 12,100 feet, high in the gulch, and produced ore intermittently (100 tons in 1887) until 1890.

Discovered in 1873, the nearby Washington Mine produced silver and copper intermittently during the 1870's and '80's. Ores assayed at a lucrative 100 to 200 ounces silver and 20 percent copper.

Neighboring Warden Gulch is Brittle Silver Mountain, host to the rich Brittle Silver Mine group on its north slope. Clustered at around 12,000 feet, the Boston, Brittle Silver, Little Nell, Peary and White Sparrow claims forged the group. Assays ran 100 ounces silver per ore ton.

An 1882 Kokomo newspaper reported 10 men working at the Brittle Silver to excavate a tunnel. "The Brittle Silver is a promising property at the surface. It shows a well-defined vein twenty-six inches between walls, with a five-inch pay streak running 3,200 ounces silver per ton. The properties of this section are invariably high-grade fissure veins in granite."

In this area, one-half mile northwest of Cinnamon Gulch's mouth you will see the Rothschild Mine. The Rothschild Tunnel opens 200 feet above Peru Creek. This ambitious tunnel penetrates Cooper Mountain a head-spinning 4,700 feet! The *Daily Mining Record* in 1903 reported, "Up at Argentine (the town of Decatur's second name), the Rothschild Company is pushing ahead on a 3,000 foot cross cut tunnel." The tunnel, complete in 1906, actually did push in the entire 4,700 feet and exposed 32 lucrative veins in the doing!

W. T. Lewis discovered the Tariff and Rothschild in 1873. Assays glowingly reported 100 to 500 ounces silver per ton and 20 to 35 percent lead. The Rothschild yielded $20,000 in 1883, then became inactive in the '90's' until 1899, when mining activity resumed. In 1907, the Rothschild produced 4,000 ounces silver; in 1922 3,544 ounces.

Cinnamon Gulch on the right, latticed with precious minerals, sprouted some rare and rich mines, among them the fabulous Delaware. Located by William Mendenhall in 1879, near the mouth of Cinnamon Gulch, the Delaware boasted a good wagon road right to the mine. Ore transport via Webster Pass to the Denver, South Park & Pacific rail at Grant in South Park proved fairly easy.

The Delaware came into notable new hands a year after discovery. An 1880 Pennsylvania Mine prospectus stated, "The famous Delaware Mine . . . has been sold in the last month to Governor H. A. W. Tabor and Major Sanders of Leadville for . . . one hundred thousand dollars."

A steady 1880's producer, the Delaware shipped three ore wagon loads (about eight tons) daily in July, 1884.

The Delaware, Delaware Extension and Sunrise claims were, according to 1800's mining savants, extensions of a colossal ore deposit lacing Decatur Mountain's fabled flanks. The historic Pennsylvania Mine perched right on top of it.

Mine buildings still stand in testimony to the Pennsylvania's long and impressive mining career. Several succumbed to a 1977 blaze — the old assay office, the bunkhouse and cookhouse/dining hall. But the rest nestle against the mountain's northwest slope about four miles from the Peru Creek Road's starting point, near the marked site of old Decatur.

Located by J. M. Hall in 1879, the historic Pennsylvania provided a lifeline to an economically-depressed Summit County during its leanest years. For the Pennsylvania, a consolidated group of lodes, operated steadily, not only through the 1893 silver panic that strangled lesser mines, but straight through to the mid-1940's.

In later years, the modern mine had a large, impressive mill run by electricity, and several short aerial trams to transport ores. Living quarters, offices, a dining hall and other buildings constituted the administrative facilities, while the mine itself burrowed beneath, developed extensively on six separate underground levels.

Owners spent the years from 1879 to 1887 just in developing the mine. Its first shipments came in 1887 and skyrocketed to 7,000 tons yearly around 1893, the mine's biggest year. In 1892, the Decatur Mining Syndicate, a British organization, leased the mine; the company's figures showed $319,275 in silver that year. In 1902, the Ohio Mines Company bought the property. A succession of later owners followed. But production never equalled the peak year, 1893. (The entire district looked longingly at Pennsylvania production figures that storied year when almost every other Summit silver mine sank into silver-panic doldrums.)

The Montezuma *Prospector*, April 14, 1906, commented, "The Pennsylvania Mine has been a steady shipper over 14 years, keeping from two to 14 four-horse teams busy hauling ore to Keystone that had a general average value of from $60 to $100 a ton."

The Pennsylvania's mineral storehouse yielded gold (594 ounces in the biggest gold year, 1910), silver (138,344 ounces in 1893), lead, copper and zinc.

Horseshoe Basin

Ruby Mountain, across the valley, recorded a rousing mining history, partly due to its isolation. (And the amoral Gassy Thompson took full advantage of this.) The Shoe Basin Mine, at roadside about five miles from the tour's starting point, is marked by a tunnel portal at benchmark 11,699. The tunnel, begun in

158

Barren, wind-whipped Horseshoe Basin, at Peru Valley head, housed stores of rich silver. Peruvian Mine produced 1874-1951. Ruined building still stands.

1911, cuts both the Shoe Basin and Peruvian Mines. Before the tunnel, shafts opened the Shoe Basin. Active in the 1870's, the mine quit after the 1893 silver panic. The Shoe Basin Mines Company resurrected the mine, completed the long tunnel in 1914 and shipped 400 tons of ore in 1914-15.

About one-half mile farther, on the left, sits the Peruvian Mine. The Peruvian, discovered in 1874, enjoyed a smash year in 1891 when the Georgetown *Courier* on the August 29 reported: " . . . it has averaged 65 tons a month this year, ore from 49 to 63 ounces of silver per ton and from seven to 20 percent lead." A 1907 Ruby Mountain mining pamphlet, a promotional piece, said the Peruvian yielded $250,000 in a recent year.

That infamous snake-in-the-grass swindler Gassy Thompson carried off one of his colorful capers near the Peruvian Mine. Absentee owners hired Gassy to assemble a crew and drive a 100-foot tunnel into Ruby Mountain. Gassy got right into the tough task, hacking away, but soon tired from the attempt to penetrate stubborn rock. When heavy Horseshoe Basin snows fell and began to pile up huge drifts, Gassy's fertile brain went to work. He began building the tunnel backward, timbering his square sets away from the mountain. The snow blanketed the timbers, creating a "tunnel" that pleased greenhorn investors when they arrived to inspect it at winter's end. They complimented Gassy for his industry and paid him handsomely. When snows finally melted to reveal the skeleton "tunnel", the charlatan Gassy was long gone!

The Ruby Mountain Mines group, next door to the Peruvian, combined 62 claims, the White Metal lodes and the Langdon lodes, and drove an ambitious 5,000-foot tunnel into Ruby's eastern slope.

159

Proceeding farther into Horseshoe Basin, one finds the National Treasury Mine on the right at milepoint 6.0. Across the road is Falls Gulch and the Paymaster Mine, one-fourth mile north of Falls Gulch, near the headwall, at 12,050 feet. Rumor said the Paymaster, discovered in the late 1860's, was Peru Creek's first mining claim.

The Paymaster, most active from 1882 to 1892, had some banner production years: 1889, with 13,670 ounces silver; and 1892, with a whopping 36,882 ounces silver!

The Paymaster ranked as impressive with its three-story circa-1882 mill and 1,300-foot tramline, plus an 80-foot shaft, adit and drifts. Mine ruins scatter the site. Two other claims, the Silver Ball and Seven-thirty, lay on the same vein. Building ruins, constructed with the old-time square nails, lay scattered about below, on the flower-carpeted alpine meadow. From here, you can see the Argentine Pass cut as it crosses the summit.

Look carefully to see the Argentine Pass Road, now a faint outline, snaking up Horseshoe Basin's steep east wall. The Queen of the West Mine clings to this wall at 12,500 to 13,000 feet altitude, 1,200 feet northwest of the arduous pass road.

Finally, below steep Mount Edwards, just north of Argentine Pass, is the Vidler Tunnel. A tunnel portal building, water pipes and gravel tailings mark the site. Hailed by turn-of-the-century Peru and Montezuma mining promoters as a dream come true, the Vidler Tunnel aimed to establish a rail passage through the Continental Divide at 11,650 feet. The Snake River mines would blossom forth wild profits once their punishing ore transport costs came into line. The narrow-gauge railway would connect from its 1880's terminus at Keystone up through the Vidler Tunnel to Georgetown and an easy route to Denver.

Honest miners awaited tunnel completion with bounding enthusiasm; unscrupulous promoters, hooligans and mountebanks began cranking out advertising to lure gullible investors into plunking their dollars into worthless mines. Every hole in the ground loomed as a potential profit-maker, because the Vidler Tunnel was coming to the Snake River Valley.

Early 1900's entrepreneurs had tackled a near-impossible task in driving the more than 7,500 foot tunnel. These dauntless developers, led by Rees Vidler, launched the project in 1901, backed by British investment funds. They began at the east side. The Snake River mining communities grew dizzy with delight. By 1911, the east portal had penetrated Mount Edwards 5,118 feet and the west portal opened to 700 feet. Only 1,700 feet separated the two. Snake River residents crowed in glee.

But high hopes dashed against economic reality. The Vidler Tunnel never reached completion. Financial snaggles, the job's sheer difficulty and other obstacles roadblocked the project. (The Vidler Tunnel, completed in recent years, now carries western slope water through the Continental Divide.)

Work crews had discovered a fringe benefit as they pushed the tunnel excavation. You guessed it! — Silver! The last vein discovered on the east side, praised as "strong enough to encourage much development", bore the frisky name of

"The Red Light" (also called the "Flossie").

How long did mining continue in the Snake River district? In 1939, the Marlin, Bullion, Maid of Orleans and Tip Top Cross still shipped ore. The Tip Top Cross continued to ship high-grade lead-silver ore until 1950, worked then by Max Dercum and Emmet Brophy. The Ida Belle produced in the 1940's and the Sts. John worked until the 1950's. And, as late as 1977, the Vega Mining Company bored into Teller Mountain seeking the old Cashier vein.

Gold and silver still seam Summit's soaring peaks. Gold values skyrocketed to more than $500 per ounce in late 1979. Yet strict environmental controls and high start-up costs work to hamper modern-day mining in mineral-rich Summit County.

Summit Ghost Camps

Summit County, seamed with silver and gold, sprouted a rash of bawdy and beautiful mine towns a century ago. Peopled with prospectors whose eyes glinted gold, these towns grew from tent communities to clusters of log cabins with no worries about urban sprawl. Street fights, lusty gambling palaces, saloons and unsanitary conditions flourished, along with heroism, determination, the Puritan work ethic and the sheer glee of knowing gold lay in the ground beneath one's boots.

Samuel Clemens, alias Mark Twain, came West with his brother in 1861. His comments on the camp: "Joy sat on every countenance, and there was a glad, almost fierce intensity in every eye, that told of the money-getting schemes that were seething in every brain and the high hope that held sway in every heart."

The scene of all this joyful greed, the mine camp, grew from a gangly group of tents, rough shanties and log cabins. If the mines proved prosperous, this raw settlement blossomed into a real town. Sawmills sprang up, and with them frame houses and shop buildings with board siding, false fronts (like some of the dance hall girls) and fashionable gingerbread trim. The final step in mine town evolution came with the construction of brick, stone and masonry buildings. These stately, sometimes pompous, monuments to affluence stamped the town with the mark of permanence. Sometimes a disastrous fire swept through the mine town, destroying log cabins and frame buildings. This devastation, though tragic, hurried the move toward stability. Property owners re-built with more elegant, substantial and fire-retardant architectural materials.

One or two main streets usually bisected the mine town. In camps built on a hillside, the main street traversed the slope. Schools, churches and homes of upstanding citizens claimed their rightful position above main street. Saloons, gambling halls and the red light district cropped up in the area below main street, bordering the less desirable creek, river or railroad tracks.

The church, a mark of respectability, stood as every community's pride. Its tower or steeple and bell advertised the town as proper for women and children. Lodges, like Parkville's 1860 Masonic Lodge, signalled stability. Arrival of traveling players, like Langrishe & Dougherty at Parkville, not only added pizazz, but marked a coming of age.

A visitor from the East once characterized a Colorado gold camp as a scene of

Stereoptican view shows 1876 Montezuma. Raw camps needed women to create community.

"vim, recklessness, extravagance and jolly progress". The zany spirit of the early camps, where bizarre and unpredictable events occurred with predictable regularity, resulted from its "crazy salad" population mix. "A motley group of rough individuals" was Bayard Taylor's description of 1866 Breckenridge population. Since male prospectors with no time for frills dominated the camps, social rules did not prevail. (Personal hygiene suffered as well. A prospector named Parsons, who came west in February, 1880, reported taking his first good bath on June 19, 1881!)

Even later, when wives and families arrived, the mine town attracted America's social rejects. "The argonauts who arrived after 1865 were the misfits, the ne'er-do-wells, and the first to be unemployed in the depression after the Civil War," states Colorado historian Robert L. Brown. "Some were psychotic personalities, hence we can explain the 'erratic characters' . . . Harry Orchard, Alfie Packer and others."

Along with the bona fide crazies came the joy boys who, freed from hometown social restraints, let their hair down in bawdy camps like old Leadville. In February, 1879 the Leadville *Eclipse* commented on these frisky fellows:

> It seems 'kinder queer' to see the chaps who are known in Denver as staid and sober church members and heads of responsible families come to Leadville, sail into the boxes at the variety shows, and with an actress on each knee, make love in the most appropriate and modern fashion. We wouldn't give the boys away for the world, so they needn't quake in their high-topped boots and blue shirts.

After the prospector's jubilant cry of "Gold!" first echoed in the gulches and the stampede to new diggings began, a certain "advance guard" of residents arrived in the mine town: The saloon-keeper (an absolute essential in mine camp life); the lawyer (where there was gold there were squabbles over claims); the merchant; and the prostitute. Although the saloon-keeper, lawyer and prostitute were always guaranteed a fat share of the miner's gold, the merchant gambled on surviving the competitive boom-town business scramble. Today's bonanza could fizzle into tomorrow's bust. Only the merchant, with sizeable investment in land, building and inventory, had much to lose. And the boom-bust cycle, along with transiency, proved very real. Sixty percent of those who beat a path to the Colorado mountain towns during the post-1859 rush left before 1870.

The real frontier "gamblers" were the blacksmiths, bakers, butchers, hotel and boardinghouse owners, druggists, livery men, bankers, barbers, general store proprietors, jewelers, gunsmiths and brewers — all the tradesmen who hung up their placards on cabin beams or across false-fronted frame buildings on a brawling, bustling main street.

One businessman, however, continued to rake in reliable profits: The dance hall proprietor owned the most roilicking establishment in town. "Men are fools and women devils in disguise. That's the reason the dance halls clear from one to two hundred dollars per night," scolded an early Leadville newspaper.

Did the busy camp really have enough fun-lovers to fill the dance halls? Or was everyone caught up in the frenzied pursuit of gold? Reverend Mark Fiester, in his *Blasted, Beloved Breckenridge* quoted an early writer who jested about the demographics of the camp:

> It is surprising what few are really workers on claims to the proportion of other pursuits. The regular average per centum might be classified as follows: Thirty active miners, ten merchants and saloon keepers, five mechanics, fifty loafers, gamblers and fancy men. Lousy with lawyers, pettifoggers and scrub doctors — six married men with their own wives — ten grass widows, three antiquated females desirous of permanent homes and partners for life — one ossified old maid, two that are hastening to ossification . . . Most of the men are sitting in their houses or tents, watching the weather, and as a *"general business"* playing "high low jack" or "seven up" for whiskey. This is the *chief* employment of almost half the population of Georgia and other gulches, from daylight to dark, throughout the week, Sunday not excepted.

When they weren't playing seven up or drinking whiskey, mine camp residents might be visiting today's charming curiosity, yesterday's necessity, the general store. This 1800's super-store carried dry goods, groceries, clothing, medicine, hardware, notions and liquor, plus agricultural implements and mining equipment. The proprietor might purchase gold and silver bullion and farmer's produce. His store might also house the local bank and post office.

But miners resented shopkeepers. Camp prices put a squeeze on the average prospector's gold pouch. His wages during the mine labor shortage in 1864-65 were $5 per day. (A dozen eggs or a pound of butter in 1860's Breckenridge cost $2.50.) By 1879, when miners flooded the work force, his pay dwindled to $2.50 per day.

Reverend William Crawford, a Massachusetts minister who came to Colorado in 1863, listed these Denver prices:

Board	$ 8.00 per week
Flour	15.00 per sack
Butter	.85 per pound
Eggs	1.50 per dozen
Potatoes	12½ cents per pound
Milk	.30 per quart

Food prices had dropped by the 1870's, but still dipped into the miner's diminishing gold dust supply.

John Irving Hastings who lived at Sts. John in 1872 took these prices from his father's diary:

Sack of flour	$5.00
One-half sack meal	2.00
Doctor's call	2.00

Carpenters earned $5 to $6 daily in 1864-65, but wages fell to $3.50 in 1879. Other laborers averaged $5 to $7 daily in the '60's, and $3 to $3.50 in the late '70's.

Miners and other workers griped about town merchants charging sky-high prices, doubly unfair since isolated high country consumers had nowhere else to shop. (Only game meat and wood were freely available to the miner, and then were often purchased to allow more time and energy for gold-grubbing. All other supplies came from the outside.)

Shopkeepers retorted that their profits remained small. High transportation costs on irregular and uncertain deliveries over storm-buffeted high passes gobbled up profits. Hefty prices paid to prairie wholesalers also pushed costs upward, they argued.

Real estate prices, too, ballooned the first year or two of a camp's existence. Then, land prices usually deflated.

Squatters hastily threw up cabins as the new camps mushroomed. Later, when the dust settled, land ownership came into question. (Lot "jumpers", like greedy grasshoppers, plagued early Kokomo. And the entire townsite of Breckenridge was jumped! Townsite rights were seized from General George Spencer and distributed to many.) Harsh words, blows and bullets often punctuated these land disputes.

Lot jumpers constituted the least of the early mine town's annoyances. The camps sprouted problems like dandelions cropping up in a late-May mountain meadow. Sanitation, with no sewers, and garbage dumps rising outside kitchen doors, probably ranked as worst. Dysentery and diarrhea ran rampant when drinking water became contaminated. (When raw sewage from shallow privies failed to pollute water supplies, mining, with its tailing minerals and chemical use, did.) Sanitation laws, enacted finally when waste and refuse became untenable, or when a death shocked the town to action, zeroed in on the community's worst offender, the red light district.

No, life wasn't all roses in the early boom towns. A stench hung over the camp, caused by manure and other decaying material, and the smell worsened in summer.

Luckily, Summit's high altitude camps lay locked in frost many months of the year. Only during summer months did sanitation present disease problems.

Epidemics flashed through early mine communities. Diptheria, smallpox, scarlet fever and other diseases account for many children's graves in Summit County cemeteries. Pneumonia also took a heavy toll in high-altitude communities.

Air pollution, considered a 20th century offender, vexed early mountain townsfolk. Fireplace and cookstove smoke hung in inversion clouds over mountain valley towns. Smelter fumes killed trees and shrubs, pervaded valley towns. Road dust in summer choked the lungs of pedestrians.

And noise pollution! Another 20th century ill? No! The early camp's huge, wide streets sometimes 60 feet across, were built to allow wagon and pack trains space to turn easily. Those same streets chorused with the activities of a busy

town day and night — freighters yelling to ox teams, screeching wagons, water-sellers peddling wares, patent medicine men hawking remedies, street fights, braying burros, dogs yelping in packs, wandering livestock mooing, bleating or bellowing.

A visitor to early Creede, Colorado, summed it up with this complaint: "I couldn't sleep with all the noise . . . hollering, yelling, horses galloping, wagons chuckling, hammering, pounding, sawing, shooting."

Worse than the noise that emanated from the street was the street itself! Roadways sprouted stumps and rocks, left there by hasty and less than meticulous road builders. The right-of-way, undefined in the early boom period, often harbored a cabin smack in the middle of Main Street. Urban planning suffered gross neglect in these early towns. Snow clogged streets in winter. Mud holes in spring threatened to swallow man and beast in their greedy brown glup. Spring run-off created little creeks that washed out whole sections of city streets. In Breckenridge, Summit County *Journal* editor Jonathan Cooper Fincher regularly lambasted the town fathers for the deplorable conditions on Main Street.

One final hazard threatened every youthful mineral camp and took its devastating toll in practically every town: Fire.

"Dearest brother, thou hast left us" laments 1864 Swan Valley gravestone.

Carelessly constructed wood buildings, parched by dry western winds and sun, waited like tinder for a spark. Roaring heat and cooking fires overheated stoves or ignited poorly-built chimneys. Lamps overturned. No matter what the cause, fire, once started, leapt from house to house on the constant mountain breeze and destroyed all in its path. Bucket brigades rushed to the blaze but their efforts often proved futile. In winter, they often found their crucial water supply frozen solid. In Dillon, like many other early towns, residents decided to dig a town well to offset fire hazard. Fire provided the threat that prompted town governments to organize. Volunteer fire companies formed and fund-raising events like dances or box-supper socials provided not only cash for equipment, but a source of merriment for townspeople. Civic pride focused on the developing fire company. In Breckenridge, today's historic 100-year-old Breckenridge fire department became an exclusive organization. Elite companies competed for prestige. Lovingly polished fixtures on fire equipment, dapper firemen's uniforms and snappy hose-handling demonstrations drew "ah's" at holiday parades.

Kokomo's 1882 fire, a typical mine town conflagration, ravaged the city's main street. Billowing black smoke clouds choked fire-fighting volunteers as raging flame consumed building after building. Breckenridge and Montezuma suffered a succession of destructive fires. Chihuahua in the Peru Creek Valley succumbed to almost total destruction in an 1889 timber blaze and was never re-built. Wheeler, in the Ten Mile Canyon, also burned.

Even today, fire threatens to destroy a heritage of fragile wooden mine buildings, ghost town structures and landmarks. The venerable Pennsylvania Mine burned in April, 1977 when heavy snow prevented fire equipment from reaching its remote Horseshoe Basin location. Another historic mine structure suffered damage in spring, 1978 when buildings at French Gulch's historic Wellington Mine caught fire.

Thirty-three once-flourishing Summit County mine camps detailed below have now faded, leaving only a bleached-bones wooden skeleton behind. Sometimes, only foundations remain, a whisper of life a century ago. If you happen on one of these old towns, please take nothing but a photograph. Leave these fading relics of gold rush days undisturbed.

A Capsule History of Summit's Century-Old "Cities"

(Note: For a history of mining around these communities, see Chapters 9, 10 and 11.)

Boston, set in a flower-carpeted natural amphitheater high in the upper Ten Mile Canyon's Mayflower Gulch, served the extensive placer operations of the Boston Mining Company and lode mines like the Golden Crest. Below towering Fletcher Mountain, with a long, dramatic view west to Jacque Peak, lie the remains of Boston, a handful of log cabins. A recent Summit visitor, born years ago in Boston, returned to the old camp in summer, 1979, to discover remnants of his mother's old brass bed crumbling there and his old toys half-buried in the cabin yard. The Colorado Mountain Club maintains a cabin at Boston to provide emergency shelter to high-country sportsmen.

Quaint Boston sprouted near Boston Placers, Golden Eagle, Golden Crest, Resumption Mines.

View west from old log structure at Boston, Mayflower Gulch town.

Braddocks was located three miles north of Breckenridge across the highway from today's Summit Motor Lodge. "Broncho" Dave Braddocks, the town's colorful patriarch, ran an 1880's stage line, operated a stable, brewed a popular temperance beer sold all over the county, cultivated a mountain garden-truck farm at 9,640 feet altitude (covered against frost at night) and staged lavish parties in his first-class hall, built in 1882. Braddocks, on the Denver, South Park & Pacific rail line, became a station in 1884 (fare from Denver: $9.80) and had a post office which served mining camps above. These mines used Braddocks as an ore station, delivering processed ore to the railway here.

Carbonateville: Who ever heard of Carbonateville? Nobody, these days. But the 1878 upper Ten Mile Canyon boom town typifies the frenzied madness of Summit's mineral rush era.

McNulty Gulch, where Carbonateville sprang up in 1878, had gained fame in 1860 when prospectors from California Gulch (Leadville) made an electrifying gold strike there at Fremont Pass' base.

"The news . . . spread like wildfire," an 1879 Leadville business directory recalled. Prospectors poured over the Ten Mile Range from Breckenridge and staked the gulch from rim to rim with placer claims. McNulty Gulch, a veritable New Eldorado, relinquished $3 million in free gold the first three seasons. But placer gold quickly disappeared.

In 1878, miners discovered new mineral wealth, in hard-rock veins this time, and a new rush began.

169

Carbonateville, on the plateau at the gulch's mouth straddling Ten Mile Creek, exploded into a log and frame metropolis. By 1879, according to the Leadville business directory, Carbonateville businesses included:

1 meat market	1 shoe store
4 miners' supply stores	2 clothing stores
2 notaries	3 contractors
1 paint store	1 druggist
2 doctors	1 general store
2 sawmills	4 grocers
6 real estate and mining companies	1 hat store
3 restaurants	1 justice of the peace
7 saloons	1 laundry
3 attorneys	1 liquor store
1 bank	3 livery stables
1 toll road company	2 lumber dealers
2 barbers	2 boardinghouses
1 blacksmith	

Carbonateville also offered six commodious hotels: The Delmonico of the Pacific, American House, Carbonateville House, Harrison House, Joplin House and Oakland House.

Finnegan, Wheeler and Company built the first sawmill 200 yards from the townsite and churned out boards for all the building activity. Colonel John W. Jenkins, one of the town's first residents, arriving December, 1878, secured a postoffice. The Merchants and Miners Bank began a brisk business in gold exchange. Colonel Jenkins published the *Ten Mile News*.

Broad streets and avenues bisected the town. Chestnut, Main, Champa, McNassar (named for Colonel James McNassar, who became rich on McNulty Gulch placer gold) were a few street names. Sherman, Lincoln and Ten Mile were some avenue names. Carbonateville served as a stop on Silas Nott's Georgetown-Leadville stage route, launched in 1879. The town bore all the trappings of a thriving community.

By 1881, Carbonateville was a near-ghost town, gasping for life. Crofutt, in his 1885 *Gripsack Guide to Colorado*, kissed off Carbonateville as "only a store and half a dozen buildings". An emerging Robinson, the powerful Ten Mile town just a mile below, drained Carbonateville's lifeblood. McNulty Gulch's promising mineral stores petered out. Carbonateville died. Climax Molybdenum Company buried the corpse decades later in its development of the huge molybdenum deposit on nearby Bartlett Mountain.

Chihuahua in the Peru Creek Valley blossomed in 1879 and snared a U. S. postoffice in 1881. Two hundred people lived at Chihuahua near tumbling Peru Creek at the mouth of Chihuahua Gulch. The town boasted two hotels, the Chihuahua and the Snively, and another lodging facility appropriately dubbed "The Snowslide House". Three restaurants, three saloons, two grocery stores, a butcher shop, the Crilly & Company general store, E. W. Grove's large dry goods store, plus a sawmill and reduction works kept Chihuahua in the

170

mainstream of Peru Creek capitalism. But this entire hallmark of enterprise disintegrated during the disastrous 1889 forest fire, when only a few cabins on a back street escaped the ravaging blaze. Chihuahua's hillside cemetery, its graves marked by native rocks, sits amidst the burn areas that testify to the town's fiery demise.

An 1882 Montezuma *Millrun* news report editorialized in the best 1800's fashion that Chihuahua residents were "honest, virtuous and happy . . . There are no physicians as their services are never required . . . The clergy seldom visit this Arcadia of the mountains, as their mission is to call the sinners and not the righteous to repentence."

Even O. Lippoldt's Cabinet Saloon, advertising in a local newspaper, righteously peddled its "pure bottled goods for family and medicinal use". A halo hung over the saintly town of Chihuahua. Yet, the devil managed a few skirmishes within its sanctimonious city limits. Sin had its day when a triple lynching followed the murder of two upstanding Chihuahua residents. Three villainous road agents waylaid the two Chihuahua prospectors, robbed and killed them. Chihuahua heard of the outrage within moments of the act and rose as one. The townsmen pursued the miscreants a few miles east to Ruby Mountain, caught them and, without benefit of trial, hung all three.

On the other hand, Chihuahua pointed with pride to its school, "without doubt the best in Summit County", according to former county schools administrator, Ruby Lowe. Taught by schoolmarm Annie Jones, the Chihuahua school, Summit School District No. 7, had 24 students in 1881-82. Some of the children came from nearby Decatur and the school was located between the two towns.

Gray's Peak, Collier Mountain and Lenawee guard Chihuahua's valley meadow site, "one of the pleasantest places in Summit County", according to the Montezuma *Millrun*. Fashionable society didn't wither from lack of light and dazzle here. Chihuahua had its fancy-dress balls. For "the social event of the season" in August, 1882, ladies blossomed forth with silk, satin brocade, diamonds and cameos, according to the *Millrun*. Dancing and gaiety were "merry as a marriage ball".

But when Chihuahua residents shed their fine blacked shoes and ostrich feathers, they returned to a life of rough, hard work. While men hacked with pick axes at mountain walls in search of mineral veins, women hauled water and boiled clothes. Mabel Carle Rice, who lived at Chihuahua in the early 1890's, cooked for hungry teamsters while pregnant with her first son, Norman. Her husband, Benjamin R. Rice, hauled ore from Peru Creek mines to the railhead at Keystone, directing six freight outfits with five drivers beside himself.

If life was hard at Chihuahua, it also had its benefits: The pristine valley, below the funnel of aspen-decked Chihuahua Gulch, ripples with Peru Creek's music, and sprouts wild flowers in dainty sprigs for those who look. Two miles north and east from the intersection of Colorado 294 (the Montezuma Road) and Peru Creek Road lies the site of old Chihuahua.

Conger's Camp on the old Boreas Pass stage route from Como to Breckenridge lay in a horseshoe-shaped meadow in Indiana Gulch, five miles above Breckenridge. Veteran prospector Colonel S. P. Conger's discovery of the seemingly-rich Diantha Lode launched the town and attracted wealthy Eastern investors.

Sam Conger, who discovered the storied Caribou silver mine near Nederland, Colorado, and helped spearhead the tungsten boom there, received assay reports of 1,000-2,000 ounces of silver per ton on his Diantha Lode. But the silver "blanket" veins in the Boreas area proved a geological curiosity. Horizontal fissures, just beneath grass roots, looked rich. But, like the Diantha, they quickly played out.

Before the rails arrived in 1882, Conger received mail and passenger service from the Spottswood and McClellan Stage Line, with modern Concord Coaches. Later, the rails came, but not directly to Conger's Camp. The railroad was three-fourths mile away.

A postoffice, sawmill, fifteen-stamp ore mill, several stores and 30-40 houses made Conger's a vibrant community in the early 1880's. A smelter was on the drawing boards then. Enthusiasm ran high: "Carbonates were similar to those found at Leadville," one report stated, "galena as fine as any around Georgetown, quartz will run 50-250 ounces." Easterners responded by buying up Conger mines. But Conger area silver claims failed to meet these expectations. Then Conger's role as a lumber camp emerged to help the town survive. The Conger postoffice, later re-named Argentine for the nearby peak, closed October 22, 1883.

Cow Camp, one and one-half miles east of the present Green Mountain Reservoir, served as a dinner stop on the old Kremmling-Dillon stage line. Horses were changed here while diners sampled ranch style fare. The stage line proved vital during the Big Snow year of 1898-99 because all narrow-gauge rail service ceased. Much-needed supplies came over Berthoud Pass and through Kremmling to Dillon in sparse, but welcome, quantities.

Curtin, located in the Ten Mile Canyon, about 1.9 miles south of Frisco, was a stop on the old Denver & Rio Grande and South Park railroad lines which both ran through the canyon. The town was named for railroad section man, Bill Curtin. Curtin served as a mining-transportation center for the King Solomon, Excelsior, Mary Verna and North American Mines nearby. Curtin had a boardinghouse and homes. Old brick foundations remain from the town's coal-fired compressor, which powered mining machinery. A tramway served mines above. The old railbed, later a county road and now a bike path, parallels the modern highway. On the path, you'll see the King Solomon tunnel and other mine tunnels, beaver ponds, the railroad rock cut and more mines until you reach Curtin.

Decatur (later renamed Rathbone and Argentine) emerged in the mid-1860's as the creation of "Commodore" Stephen Decatur, a promoter who laid out the town. Decatur got off to a slow start because early discoveries yielded only mediocre ores and transportation costs ran as high as Decatur's lofty altitude. The "Commodore" set his namesake town below steep-walled Horseshoe Basin at the foot of the pass road he helped develop — 13,132-foot Argentine Pass, highest U.S. Rocky Mountain road crossing.

Colorado's famed "Snowshoe Itinerant", Fr. John Lewis Dyer, preached at a fledgling Decatur in the mid-1860's, the Montezuma *Millrun* reported later. In 1865, he also "preached to eight persons in Commodore Decatur's cabin at the Horseshoe Basin above Decatur".

Samuel Bowles, in his 1869 *Colorado: Its Parks and Mountains*, visited Commodore Decatur at his tiny Horseshoe Basin settlement:

Abandoned 1930's Argentine home decays but Pennsylvania Mine worked to '40's.

173

> Here, the grass was abundant, the stream ran pure and strong, unpolluted by miner's mud, fuel was plenty, even the mosquitoes sang a welcome, but no Ashley Franklin, no pack-mule was to be seen, no blankets, no food, no nothing, that belonged to us, but weariness and hunger. We sounded the war-whoop of the country, — a shrill, far-reaching cry; and back the voices came, not only from our lagging outfit, but from miners here and there among the hills, just finishing their day's work, and wondering who had come into their wilderness now. The mules took up the refrain, and bellowed from "depths that overflow" their welcome to each other. Soon we were at home, the coffee brewing, the ham stewing, and a hole through the peach can; Commodore Decatur, the prince of prospectors, the character of all Colorado characters, dropped in to bid us welcome to his principality, on his way from mine to cabin; under the frosts of night and the smoke of the camp fire, the merry mosquitoes flew away; our tent was raised our blankets spread; and the peace of Saturday night and a day richly spent reigned over us four and no more.

Illinois Lt. Governor Bross, who traveled with Bowles, had come to Colorado to reclaim his long-lost brother, Stephen Decatur. But the Commodore vigorously denied the relationship. The two must have made an uneasy peace.

Decatur's history unfolds as mercurial as the town's enigmatic founder. While the Commodore vacillated between service as a Colorado statesman and a hidden life as an alcoholic and bigamist, the town of Decatur experienced the same glory-and-bust syndrome.

In 1879, a dazzling Pennsylvania Mine silver strike boosted Decatur's growth. A 300-strong population in 1881 took steps toward town incorporation. Decatur held its first election in spring, 1882.

And then, a downer: In 1885, dwindling population forced the Decatur post-office to close.

The Silver Panic of 1893 hit hard at the entire Peru Creek-Montezuma mining region, but the strong Pennsylvania Mine managed to weather the devastating effects of silver devaluation. In 1893, the town obtained a new postoffice. When the postal service again awarded a postoffice, it required a new town name. So Decatur residents renamed their town Rathbone. The town arose from the ashes, riding high again.

But disaster lurked, awaiting its chance to strike again. The glory-bust cycle prevailed. After the "Winter of the Big Snow", 1898-99, when snow reached second-story rooftops in Summit County communities, came a spring of blockbuster snowslides. One day, gunshot-like reports split Rathbone's air. Instants later, a giant crush of snow demolished the town. Gray's Peak snowmelt had set off a massive avalanche that reduced Rathbone to splinters on a fine spring 1899 day.

Townspeople found little incentive to rebuild until after 1900. New strikes then revved up operations at the Pennsylvania Mine. By 1902, both the Pennsylvania and the Rothschild Mine operated full-time with 200 men on mine payrolls. Hammers rang and saws scraped as new buildings took shape. A school opened. And yet another new name — Argentine for the neighboring pass — crowned Commodore Decatur's off again-on again Peru Creek community.

Lula Myers, whose restored cabin now proudly rests at Dillon's Summit Historical Society Museum, remembered an unusual ride from Argentine to Dillon one moonlit night in the early 1900's. Edna Dercum recounted the story in *Women As Tall As Our Mountains*:

> There was one other "turrable" beautiful moonlit night that Lula remembered with humor. Way up Peru Creek road is a big mill and mine called the Pennsylvania Mine. It was a big operation in the early 1900's and a telephone line had been strung all the way from Dillon to the mine. One night, the phone rang at the Myer's home. There had been an accident at the mill and a man had been killed. Could Dimp come and bring the body back to Dillon? So, Lula not wanting him to have the long trip alone, dressed in warm clothes and went along . . . The miners loaded the stiff body of the unfortunate miner onto the flatbed of the dray wagon. With the full moon it was much easier to see the road. To cheer themselves up, Lula and Dimp started to sing and the horse went on at a good clip as the grade was a nice, gradual downhill. They reached the corner of Montezuma and Keystone roads and Lula looked back to see only an empty wagon. "Dimp" she cried out. "The body is gone." So turn around they did and the long trip back began. Finally, part of the way up Peru Creek road on the curves just beyond the Montezuma turnoff they found the body, which had bounced off during the swaying and jolting ride. The rest of the return ride was more sedate and "more somber".

Decatur's site, marked with a sign and a few foundation sites, lies above the old Pennsylvania Mine, about 4.5 miles in on the Peru Creek Road.

Delaware Flats, located on the Swan River east of the Blue River above fabled Gold Run Gulch, thrived as an 1860's placer mine town. William Byers, *Rocky Mountain News* editor wrote in his new publication, the Tarryall *Miners Record*, in summer 1861: "Delaware Flats . . . is all the excitement these days. They have a theater in Delaware Flats already, and as soon as the billiard table arrives . . . the city will be 'finished'." "Twenty or thirty houses stood where a week ago there were but three or four cabins". A postoffice opened in November 1861 with George W. Anders as postmaster. Placer mining, aided by the creation of water ditches from the Blue River flourished at Delaware and nearby Buffalo Flats, which was the old name for the area below Gold Run Gulch's mouth.

Dickey, now mostly submerged by Dillon Reservoir waters, was a railroad town located six miles north of Breckenridge near today's Farmers Korners. Earlier called Placer Junction, Dickey had a railroad roundhouse and a coaling station for the coal-stoked narrow-gauge locomotives of the South Park rail line. Ranching and stock raising flourished here. Mary Cluskey Ruth, longtime Summit resident born in Breckenridge in 1902, lived on her family's ranch at Dickey. The Cluskey children tramped to school in Dillon across land today submerged by Lake Dillon, and caught the afternoon train back to Dickey after school.

Dyersville sprang up in a heavy stand of evergreens near the mossy headspring of Indiana Creek in Indiana Gulch below the Boreas Pass Road. Dyersville was founded in 1881 by Colorado's own Fr. John Lewis Dyer who traveled on heavy miner's skis to bring Methodist religion to the godless gold camps. Fr. Dyer hauled lumber up from Breckenridge daily to build his 17 x 17, one and one-half story home topped off by a pine brush roof. The Warrior's Mark Mine nearby kept

Dyersville thriving, while nearby Angel's Rest, Jerry Krigbaum's lively watering hole, provided food, drink and merriment to local revelers, much to Father Dyer's chagrin.

Dyersville had a branch of Adamson's Blue Front Store, a Breckenridge clothier. A school, in Summit School District No. 9, educated Dyersville's young. Thomas West, C. H. Pike, John Zwergle, John Stuber and Messrs. Wood and Abbot lived in the town in 1887, according to *Blasted, Beloved Breckenridge*. Dyersville remained an active mining camp due to the long-term production of the Warrior's Mark Mine. Other mines nearby included the Snowdrift, LeRoy, J. L. Dyer, Lookout, Empire, Josephine and Saukey.

Four cabins remain in the rich woodland at Dyersville. The rough jeep trail takes off downhill from the 7:40 Mine ruins on the Boreas Pass Road to Dyersville.

Excelsior served as a ticket stop on the rail line through the Ten Mile Canyon southwest of Frisco. Ores from the Excelsior's concentrating mill bumped down a wagon road leading southward to meet the rail stop here. The big Excelsior Mill dominated the canyon scene just outside Frisco's west boundary. Ruins of the mill can still be seen there. Foundations and the main tunnel entrance dot the slope above the mill skeleton.

Farnham reigned as a miniature kingdom high in the rich McBarnes Mining District, eight and one-half miles above Breckenridge. Ores from W. H. Iliff's 7:40 Mine, one-tenth mile away, and from the Warrior's Mark below, were loaded on rail freight cars near Farnham.

The town occupied a splendid site in an open park on Bald Mountain's south slope, one mile below the Continental Divide. W. H. Farnham built a spacious sixteen-room summer resort hotel, with large parlor, dining hall and porches to take advantage of the superb mountain view of Baldy, Lincoln, Hoosier, Silverheels and Pacific peaks. Though Farnham tried to promote his town as a resort, it survived as an adjunct to area mines. Dynamic Farnham resident Calvin H. Pike once operated the Farnham general store, owned a mine, served as railway ticket and express agent, acted as postmaster in 1885 and worked at the 7:40 mine as local rail agent. For all his trouble, the railroad destroyed his home by spraying hot cinders upon its dry wooden frame and causing it to catch fire. Other Farnham residents were W. Wood, 1885 general store proprietor, J. S. Dowling, notary and justice of the peace, J. R. Muldoon, Henry Boaber and John Mix.

Farnham, developed in 1884, had 50 residents by 1885. The town served as a rail stop through 1906.

Haywood, an 1880's pit stop on the High Line stage route over Loveland Pass between Georgetown and Kokomo, stood near the present Loveland Pass Motel site on Highway 6 east of Keystone. Passengers and wagon freighters from the much-used Webster Pass stage and wagon route also made a rest stop here. Mrs. Kate Haywood served as postmistress. A hotel and restaurant housed in one building with the postoffice catered to stage travelers. One High Line stage passenger praised Haywood: "The stage station at this place is one of the most pleasant in the mountains." Haywood, though important to 1880's Summit life,

Disappointment and hard work faded from miner's memory when dance hall girl smiled.

never became a real town, just a few cabins clustered around the stage station.

Old Keystone, located on Soda Ridge Road, one-half mile west of the classy Keystone resort, preserves the 1880's rail depot and neighboring hamlet, now part of the Keystone Equestrian Center and Keystone Center for Continuing Education restoration project. As Snake River Valley railhead for the old South Park line, Keystone served as a depot for the town's sawmill products and Montezuma Mining District silver ores enroute to Denver. Passenger fare from Denver to Keystone was $10.75, a service for visitors and residents of nearby Sts. John, Montezuma, Chihuahua and Decatur.

The Denver, South Park & Pacific narrow-gauge locomotive made a Y-turn here in a large meadow switching area called Jackstraw Flats (terminus of "jack" or burro trails). The meadow sits on the south side of today's Soda Ridge Road. The train navigated the turn-around, then left the depot, which today still stands, alone in the meadow.

The railroad never proceeded beyond Keystone into Montezuma, although ambitious developers intended to carry the line much farther. Grading and some ties laid past Keystone toward Montezuma were preliminary steps toward a lucrative rail connection from Keystone across the Continental Divide to Georgetown. Incredible labor went into the almost-completed excavation of the Vidler Tunnel beneath the Divide in the early 1900's. But the effort proved futile, and Keystone remained the South Park rail terminus for 54 years.

Visitors can view the restored town of Keystone on Soda Ridge Road by car or foot from the new Keystone, a four-seasons resort. Keystone is steeped in history, not only as the old railhead, but also because the historic Keystone Ranch, a golf club, preserves an 1860's Soda Creek dairy ranch. The property later became the Smith-Reynolds Ranch.

Lakeside: Old Dillon isn't the only town submerged by reservoir waters. Lakeside lies beneath the Green Mountain Reservoir. Situated between Otter and Black Creeks, this ranching-mining community listed an 88 population (eligible voters, male only) in the 1892 census.

The Guyselman Ranch at Lakeside, about 20 miles north of Dillon, served as a stage stop on the Dillon-Kremmling route. Food, rest and a change of horses awaited stage drivers and passengers on the dusty, snow-clogged or muddy (depending on the season) 41-mile trip. The original ranch barn building, still standing today, became the Lakeside Post Office, the "Mail House". Lakeside grew and in the 1890's a school opened alongside the Mumford Ranch, with classes held May through November.

In 1899, Breckenridge resident William Knorr bought the ranch and in 1900

married Corinne Guyselman. The energetic pair expanded the ranch to an 8,500-acre success. Though neighbors scattered across the remote countryside, they banded together to build a clubhouse at Lakeside. Named for a small lake on the Knorr property, Lakeside with its clubhouse meetings and parties became synonymous with "good times". Gail Culbreath in *Women As Tall As Our Mountains* describes the annual Lakeside dance:

> What a delight to see folk, after many months. The music was usually donated by a piano player, a fiddler and sometimes a drummer. Weeks before, the Lakeside ladies had planned as bountiful a midnight "supper" as one can imagine. The highlight of this was the fried mountain trout which they prepared in the makeshift kitchen of the clubhouse . . . At dawn, regretfully, good-byes were said . . . The children came with their parents — and after several hours fell asleep on benches, amid the hullabaloo. Finally, the dance over, they were tucked warmly in the waiting wagon boxes.

In 1943, Green Mountain Dam flooded a large part of Lakeside and the Knorr Ranch.

Lincoln: Harry Farncomb came with the early prospector rush to the 1860's Blue River Diggings. Shortly after his arrival, Farncomb moved to French Gulch, named for Canadian French Pete who lived in the gulch in 1860. The newcomer stumbled upon gold — but a very special kind of gold. Farncomb's find twisted in interlocked strands of pure, highest-quality crystallized gold. He hurriedly hunted his treasure's source, knowing placer gold usually washes down from a neighboring mountain. On the hill immediately above his placer claim, Farncomb found his stunning "wire patch", a deposit of rich, sculptured wire gold. He spent the next several months quietly purchasing property on the hill.

Word of fabulous wire gold leaked out. Resentment flared when miners discovered that Harry Farncomb owned practically every known wire patch claim.

Greed then prompted the infamous "Ten Years War", a protracted squabble over ownership of Harry Farncomb's wire-gold nugget patches on Farncomb Hill. Denver capitalists formed a group to dispute Farncomb's rights to several acres in claims. Their legal battle to wrest control of this wildly rich acreage from Farncomb constituted the first phase of the Ten Years War. Colorado mining lawyers focused their energies on the case for years. Hundreds of thousands of dollars were "fired" as ammunition. The sole casualty: A Denver bank, involved in the strife, went broke.

Legal means failed. Litigants took up their guns and a real battle filled French Gulch with gunsmoke and bullets. Forty men fought the shoot-out battle that ranged up and down French Gulch for seven hours in the finest Western tradition. Three men died, many lay wounded and the ownership question remained unsolved.

Finally, an outside party purchased the disputed French Gulch land. Squabbling stopped, and an embattled French Gulch began mining again. Harry Farncomb emerged a richer man; his bonanza Elephant Mine had already made him a Midas.

While the Ten Year conflict was beginning to blister, Lincoln mushroomed into a thriving town. Originally called Paige City for an early resident, the town's earliest site stood one mile from its present French Gulch location, according to Colorado ghost town historian, Muriel Sibell Wolle.

Methodist preacher, Father John Lewis Dyer, became an early Lincoln resident. He headquartered his high-country missionary work there in 1862-63, purchasing an 18-square foot cabin with earthen floor, gunny-sack carpet and a table which he covered with two copies of the *Northwestern Christian Advocate*, as a makeshift tablecloth.

The Speer and Conant smelter, listed in an 1875 *Colorado Business Directory*, filled a vital need for French Gulch mines with its ten-ton per day furnace.

Crofutt's 1885 guide lists Lincoln as having one store, two hotels (the Wheeler and the Perkins), three refining furnaces, one stamp mill with 15 stamps to crush ore, one steam sawmill and several companies engaged in hydraulic mining.

The 1885 *Colorado Business Directory* also mentions Mrs. Ganger's Eckhart

Mine worker made $3 daily in 1880's, risked cave-ins, frozen limbs, blast injury.

Pioneer Giberson and Ruth families pose at 1908 Curtin. Tiny rail depot is right, rear.

House lodging, G. F. Williams' Lincoln City Hotel, Shea and Cook's Saloon, George Perkins' grocery and general hardware store, along with mine offices for the Elephant, Ontario, Morgan, Cincinnati and Franklin Mines. J. D. Bayes served as 1885 postmaster. The annual business directory was probably more up-to-date than Crofutt's guidebook.

Lincoln population figures vary. Some historians say that thousands lived in and around Lincoln. The 1885 *Business Directory* lists Lincoln population as 100.

The town had a school, in Summit School District No. 5, with 18 students in 1881-82. W. R. Pollack's private school at Lincoln, opened in 1862, was reportedly the first school in Summit County.

During Lincoln's early years, before the town obtained a postoffice, French Gulch miners took turns hiking to Breckenridge for mail. The town postmistress, who was drying some wire gold in her oven one day, busied herself hunting for the various miners' mail. The waiting French Gulch miner saw his chance. He slipped the gorgeous hunk of twisted gold into his shirt.

Yee-ow!!!

Forever seared into the skin across the miner's burly rib cage was a burning message: Honesty is the best policy.

Masontown, located one-half mile above and southeast of Frisco on the lower slope of Mount Royal, stands out as Summit's most disputed ghost town. Old-timers chuckle over reminiscences of the lively "Masontown fiddler", who made nearby Frisco "the quickest dancin' town in the Rockies". Other old-timers insist that the Masontown fiddler never existed — but that Frisco's own Ike Rouse fiddled up the music for those rollicking dances. Some story-tellers chronicle

Masontown's demise in a giant avalanche that smashed the town to smithereens on New Year's Eve 1912 — while Masontown residents reveled away the old year safely down in Frisco. Others, like Breckenridge's Helen Rich contended that a "slide", not an avalanche, may have slammed Masontown, but certainly not on frigid December 31, when snowslides are rare. No, the destruction occured in spring, when slides of heavy, compacted snow commonly break loose — and *not* in 1912. The town sat away from the main slide area and wasn't demolished until a fluke slide hit, probably in 1926.

Masontown's population inspired another debate: Helen Rich said the Mount Royal mine site never became a town at all. Mark Fiester, in *Blasted, Beloved Breckenridge*, estimated probably 10 to 12 cabins and buildings stood at Masontown. This history points to evidence of heavy dollar investment in Masontown mining and a population of several hundred.

No matter what the uncertainties about Masontown, one thing is sure: The men who moiled for gold and copper there all got busted. Huge dollar outlays went into Masontown. But almost nothing came out.

General Buford, an early Breckenridge settler, developed the old Victoria Mine in 1866 when its gold and copper potential emerged. Buford built a very expensive mill — and then vanished! In 1872, the Masontown Mining and Milling Company built a $75,000 reduction works with 20 stamps and a cyanide process facility, and renovated Buford's old mill. Finally, Masontown, named for its investors home, Masontown, Pennsylvania, swung into full operation. Backers, including A. E. Keables, Summit County Mining Exchange business manager and respected local mining authority, hoped to produce an $800 to $1,000 daily ore yield. A boarding house and new homes appeared. Several hundred people took up residence at Masontown, prospecting or working in mines or mills. Five main tunnels were excavated on mine sites. The mine shipped gold and silver to the Denver Mint. While shipping costs made staggering cuts in profits before the railroad arrived, the rail's proximity after 1882 solved these problems.

The Breckenridge *Bulletin* listed Masontown company officials in June, 1904. They were J. V. Hoover, president; A. E. Keables, secretary, superintendent and general manager; and S. R. Provins, treasurer. David Lawrence was mill superintendent.

Masontown's flurry of prosperity played out, along with Frisco-area mining in general around 1910. Later miners had little luck at Masontown. A Mr. Morrison leased the mine and sunk $5,000 into improvements. His yield: Nothing.

Fred Echternkamp worked the mine around 1915 for two years. Every few months his progress toward the main vein created excitement — but no big strikes ever emerged.

One thing that Masontown *did* produce was illegal whiskey during Prohibition. Bootleggers holed up there and locals whispered about a still.

In spring, 1926 (probably), a cornice broke loose and the resulting slide demolished Masontown, except for a few cabins on the town's far north side. The scar remains clearly evident on Mount Royal's slope. An earlier snowslide in 1912 probably destroyed Buford's old mill. A nice hiking trail leads from Frisco to Masontown. But don't walk it in spring. We know something that early Masontown residents apparently missed: Ill-starred Masontown sits on a long-established avalanche path!

Montezuma is not a ghost town in the true sense because people still live there. But "ghosts" abound from the 1880's heyday of this Snake River Mining District capitol. For a full profile of this intriguing and historic town, see Chapter 5.

Naomi, at the mouth of Rock Creek north of Silverthorne, provided a shipping point for mines in the Gore mountains above. Travelers on rough Post Road 32 to Kremmling stopped at Harry and Sadie Forche's Naomi Hotel, today on the privately-owned Rock Creek Ranch site. Naomi's slim population grew when lode mines were discovered in 1881 and '82. By June, 1892, male population totalled 80. Naomi received a postoffice with Harry Forche as postmaster.

Sadie Forche's sister, Esther Denecamp Hill Albee, arrived at Naomi from England in 1879. She was 16. Esther met and married one of the newcomers, lode miner Frederick Horatio Hill, a Maine native employed at the Boss Mine up in the Gore Range west of Naomi. The Hills later lived at Kokomo, Cripple Creek, Denver and Seattle.

In later years, the Naomi townsite passed into the ownership of the Gould brothers who ran a store, hotel and mine. They operated a sawmill for the mine and to make ties for the railroad already grading a path down the Blue from Dillon to Kremmling. (This route later fizzled.)

An intriguing account of how fate determined current ownership of old Naomi appears in *Women As Tall As Our Mountains*. Veronica Kohl writes that Gould ownership passed to a niece after death and later, through inheritance, to the niece's children, Marjorie and Eugene Lott. Fate intervened when Marjorie Lott met and married the grandson of pioneering Naomi residents Esther and Frank Hill, Raymond Hill, Jr. "Neither Marjorie or Raymond knew of Naomi's previous history or of their relationships to the property," Veronica Kohl writes.

Fire partly destroyed the old Naomi hotel during Gould ownership, but remnants of the century-old building still stand.

Parkville, a genuine gold rush boom town, spread at Georgia Gulch's mouth, five miles east of Breckenridge. Parkville soon emerged as "the" town in early Summit County. (Election rolls show 1800 male voters in 1860.) Elite of the pick and pan society gathered at Parkville, Summit County seat, where top touring stars and troupes, a brewery and one of Colorado's three early mints, soon flourished. Summit's first city declined quickly. By the 1880's, Parkville was ignominiously buried by its own tailings. A Masonic monument, marking the first Masonic Lodge west of the Divide, identifies Parkville, but was vandalized in recent years. (For more details on this Georgia Gulch metropolis, see Chapter 16.)

Preston perched atop Gibson Hill's north side on a good wagon road from the Gold Run Diggings. A postoffice, established July 13, 1875 under John Shock, postmaster, served a substation opened in October, 1887 at the prominent Jumbo

Mine. Discovered in known gold-bearing ground, the Jumbo strike triggered a stampede to the Preston area. A boardinghouse, sawmill, cabins and mine offices sprouted. Postmaster John Shock ran a produce store (fresh fruits and vegetables were a rare treat for miners) as well as the Preston boardinghouse. J. C. Wilson rounded out the miners' diet by launching a dairy business in 1888. Mrs. Hattie Shock delighted local ladies when she opened her millinery and dress-making shop in the mid-'80's.

Offices for the Gold Run Mining Company, Gold Run Placers and Consolidated Preston Mining Company headquartered at Preston.

The Jumbo Mine, a longtime producer, helped Preston survive the boom-bust cycle. Desolate poisoned trees and chalky white tailings below the Jumbo indicate the use of cyanide as a gold-refining chemical here.

Recen, a mining camp on Ten Mile Creek neighboring Kokomo, sprang up during the 1880's lode boom. The Recen brothers, early canyon pioneers with a mine bearing their name, founded the town on their 1873 placer claim site, a sandy bar off the Ten Mile River at the mouth of Searles Gulch. Kokomo and Recen, twin towns, merged into a single community after Kokomo's 1882 fire. (See Chapter 16.)

Rexford, set in a grassy meadow high on the Swan River's North Fork, offered a civilized collection of general store, assay office, saloon, boardinghouse-hotel, postoffice and the Rexford mine, just above town. Log cabins, built with the old square nails, remain at Rexford, but the wood frame general store has collapsed. This was a company town, like Sts. John. The Rexford Mine Company, listed in the 1884 *Colorado Business Directory*, owned properties all over the state, but headquartered at Rexford.

Old references mention a road from Rexford crossed the range to Montezuma and the Snake River Valley. A twice weekly mail delivery traveled this route over an 11,750-foot gap to the head of Sts. John Creek and down to Montezuma.

Despite large cash outlays, the Rexford Mining operation went under when the main lode, the Rochester King, pinched out.

Robinson sank community roots into rocky upper Ten Mile Canyon soil on a Sheep Mountain slope near Fremont Pass. Silver-laced Robinson once ranked as a leading Summit city, rivaling bustling Breckenridge. Leadville merchant George Robinson, spearheaded an admirable town with the Robinson Hotel, a bank, smelting and milling works, newspaper, church, school, sawmills and a variety of flourishing businesses. Robinson now remains buried under Climax Mine tailings. (To further explore Robinson's dynamic history, see Chapter 16.)

Sts. John, a prim, starched-collar replica of Boston, the home of its investors, blossomed in a meadow beside Glacier Mountain above Montezuma. Swaying skeletons of old structures still remain to testify to Sts. John's fascinating history, beginning in 1863 with Colorado's first silver strike there. (For a closer look at old Sts. John, see Chapter 16.)

Spencerville: W. W. Spencer founded this town in December, 1860, after discovering gold. Spencerville, only a temporary town, was located in Dry Gulch, a ravine near gold-abundant Georgia Gulch.

Swan City: Delighted prospectors held a miner's meeting on May 1, 1880, to organize a new town near their recent, and highly rewarding, gold strikes. Situated in a timber forest on the Swan River at the mouth of Brown's Gulch, Swan City had a postoffice by August, 1880, a store, hotel and Dickson's Saloon. Both placer and quartz (lode) mines flourished here, with ores assayed at values of $800 a ton. The historic Cashier and IXL Mines triggered a population influx to Swan City, which grew to sizable proportions. Big mines in the nearby gulches established offices here. Broncho Dave Braddock's stage ran from Breckenridge to Swan City in the 1880's (with Dave hand-shoveling in winter to maintain service). Ore wagons lumbered from the Hamilton, Cashier, IXL and others down the road from Swan City to Braddocks and the rail line.

Swan City's school opened for classes on February 11, 1884.

Residents enjoyed an abundance of game in nearby forests. Early writers glowed over the area's plentiful deer, bear, elk, grouse, turkeys and fine trout.

A few cabins remain in the woods at Swan City, but the dredges smothered this once-dynamic community with a fatal dump of gravel tailings.

Swandyke, on the Swan River's Middle Fork below the soaring Continental Divide, sits in a vast natural amphitheater. Gold lay close to the surface here. Lode mines proliferated. The Brilent Mine, above Swandyke, perches at 13,000 feet. Two hundred residents lived in Swandyke or nearby. The town blossomed in the late '90's, with a postoffice established April 12, 1899. A February 5, 1898 Summit County *Journal* detailed the progress of this late-bloomer during the famous Big Snow winter: "The reports from Swandyke are encouraging for those who have braved a cold but beautiful winter in that gold-bearing camp." A new butcher shop, saloon and barber shop, plus a boarding house, were part of a "summer building boom", according to the *Journal*. Swandyke also had a general store, blacksmith shop and ore mills nearby to accommodate mines. Stagecoach service from the railroad at Jefferson in South Park brought Denver visitors to Swandyke in a one-day trip, despite the hairy descent from Georgia Pass.

A few cabins remain on a grassy hill at Swandyke. A jeep road to the site became nearly impassable in summer, 1978.

Tiger, located on the Swan River about five miles east of Highway 9, lasted until the early 1970's, as an intact "ghost" town. (Some buildings had fallen victim to dredging, but many remained.) Furniture, pot-bellied stoves and utensils left in buildings reminded the curious of Tiger's high-riding days as a vigorous mine community. Today, the old assay office, built with square nails, still stands, rescued by the Summit Historical Society and U.S. Forest Service when the rest of historic Tiger burned. Transient residents of the 1960's flower-power generation had overtaken the old town of Tiger, despite repeated warnings by the U.S. Forest Service and Bureau of Land Management (BLM) to *get out!* Finally, in 1973, the Forest Service, Breckenridge Fire Department, and BLM torched all the buildings at Tiger, except the assay office, to roust out the non-paying tenants there. Furnishings had disappeared from houses, but the assay office, with its brick retort oven, remained intact. Today, even the old oven has

185

Rent, light, water and medical service were free at idyllic mine company town, Tiger. But tragic 1918 flu siege killed many. The Martins (2nd and 3rd from left) succumbed.

been torn apart by souvenir-seekers.

The 1900's town of Tiger emerged when the Royal Tiger Mines Company's John A. Traylor discovered untapped profit potential in the abandoned IXL lode (one of neighboring Swan City's heavy producers in the 1880's and 1890's). Traylor purchased the IXL in 1917, built a 500-ton mill and pushed through the IXL tunnel to connect with Swan City's old Cashier Mine.

The names "Tiger" and "Royal Tiger" derive from the Spanish custom of using the name for prominent mines. Spain's famous "Tigre", as well as Mexican and South American mines repeat the name.

Like Sts. John and Rexford, Tiger became a company town maintained by the most solicitous of early 1900's companies. Nothing was too good for Royal Tiger Mines Company employees. Electricity, a steam heating plant and a water works supplied the town. Tiger boasted a good school, Mrs. J. B. Ahearn's hospitable boarding house, a bunkhouse, office building, mill, blacksmith shop, Oliver Swanson's sawmill and the assay office. Free movies and dances livened up the weekends. And a company physician, Dr. W. G. Smith, offered his services to a 250-population.

The doctor must have been busy during the tragic Summit flu epidemic that hit hardest at Tiger in 1918. A 15-year-old Mary Cluskey Ruth, who waitressed at the Tiger commissary during mealtimes and sorted ore the rest of the day, had the flu three times. Her father, Chris Cluskey, worked as head teamster with 18 teams to oversee. During the flu siege, he took on the sad task of driving flu victims' bodies to Breckenridge — sometimes as many as four bodies daily.

A depression-ridden Summit County basked in the prosperity of the Royal Tiger Mines Company and its heavily-subsidized town. Tiger school children composed and performed a song in gratitude. A few lines from "Tiger":

Oh time will tell the tale, of the richness of the ground
Lead, gold and silver shipped out yearly
And there's pretty rainbow trout in the waters all around.
Tiger, the place we all love dearly

Tiger mines produced enough gold to keep men and machines busy until the late 1930's. The pretty little school had already closed, and the Tiger Club had taken over its building. Tiger's postoffice closed in November, 1940.

When the Royal Tiger Mines shut down, significant mining in the incredibly-rich Swan Valley, begun in February, 1860 with the discovery of Gold Run, ground to a halt. But Tiger ranks as outstanding among Summit mines because its blue-ribbon lodes delivered ore almost steadily from 1864 to 1939, a 75-year output.

Valdoro: When the Colorado Gold Dredging Company contracted with Milwaukee's Bucyrus Company to build two new electric dredges on-site beside the lower Swan River, a little construction camp called Valdoro emerged. The year was 1907. The site was about one-half mile in from the Swan's confluence with the Blue River, just below dredge pioneer Ben Stanley Revett's elegant home, Swan's Nest.

Valdoro became a thriving camp, boosted by an equally thriving dredge industry. In March 1907, Colorado Dredging Company superintendent Tuttle oversaw construction of an "immense" boardinghouse and bunkhouse at Valdoro. A railroad spur traveled the half-mile from the Colorado & Southern main track along the Blue to serve Valdoro. The town's boardinghouse became the scene of merry dances, with a bounteous midnight supper to cap the fun for Breckenridge's high-spirited young.

The two proud new dredges, built at Valdoro, launched operation May 1, 1908, with townspeople cheering the gold boats' debut. But dredge tailings, depositied by the gold barges, eventually inundated once vigorous Valdoro.

Wapiti was called Victoria until March, 1894. This tiny town atop famous Farncomb Hill produced the beautiful crystallized "wire" gold that made Breckenridge — and Wapiti owner John Campion — renowned. Wire gold snared first prizes at the 1893 World Columbian Exposition in Chicago. Its nuggets were so beautiful that they were used for jewelry and keepsake items, rather than to convert to cash. John Campion's unrivaled 200-nugget wire gold collection from near Wapiti is Farncomb Hill's largest.

Ben Stanley Revett managed Campion's Wapiti group before he spearheaded his first gold dredge on the Swan River. A large building at Wapiti housed mine office, living quarters, and postoffice, granted in 1894. George Moon was Wapiti's first postmaster. Fire has destroyed a nearby stable-barn, but the old headquarters still remains.

Wild Irishman Mine Camp: Situated in a pretty, wooded meadow near timberline, on Glacier Mountain, the Wild Irishman became a heavy producer of silver in the late 1870's. The "legend" of its origin goes this way: A free-spirited Irish New York policeman, Michael Dulhaney, came west to Colorado and struck it rich at the mine site high above Montezuma and Sts. John. They say his whoops of joy backed up the rushing waters of Sts. John Creek and washed away three silver camps!

The hard-working, hard-playing Dulhaney, always wore his battered police-man's hat. His mine camp never became more than a small settlement, but it still stands, with three cabins in good condition. The old mine, with its little railway, stands nearby.

Wheeler, an 1880's town located in the Ten Mile Canyon at the base of Vail Pass, has blossomed today into a ski resort community — Copper Mountain. A century ago, Judge John S. Wheeler's hay fields spread across the valley and provided grazing for his cattle. The Wheeler hiking trail, climbing the Ten Mile Range and crossing over alpine tundra to South Park, was Wheeler's old stock trail.

Wheeler pioneered a much-needed sawmill for Wheeler Flats in 1878 to supply timber to bustling Ten Mile mine camps and to furnish ties for a coming railroad. Eventually, a town sprang up at Wheeler Junction. Half a dozen sawmills, saloons, a billiard hall, blacksmith shop, wagon shop, notary office, postoffice (in April, 1880), lodgings (including a hotel with real china dishes instead of tin plates) and Judge Wheeler's general store served a peak population of 225 lively local residents and more in outlying camps. The Summit County *Journal* described Wheeler as " . . . the wildest spot in the county".

Crofutt's *Gripsack Guide to Colorado* lists ore assays on "prospects" as $40-$90 per ton silver in the mountains around Wheeler. Nearby Graveline Gulch boasted some well-known silver mines.

Sawmills also sprouted in the wooded mountains near Wheeler. Twenty-nine sawmills hewed logs from the canyon's timbered slopes into boards, beams for mines and rail ties. Smoke puffed from their steam engines up through the trees and their racket echoed against mountain walls. According to Ten Mile Canyon history buff Penny Lewis, all this logging activity attracted Swedes, traditionally skilled loggers, and these immigrants became the majority population in the Wheeler area. Two Swedish loggers built the Ollie Lind cabin in the late 1880's. (Swedish newspapers covered logs inside and an original wood stove remains in two cabins preserved at Copper Mountain.)

Probably one of the least boisterous members of the Wheeler community was the county superintendent of schools who walked daily from Frisco to his Wheeler office. The superintendent's annual salary in 1882-84 came to $268.60.

Like many high-country towns, Wheeler suffered devastation by fire, in April, 1882. The Kokomo newspaper reported:

FIRE AT WHEELER
The Little Gem in the Ten Mile Valley Almost Obliterated

A serious loss occurred to our esteemed fellow citizen Judge Wheeler, last Thursday afternoon at 3:30. Some persons on the street noticed a smell of fire, and had no sooner given the alarm than flames were seen to burst forth from the upper windows of the building next to the post-office. The fire spread with such rapidity that the cluster of buildings, including the general store, post-office, milk house, store room and the judge's private office were soon a mass of embers.

No appliance to successfully fight the fire being at hand, the attention of all was directed to saving the goods, but owing to the rapidity of the fire but a small portion were saved. The post-office fixtures, grocery store, wagon shop, tools, etc. went like a flash.

Great credit is due to two of the saw mill men for their efforts to save the premises; also to four Cornish miners, who were passing by at the time. The Judge's dwelling house was saved principally by the efforts of the D. & R. G. station agent, who worked like a hero. At one time it was thought the whole village would have to succomb to the flames.

During the excitement Mrs. Wheeler sprained her ankle severely, and is at present confined to her room.

The property is insured in the Home, Columbus, Ohio, for $750, and in the Argentine of Denver, for $1250. Summit county extends its sympathy to the Judge in his affliction, and it is to be hoped the insurance companies will come promptly forward and adjust the loss.

During winter, 1898-99, slides and drifts 20 to 30 feet buried the wagon road near Wheeler. Snowstorms had already forced a railroad shutdown. Travel all but ceased. However, the New York *Times* reported on February 13: "Two prospectors on snowshoes arrived in Leadville today from Wheeler. It took them four days to make the trip . . . There is enough food at Wheeler . . . to last 10 days with care . . ."

More mine camps than those detailed here existed in Summit County. Most of them experienced the boom-bust cycle so quickly that no information on their brief histories remains.

Ox, Burro and Mare:

The Summit Transportation Story Till the 1880's

Prospectors pushed over Summit passes in droves, seeking silver and gold. They battled dangerous dust-choked or mud-clogged trails in pack trains, bumped and jostled on ox-drawn freight wagons and, later, hazarded stormy high passes in stage coaches.

Before the railroad came to Summit County in 1882, miners faced a big problem: How to get needed machinery and supplies to isolated high-country mine sites. And, how to get cumbersome gold and silver ores to mills and smelters without pinching profits. Scaling tortuous Continental Divide passes on rough, rock-strewn roads with loaded ox-drawn freight wagons proved a horrendous feat in summer, an impossibility in winter.

Wagon rates averaged about $18 per ton, but could run as high as $29 per ton, more than the per ton cost of the ocean route from New York to California via Cape Horn. Wagon freight rates could double during winter months.

Lucrative freight-hauling business finally opened Summit County, luring entrepreneurs to build toll roads linking Denver to the mountain mining districts, and prompted the race between competing rail lines to lay track to the new boom towns. Railroad moguls, like the Union Pacific's Jay Gould, believed they could cut the $18 wagon rate to $10 per ton and corner the big mining boom freight market.

Summit County transportation routes had been established centuries earlier by wandering buffalo, game and Ute Indians. Colonel John C. Fremont, exploring the Blue Valley in 1843, easily chose Hoosier Pass as his route south because the trail was well-tramped by migrating buffalo.

But travelers did not find these routes in and out of "crow's nest" Summit County easy. Of eleven mountain passes used before 1882, nine ascended the Continental Divide, from the nation's highest Rocky Mountain pass, soaring 13,132-foot Argentine to a relative "piece of cake", demure 11,318-foot Fremont, which gently climbs the Continental Divide from the Ten Mile Canyon to Leadville.

The Passes:

Early prospectors, miners, settlers and travelers in Summit County traversed these eleven passes:

Boreas Pass, 11,482 feet, from Breckenridge to Como in Park County, crossing the wind-swept Continental Divide with steep grades and, in winter, incredibly deep snow and drifts. Breckenridge Pass, Hamilton Pass and Tarryall Pass were its early names.

Georgia Pass, 11,598 feet, a steep ascent from old Parkville, the former county seat, and the south fork of the Swan River across the Divide, beside towering 13,370-foot Mount Guyot, to Jefferson in Park County.

French Pass, 12,057 feet, from French Gulch across the Divide toward Tarryall in Park County.

Hoosier Pass, 11,541 feet, from Breckenridge over the Divide to Alma and Fairplay in Park County. Homesick Indiana prospectors named it around 1860.

Argentine Pass, 13,132 feet, a wind-blasted, steep, snaking climb from old Decatur in the Peru Creek Mining District to the Continental Divide summit, then an easy roll down to Georgetown in Clear Creek County. Called Sanderson Pass in the 1860's for a pioneer stage coaching family, it became known as Snake River Pass in 1870's.

Webster Pass, 12,108 feet, heavily-used Continental Divide route from Montezuma via Handcart Gulch and Hall Valley to Webster in Park County.

Fremont Pass, 11,318 feet, from old Kokomo and Robinson past Climax and over the Divide to Leadville in Lake County. Once called Alicante Pass, it bears the name of Colonel John C. Fremont, who never crossed it.

Pack train crosses log bridge enroute to Peak 10. Look for "jack" trails, snaking easily down the steepest slopes, in mining areas.

Grizzly Pass, 13,093 feet, ascends Grizzly Gulch from Bakersville to cross the Divide and descend via the Snake River's North Fork. Also called Irwin Pass and Quail Pass, the route was once planned as a wagon road.

Loveland Pass, 11,992 feet, from Dillon east to old Haywood-Keystone area followed the Snake River's north fork over the Divide to Georgetown in Clear Creek County. William Austin Hamilton Loveland built it in 1879 hoping the pass would become a rail route for his Colorado Central Railway.

Ute Pass, 9,524 feet, an ancient Indian route from the lower Blue Valley, crosses 11 miles to the William's Fork Road in Grand County. Ute Pass does not cross the Continental Divide.

Vail Pass, 10,601 feet, from Eagle County across the Gore Range to Wheeler Flats (today's Copper Mountain village area). This relatively low pass, not a Continental Divide crossing, served as an Indian route in early years; gold rush traffic came over passes from the Eastern Slope.

Bayard Taylor, the genteel and gentlemanly traveler of the 1860's, ascended Hoosier Pass following his visit to Breckenridge in 1866. Despite the fact that it was June, he found deep snow on Hoosier. "The snow-drifts lay thick all around, the grass was just beginning to shoot and the three months summer of the higher ranges . . . had barely made its appearance."

Summer is like a passing breeze on those high mountain passes.

Taylor went on to characterize some of the county's mountain transportation routes:

> There has been some doubt concerning the practicability of the pass . . this is called, I believe, the Hoosier Pass; a little to the east of it is the Tarryall Pass, from Hamilton to Breckenridge (Boreas), which is traversed by vehicles, even during the winter. There is also a direct trail from Breckenridge to Georgetown, near the head of the Snake River (Argentine Pass).

Then Bayard predicted the only major Summit transportation route available today that early miners didn't use: "Without doubt other and probably better points for crossing the mountains will be found, when they are more thoroughly explored." The final pass is the Eisenhower Tunnel which is undoubtedly better because it goes under, not over, the Continental Divide.

Samuel Bowles traveled Boreas Pass in 1868 and wrote this description:

> There was a good wagon road all our way, leading from Breckenridge to the summit of Breckenridge Pass, through open woods, flower-endowed meadows, a broken, various and interesting mountain country, often giving majestic views of the higher and snow-crowned peaks, with glimpses of valleys and parks below and beyond. The Pass is just above the timber line, about twelve thousand feet high, and as we mounted it, a cold storm gathered upon the snowfields above us, wheeled from peak to peak in densely black clouds, and soon broke in gusts of wind, in vivid lightning, in startlingly close and loud claps of thunder, in driving snow, in pelting hail, in drizzling rain . . . The rapidity of its passage from side to side, from peak to peak was wonderful; the crashing loudness of its thunderous discharges awful; one moment we felt like "fleeing before the Lord," the next charmed and awed into rest in His presence.

Geologist William Brewer described a stormy Argentine Pass in 1869 when he wrote:

> . . . a desolate trail . . . the howling wind which at times swept in fierce gusts past us, the fog seething in the abyss below like steam in a giant cauldron, of which we would catch occasional glimpses . . .

Early prospectors poured over the range from South Park via Boreas, Hoosier and Georgia Passes. Later, Webster Pass became a main freight route between the Montezuma and Peru mining districts and Denver, via South Park. Boreas Pass, to South Park and Denver, served Breckenridge as a route to the ore markets.

Since silver-laced Leadville stood as the destination of many travelers from Denver, the most used routes after the 1878 silver boom there were Loveland and Fremont Passes. When the Denver, South Park & Pacific Railroad crossed Summit County enroute to Leadville, it came over Boreas to Breckenridge, down the Blue to Frisco, then it turned up the Ten Mile Canyon and over Fremont Pass to the silver capitol.

Both pack trains and freight wagons hauled supplies into a thriving Summit County. Pack trains cost two or three times more than wagon freight, but the trains could travel roughter terrain. (Builders soon learned to order lumber longer than needed because the packers hauled it Indian style, with the boards dragging behind the pack animals.)

Horses, mules and burros provided pack train pulling power, but these same horses, mules and burros often succumbed to the rigors of mountain winter trail work. Early 1860's Georgia Gulch miner Daniel Conner told the story in his Journal:

Pack trains traversed tougher terrain than wagons. Summit's first wagon roads were built in 1860's, but pack trains continued in use.

During the winter, when a pack train would come over to the gulch, some of the animals were sure to miss the beaten trail, which was constantly hidden by the constantly drifting snow from the action of the winds, and when once off the trail the poor creature was lost. The pack of provisions would be taken off, and the animal left to work deeper into the snow as he struggled, until he was finally left to be drifted over by the ever-changing snow. A little burro could be lifted upon the beaten trail again when he was unlucky enough to wander off of it, but the larger mules and horses were promptly deserted when they made the fatal misstep.

Pack trains provided an early answer to Summit supply problems, but clearly wagon roads had become a must.

Post Roads

Toll roads, the answer to road-building incentive, came early in Summit County's history. The Colorado Territorial Legislature, beginning September 9, 1861, passed incorporation of toll roads. The earliest Summit toll roads served the Breckenridge mining region.

On October 11, 1861, the Denver, Bradford and Blue River Road Company incorporated. Its route: Denver to Bradford in South Park, along the north fork of the Platte River and on to Hamilton, then over Boreas Pass to Breckenridge.

On November 6, 1861, the Park Junction, Georgia and French Gulch Road Company came into being. This toll road would run from DeHart's Ranch in South Park to Jefferson over "Swan River Pass" (Georgia) to Parkville, in Georgia Gulch, then to Humbug and French Gulches.

On November 8, 1861, the Breckenridge, Buckskin Joe and Hamilton Wagon Road Company announced its plans to cross Hoosier Pass from South Park.

On August 15, 1862, the Empire City, New Pass and Montgomery City Road Company planned to pass through Summit County from the north, cross Hoosier and terminate in the old town of Montgomery, a flash-in-the-pan camp just below the Hoosier summit.

On February 5, 1866, the South Park, Blue River and Middle Park Wagon Road Company announced its intention to connect South Park with the Blue River mines and travel down the Blue River to Kremmling.

On January 11, 1867, the Georgetown and Breckenridge Wagon Road Company stated plans to route a post road from Georgetown up Clear Creek to Grizzly Fork, then over Irwin Pass to the north fork of the Snake River down to the junction of the Snake and Blue (later to become the site of Dillon) and up the Blue to Breckenridge.

Most of the post roads consisted of a wagon track with boulders and large rocks removed. The roads were anything but level. Heavily-loaded ore wagons and, in winter, sleds could, and did, tip over. But road builders did their "level best" in rocky mountainous terrain without modern tools or machinery. Neither steam shovel nor air drill existed. Dynamite, invented in 1866, was costly to ship.

These roads served Summit placer miners in the 1860's. The development of lode mining here lingered, particulary in the canyon-locked Ten Mile Mining District and the rugged Snake River District, because, as 1880's historian Frank Fosset pointed out, there were no good wagon roads for transportation of ore.

On October 18, 1878, the Snake River and Hall Valley Wagon Road Company opened its toll gates. The company had organized with outstanding Snake River Valley citizens, Franz Fohr, John Yonley, Colonel Sampson Ware and William Candler from the Sts. John Mine and W. P. Haywood as trustees. The company sold 1,000 shares at $10 each. William and Emerson Webster of South Park cooperated with the Montezuma mining men to build the pioneering road from Webster in South Park to Montezuma. Stephen Decatur in the October 18, 1878, *Colorado Miner* heralded the road as a landmark to "Progress":

> The blockade on the mining industry of the Snake River Mining District has been raised. The Snake River and Hall Valley Wagon Road has been completed. Hipla! Hurrah! Carry the news everywhere! A new route to Leadville — Montezuma the halfway station! . . . The road just finished is said to be the smoothest and have the easiest grade of any pass in the state. There is joy in the Halls of Montezuma!

Webster Pass, Post Road No. 40, became a main shipping route for Montezuma ores to Denver, unlocking the ore jammed up in the isolated Snake River Valley.

In 1869, Stephen Decatur's "baby", the Georgetown and Snake River Wagon Road over skyscraping Argentine Pass, opened. The road connected with the Colorado Central Railway from Denver to Georgetown. The road climbed Argentine from Georgetown, descended the pass to Decatur at Argentine's western foot, went on to Chihuahua and Montezuma. The toll gate, located on the old road between Chihuahua and Montezuma, bore the warning that gate crashers would pay a stiff fine of $10. (Slipping past toll gates without paying became a tempting challenge for 1880's travelers.)

Georgetown and Snake River wagon road had toll gate near Chihuahua. Forks, still visible, led left to Montezuma, right to Keystone-Dillon.

Toll rates on the Argentine Pass road were slightly lower than the average charges, which were:

    1 vehicle with 1 span horses, mules or cattle $1.00
    each additional pair draft animals   .25
    1 horse or mule with rider   .25
    loose horses, mules, cattles or asses   .10
    sheep, hogs or goats   .05
    funeral processions   free

The Argentine route, arduous and accident-prone, served as a post road until 1883, when the railroad arrived at Keystone.

Another, better road, completed in 1879, provided a more manageable link with the Colorado Central at Georgetown. The new "High Line" wagon road scaled Loveland Pass as Post Road No. 13, crossing the Divide 1,500 feet lower than Argentine and providing a route 70 miles shorter than any other route from Denver to Leadville. Enthusiastic backers of the new Loveland Pass road began work in February, 1879, in deep snow.

"The road will cost three times what it would if built in the summer," the Georgetown *Courier* reported February 20, 1879, "but as the company are anxious to turn the spring travel over the route, they are willing to make the sacrifice . . ."

Mother Nature smiled on W. A. H. Loveland's road-building efforts. Scanty snow that 1878-79 winter smoothed construction along. The 60-mile dirt track, completed June 1, 1879, proved a full day's trip for a four-horse team. (Automobiles today skim the modern Loveland Pass highway route in 25 minutes.)

Local residents also used the toll road concept to solve the problem of local freighting from individual mines into nearby towns. Douglas Walter, in his "Historic Sites in Summit County", provided this quote from the Breckenridge *Daily Journal,* June 7, 1881, which shows how a road to Crystal Lake was created:

> On the north fork (Spruce Creek), the road can be built for $750 to Crystal Lake and all mines reached by short trails; various plans have been proposed, but the most popular one is to secure a charter for a toll road and issue stock to those who perform labor on the road. On Monday twenty men commenced work and the road will probably be passable before next Saturday night . . .

The Stage Lines

Stagecoach lines crisscrossed Summit County to serve local travelers and the bustling business of passenger travel between Denver and Leadville.

Local stage lines, like Broncho Dave Braddock's service from Breckenridge to Swan City, Delaware Flats and Galena Gulch along the Swan River, were launched by enterprising individuals. Broncho Dave's stage, begun on February 21, 1881, later expanded with a route from Breckenridge to Lincoln City in French Gulch.

Braddock battled all kinds of difficulties, from malicious mischief done to his horses, to deep snow, to keep his line running. The Summit County *Journal* reported: "The irrepressible Braddock, in order to keep open the road from

Braddockville to Swan City, during the later weeks of winter, had to shovel nearly the whole distance."

Six major stage coach lines linked Summit County to the outside world in the early 1880's. The best used four- and six-horse Concord coaches and charged passengers 12-15 cents per mile. The worst used rough open wagons at lesser rates. Six main routes were:

1. Georgetown via Peru Creek Valley to Kokomo in the North Ten Mile, daily during summer

2. Breckenridge to Hot Sulphur Springs in Middle Park via the Blue River, once weekly.

3. Breckenridge to Kokomo, via Frisco (26 miles), three times weekly.

4. Webster to Breckenridge, via Montezuma, then Sts. John, next to Preston, Lincoln City and Breckenridge (39 miles), Monday, Wednesday and Friday.

5. Como and Hamilton to Breckenridge, 18 miles over Boreas, six times weekly in Spottswood and McClellan's Concord coaches.

6. Georgetown to Kokomo (and connecting to Leadville) via Montezuma and Frisco, daily in Concord coaches.

Ore wagons, like this one hauling 1909 Princess silver ore, rumbled regularly along Summit roads. Princess was 1866 Sukey, then '80's Silver King.

The story of the "High Line" stage over Loveland Pass and its dynamic developer, Silas W. Nott, typifies the enthusiasm and energy of Summit's lively 1880's. The Georgetown *Courier* ran regular and glowing reports of Nott's progress in pioneering the new stage route that would transport Denver rail passengers from Georgetown all the way to Leadville in a one-day coach trip.

(Nott, a well-known Georgetown livery stable owner, originally planned to use Argentine Pass, but the 1879 completion of the Loveland Pass road coincided with the debut of his stage line's opening and provided a less treacherous route with shorter mileage.)

Silas Nott had a guaranteed market. "The company will have a pledge from the U.P. (Union Pacific) and the C.C. (Colorado Central) that they will send their passengers from the East direct to Georgetown, so they can leave here in the morning and reach Leadville the same day," the *Courier* reported on March 6, 1879.

On June 26, the *Courier* said:

> S. W. Nott started a passenger and express line from Georgetown to Kokomo, which, for the present, will be run tri-weekly. Teams will leave Georgetown Mondays, Wednesdays, and Fridays, and returning will leave Kokomo on Tuesdays, Thursdays, and Saturdays. Travel on the road is increasing and we presume it will not be a great while before a daily line will be established.

In July, Mr. Nott snared the U.S. postal service contract to carry daily mail between Georgetown and Kokomo. Daily stage service was a boon to travelers, the *Courier* wrote on July 2, 1879: ". . . the shortest, cheapest and most direct route from Denver to Kokomo, Leadville, the Gunnison country, and the whole of that vast country beyond the range which is now rapidly filling up with newcomers."

One passenger marveled that in the very heart of the Rocky Mountains a stage could travel 30 miles without ever encountering a hill. From the base of Loveland Pass through Frisco to Kokomo, this was true.

Nott's advertised fares were $7 to Kokomo and $10 to Leadville, with "no walking — no dust — no danger". Summer traffic began at 10-15 passengers per day. But by September, 1879, Nott purchased and put into service three new Concord coaches with double six-horse teams to handle the surging popularity of his brisk new line. The *Courier* lavished praise:

> Staging with all its pristine glory has been revived in Northern Colorado by the Nott line from this place to Leadville. Six-horse Concord coaches, in charge of the best drivers in the Rocky Mountains make the trip by daylight; and on no other road in the mountains is their time equalled. Pearly Wasson and Ed Cooke, two men who, we may say, have been raised on the ox, handle the lines, and in their charge the patrons of the line feel as safe as at home. This route is now by far the pleasantest and safest from Denver to the carbonate camp, and the growing business shows that the traveling public appreciate it.

Winter snows failed to daunt Nott's dedication to keep the "High Line" running. He switched from coaches to sleds, as the *Courier* noted on November 14, 1879: "While the coaches from the terminus of the South Park road to Leadville found it almost impossible to cross the range during the snow storm last week, the High Line coaches from this place passed through without difficulty."

Avalanches, perilous road conditions and punishing snows characterized mountain winter travel. Nott's enterprising stage line encountered his share of these, as a report from Kokomo's Summit County *Times* reveals:

> The Loveland coach, which left Kokomo on Saturday afternoon, encountered a great storm in the heights of the Rockys on Sunday. Aboard this coach was the writer and a half a dozen other passengers with a very sick man. The storm raged with fury in the early morning, but not until reaching an altitude of twelve thousand feet did it burst with full force upon the benighted passengers. Commingled with snow and sleet, it came upon us, never letting up, never abating. The summit was reached and descent began. When just above timberline, the sleigh was stopped by a formidable snow slide just ahead. To clear it away all hands were employed for an hour, and the long train of sleighs, freight wagons and horsemen started again, when a second slide much greater and more powerful than the former was encountered. It had fallen from the crest of a mountain and filled the road and bridge across a gulch to a depth of from six to ten feet. This again necessitated considerable delay and much wearisome labor. Finally about four o'clock, after the lead horses were turned loose and urged to escape from the drifts, the train made its safe exit from the ordeal of trial, and the coach reached the way station down the summit an hour later. At eight o'clock, the snorting six-horse team had unloaded its precious load of freight.

Horses slipped on icy roads and their shoes cut into their feet, so Nott's teams went unshod in winter. When the animals stepped off the packed snow surface, they sank into deep snow. Quick action prevented their burial. Drivers placed a blanket roll beneath the horse's head to avoid suffocation, then rigged a block and tackle using the wagon tongue as a derrick, to lift the horse from the deep drift.

Getting across the summit of Loveland Pass in the face of icy, stinging winds that swept the area above timberline provided a challenge. Just before the summit, the horses were given a short breathing spell. Then came a sprint across the mountaintop, a rush down to the protection of the tree line.

Drivers bundled up in long coats and caps, with burlap wrappings on their feet. Burlap offered more grip and more warmth than overshoes.

The "High Line" continued to operate through the winter of 1879-80. On February 12, 1880, the *Courier* reported:

> Business over the High Line is steadily increasing. On Tuesday morning Nott sent three coaches out carrying 21 passengers. Two coaches leave every morning now, and as soon as the weather moderates a little he will probably send three or four out every morning.

Mr. Nott's efforts did not go unappreciated. The Kokomo newspaper lauded his industry in March, 1880:

> Mr. S.W. Nott, the pioneer stage man of the High Line road, is doing more for Summit county than almost any man in it. In addition to projecting the main route through the deep snow of late last winter, and making it the favorable route, he has established branch lines to Decatur, Chihuahua and Breckenridge. Mr. Nott deserves great credit for his efforts, and every enterprising citizen will commend him for his business industry.

Nott redoubled his efforts. The *Courier* announced on April 29, 1880:

> Mr. S.W. Nott received seventeen fine Iowa horses on Thursday last,

which will be used on his Leadville and Breckenridge coach line. He now has one hundred horses on the line and nine drivers. He has a force of twenty men employed at shoveling snow and placing the road in good condition so that further use of sleighs this season will not be necessary.

Heavy spring snows and warm weather created soft snow conditions that almost stopped travel on the High Line. Horses became stuck in the deep, slushy snow and coaches couldn't travel atop it. Finally, around May 20, Nott dispatched a large crew of shovelers to clear the snow from the road over the range.

An unusually stormy winter the next year, 1880-81, dumped continual heavy snows on the Loveland Pass road. Nott's sleighs, plagued by impassable roads, snowslides and horses mired in deep snow, had to cease service temporarily. The mail traveled the range by snow-shoed carrier or, when possible, by horseback over Argentine to connect with sleighs at Decatur.

(Argentine Pass, because of its extreme height, was scoured clean of snow at the summit by strong, sweeping winds. Thus, it became a winter route alternate. But coaches couldn't travel the tight curves of tortuous Argentine. A Stoddard wagon, pulled by four horses, normally served on that challenging pass.)

Nott's drivers (among them Adolphus "Tip" Ballif, who would become an early Dillon resident) had a good safety record. Accidents vexed mountain stage lines; the newspapers regularly reported them. But even the most cautious

Hard-working horses enjoy dry road in August, 1914, but spring mud mired many an ore wagon. Miner's sign reads "Ford's Hill"

driver had to hazard rough, often icy roads. Nott's line had its accidents, such as the coach that overturned with 16 passengers near Fiske's Mill in the Snake River country in October, 1880.

But the worst tragedy occurred in 1881 on Argentine Pass when a neckyoke on one of the horses broke, throwing the animal to the ground. He crowded a second horse over the edge of the narrow road that clung to a cliffside. As the wagon tipped, it threw two passengers over the cliff. Two of four passengers jumped out before the wagon jolted, but the victims, both Frenchmen, were a blind man and a cripple. The blind man died; his companion suffered injuries.

Bridges presented danger when spring run-off coursed in torrents to weaken or wash them out. Stages carried huge planks for use in crossing road washout areas and to strengthen damaged bridges.

Passengers probably breathed a sigh of relief when they finally reached Warren's Station near the western foot of Loveland Pass. Built in 1879 by Chauncey Warren who later became mayor of Dillon, the hostelry was abandoned when rail service made stage coach travel obsolete. (One delighted visitor to Warren's Station pulled in a four and one-half foot long trout in the stream there.) The station burned in a December 16, 1882 fire.

Haywood, another rest stop, served travelers from Agentine and busy Webster Pass, as well as Loveland. Located on today's U.S. Highway 6 east of Keystone, about where the Loveland Pass Motel now stands, Mrs. Kate Haywood's station served travelers until the 1890's.

High Continental Divide passes provided thrills and spills for stage coach travelers. But authoress Alice Polk Hill encountered adventure on a simple stagecoach ride from Breckenridge to Frisco — practically a flatlands excursion. Her coach ran through a flash forest fire! She told the tale in her book, *Colorado Pioneers in Picture and Story*:

THE STAGE RIDE

Now arose a debate whether we should go to Leadville by way of Como or Frisco. We were informed that the coach left for Frisco every morning, and the road was level and smooth, through the prettiest valley that ever was seen.

The stage ride — that decided me. Mr. Smith, a walking embodiment of common sense, and the "brake and balance wheel" of the party, gave us the advice that Punch gives to people about to get married — "don't." But he might as well have said "do," for we immediately engaged passage in the stage, and I commenced to plan for myself a seat with the driver; for drivers are said to be living, breathing, talking encyclopaedias of western lore.

Promptly at the appointed hour the horn blew; we gathered our traps and were soon on the veranda of the hotel. But where was the coach? We anxiously looked about for one of those gaily decorated affairs, like the chariots in the circus... To our utter amazement "the coach" was a large three-seated spring wagon, painted in black and "old gold," and strikingly suggestive of an undertaker's rig.

I bounded to the front seat, eager that my chat with the driver should not prove a delusion also.

The driver regaled Mrs. Hill with stories of lost love in the San Juans. But suddenly, the stories ceased:

> There was no more time for talking, for we were drawing near a "fire in the mountains."
> The sight was grand; the long red tongues of fire were twining and lapping around the lofty pines up to the very top, and flying off in flags and sheets above.
> We began to feel their warm caresses, for the wind was in our direction. The flames had closed back of us, cutting off all retreat, and onward we must go.
> I hoisted my sun umbrella to keep off the sparks. Vesuvius couldn't hold a candle to them. The "whole region 'round about'" seemed on fire. My umbrella was reduced to a skeleton.
> Finally we all curled down in the bottom of the wagon "like breakfast bacon in a frying pan," except the driver, for he had to bend his energies to keeping the frantic horses in the road; as it was they traveled considerable zig-zag country. He would occasionally tell us to "keep cool." But it was a difficult thing to do under the circumstances.
> We were a sorry looking outfit when we arrived at Frisco. "O my!" and "Duty" were minus mane and tail, and cooked in spots. It was a burning shame.
> The driver's face was so black with smut, he looked like a coal heaver. He said, "That takes the eyebrows off of any fire I have ever seen."

It's this kind of surprise twist that jazzed up travel in the mountains 100 years ago. Today's skier traffic snaggles are ho-hum by comparison.

From 1859 until 1882 when the rails arrived, ox, burro and mare provided the go-power for passenger and freight travel in Summit County. When the brawny narrow gauge locomotives chugged onto the Summit scene, wagon, pack train and stagecoaches began their exit. But adventure — and misadventure — remained aplenty!

America's Highest

Narrow-Gauge Railway

One-hundred years ago, the dauntless Denver, South Park & Pacific Railroad raced it competitor, the Denver & Rio Grande, to complete rails to Colorado's rich mining camps. On August 7, 1882, its first, shiny, black, narrow-gauge locomotive chugged into Breckenridge. Having challenged and conquered steep, 11,482-foot Boreas Pass, the South Park line became the nation's highest narrow-gauge railway.

More anxious than most for the rails to arrive were the gold-rich placer and lode camps of the Blue River mining district, centered at Breckenridge, and the isolated silver towns perched high in Montezuma Canyon. For these Summit County towns, rough wagon toll roads over Continental Divide passes like Argentine to Georgetown and Boreas to South Park (or the less strenuous Hoosier Pass) provided only a fairweather link to the outside world. No reliable way to transport ores was available. As the Denver, South Park & Pacific (D. S. P. & P.) challenged the winding narrow river canyons and the windswept high passes to reach these Summit County communities, the little narrow-gauge road consistently met and overcame impossible odds to create the most colorful railroad in Colorado history.

Railroad authority Gordon S. Chappell describes the D. S. P. & P.: "Its extremely arduous routes made it the most scenic narrow gauge railway that ever ran in the Colorado Rockies."

This tough little railway maintained service for more than fifty years over wind-pommelled Boreas Pass, and deposited the daily mail at the nation's highest U.S. postoffice atop the Continental Divide there. Constantly plagued with financial woes, among them the cost of winter maintenance at Boreas, the Denver, South Park & Pacific mingled aspects of the ridiculous and sublime. The road that challenged near-impossible grades and persevered against the toughest climatic conditions was "poorly surveyed, poorly engineered, poorly financed", according to Chappell, and stood lamentably as "a streak of rust from end to end" for many years of its operation. Its much-touted Mason "Bogie" engines proved impractical. The road's main line to Gunnison, built and maintained at great expense and loss of life (especially at the 11,600-foot Alpine Tunnel), lasted less than thirty years. And in its frantic races with its aggressive rival, the Denver & Rio Grande, the D. S. P. & P. lost every competition.

Chugging its perilous path through some of Colorado's most spectacular mountain terrain — the sweeping vistas of pastoral South Park from Boreas Pass, the chasm of the rock-rimmed river canyon at craggy Ten Mile — the D. S. P. & P. became a legend. And the little railroad, in a less spectacular way, also became an artery pumping lifeblood to sequestered Summit County.

Jubilant citizens of Breckenridge had gathered to watch as the first Denver, South Park & Pacific train chugged triumphantly into their Midas-rich mining town. The shiny, black, narrow-gauge locomotive had surmounted steep Boreas Pass, straining against its steep four and one-half percent grades, clinging to narrow ledges around hairpin curves, in a feat of railway engineering. (Even the narrow gauge, designed to handle curves, had to struggle on the 21.7 mile pass, where total curves add up to twenty and one-half complete circles.) The shiny new track followed a formerly-bustling stagecoach route up Boreas from Como, over the wind-buffeted Continental Divide, then snaked down through mushrooming mine camps and gold-rich gulches to Breckenridge.

The new D. S. P. & P. "High Line" branch linked Breckenridge (and by 1883 the silver communities in Montezuma Canyon) to Denver. The route divided at Como. The main line of the railroad extended from Denver through South Park to Buena Vista, then on Denver & Rio Grande shared track into Leadville, and finally through the 1,800-foot Alpine Tunnel to Gunnison. Lucrative ore freight provided the lure for the D. S. P. & P. to hack its way through the mountains to these mine communities.

The busy Summit County branch hauled precious gold and silver ore, along with lumber supplies to Denver. Railroad cars returned with beans, hardtack (and hard liquor), bacon, laces, fine linens and other luxuries for the socially disparate population of Summit County.

Locomotives with names like "Dillon" (built in 1882), "Breckenridge" and "Fairplay" were specially-designed for heavy service on steep grades and hairpin curves. Companies such as William Mason Machine and Locomotive Works, Taunton, Massachusetts, built them, locomotives with low drivers and low centers of gravity to handle the backbreaking demands of mountain railroading. Between 1878 and 1880, the D. S. P. & P. acquired nineteen of the 2-6-6T Mason "Bogies", thought then to be the finest of their kind. These proud little Masons, and the Dawson & Baily's, Grants and Baldwins like them, challenged the perils of early Rocky Mountain railroading.

And perils there were. Steep grades, ice glazed track and primitive braking equipment caused fatal runaways.

One notable runaway occurred when Union Pacific mogul Sidney Dillon, D. S. P. & P. chief engineer Leonard Eicholtz and other rail dignitaries settled themselves into a Pullman sleeping car. On a plunging descent, the engine went out of control. The train careened wildly downward. A panicky conductor roused the tousled, pajama-clad captains of industry with the cry, "Jump!" The engineer regained control — but back in the bushes were some bruised, banged-up railroad officials, one with a broken ankle.

Avalanches and snowslides, thundering down when Chinooks loosened tons of wet snow, devastated the track, smashing large sections of laboriously-built snow fence in their ruinous path. During the heavy snow year of 1884, slide-damaged track could not be repaired until July in the high places.

An undated news clip described a typical winter rail wreck, caused by a February avalanche during a "dreadful snow and wind storm".

"Engine 263 and the mammoth rotary plow are lying in the ditch some 20 feet from the track," the newspaper reported. "The huge avalanche of snow covers the track for a distance of 200 feet in length and the depth ranges from eight to twelve feet."

The worst loss lay not in ruined rail equipment, but the tragic deaths of crew members. "The mangled body of Engineer Lynch was extracted from under the rotary boiler." The missing body of Fireman Smith had not yet been found.

Avalanche snowpack proved so solid that crews with picks would have to remove it, according to the news story.

Wooden bridges remained vulnerable to the ravages of fire. Spring floods churning down through narrow gorges also wrought havoc to bridges. The history of Rocky Mountain railroading is peppered with stories of trains rounding a bend to discover a bridge wiped out — sudden disaster.

Another hazard, fallen rock, which still plagues modern mountain highways, also stood among the perils of early alpine railroading. Wreck stories proliferate — as do yellowed wreckage photos, like the one showing a rock-mangled D. S. P. & P. locomotive at Peabody on Boreas Pass.

But the most awesome threat to the early days of the Denver, South Park & Pacific rail service to Summit County was the ill-tempered and unpredictable Boreas, mythical god of the north wind, who guarded his stronghold atop Boreas Pass in blustery grandeur. Bitter cold and superabundant snowfalls above timberline on Boreas Pass presented one challenge; the relentless breath of Boreas, sweeping acres of snow across the track and sending temperatures plummeting through wind chill made the winter maintenance of train, track and station at the summit a grueling task.

Crews numbering 100 and more, armed with shovels, attacked the thick eiderdown of snow. They would complete the exhausting work of digging out the track only to have mischievous Boreas blow snow all over it once again. When March brought warmer temperatures, the shoveling team used dynamite to blast the compacted "lead" snow, and layers of ice, from the track.

In March, 1889, the railroad proudly unveiled its new — and revolutionary at the time — Leslie rotary snowplow. The plow, designed by Cooke Locomotive Works, featured a huge steam-powered fan which cut through the snow. The rotary proved to be most effective of all devices tested by early Colorado rails. It certainly beat the hand-shoveling in practice until 1889. But drawbacks arose.

When the rotary encountered a slide across the track, it ate through the heavy snow only to strike slide-carried rocks that damaged or broke its blades. Crews were forced to hand-clear slide areas.

The pugnacious little rotary plow, nudged up the steep grades of Boreas by five narrow-gauge locomotives (the last one backward to retrieve the others when stuck), created quite a scene.

During the famous "Big Snow" winter of 1898, when snow began to fall in November and fell steadily to mid-February, people used snow tunnels to get around Breckenridge. Those snow-shoeing on the snow's surface above found their heads level with two-story buildings!

What a year for the surly storm-king Boreas. He buried the station atop the Pass, inundated the track, and managed to blockade Breckenridge for 79 days. All the efforts of men and machines proved futile — the train could not get through.

Starved for fresh food, mail and supplies, the men of Breckenridge volunteered about March 1 to shovel out the wagon road over Boreas Pass to Como. The task took ten days of backbreaking labor, but succeeded. Supplies and mail came by sled until rail service resumed April 24. Rail crews had labored for six weeks, using a rotary plow pushed by as many as twelve straining engines, to open the Pass by late April.

The dauntless Denver, South Park & Pacific met and mastered all these chal-

C&S locomotive toppled just before Ten Mile creek rail bridge at Dillon, August 14, 1902. Cause? Rain-softened earth probably sank far rail.

lenges, going on to create its own colorful history.

When P. T. Barnum brought his much-heralded circus to Breckenridge, the circus train struggled, then finally stopped, unable to prevail over Boreas' steep grades. But the train's heftiest passengers saved the day. The elephants were unloaded and used to push the circus train up three miles of the steepest track!

A mining era celebrity, nicknamed "Tom's Baby", numbers among the railroad's most mysterious passengers. Discovered July 23, 1887, Tom's Baby, perhaps Colorado's largest gold nugget, weighed in at a remarkable 13 pounds. The nugget left Breckenridge on the D. S. P. & P. enroute to its owner, Colonel M. B. Carpenter of Denver. Although its receipt was documented, the nugget soon after disappeared. For years, no one knew where the record-breaking "baby" had gone. Decades later, after a tireless search by Rev. Mark Fiester, a long-forgotten locked box in the Denver Museum of Natural History was opened in 1972 — and there among specimens of Breckenridge's famous "wire gold" lay the long lost 13-pound whopper, Tom's Baby.

Another colorful facet in the history of the South Park line was its impact on the town of Breckenridge and Summit County. When tracks came to Breckenridge, there came, inevitably, the "other side of the tracks". A train station, erected in west Breckenridge at Main and Watson, marked the birth of a red light district.

Throughout its 55-year history, the railroad acted as a vital conduit to Summit County. In mining days it carried ores to market. With the demise of those dynamic days, the railroad helped keep sleepy Summit County from lapsing into rest eternal. Ranchers shipped cattle, sheep and hay to Denver by rail. The rail helped to keep the Keystone sawmill alive. It provided the residents with a needed link to Denver and Leadville, where goods and services unavailable in Summit County could be procured.

Standing today on the Boreas Pass road, with aspen trees creating an arch of fresh greenery over the old railbed, one can picture the vivid days of the early railroad. Imagine, perhaps, a journey from Denver to one of the Montezuma Canyon towns, Sts. John, for example. You, the traveler, have ridden the D. S. P. & P. from Denver to Como and are ready to change trains for the High Line route.

(Perhaps you engaged a berth in the sleeping car, the first narrow-gauge Pullman ever built. You relaxed in the elaborate trappings of mahogany, crimson plush upholstery, silk curtains and silverplated lamps.)

The proud little locomotive "Dillon" stands ready on the turntable outside the 19-stall Como roundhouse. After hooking up with its maximum one-engine load — one coal car and one passenger car — the pompous engine begins to parade its might before an appreciative audience. With a salvo of steam, throbbing machinery, a noisy build-up of chugging and the finishing fillip of a surprise "tooooot", the little locomotive is ready to roll.

Passengers scramble aboard. The train chugs across South Park toward the nearby mountains. You travel higher and higher, and soon will have passed Hamilton, Tarryall, Peabody's and Halfway, at Halfway Gulch, where a water

Crews worked six weeks with rotary plow to clear Boreas Pass after 1898-99's mammoth snowfall. On April 10, 1899, snow alongside track rose to 12 and 15 feet. Breckenridge citizens assisted final effort, blockade ended April 24.

tank, section house and bunkhouse once stood. Later, a lone cabin used as a wait station stood available to shelter miners who wished to wave down the passing train. Today's road, constructed in 1952 on the old rail grade, circumvents treacherous Windy Pass on the old rail route.

Behind, you view the vast and sleepy spread of South Park, rimmed by mountain walls. Ahead is the steep climb to the summit. The narrow-gauge locomotive now sweats and struggles to conquer the incline. Majestic mountain views appear. You enjoy the intimate contact with nature as you travel slowly upward. Wild roses flourish in the sunshine. Aspen leaves brush against the cars. There in a glade flutters a patch of fragile blue Columbine. Ground squirrels, birds and other wildlife rush to escape the noisy locomotive.

You pass Selkirk Spur, and finally... the summit. You disembark in the pitch-blackness of a 600-foot long snowshed covering the track to the depot. Passengers stretch their legs as the mail is unloaded and received at the only U.S. postoffice straddling the Continental Divide. The postal station, established January 2, 1896, closed January 4, 1905. A five-room, one and one-half story log section house (the remains can still be seen), a large, impressive 1884-built stone engine house with turntable, the station, a huge coal bin, 9,156-gallon water tank and an engine house snowshed plus 190-foot snow fence comprised the station facility.

Breckenridge residents called Minnie Donella Fletcher, born May 3, 1882 atop Boreas Pass, the "highest born lady in Colorado".

Alice Polk Hill rode the Boreas rail route soon after it opened and described her trip in *Tales of the Colorado Pioneers*:

> Taking the Breckenridge branch, we immediately commenced the ascent of a succession of hills. Everyone sat in the open car and laughed and chatted and apostrophized the wonderful scenery.
>
> As our train followed a groove in the mountain side, we looked down upon a green exquisite little valley... The mountain sides were all aglow with rainbow tinted flowers, and it seemed that we were being literally "carried to the skies on flowery beds of ease."
>
> At Boreas, the summit, the train stopped long enough for us to gather bouquets, and look down the valley of the Blue river, over which nature has thrown a beautiful blue mist, like a veil — the effect was enchanting.

C&S climbs Boreas 1898. Note route over Gold Pan trestle, up Ford Hill.

With a spray of cinders, a grand lurching of cars and a screeching goodbye, the train is off again, this time sailing happily in descent until curves or steepness call forth a squeaking of brakes and a show of caution.

209

Boreas Pass Rail Route

Miles from Breckenridge	Location	Miles from Denver
	Breckenridge Depot Main & Watson Sts. frame depot with living quarters and freight house.	110.0
0.	Gold Pan (later Tonopah) Shops: Near today's Breckenridge Inn. 31-car spur entered shops building.	109.40
0.8	Wakefield: Auto road diverts from rail route here, rejoins rail at first left-hand hairpin curve, Gold Pan Trestle site. (Big trestle was 158 feet long, 16 feet high.)	
	Puzzle Spur, 440 feet long	108.70
	Little Mountain Spur, 212 feet long	108.60
	Jacot Spur, around 400 feet	108.50
	Smith Spur, 403 feet	108.40
	Sutton's Spur, 297 feet. Used before 1890. Trestle nearby.	108.20
2.3	Mayo Spur, 564 feet long and located on track's east side. Served area mines 1889-1906	106.48
2.9	Washington Spur, 322 feet long, serving Washington Mine. Hydraulic mining site nearby.	105.78
3.5	Pittsburg Spur	105.30
3.85	Rocky Point, scenic spot	104.90
4.9	Argentine (Conger's Camp is below), later called Bacon. View of Goose Pasture Tarn and Upper Blue Valley nearby	103.70
6.0	View of Indiana Gulch	
6.5	Baker's Tank	102.16
7.0	Rock Carvings	
7.7	Dwyer Spur (later called Belmont), 738 feet long	100.80
8.3	7:40 Mine and jeep trail down to Dyersville	
8.5	Farnham	100.0
9.0	Old Stage Road	
9.7	Boreas Station: Section house, snow shed stone round house among buildings here.	98.84

Next stop: Farnham, located just below timberline one and one-quarter miles from the Continental Divide on the Pass' west side. A cindered area today marks the remains of Farnham, eight and one-half miles above Breckenridge. Here, Mr. W. H. Farnham, postmaster, received mail at the station. C. H. Pike served as 1885 rail agent.

The Farnham Spur, into the McBarnes mining district known for its high-grade ore, served as a major ore shipping point on the rail. Ore was loaded here from the 7:40 Mine on Bald Mountain just above, using an aerial tram, and concentrate came up from the rich Warrior's Mark Mine on Indiana Creek below. Ruins of the tipple at the tram's end and two 7:40 buildings remain in decay near Farnham.

From Farnham, a challenging jeep road descends through Indiana Gulch to Warrior's Mark. Colorado pioneer, Father John L. Dyer, discovered the lode here in 1880. Located at the head of Indiana Gulch, six miles above Breckenridge, this prosperous mine had already yielded $96,000 worth of silver from shallow diggings before 1920, when it was re-opened. In the late '80's, when a bushel of tomatoes sold for ten cents, $96,000 was a fortune.

Nearby lay Dyersville, resting in a heavy stand of evergreen on bubbling Indiana Creek, the home of the state's famed "snowshoe itinerant", the Methodist Fr. Dyer.

Despite Fr. Dyer's inspiring presence, the pure mountain air of Dyersville rippled with the exploits of one Jerry Krigbaum, purveyor of food and spirituous liquors at Angels Rest, a rollicking watering hole opened in 1881, the same year the teetotaling Fr. Dyer built his cabin there.

The train proceeds, hugging the east ridge of Indiana Gulch. The 738-foot Dwyer Spur, later called Belmont, was a frequent ore stop. Soon, the thirsty engine squeals to a stop at Baker's Tank, where much-needed water is taken on. A D. S. P. tank, which replaced the original Baker's Tank, still stands here, amazingly well-preserved, with a pretty picnic ground nearby. The old tank held 9,305 gallons of water. Ore from the nearby Mountain Pride Mine came on here. A coal station and 350 feet of side track stood near Baker's Tank.

The train didn't go directly to Conger's Camp (known after 1891 as Argentine, for the nearby mountain of that name). But it dispatched two daily mails to Diantha Conger, postmistress at the busy camp three-quarters of a mile from the rail. Later, the railroad used the name Bacon for a stop in this area, but this stop was on the rail line. A two-story frame section house stood at Bacon at 10,604 feet altitude. And 814 feet of side track served the Bacon rail facility.

The train continues, blasting forth steam, dusting all in its wake, including passengers, with cinders.

When the train arcs through the cut at Rocky Point, bystanders often wave at passengers, for Rocky Point is Breckenridge's favorite picnic and outing destination. The Little Giants, huge hydraulic nozzles, are at work, gutting a hillside washing gulch gravels for placer mining purposes as the train passes Washington Spur beyond.

The narrow-gauge train squeals from the strain of braking down the steep descent. After rounding Engineers Curve on Nigger Hill, the train shoots across the spectacular 158-foot long Gold Pan Trestle, spanning the gap at Illinois Gulch's mouth. The wood-frame Gold Pan Trestle stood at the first left-hand hairpin turn ascending the present-day Boreas Pass Road. The rail route entered the Wakefield area and crossed a smaller trestle (still standing) to loop around past Little Mountain here, thus diverting from today's auto road route.

The engineer takes his train through the snowshed on hairpin Hookeye Curve and possibly stops at one or all of the five spurs serving Wakefield mines. The train emerges where the present "Wakefield Home" sign is located and steams on toward Breckenridge.

After 1900, the train would probably stop at the Gold Pan Shops, biggest machine works west of the Mississippi, located on the site of today's Brecken-ridge Inn at the town's south end. A spur there entered the shops building.

Soon the train chugs into Breckenridge depot, altitude 9,568 feet, located north of Watson Avenue on the Blue River's west side. F. W. Janeman served as agent here in 1885. A flurry of activity marks the desembarking of passengers, transfer of mail and other shipments. Then the train steams forward again, northward into the Blue River Valley, past the French Gulch water tank toward Braddock. There, at the junction of the Swan and Blue Rivers, near today's Summit Motor Lodge on the highway's west side, stood Broncho Dave Braddock's ranch buildings and a few cabins. Broncho Dave somehow managed to wangle a rail station and postoffice for his "town" in 1884. They lasted till 1890. Dave also managed to coax vegetables from the cool alpine soils (official growing season: 12 days) and a big following for his home-brewed "temperance beer".

Braddock stood at milepoint 113.29 and the next stop, Valdora, at 113.79. The train crossed a trestle over the Blue between the two stops, one of three trestles spanning the river. Valdora, altitude 9,205 feet, had a 13-car spur.

Next stop: Dickey, like Como a railroad town, now mostly submerged by the waters of Dillon Reservoir. Located near today's Farmers Korners, six miles north of Breckenridge at 9,004 feet altitude, Dickey hosted a three-stall railroad roundhouse and substantial coaling station, vital to the coal-stoked steam locomotives. In 1906, for example, Dickey loaded 12,772 tons of coal, second to Como's 24,933 tons. Dickey, originally called Placer Junction, had a 20 by 63-foot depot/freight house, a 47,500 gallon water tank, a pump house and a large wye with 4,383 feet of side track. V. Jackson was agent in 1904.

The Dickey depot was demolished in a bizarre December 11, 1897 accident. Six cars of ore tied up at Breckenridge broke loose and rolled with gathering

D. S. P. & P. OWNERSHIP

1872: Denver, South Park & Pacific Railroad spearheaded by former governor John Evans.

1881: The Union Pacific gained control of the D. S. P. & P.

1882: D. S. P. & P. launched service to Summit County

1889: A bankrupt South Park line, placed into receivership in August, emerged as the Denver, Leadville & Gunnison (D. & L. G.) Railway, still controlled by the Union Pacific

1894: Denver, Leadville & Gunnison placed in receivership as part of Union Pacific financial crisis

1898: Colorado & Southern Railway Company (C & S) organized when investment group purchased D. & L. G. and other lines. C. & S. ran Summit County route till 1937

momentum six miles north to Dickey. The Dickey switch was set for the turn to Frisco and Leadville. The ore cars could not navigate the curve. They jumped the track and smashed into the depot, destroying the ticket office, waiting room and a bedroom in the station's living quarters.

Dillon, 2.7 miles from Dickey at 8,839 feet altitude, received rail service as early as December, 1882. The town shifted its location to be on the rail line. Dillon had a 24 by 80-foot frame depot, shared with the Denver & Rio Grande, a bunkhouse and freight office. W. E. Handy served as agent in 1885.

After a stop at the Dillon station, the train gathers steam for the last leg of the journey. The engineer makes an ore freight stop in another one-half mile at the Oro Grande mine spur, a 233-foot spur later called Nichols Spur, then renamed Sterne Spur. The Oro Grande made 1897 news with its hydraulic elevator pit mining near Dillon.

As it makes its noisy way into the rail terminal at Keystone, the train is met with a rush of activity. For Keystone served as the early railhead to the rip-roaring mining towns of Montezuma Canyon above, as well as a wagon road stop for the Argentine, Webster and Loveland Pass routes. Most of the mining towns have disappeared today, but they loomed large in the 1880's and Colorado mining history.

Keystone, altitude 9,153 feet, had a large coal bin, ore platform, 1,900 feet of side track and a big rail wye in the nearby meadow. The town, 35 miles from the Como starting point on the High Line, was four hours and ten minutes in time, with good weather. In 1883, the train departed Como at 2:30 p.m., reached the Boreas summit at 4:05 p.m., Breckenridge at 5:40 p.m., Dillon at 6:20 p.m. and Keystone at 6:40 p.m.

At Keystone, the old rail depot remains in Old Keystone in a meadow off Soda Ridge Road. In later years, after mining's demise, the train traveled the 4.2 miles from Dillon to Keystone only when lumber and rail ties from the town's busy sawmills needed hauling.

The D. S. P. & P. planned to mount the Montezuma Canyon and penetrate the Continental Divide via the Vidler Tunnel to connect with Georgetown, but this ambitious plan failed. Evidence of grading beyond Keystone and into the canyon remains.

So the trip by rail from Denver and Como to Keystone ends. Yet, as an imaginary traveler heading up the canyon to your destination, Sts. John, you see ample reminder of the railroad. Well-furnished homes, flourishing businesses and mine-related development underscored the South Park's contribution to the civilized growth of Summit County.

In the early 1880's, when Rocky Mountain mining towns reached their heyday, mountain railroading proliferated. Feeder lines into the Rockies extended naturally from a railroad boom that rocked the nation. Chicago humanist and physician John Evans, Lincoln's choice as Colorado territorial governor and founder of Northwestern University, originally organized the Denver, South Park & Pacific. Evans' railroad eventually became a subsidiary of the big Union Pacific, the lengendary line that spanned the continent. Union Pacific's Jay Gould saw that the railroad could not exist on transcontinental traffic alone. Feeder lines meant earnings. The mineral-rich Rockies beckoned the profit-hungry railroads.

Stymied in his attempt to gain control of the Denver & Rio Grande (D. & R. G.), Jay Gould shifted his acquisition goal to the South Park line and began buying up stock. Immediately upon the Union Pacific's final 1881 take-over of the little railroad, troubles cropped up. Gould had pledged the D. & R. G. that the Union Pacific would not extend feeder lines into the mountains. Buying the D. S. P. & P. broke the spirit of this Joint Operating Agreement. Since the two rails shared track to Leadville and cooperated in lending equipment during emergencies, a new sense of suspicion caused hostilities to flare. The mismanaged tangle marked the beginning of a battle between the two roads and the downtrend of the Denver, South Park & Pacific.

At the time of purchase, the South Park line stood as a solid investment. Prominent Denverites originally financed the railroad. Governor Evans, an aggressive and pragmatic entrepreneur, had headed a group of investors including banker David H. Moffatt, Jr., attorney Bela M. Hughes, civil engineer Leonard

H. Eicholtz, financier Walter S. Cheeseman and banker Charles B. Kountze. (The list sounds like a "Who's Who" of early Denver.) In August, 1880, for example, the railroad paid a very credible four percent dividend despite heavy construction costs. But by 1883, under the Union Pacific umbrella, the line began steadily losing money. The debt grew to $2 million as the mining industry started sliding downhill and by May, 1888, default loomed. The Denver, South Park & Pacific Railroad went bankrupt, and entered receivership in August, 1889.

Heavy-handed absentee management by the Omaha-based Union Pacific had loosened an avalanche of troubles upon the D. S. P. & P.

The U.P. boosted freight charges so drastically that the line lost its lucrative Leadville freight business to the D. & R. G. Since the South Park line had contracted to pay $10,000 yearly to the Denver & Rio Grande for the use of its shared track from Buena Vista to Leadville (when the D. S. P. & P. retained only 10-15% of the freight business), bitter feelings arose. The D. & R. G. refused to lower the yearly fee. An angry U.P. management then made a disastrous decision: Rather than continue to share track, the U.P. launched construction on a new South Park track from Dillon/Dickey to Leadville. The Denver & Rio Grande had already penetrated Summit County with its branch line from Lead-

Spring thaw had already reduced snow depth at 1899 Boreas Station. Tunnel and stovepipe mark America's highest postoffice.

215

ville through the steep Ten Mile Canyon to Frisco and Dillon. Now the South Park line embroiled itself in a squabble with the D. & R. G. over rights of way in the narrow canyon where the South Park was attempting to lay track almost side by side with its competitor's rails.

And the new track into the Ten Mile Canyon demanded a huge financial outlay, born heavily by the D. S. P. & P. The little road flailed.

Exorbitant construction costs propelled the D. S .P. & P. to economic doom. The competitive D. & R. G. employed the quickest and cheapest methods of construction (trestle instead of land fill, easy, long routes instead of precipitous short ones). But the D. S. P. & P. painstakingly built a permanent and expensive railroad. For example, the Denver & Rio Grande won the rail race to Gunnison in one year, while the meticulous South Park line spent two and one-half years building a great stone wall at the Palisades and shoring its Alpine Tunnel.

The D. & R. G. quickly discontinued its Blue River Branch when mining profits began to play out around 1911.

But the faithful Colorado & Southern (formerly Denver, South Park & Pacific) interrupted service to Summit County only once, in late-winter 1910. Snowsheds atop Boreas Pass burrowed a path to the section house. When the rail closed, mountain lions moved into these dark tunnels. Workers had to evict the snarling squatters in 1913 when rail service resumed.

In 1909, the proud stone engine house succumbed to fire. A wye was constructed at Boreas to replace the fine 49 ½-foot wrought-iron turntable lost in the engine house fire. In 1934, fire again swept through Boreas Station, destroying much of the second highest rail depot in the world. Only a few remnants remain today.

The Denver, South Park & Pacific, conceived by men with profits glittering in their eyes, had survived financial woes. The rail went into receivership twice, but refused to die. Reorganized once as the Denver, Leadville and Gunnison Railway, then again as the Colorado & Southern, the line served Summit County until 1937, creating a lifeline to Denver that longtime county residents remember warmly.

Dillon resident Hank Emore remembers, "I took the railroad in 1936 between Christmas and New Years. It took forever to get to Denver," Emore chuckles.

"You could walk up Boreas Pass as fast as the train went. I think the trip to Denver took from 8 a.m. till 4 p.m." (Today's driving time is one hour, 15 minutes.)

Mary Ellen Cluskey Ruth, born in Breckenridge in 1902, grew up with the railroad. "We lived at Dickey. My father had a sheep ranch there.

"The roads to Breckenridge — even the roads between Dillon and Frisco — were closed in winter time, so we really needed the train for daily transportation," Mary Ruth explains.

The railroad funneled needed tax dollars into the spare coffers of Summit County and provided some jobs. But its significance to the old-time residents went far deeper than that.

The railroad was linked to a way of life for Summit County, and when it died, a way of life went with it.

Rival Rails in the Ten Mile Canyon

The rival railroads kicked up a legendary fuss in the Ten Mile Canyon when the Denver, South Park & Pacific began to elbow its way in there in July, 1883. Fuming over high annual fees imposed by the Denver & Rio Grande on the D. & R. G. track the two rails shared from Buena Vista to Leadville, the South Park line began laying its own track to Leadville — from Dickey into Frisco and then side-by-side with the Denver & Rio Grande rails in the lower Ten Mile Canyon. The D. S. P. turned its first shovel full of canyon dirt on August 3, 1883.

The South Park line could have followed the D. & R. G.'s easier path from Buena Vista to Leadville, but the company always chose the shortest route, no matter how difficult or expensive. Even though it crossed the Continental Divide twice, the Denver to Leadville route proved 21 miles shorter via the Ten Mile Canyon — so the determined D. S. P. & P. people pushed into the tight canyon.

D. & R. G. attorneys ran screaming into court. They wheedled the judge into ordering the D.S.P. & P. to stay 50 feet away from the D. & R. G. track on each side — a tricky task in the narrow Ten Mile Canyon.

While tie hacks busied themselves cutting trees for 3,000 spruce ties for every rail mile and Ten Mile Canyon sawmills rushed to cut them to narrow-gauge size, the railroads' executives raged in dispute.

The Denver & Rio Grande threw up every physical and legal obstacle available to prevent the construction of the new track. The South Park was forced to maintain an armed guard on its newly-constructed track. The company placed

218

loaded trains on the line as fast as the rails were laid, to prevent Denver & Rio Grande men from tearing it up, according to the *Commercial and Financial Chronicle* quoted by railroad authority M.C. Poor. The D. & R. G. used every available ploy, from parking a locomotive at a point where a D. S. P. & P. track had to cross D. & R. G. rails, to the August 27, 1883 injunction to prevent the South Park line from entering on a D. & R. G. right of way at Kokomo. Moreover, the injunction forbade the South Park to alter the Ten Mile Creek's course, which the rail had to cross occasionally. The court order also protected 50-foot easements on Denver & Rio Grande snow fences, snow sheds and telegraph lines along the D. & R. G. right of way area, plus the depot grounds at nearby Robinson.

Jay Gould was no man to spite. His Union Pacific held the whip of ownership over the South Park line and this time he cracked it. Against sizeable odds and constant harrassment from the D. & R. G., the railroad pushed construction on toward Kokomo.

At Kokomo, high in the canyon's southern reach, natural hillside topography and the Denver & Rio Grande's location rendered D. S. P. & P. rail construction almost impossible, without infriging on D. & R. G. right of way. D. & R. G. track was on the river's west side, blocking D. S. P. & P. entrance to Kokomo. The South Park finally concocted the idea of a complicated switchback above Kokomo which skirted the D. & R. G. right of way. Though a nuisance to operate, the switchback seemed a heaven-sent solution.

As work teams approached the upper Ten Mile Canyon silver community, Denver & Rio Grande representatives attempted a last-ditch effort to halt construction. They persuaded a Kokomo land-holder to hike his price on needed rail switchback property to outrageous highs. The Denver, South Park & Pacific had a prior agreement on the 3,000-foot strip of land — but contract deadlines appeared impossible to fulfill. On the night before the land agreement expired, the South Park worked frantically all night. Workers raced to lay track by lantern light, without even bothering to grade! The new track reached Kokomo by the time people emerged from their homes next day. But the reward for all this hard labor came later when Leadville's Sheriff Hanley arrested the entire construction crew and threw them all in the slammer for two days.

For the poor immigrant workers employed on the D. S. P. & P. construction gangs, jail may have seemed palatial. The railroads exploited Italian and Mexican workers, with pitiful wages and starvation conditions. Gang bosses issued thin jackets and poor shoes for paltry protection against harsh high country winters. In fall, 1883, the Leadville *Chronicle* reported 1,200-1,500 men at work on the line. These immigrants "nearly freeze as many of them have no blankets," the newspaper stated. ". . . it has snowed every day for two weeks."

The Denver & Rio Grande had a right to be mad about the upstart D. S. P. & P. shouldering its way into the Ten Mile. The Canyon was hard-won D. & R. G. territory. The determined D. & R. G. had battled deep snows and stinging winds to scale Fremont Pass from Leadville in the winter of 1880. Its first train steamed into the upper Ten Mile's silver-rich Robinson on New Year's Day, 1881. Miners kicked their hobnailed boots in mid-air for joy, because rail ore freight service meant profits for area silver mines.

The Denver & Rio Grande had faithfully hauled Robinson and Kokomo silver ores to Leadville markets since 1881. And the line built track down the Canyon to Wheeler by September, 1881 and all the way to Dillon by December 7, 1882. The D. & R. G. had gained a firm foothold in Summit County. Grading crews continued 38 miles down the Blue Valley toward Kremmling and, ultimately Salt Lake City. Evidence of grading remains along the Blue today, but no ties or rails were laid for track.

Nevertheless, the rival railroads soon patched up their differences. They had to, in order to survive the challenges of railroading in mountain-bound Summit Country. Every kind of misadventure befell the struggling railroads. Cars froze into snowdrifts. Steep canyon walls let loose avalanches that buried the route. Ice glazed the track on steep and dangerous grades. Derailments, smash-ups and tragic loss of life marked the history of Summit railroading. The two rail lines lent snowplows, traded freight cars, shared equipment and manpower whenever emergencies arose.

And they arose right away for the South Park. Launching Canyon service in 1884, the South Park ran smack into Summit's second-worst winter of the late 1800's. (1898-99 took the cake as Summit's snowiest season.) Heavy snows inundated the freshly-laid track. New track, especially vulnerable to weather damage, caused constant problems. The snow finally melted in July, 1884, and unused track had to then be cleaned and repaired. Service finally began September 30, 1884. The D. S. P. & P. was off to a bad start.

The following railroad mishap typifies winter hazards:

Picture a snarling snowstorm on the bitter night of January 28, 1909 deep in the cliff-lined Ten Mile Canyon. The narrow-gauge Denver, South Park & Pacific chugs through the blinding storm from Frisco toward Wheeler Junction, present site of Copper Mountain ski resort. The sturdy little Mason "Bogie" locomotive stops at Wheeler to pick up several cars there — only to discover them locked in icy snowpack. The crew spends three or four precious hours to chop them out. Will the train reach its destination, the mining center of Kokomo, before the next scheduled train roars down the track?

Hope diminishes when an engine stalls just four miles below Kokomo. Conductor J. D. Snee cuts off the head engine, takes four cars and leaves the rest of his train, intending to return from Kokomo with the increased muscle of an additional locomotive. He reaches Kokomo just as Engine 41, pulling freight, readies for departure. There is shouted conversation through the storm. "Watch out! I left a stall on the track!"

In the storm's confusion, the engineer misunderstands the location. Back at the stall site, the rear brakeman, who has remained with the immobilized freight, sees something emerge through snow-blurred darkness. Relief! "The extra engine," he breathes. But it is Engine 41, bearing down with frightening speed. Desperately, he tries to back up, blowing his whistle in panic. But four cars of logs have already frozen into the snow. He jumps for his life. Engine 41

Leslie rotary snowplow, invented 1889, kept High Line open year-round.

smashes the stalled freight with terrific force, destroying valuable rolling stock and freight, tying up the South Park line at a most miserable time.

A famous rail foul-up came with the incredible Uneva Lake Slide, when an avalanche covered track with snow 50 feet deep. Boulders, trees and debris were embedded in the slide snowpack.

Despite accidents and hardship, Ten Mile Canyon railroading was also lots of fun. Balmy summer days provided ample opportunity for a scenic passenger jaunt to the lively mine communities at Fremont Pass' base. Kokomo, for example, had shops to entice the ladies by day and hair-raising revelry to draw "the boys" by night.

You can board at the Frisco depot for an imaginary train ride through the Ten Mile Canyon. The South Park line cut over from Dickey to its station at the base of Mount Royal. (The rail grade remains clearly evident near the Blue Spruce Inn and just north of the Frisco library.) The Denver & Rio Grande, chugging up from Dillon, cut through the alley between Main and Galena Streets before entering the canyon. Frisco resident Wayne Bristol reported the D. & R. G. rail ties remained in his alley until 1965.

It is a bright autumn day in the early 1900's. Aspen groves run like rivers of gold against rich green pine forests. The train sends forth a volley of steam, a noisy whistle and a mischievous blast of sooty cinders to dust bystanders on the

The gay '90's were gayer at blissful Uneva Lake where railroad companies created summer resort. Glacial lake is in Ten Mile Canyon.

platform. Then it chugs along narrow-gauge rails past Mount Royal into the narrow, cliff-walled canyon.

Just inside the canyon, you see the Square Deal Mine's lower facilities, and climbing a cliff on the left, the mine buildings and big concentration mill of the Excelsior Mine. On the right is the bustling King Solomon Mine, with a 6-car rail spur for ore freight. Farther along, still at right, you see the Mary Verna Mine, with its big power house and tunnel ore dump beside the track. The Kitty Innes Mine neighbors the Mary Verna.

There are ticket stops at Excelsior and tiny Cunningham. But the first real town is Curtin, with its prim log depot, one and one-half stories high. The Webb Giberson family lived there in a cabin near the power house which served both the North American and Mary Verna Mines. Pump station, foundations, scattered brick and square-nail constructed cabin remnants remain at Curtin, 2.1 miles into the canyon from Frisco's rail depot. Just beyond Curtin is the North American, marked by its steel-gray tailings pile.

The old county dirt road paralleling I-70 recently underwent a face lift and became today's scenic bicycle path. Those who use it might enjoy knowing that the path is the old Denver, South Park & Pacific rail route. Just a stone's throw from the D. S. P. & P. track lay the Denver & Rio Grande rails, west of the South Park and obliterated by today's I-70 highway.

The next stop served visitors to Lake Uneva, a privately-owned lake hanging in the canyon about four miles from Frisco. Tourists enjoyed Lake Uneva as a railroad-developed resort area as early as 1899. A dude ranch flanked the one-mile long Lake in early days. A balmy retreat for local residents as well, Uneva Lake is remembered by old-timers for its voraciously-hungry mountain trout.

Bottom, they say, has never been found at Uneva Lake.

Officers Gulch, the next stop, is today the site of a $2 million highway interchange. In early days, a wood tower with a trolley up to the Monroe Mine, above and east across the canyon, shuttled ore down to the train stop. The cut for the trolley remains, near an old cabin perched on the cliffside.

The little narrow-gauge locomotive chugs along beside the rushing Ten Mile Creek all the way to Wheeler, laid out below the big, forested mountain that in 1972 became Copper Mountain Ski Area.

Judge John S. Wheeler, a South Park rancher, had grazing lands at Wheeler Flats. Before the canyon's blustery winter arrived, Wheeler drove his cattle over the long Wheeler trail which mounts the Ten Mile Range and crosses the flanks of Peak Eight and Nine to south of Breckenridge. Copper Mountain resident Penny Lewis remembers the Wheeler site as strewn with arrow heads and old glass bottles when she first stopped there in 1956. The remains of an old hotel, postoffice, well and town dump still visible gave evidence to the rip-roaring town that once flourished at Wheeler. (See Chapter 12 for more on this ghost town.)

During the Big Snow Winter, 1898-99, several Rio Grande rail cars froze into the snow at Wheeler. Terrific storms at the same time caused both railroads to abandon service. A stranded crew at Wheeler lived for two or three weeks, eating supplies from the merchandise car. Then, the men made skis from snow-fence planks and skied to Breckenridge. A remaining passenger later made an ill-starred attempt to reach Como. His body wasn't found till May.

While the Rio Grande stopped at Wheeler, the South Park made its stop just across the way and called it "Solitude". Solitude, altitude 9,737 feet, had a 47,500 gallon water tank, fed by a nearby spring and 1,596 feet of side track. Benson's and Graveline, at silver-rich Graveline Gulch, ranked as official stops on the Ten Mile Canyon rail route. In 1934, after mining's demise, a passenger wrote: "Now we are coming to Solitude, where we take on water. The place is aptly named for there isn't a human habitation in sight."

Woodside, a little more than two miles from Solitude/Wheeler, and Wilder's Spur another two miles, were also rail stops, along with Deneen, about five miles past Solitude.

The shiny black Baldwin locomotive steams farther into the canyon, below sunny splashes of golden aspen trees dazzling against heavy, green, pine-forested mountainsides. The train chugs up toward Kokomo, stopping one-half mile from town at the 47,500 gallon railroad water tank to refill. Engine and coal rooms stood beside the tank.

At this bustling silver city, the Denver, South Park & Pacific had constructed its complicated switchback to skirt Denver & Rio Grande track. But the railroad used the switchback only a few months. On December 21, 1884, the D. S. P. & P. completed two trestles which its trains used to bridge the D. & R. G. The first trestle measured 132 by 26 feet; the second 200 by 29 feet. When the town shifted locations after its 1882 fire, early D. & R. G. trains stopped at Recen depot. Passengers had to hike uphill into town from that station on the town's outskirts. The D. S. P. & P. built its first depot just above its old D. & R. G. crossover. Then the railroad relocated its train depot three-fourths mile north, near Kokomo's business district. (See Chapter 16 for details on Kokomo.)

The 1.1 mile Wilfley Spur at Kokomo served the big Wilfley Mill, in Searles Gulch. A. R. Wilfley's revolutionary 1895 Wilfley table, invented there, is still used in ore processing today at operations like the nearby Climax Molybdenum Mine. The train picked up ore at Wilfley's Mill and also at Breene's Spur (Peter Breene's mining operation) nearby. Breene's Spur, built in 1908, was a 20-car spur, an offshoot of the Wilfley Mill Spur. These spur rails were gone by 1934. (Chapter 10 discusses mining near Kokomo.)

The train lurched out of Kokomo station, cars swaying crazily, and gathered steam for the 1.8-mile trip to Robinson, the largest community in the early Ten Mile Canyon.

Robinson, with an 850 population as early as 1881, sprang up to serve the stunningly-rich Robinson Mines Group, discovered in 1878. Stable and prosperous, the silver community suffered a blow from the tragic death of its enterprising founder, George Robinson. (See Chapter 16.) The town had a 1,412 square foot freight platform and 1,175 feet in side track. T. J. Flynn was the rail agent in 1885.

Robinson, now buried by molybdenum tailings from the Climax Mine, once ranked as the Ten Mile Canyon's answer to Leadville.

Leaving Robinson, the engineer eyed the path up toward the Continental Divide. He would negotiate the ascent to nearby Buffehr's Spur, 1.3 miles, then climb 11,320-foot Fremont Pass. Carbonateville, one mile southeast of Robinson, sprang up in 1878 with the discovery of silver ore nearby. Carbonateville, on Ten Mile Creek, typified the craziness of the silver boom era. The town boomed with scores of businesses lining its streets and a massive prospector influx. And then Carbonateville went bust. The town that flourished and reached its peak in 1879 became a ghost town by 1881.

McNulty Gulch, a once-famous placer gulch that yielded $3 million in free gold 1860-62, lay just east of Carbonateville.

Early railroaders named the 11,320-foot altitude settlement atop Fremont Pass "Climax" to indicate their triumph over rail difficulties in constructing track to that lofty point. In 1889, Climax had a rail turntable, coal station, telegraph office and 1,854 feet of side track. The engine house and turntable burned in 1907.

In later years, after the D. & R. G.'s 1911 Blue River Branch shutdown, the D. S. P. & P. still served the Ten Mile Canyon, under its long-time Colorado & Southern title. The C. & S.'s biggest customer after 1917 turned out to be the producer of a little-known metal called molybdenum. The Climax Molybdenum Mine, straddling the county line atop Fremont Pass, transported its ores to Leadville via the sturdy little C. & S. for years. The C. & S. ran from Leadville to Climax even after its High Line shut down Summit County service in 1937. The line still runs to Climax from Leadville's Malta substation.

Passenger train engineers were forbidden to exceed 22 miles per hour in Summit County. Freight trains had to crawl along under 12 miles per hour on

Boreas Pass and through the Ten Mile Canyon. The D. S. P. & P. initials produced a popular saying: "Damn Slow Pulling & Pretty Rough Riding." In 1922, with improved equipment, the train left Frisco at 4:11 p.m. and arrived at Climax at 5:29, reaching its Leadville terminus at 6:25. A trip to Denver via Boreas Pass took around nine hours from Frisco.

Of course, long trips could be fun if the passenger had the price of a berth in the train's elegant Pullman car. The Denver, South Park & Pacific boasted the nation's first narrow-gauge Pullman car — a treat for the affluent traveler.

The early locomotives made travel in the Ten Mile, and everywhere else, a much slower process in the 1880's. Early engines like the Denver & Rio Grande's first locomotive, the "Montezuma", had to stop to take on water every 15 miles. The 12½-ton Montezuma, debuted July 3, 1871, had a top speed of 25 miles per hour with four cars. Her engineer, William Walk, said:

> There was a sweet little engine for you; she was perfectly balanced, not top-heavy, and took the curves like a piece of tangent track, yet she never so much as spilled a drop of water from a glass set in any of the windows of the cab.

Walk remembered the early passenger cars as fairly comfortable, although small windows made for poor lighting aboard. "We could seat 36 passengers if they were not too fat," he reminisced.

All-too-frequent wrecks halted rail traffic. Maintenance was challenge in Ten Mile Canyon. This wreck probably occurred at Robinson.

Today only a few relics remain to remind the curious of early railroading in the Ten Mile Canyon, Among the most intriguing of these remnants is a mysterious collection of stone huts and small domes that have given rise to some wild speculation among Summit local residents. The hut structures stretch from the north (Frisco) end of the canyon to Wheeler Flats (Copper Mountain). Locals began referring to the native stone structures as the "Chinese huts". Instant legends, depicting rail construction gangs of slant-eyed, yellow-skinned, pigtailed Orientals who occupied the tiny huts, began to circulate. Unfortunately, truth failed to rival fiction in the matter. A Denver & Rio Grande lineman recently explained the mystery: The 8 by 12-foot stone houses, found in various states of disrepair particularly in the area stretching from Officers Gulch and Uneva Lake to Wheeler Flats, housed Mexican immigrant rail laborers. Not Chinese. The immigrants used the native stone huts, with their rough floors and corner hearths, as temporary dwellings. They built cookfires in the huts and attempted to stave off the threat of exposure to the Canyon's challenging elements. (These rail workers, many of whom contracted pneumonia, filled Leadville's hospitals and poorhouses to overflowing when they became ill and unable to work.)

The story's Chinese twist probably sprouted from the gang boss' practice of hiring a Chinese cook. The cook, one of the only crew members to contact townsfolk and local merchants during supply trips to nearby communities, came to represent the whole group of foreign workers.

A second series of stone structures, a curious collection of domes extending from Wheeler Flats to the north appeared unsuitable for dwelling use. These domes, with charcoal remains still evident, served as ovens in which hot fires were built for use in bending rails. Similar domes appeared along D. & R. G. track in other canyons, where curved rail was necessary, particularly the Phantom Canyon, according to Copper Mountain historian Penny Lewis.

Today's motorists skimming the modern highway through the Ten Mile Canyon probably remain unaware of its history as a transportation corridor. The glacier-carved canyon served as an Indian route from the Vail Pass hunting grounds to the South Park buffalo pasturelands since 5,000 B.C. and before. Before road-builders penetrated the canyon, miners ran pack trains through the cleft. Sure-footed little pack animals, burros and mules, formed a "narrow-gauge" pack train to traverse the canyon's tricky trails. Burros toted 200 pounds of ore each and a mule hauled 300 pounds. Teams of 60 to 100 animals could navigate under the guidance of only two or three drivers and shepherd dogs.

Later a stage line ran daily through the Ten Mile, connecting Denver and Leadville via Georgetown, Dillon, Frisco and Kokomo.

In 1880, the Denver & Rio Grande, dubbed the "Little Giant" for its dauntless penetration into the rugged Rockies, first rolled down off Fremont Pass to enter the Ten Mile Canyon. The pioneer narrow-gauge line served the area until 1911. In 1884, the colorful Denver, South Park & Pacific steamed up the canyon from Dickey and Frisco, launching a 53-year history of Ten Mile Canyon service that ceased in 1937, on April 10, when a sentimental crew of old-timers manned Summit's last railroad train.

A rugged, rock-strewn dirt road, laughingly remembered by old-time Summit residents, offered the only access to Leadville after the railroad shut down. (Leadville provided vital services, including medical and dental facilities, for isolated Summit residents.) U.S. Highway 6 later served motorists as a transcontinental route. Today, a modern interstate highway speeds travelers through the rock-rimmed Ten Mile Canyon. The whispers of ghosts from days gone by are now becoming almost inaudible.

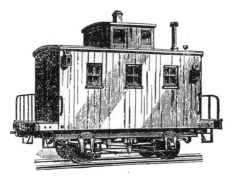

Summit's Star Cities

PARKVILLE

It was 1861. Mounting Civil War tension that turned Northerner and Southerner against one another across the land had permeated the far reaches of Summit's isolated Georgia Gulch.

There, at the mouth of Georgia Gulch blossomed the town of Parkville, *the* early mine camp of Summit County.

On this particular 1861 day, two incensed Parkville patriots, a Rebel supporter and a Union man, armed with heavy six shooters, gazed murderously at one another across a small table.

Each left hand held a corner of a large miner's handkerchief stretched between them. Each right hand held a deadly pistol aimed at a former neighbor. The two, engaged in a duel which culminated the quarrel between Yankee and Rebel factions in the high country mine camp, waited as their seconds carefully loaded their guns. These men covered the charge in the revolver's cylinder with tallow, to make the pistol shoot slick. The combatants had waxed their bullets as well.

Two additional men, each toting six shooters, stood unflinchingly beside each duelist. Their duty: To shoot down the duelist who might seize the advantage and fire before the signal was given.

As nerves grew taut, onlooker Daniel Ellis Conner, a Kentuckian who arrived in the Blue River Mining District with early white prospectors in May, 1860, remembered with dread the dire events leading to the impending catastrophe:

A drunken miner, bellowing "Hurrah for the North", had caroused through the streets of Parkville a day earlier. A miner from Georgia, sitting in the butcher shop doorway greasing his boots with a lump of tallow, replied by shouting "Hurrah for the South!". "Then the Yankee shot at the Rebel, and the Rebel shot at the Yankee," according to Conner's journal, "and both repeated the pleasantry, which ended by the Yankee being shot directly through the body. This was followed by another 'Reb' stepping into the street and emptying both barrels into the U.S. flag over the Union war recruiting office, riddling it into tatters."

Two patriots took up the argument, Conner recalled, and agreed to settle it sensibly — the result being the duel, about to begin now, as deathly silence pervaded the crowded one-room miner's cabin.

"Make ready." The two cocked pistols held steadily in unfaltering grip rose above the table till they came into position, nearly breast to breast.

"One, two, three!" A blast and smoke as two men fired and fell. Each pros-

228

trate victim's coat was stripped from him. Dr. Stewart, a Virginian, knelt quickly, and felt each man's pulse, then passed rapid opinion on him.

Conner relates the culmination of this cold-blooded event with these words:

> Then pulling open the shirt to search for the wound, and as there was none, he remarked the fact in surprise, as he hastily examined the other with the same result. This announcement from the doctor encouraged the wounded men enough to induce an effort to get up, which they did, by blundering to their feet, looking like two mortals just out of a painful and confused dream. The doctor said amidst his puzzled stupor that each man had a red spot on his chest, but there was no bullet hole in either of them. Now those who were in the trick burst into uncontrollable laughter which could have been heard for a mile. They had duped both the principals and the doctor by charging the pistols with powder only . . . that made the two red spots at such close range.

The doctor left, asserting ominously that he carried a pistol that *did* have bullets in it.

Conner, native of Bardstown, Kentucky, had first heard of gold discovered at Denver's Cherry Creek in fall, 1858, while residing in Leavenworth, Kansas. He joined a party of Colorado-bound gold-seekers to become part of the famous and historic 1859 Pikes Peak Gold Rush. But his group spurned Pikes Peak. They pushed on, pausing to refresh themselves with the bubbly water at "Soda Spring", today's Manitou Springs. (The soda water made excellent bread, they discovered.) From there, the party penetrated the mountains via Kenosha Pass to South Park. They crossed the grassy park, swarming with buffalo, and made their way to the base of the "Snowy Range" (the Continental Divide mountains between South Park and today's Summit County) by the end of May, 1860.

Conner's journal details the journey:

> . . .We arrived at the foot of the cordillera or Snowy Range. A grand confusion of mountain crags, peaks and ranges of the most imposing proportions, all covered with snow. . . . Many fearful gorges and at-tritioned fissures lay hidden far beneath the surface of the drifted snow here and there and everywhere. The innumerable and distant white snow-crested peaks, with their bases hidden behind others as they arose higher and higher and further away toward the top of the main divide, presenting a magnificent picture of gloom and starvation.

The determined gold-seekers, who had so far permeated the Rockies with wagons and a team of oxen, decided to take only their lightest wagon, loaded with 500 pounds of provisions and hitched up with "six pairs of work steers" to scale the snow-covered Continental Divide.

"We soon came to where the snow was too deep to proceed without tedious difficulties." The early June snow presented a solid crust on the ridges, but in the countless ravines the wagons and oxen sank deep into the snow.

"Across those places we began to cut grades with long-handled shovels . . one to a man. Thus we cut a railroad grade in appearance . . . " Near the summit, the determined travelers dug in snow so deep they couldn't throw it up out of their trench, but had to carry it out to each end. Thus, by hacking their way through snowpack, occasionally plunging into icy creeks hidden by the deep snow, and incredible back-breaking labor, the discouraged oxen and exhausted gold-seekers reached the Continental Divide summit.

The next day, the group reached the headwaters of a river which they believed to be the Blue. Conner wrote in his journal, published in recent years as *A Confederate in the Colorado Gold Fields*: "We were now in the boundaries of the new Eldorado, our predestination. This section was then in Utah Territory, but soon after became Colorado Territory, whose subsequent legislature named our locality Summit County."

What Daniel Conner and his friends discovered in Summit County (while those more fortunate were discovering gold) was a sylvan paradise where contented herds of "black tail" (mule) deer and antelope frolicked unafraid, fish flashed silver in the streams, ptarmigan strutted and bighorn sheep grazed. More treacherous was the Rocky Mountain cougar. Its piercing scream in the dark woods, says Conner, "entered my very soul". And the huge, powerful grizzly, raging in fury when wounded, gave Conner and his friends some breath-taking chases.

Conner prospected all over the Blue River Mining District but never found the golden wealth he sought. He was always out hunting, encountering close calls with grizzlies and Ute Indians when someone else made a big strike. (The cry of "Gold!" always created a "rush" to the area of discovery.)

One such strike was made at Georgia Gulch, located on the south fork of the Swan River, on the north side of now-famous Farncomb Hill, about five miles east of Breckenridge. Said Conner:

> Another rush was made from Miner's District to the newly discovered "Georgia Gulch", a tributary to Swan River . . . this was about the first of June, 1860. On arriving there it was all claimed up, tributaries and all. It proved to be the richest diggings ever found in this section of the Rocky Mountains. It was found by a little party under the leadership of Mr. Highfield, a Georgia gold miner, hence the name of Georgia Gulch.

Conner wintered on the warmer side of the Divide and returned to Georgia Gulch the following spring on April 27, to discover that many had endured the bitter high country winter there.

"I found the little park at the foot of Georgia Gulch pretty well covered with cabins," he wrote. "This season there were about 500 men in Georgia Gulch at work either as owners of mines or hired laborers."

Prospector Lew Wilmot mined a Georgia Gulch placer claim in summer 1860 with his father, Benjamin Wilmot. He quoted a Canon City *Times* February 16, 1861 report that stated 400 people were wintering in Georgia Gulch.

Conner departed on one of his extended hunting trips. When he returned to Georgia Gulch, he found jubilant miners taking out $300-$500 per day of high quality dust from mines worked by three or four men. Population had soared. Colorado historian Charles W. Henderson reports that individual claims produced as much as $10,000 in a single season during the placer-mining peak in Georgia Gulch. Three million dollars in gold, during days when a bushel of tomatoes sold for a dime, came out of Georgia Gulch in the short summer work seasons from 1859 to 1862 alone.

With gold dust aplenty and plenty of cause for celebration, Parkville sprang into bawdy existence. The 1860 election rolls recorded 1,800 voters here. In the early '60's estimates of population in the area (including French Gulch, Gold Run and other nearby gulches) vary from 8,000-10,000. Parkville quickly became "civilization" west of the Divide in Colorado. The boom town became the county seat of then-huge Summit County, encompassing the entire northwest corner of Colorado. The flourishing community took its place as a social and supply center.

Parkville came close to being the territorial capitol in February, 1861, according to Wallace La Bauw in "Nah-oon-Kara". The town lost the honor by only 11 votes.

Conner reported:

> (Parkville) was not yet two years old, but including the cabinites along the gulch and its tributaries, there was probably a thousand men upon an average, while thousands probably came and left, keeping up a constant flow to and from the place. A sawmill had taken the place of the whipsaw; a theater was established; plenty of billiard saloons . . . The different games known to professionals were constantly exercised for winnings, great and small — eucher, seven-up, cribbage, faro, monte, roulette, rondo, keno, tan, diana, and all other games known to the profession (for) gain and frolic.

Three saloons, the Bedrock, Metropolitan and Gayosa, provided Georgia Gulch miners the opportunity to use their dust in these games of chance.

Parkville had its share of gamblers, high-livers, loafers and miscreants. An August 21, 1861 letter to the *Rocky Mountain News* quoted in *Blasted, Beloved Breckenridge*, reported: "Great numbers throughout these places, nevertheless are loafing and eating away their time — neither owning claims nor wishing to work if claims were donated to them."

The Tarryall *Miners Record*, July 20, 1861, intoned: "Loafing, saloon-keeping and peddling are assiduously patronized . . . "

But the good old Puritan work ethic also flourished in Parkville. A lively grab-bag of commercial enterprises hawked wares, services and rowdy entertainment to the gold-toting miners. On a stroll through old Parkville, an early 1860's visitor would see:

> Louis Valiton's drugstore, Parkville's first pharmacy (apothecary).
> George E. Kettle's meat market, Parkville's first butchery.
> Gallatin's saddle and harness shop.
> Chapin House, J. B. Chapin's fine hostelry that could (and did) serve 50 at a meal, breakfast, lunch and dinner. Called "the best hotel this side of sunset".
> Jones, Clifford & Company's water-driven sawmill, built May, 1861.
> The Henry Weiss Brewery, makers of a fine lager for which the miners gladly parted with their gold: " . . . its manager is making lots of money out of it, as much as he could out of a 'discovery' claim."
> The Masonic Temple, Colorado Lodge No. 2. The first Western Slope Masonic Lodge was built in 1861 and dedicated on May 6 by Parson John M. Chivington, a man of God now infamous for his ungodly role in the brutal Sand Creek Massacre. The Lodge, discontinued in 1864 with Parkville's demise, was next door to Gayosa Hall.

231

Whittemore's General Store occupied the two-story Masonic Lodge's lower floor. (Whittemore, an 1859er and Breckenridge storekeeper, rented his first store to the Silverthorns for use as a hotel and residence.)

Peabody and Company's General Store, E. C. Peabody, another '59er, wintered with a hardy handful of prospectors in the Blue River Diggings discovery year.

Willand and Company, owners of a large building that contained a storehouse and a grand hall where nightly dances took place. These "balls" were usually stag, as there were no ladies in early Parkville.

The Langrishe and Dougherty Theatre, a large fashionable theatre with a 30 x 40 foot stage.

Gayosa Hall, where the "Colorado Minstrels", featuring the fetching Mlle. Haydee, performed.

The Pioneer Theatre, housed in a large tent.

The United States Post Office, established December 13, 1861.

Humbug and Georgia Gulches ran together. Humbug Gulch stood a little above Parkville and its businesses were at first separate from the county seat town, but later the communities merged.

Despite all this gainful enterprise, the poor preacher, Father Dyer, never seemed to get a share in Georgia Gulch's free-flowing gold.

Father John Lewis Dyer, Colorado's famous "Snowshoe Itinerant", preached to a Methodist congregation at Georgia Gulch, but also, according to Father Dyer, "the boys" went "rather long between collections". Father Dyer's pants wore thin, yet the miners still failed to pass the hat in support of the tireless missionary. Father Dyer writes in his book:

> I reached Georgia Gulch on the second day of April, (1862) and was received kindly . . . I gave out preaching for the next Sunday at ten and a half o'clock and at French Gulch in the afternoon. The hall was well-filled in the morning, and there were about forty hearers in the afternoon. There was a friendly Jew at Georgia Gulch, who proposed to raise the preacher something, and took a paper and collected $22.50 in dust; for that was all the currency then. This amount was quite a help, as there were only ten cents in my purse when I got there.

When the first young lady arrived at Parkville, the cry went up, "Boys, thar's a gal in the gulch!" "Sis", a pretty young thing, served drinks in her mother's grog shop. ("Deadfall" was the prospector's term for a liquor establishment.) Miners traveled good distances to buy a drink from Sis and the old lady's spirituous sales soared.

Other enterprises flowered. J. J. Conway's Parkville mint coined $2.50, $5.00 and $10.00 gold pieces to keep commerce flowing smoothly. Samples of these historic coins are displayed at the Smithsonian Museum.

No other Conway Mint coins are known to exist, according to local historians, but the mint's original 1861 dies were found in a Denver attic by Mrs. Carl Modisett and given to the Colorado State Historical Society.

The Conway Mint was one of three in early Colorado. The others were Clark, Gruber and Company and Hamilton's (South Park) Parsons and Company.

According to Colorado historian Frank Hall, a miners' meeting settled the question of Parkville gold's dollar value. Traders attempted to price the gold at $14 or $16 per ounce. " . . . the miners held a meeting and settled the question by resolving not to deal with'any man who refused to take it at $18," Hall said. (Prospector power!)

As Parkville flourished, a bit of culture began to temper the town's raucous nature. Top entertainers and troupes of the day visited the bustling camp. The famous Central City team of Langrishe and Dougherty opened a large theater and produced many lively shows for overflow crowds. The troupe, which began the entertainment tradition that culminated in the famous Central City Opera House, relied on mountain talent, developing miners and dance hall girls into polished performers. Their success lured top stars such as Lillian Gish, Frank Fay, singer Eleanor Steber and others to the gold-rich Colorado camps.

Bawdy mine camp audiences sometimes displayed a deplorable dirth of social grace. During a melodrama performance at the Parkville theater, a thwarted lover grabbed an innocent heroine, about to carry her off. Suddenly, a barrel-chested miner, rum reeking from every pore, rushed the stage with a loaded revolver shouting, "No you don't, Mister! Just drop that gal or I'll blow the top of your head off." A panicky change of script soothed the offended sensibilities of the red-eyed miner and the play proceeded with alacrity.

By 1862, the ambitious residents of Breckenridge, anxious to secure their town's position as Summit's gold capitol, tiptoed into Parkville and stole the county records from beneath the noses of sleeping residents. The last county meeting in Parkville had occurred in March, 1862. These high-handed highjackers were probably prophets anyway, for the demise of Parkville and Georgia Gulch proved imminent.

(Another version of this story, less colorful, excludes the midnight caper from the tale.)

While the rollicking residents of Parkville lived it up in town, miners high in the gulch had less luxury, particularly during the heavy winters. Alice Polk Hill, in her *Tales of the Colorado Pioneers*, related this Georgia Gulch story:

Have they told you of the two boys who had a camp way up yonder in Georgia Gulch? That was a bitter winter.

> We had the heaviest snow storm that winter that ever sifted down on these mountains, and the two boys in Georgia Gulch were snowed in for weeks and weeks, until their larder ran pretty low — it went plumb to the dogs, I might say, for they had decided that the poor, woe-begone 'yaller purp' must serve them for the next meal.
>
> Neither of them could scrape up courage to slaughter the brute, for a miner's dog is dear to his heart; they talked about drawing straws, and finally concluded to chop off its tail, out of which they made soup; the famishing are never very choice. They gave the poor dog the bone, and being refreshed by their porridge, went in search of game. Success crowned their efforts, and they returned in the evening with enough to keep them from starving until the snow melted; but the mutilated pup was sorely grieved.

Environmentalists of today would gaze in horror at early prospectors who leveled the green forests for firewood and tore open the belly of the earth in their relentless search for gold. When Conner returned to Georgia Gulch from South Park one spring, he "found the steep mountainsides stripped of timber." Curiously, many stumps appeared five, ten and fifteen feet above the April snow. But the heavy winter snow had reached that height when miners felled the trees.

Conner tells the story of one hapless miner, Jim Bennett, who mounted a steep hillside in search of firewood. He cut a long, heavy pole and began to descend the mountain, dragging the log with his ax handle firmly embedded in the wood. Bennett wore the old-timer's "snow shoes". We call them skis, but clumsy ones, with their average length of eight feet and sturdy width of four inches.

Bennett slid easily down a ridge on his skis, gripping the ax handle with the log as incongruous rudder. Snow blanketed the many stumps there, except one, a huge hazard halfway down the hill. Unfortunately, the luckless logger soon discovered that the weight of his timber propelled him faster and faster down the steep incline. He practically sat down on his skis, clutching the ax handle in sheer panic as he shot down the hill with now-terrifying speed. As fate would have it, he hit the lone stump with shattering force. The impact sent him flying in an airborn somersault. The log went skidding into a creek. Skis went down one side of the ridge; personal belongings went down the other. Bennett, who lodged miserably in some deep snow where the crust broke and held him, emerged brusied but unharmed.

The fate of Parkville was a downhill slide as well. Celebrated placer claims played out. Destructive dredges finished off Parkville, but the town first destroyed itself. Summit County's first city, its earliest county seat, was ignominiously buried by its own tailings by the 1880's.

John Carter, a Tarryall *Miners Record* reporter, served as the first harbinger of Parkville's fate. " . . . they are tearing up the mother earth at a fearful rate and undermining houses," he wrote on September 14, 1861.

Twenty-one years later, the Denver *Times* headlined its January 8, 1882 article, "A Buried City". The *Times* reported that hydraulic mining after Parkville's heyday had washed down gold-bearing glacial-deposited gravel beds and almost buried the city.

The *Rocky Mountain News* witnessed Parkville's final death throes when it announced the town had been swallowed by 20 to 50 feet of mining debris.

"Naught but the cones of a few roofs are to be seen," said the Denver *Republican* in a January 6, 1882 Parkville "obituary". "In future years some nomadic adventurer may prospect at Park City, and finding these old remains may conclude he has discovered a town engulfed by an earthquake."

What remains at Parkville today? On a hillside south of the townsite some rotted logs, notched for cabin construction, remain around eroded foundations. A small cemetery, with six unmarked stone-ringed graves, rests among the trees. The Masonic Monument, long a landmark, suffered destruction by vandals during the 1977-78 winter.

Sts. John

Tumbling, rock-strewn Sts. John Creek bisects a sweet wooded valley at 10,800 feet in the silver-rich Montezuma Canyon. Here, beside towering Glacier Mountain lies a ghost town unique in Colorado, the cultivated 1880's community of Sts. John.

Perched precariously on the side of silver-studded Glacier, two miles southeast of Montezuma, the bleached-bones skeleton of the town today looks as steady as an octogenarian on roller skates. And the monumental mine slag pile on the steep sides of Glacier looks ready to roar down to finish the old town off.

Though Sts. John claims history-book status as the site of Colorado's first silver strike in 1863, its real uniqueness arises from its prim and proper personality. Another lusty, bawdy and sinful mining town would be ho-hum; Sts. John, impeccable as the starched white collars of its Bostonian founders, is anything but average.

For example, Sts. John had no saloon. But the town did boast a 350-volume library with regularly-received Eastern and European newspapers. And, in its isolated near-timberline locale, where roads remained closed by snow all winter and summer's thaw revealed only a steep, rough and rocky track, Sts. John managed to create one of the showplace homes of the early Rocky Mountain West. The elegant, two-story mine superintendent's residence, furnished throughout in exquisite and expensive Sheraton pieces, shone like a gem in a rugged high country setting. Built for Captain Sampson Ware, the home was abandoned following the silver crash of 1893. Vandals made off with the Sheraton antiques in later years.

The Sts. John story really began with a man named John Coley, who first unearthed the rich silver lode around which Sts. John grew. Coley, who lived in Empire, Colorado, received one day in the early 1860's an intriguing letter from prospector friends in Nevada. The pair had fashioned crude bullets from lead while deer hunting near Glacier Mountain. Later, working with similar ores in a Nevada silver mine, they recognized their Glacier Mountain lead as rich silver ore. Coley, a loner, could travel with only "a bit of flour and salt on his back,

Sts. John superintendent's home still stands. 1979 photo (left) duplicates 1880's shot (below). Sheraton antiques and porch are gone, but century-old structure survives harsh winters. Mess hall (left) has collapsed. Berry home (right) remains sturdy.

trusting to kill game for sustenance" according to the Montezuma *Millrun's* first edition, an historical issue, June 24, 1882. He didn't need much prodding to hasten to the isolated source of these silver bullets.

Coley found Glacier Mountain and made history there with Colorado's first silver strike in 1863. He jerry-rigged a crude smelter-furnace from rocks and clay, which he packed over a hollowed-out log. When he lit his first smelter fire, the log burned away, leaving a perfect stone flue. Then Coley began to smelt silver ingots. His furnace remains, one-quarter mile from the town site. When "the boys" in Georgetown eyeballed Coley's ingots, the Montezuma Canyon silver rush was on!

Edward Guibor and Oliver Milner erected the first cabins at Sts. John in 1865-66 according to the *Millrun*. (Milner later became "Mailman Milner", struggling against heavy snows and bitter temperatures to carry the mail over the mountain trail to Breckenridge for a fee of $15 round trip.)

Sts. John, originally called Coleyville, was renamed in 1867 by a group of Freemasons to honor their patrons, Sts. John the Baptist and John the Evangelist. Prospectors there had in 1865 uncovered the dazzling Comstock Lode, a perpendicular stand of silver ore averaging four to five feet thick, at 12,000 feet on the southwest face of Glacier Mountain. Combining the Coley and Comstock Lodes, the Boston Silver Mining Association created the rich, productive Sts. John Mine.

The enterprising Bostonians took a giant step for Colorado silver mining progress when they constructed in 1872 the most modern and complete mill and smelter works of its kind at Sts. John. To build this mini-miracle at 10,800 feet in isolated Montezuma Canyon required an enormous outlay in money and manpower. Bricks imported from Wales and machinery fabricated on the East Coast were painstakingly transported to Sts. John by sailing vessel, railroad and ox team.

Called in to construct the stamp mill at Sts. John was a 30-year old Denverite who moved his family to the high-country mine town for a year in 1871-72. His son, John Irving Hastings, a small boy at the time, later published the elder Hastings' 1871 diary.

The grueling work of wrecking the old quartz mill and building the large new one, struggling through 12-foot snow depths to do it, provided quite a challenge. But, for the family, mountain living in isolated Sts. John may have proven an equal challenge. Mrs. Hastings soon learned to start Sunday's beans cooking by noon on Friday, because Sts. John's lofty altitude meant a low boiling point. The children learned the value of mountain ecology when avalanches roared down from steep valley walls, stripped of their protective timber by greedy miners. Mr. Hastings adopted the curious costume of high country travelers — a black suit, soot-blackened face and snowshoes to protect himself from harsh high-altitude ultraviolet rays. Sunglasses and sunscreen lotions were not available to combat the sun-on-snow brightness of the alpine winter day.

For the children, winter in the mountains meant staying indoors. They floundered in the fine Colorado powder snow, deep as their porch. But on New Years Day, 1872, Mr. Hastings "finished the children's snowshoes, after night."

"We were literally confined to the house without them," writes young Hastings. "Mine were six feet long, while my sister's were eight feet in length. They were a delight and we soon learned to use them. We may have had a few falls, but nothing serious in the soft snow."

Mr. Hastings had made the snowshoes, forerunners of today's skis, with four-inch wide spruce boards, one-half inch thick. The tips soaked in boiling water till they could be turned up. And a toe cap, fitted with lashings, served as the binding. A five-foot long pole provided steering and braking power.

While his father attempted to cope with shipping and building-supply problems in snow-bound Sts. John, John and his mother waited for mail. Letters and a few newspapers came over the snow-blanketed Range from Breckenridge on the mail carrier's back, during the early years. After Montezuma received its postoffice, mail came up from there by saddle. "Possibly there were two or three newspapers," young Hastings writes, "and they would be read to shreds."

The family probably possessed few books of their own in Sts. John because travel from Denver over hazardous Argentine Pass demanded transportation of bare necessities only.

"Family arrived at Sts. John 10 p.m. after a week's hard travel," read Mr. Hastings' journal entry for October 7, 1871. When Argentine Pass got windy, travelers sometimes had to crawl, on hands and knees, over the blustery summit. Young John remembers peering over the edge of a narrow shelf and "seeing below a brawling mountain stream..." with "...what remained of a broken wagon and some household furniture, belonging to some family whose wagon had failed to get over the pass as we did."

On July 1, 1872, Mr. Hastings' proud new stamp mill crushed its first ton of silver ore, ready then for processing in the new smelter. Soon the new mill ran day and night.

Progressive Sts. John Mine owners built mill in 1872 to crush ores stockpiled from district's first silver lode. Photo, 1898.

Town fortunes fluctuated with silver value. Smelter appears (rear) in '80's photo.

A monstrous hurdle in the development of mining at Sts. John had been scaled. Before 1872, bulky silver ores had to be shipped overseas all the way to Swansea, Wales where costly refining processes separated the precious metal from the lead ore in which it occurred.

In 1878, the company changed hands and the Boston Mining Company took over. Under its cultivated care, the company town began to blossom into a cosmopolitan community, the envy of surrounding camps.

Stephen Decatur, impetuous and highly-verbal Montezuma Canyon community leader, reported in the Georgetown *Colorado Miner* on December 19, 1879:

> Is this a section of Boston, Massachusetts, transplanted to the Rocky Mountains? The buildings, mills, furnaces, reducers, and offices, 50 in number, are not quite so pretentious in their architecture and material, but the neatness of the place, the thrift and energy and cultivated society of Sts. John, reflects credit on its founders, Boston Capitalists, who have built up this gem mining camp of Colorado. Here are no doctors, lawyers, or saloons where "liquid damnation" is sold for gain, but there is a library of 350 volumes of rare literary merit, piles of home and foreign magazines, and a great many files of stately newspapers.

Sts. John boasted an assay office, which housed its library, a company store, sawmill, two and one-half story boarding house, postoffice, guest house, ornately-trimmed residences for the superintendent and foreman, a mess hall, a blacksmith shop (burned in 1872), and many miners' homes, plus the stamp mill and smelter. Since the town sanctioned no saloon, local miscreants were forced to travel the steep, hairpin-strewn track down to Montezuma in order to sin — the proverbial road to Hell was not paved!

One of these citizens, Bob Epsey, returned to town in a deplorable state one night and felt obliged to sleep off his night's libation under a friendly tree. Next morning he awoke and groped for a rock to steady the world whirling about him. The rock worked loose and — you guessed it! — old Bob scored another silver strike at Sts. John.

Not all of the Sts. John residents were of Epsey's stripe. Most led flawless moral lives, often dedicated to higher values. Such a man was the British-born mine manager, Mr. Mumby, a physical fitness devotee.

Mumby maintained the practice of an early morning cold bath. Daily, he jogged the two miles to Montezuma and jolted his sluggish metabolism with an icy splash in a pool that had been dammed in the river.

Unfortunately, Mumby's daily dip was frowned upon by those Montezuma families who had built the pool. Having constructed pipes from the pool to their homes for a summer supply of running water for cooking and drinking, these families voiced their keen distaste to the health faddist. Mumby was indignant, as only a British gentleman can be. Happily, winter soon set in, and Mumby took to diving from his second-story balcony into a snowbank for his daily pepper-upper. He emerged "pink and glowing, full of energy".

Winter skies always dumped an abundance of snow at Sts. John. In 1873, for example, a news story reported snow depth averaging nine feet at Sts. John. A shoveling crew cut through four remaining feet of snow in June to open the road between Sts. John and Montezuma. But the year of the "Big Snow" made these snow depths seem humdrum.

Winter 1898 yielded colorful stories from all over Colorado. At Sts. John, where steep, glacier-sliced canyon walls made avalanches a dreaded common occurrence, resident Carl Clinesmith counted ten major slides in 1898-99. The entire town of nearby Argentine was wiped out by an avalanche, probably during that famous winter.

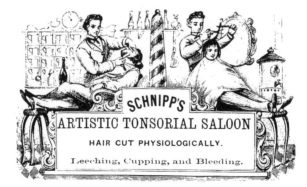

Smelter stack, shown, 1954, lasted till '68.

A slide area, still evident on the mountain west of Sts. John remains from an avalanche that once crushed the north end of town.

The Clinesmith family lived next door to the two and one-half story Sts. John boardinghouse, which had an upper window just above the snow's surface. Carl, a child during that magical winter, took great delight in the mammoth snowfalls that closed his school. His parents assigned him a big job, however. Carl's task: To keep open the entrance to the boardinghouse, which his mother managed. He cut a stairway from the surface of the snow to the boardinghouse doorway. He placed a door on this frame, creating a trapdoor. When it snowed, he climbed out the high boardinghouse window, careened crazily down the

241

slippery snowbank and shoveled off the trapdoor. Thus Carl maintained the entrance.

However, in 1898, Sts. John had already launched into its downward spiral. The Silver Panic of 1893, which created ghost towns all over Colorado, cast a somber pall over Sts. John. The mine shut down, then produced intermittently in later years, as it did from 1913-16. But its early successes during silver's heyday could never be equaled.

Tumbledown piles of weathered gray boards haphazardly arranged on stone foundations, withered carcasses of buildings and a few still-standing structures remain today to bear silent testimony to the Sts. John that once was. A small brick chimney stands preserved; the landmark Welsh brick smelter smokestack suffered destruction by vandals in 1968. Ten years earlier, a harsh winter had reduced the mill itself to rubble.

Sts. John, situated in a beautiful, glacier-carved valley, with views to soaring Grays and Torreys Peaks, lies below timberline in a snow-carpeted meadow. In summer, multi-hued wildflowers punctuate the green valley floor with bright color. The creek splashes crystal on the rocks. Blossoms peek out from behind gnarled, weatherworn remnants of logs. Nature is charming in disarray.

As you leave Sts. John, you can almost hear an echo of the lively past, the firm footsteps of the town's prim populace, the whirring of mine machinery. As you descend to Montezuma, voices of the past whisper a tale of days gone by... of bustling Montezuma, with its 100 buildings and flourishing newspaper ... of nearby Chihuahua, Peru and Decatur, sterling-silver towns that helped make the Montezuma Canyon one of the biggest silver producers in the U.S. .... of profitable Pennsylvania Mine, still visible today along Peru Creek, a dazzling star in a galaxy of famous Summit County mines.

All of these are echoes of a provocative past. And in the pristine silence of the glistening, snow-frosted woodlands surrounding Sts. John, you begin to really hear them.

Sts. John ghost town evokes memories of by-gone days. Prim Bostonian community has a history unique among Summit's lusty camps.

Winter 1916 snowfall blankets Kokomo's Ten Mile Avenue.

Kokomo

How the upper Ten Mile town of Kokomo began a century ago is the subject of lively dispute. Tale-spinners spun one tall enough to challenge the soaring Ten Mile peaks surrounding old Kokomo. They called it "The Story of the Dead Man Mine":

Icy wind blasts stung the faces of a Leadville prospecting party on Fremont Pass one moonless 1878 night. As the group forged through a bitter snowstorm down the Pass into the Ten Mile Canyon, cold sapped the vigor of one, a Scotsman. He died that night.

"The boys" wanted to give Scotty a good burial, so they found a prospector next day and paid him $20 to dig a grave through six feet of snow and six feet more of frozen earth. They stuffed Scotty in a snowbank to await the preparation of his final resting place.

Next day, the men had heard nothing from the gravedigger, so they returned to check. They found this note nailed to a tree:

"Struck it rich at four feet below grass roots. Gone to town to record location. Will be up to plant old pard in the morning!"

So the lucky gravedigger recorded his claim in Leadville and around the silver strike a new town sprang up: Kokomo.

A less colorful, but probably more factual version of Kokomo's beginnings appears in an 1879 Business Directory of Leadville, Kokomo and Carbonateville issued by Clark, Root and Company. Their Kokomo section asserts that Denver's Captain Amos. C. Smith, led a prospecting party into the Ten Mile Canyon. On February 8, 1879, the hardy Captain pitched a tent on Sheep Mountain's eastern slope just south of Kokomo Gulch. Despite deep and drifting snows, Smith took a shine to the place. He platted a 320-acre townsite there. Captain Smith, who later helped form the Ten Mile Land and Mining Company, then sat back and watched his new town grow.

Silver crazed miners flooded over Fremont Pass following Charles Jones and Jack Sheddon's smashing fall, 1878, discovery of the rich Robinson Mines Group. The White Quail Lode, struck soon after, further whetted their excitement.

Kokomo faced some stiff competition for town supremacy. Carbonateville, a sizeable, though short-lived, town at Fremont's base, and Robinson, two miles from the Kokomo site, had already sprung up on the silver-studded mountain slopes along Ten Mile Creek.

Kokomo boomed anyway. Miners swarmed to the camp. Three months after the February town platting, Kokomo held an election to incorporate. The number of voters more than doubled the total polled by big, bustling Leadville in its first election a year earlier, according to the Clark-Root Directory. Kokomo voters obtained town incorporation on June 3, 1879.

Mine historian Frank Fosset, boggled by the Ten Mile's lusty, sprouting and sprawling camps, reported:

> The embryo cities of Kokomo, Summit, or Ten Mile, and Carbonateville presented a strange medley of log cabins, tents, and primitive habitations, and the prices of town lots compared in altitude with the places in which they were located. There were from thirty to fifty arrivals daily all through the spring (1879), when the melting snows made the imperfect roads almost impassable.

By 1879, Kokomo's rapid-fire growth produced a population of 1,500, a good chunk of Summit County's total 6,000 population. (Summit population stood ready to skyrocket, as the 1880 lode mining boom began.)

Kokomo clung to the Sheep Mountain slope near the confluence of Kokomo and Ten Mile Creeks, with "the little stream of Kokomo (Searles Creek) bounding the town on the north. Its altitude, a dizzy 10,618 feet, made Kokomo the highest incorporated town in Colorado.

"Kokomo" an Indian word, means "young grandmother". Miners from Indiana named the Ten Mile mine camp for their home town. Kokomo had a twin town, a Siamese twin, in fact, named Recen. The Recen Brothers platted their new town in the valley just below Kokomo across Searles Creek. The two towns grew together. The Recen Brothers (pronunced Re-*seen* and sometimes spelled Recene) were Swedish immigrants who struck Ten Mile Canyon silver at the fabled Queen of the West Mine in December, 1878. The brothers had placer mined in the area for several years. Harry built Frisco's first cabin in 1873. Mrs. Harry Recen, story says, was the first woman in the Ten Mile Canyon. Daniel Recen made a big secondary strike at Jacque Mountain's Queen of the West in 1881. The pair had a placer claim, the Herculean Bar Placer, on a sandy flat just below Kokomo, filed and worked since 1875.

This claim proved the downfall of railroad executives who planned a town just below Kokomo. The Denver, South Park & Pacific Railroad was enroute to the Ten Mile. 1880's rail promoters got rich by platting towns along the rail line. "Junction City", a soon-to-flourish rail depot town, with lots already on sale, took a fatal nosedive when the Recen Brothers showed up and claimed ownership of the site. According to the April 26, 1879 Denver Daily *Tribune*, "the possession of title lies clearly with the Recen Brothers, who have their flumes in their ditches built and reservoirs made, ready for extensive mining operations this year".

Another Kokomo "suburb", Clinton City, also had its lots staked off and streets laid out, plus a single log structure built. But Clinton City never passed the embryo stage.

Transportation proved Kokomo's biggest problem. The Loveland Pass road had opened in 1879 and stagecoach service from Georgetown to Kokomo began. Thus passenger service from Denver (using the railroad to Georgetown) was assured. But ores had to travel by pack train to Leadville and food supplies had to come via pack train from that mining mecca as well. Upper Ten Mile miners and settlers soon pitched in to construct a road from Kokomo to Leadville. But ore wagons had to wait half the summer for the mud-clogged road to dry, as the last of winter snows melted in the high meadows.

". . . the bad roads render freight rates so high that prices seem almost unreasonable," the Denver *Tribune* observed. " . . . flour, sells here at $12 a sack, and ham at twenty cents and sugar at the same price. I saw a grocer receive a barrel of vinegar on which the freight from Leadville was twenty dollars."

Despite its considerable drawbacks, Kokomo mushroomed "so that after an interval of a week or two, one scarcely recognizes the place". Kokomo burgeoned into a construction city, with hammers ringing, saws buzzing, workmen shouting and oxen bellowing. The air rang with this joyful racket.

"Four sawmills are running night and day at full blast, with people standing around awaiting their turn to get lumber at $50 per 1,000," said Muriel Sibell Wolle quoting an 1879 source in *Cloud Cities of Colorado*.

The construction scramble did little to alleviate sky-high prices.

One of Captain Amos Smith's two-story buildings, with basement, leased for a year at a $200 monthly rental, a shocker by 1880 standards. E. B. Ketchum purchased a corner lot at Ten Mile Avenue and Kokomo Street for a scandalous price — $650. But Ketchum recouped his purchase price when a contractor excavated a basement for the elegant three-story building and discovered — Silver! The "true fissure vein some four feet in width" assayed from "311-728 ounces of silver to the ton", according to the Clark-Root directory. Ketchum named his basement mine the Jennie W.

(Two homeowners also struck silver while digging cellars, Kokomo legend relates.)

The ne'er-do-wells, and rogues that populated every camp had a heyday in old Kokomo, where the illicit practice of claim-jumping went one villainous step further to "home-jumping". When lumber ran scarce and rascals were plentiful, scenes like this May, 1880 Kokomo house-jumping occured:

> A gang of enraged residents all armed to the teeth rode into town at breakneck speed and reaching the building demolished the door and took possession. Five hundred citizens joined them and tore the building in fragments and scattered it upon the streets. Public sentiment is so strong against jumpers that hanging is openly discussed.
>
> (Leadville Weekly *Democrat*, May 22, 1880)

These skirmishes failed to dampen Kokomo's dynamic growth. Its postoffice opened May 5, 1879. Summit County's first newspaper (and its highest), the outspoken Summit County *Times*, debuted in Kokomo on September 27, 1879. The weekly *Times* appeared each Saturday under the firm editorial hand of Thomas Gowenlock (also Kokomo's 1882 mayor), who predicted "stagnation and death" for the town if it failed to support his newspaper. Gowenlock claimed the *Times* ranked not only as Summit's loftiest, but the "world's highest newspaper".

By 1880, Kokomo had a school, in Summit's third school district. The school opened for a three-months session that summer. By 1881-82, the Kokomo school grew to 104 students.

The Masons built Kokomo's pioneering Masonic Lodge in the early '80's, the "highest Masonic Lodge in the world, except for Peru". In later years, Masons moved the Lodge's exquisite old furnishings to Leadville, where they occupy a special room in that town's Lodge. "The old organ works just as it used to," said Edna Enyeart in a Summit Historical Society taped lecture. Kerosene light fixtures and all accessories remained intact.

As early as fall, 1879, Kokomo boasted an impressive roster of businesses lining its streets and avenues. The town had two smelters to serve hundreds of area mines — Graff & McNair's and Davidson & Company. To lighten the cares of hard-laboring miners, Kokomo also featured four "concert saloon" and dance halls. Their frisky names: Red Light Dance Hall, the Light Fantastic, Variety Theatre Comique and Jardin Mabille.

A partial list of fall, 1879 businesses taken from the Clark-Root directory includes:

Assayers	1	Druggists	4
Attorneys	5	Dry Goods	4
Bakers	5	Freighters	4
Banks	1	Furniture	1
Barber Shops	1	Gentlemen's Goods	4
		Groceries	17
Blacksmiths	3	Hardware	4
Billiards	1	Hotels	11
Boots and Shoes	7	Liquor Establishments	
Bowling Alley	1	(with 8 "clubrooms")	23
Butchers	3	Livery	7
Carpenters and Builders	24	Physicians	2
Cigars	30	Restaurants	19
Civil Engineers and Surveyors			
	5		

In 1879, Kokomo stood as unique among Summit's mountain mining communities: Kokomo had a fine *brass band*: Professor Graff, Musical Director, led the splendiferous musical troupe.

Hospitality flowed from Kokomo's public lodgings. Herman Stern's Pennsylvania House offered the traveler "a hearty welcome and pleasant people," according to the April 26, 1879 Denver Daily *Tribune*. "Mr. Stern's little daughter was the first maiden in the new town and received presents of one or two lots on that account." Woods Hotel owned by Henry Woods and John Gallagher, "two very pleasant and genial gentlemen" was rated a "first class" hotel by the *Times*. The hotel had started as a collection of tents. Kokomo had an impressive eleven hotels in early 1879. Boardinghouses also served lodgers, but some of these were simply tents, chilly accommodations in lofty Kokomo.

Ten Mile Avenue served as Kokomo's main street. Woods' Hotel, Harder's Bakery and Restaurant, Sanders Place (selling wines, liquors, cigars), Lippelt and Bowman, Druggists and Apothecaries, and other enterprises lined the busy street.

Business began as usual one brisk morning in October, 1881, with pack trains unloading in the street, shopkeepers unlocking their doors and saloon owners polishing their bars. But by day's end, Ten Mile Avenue stood in smokey, charred ruins. Fire broke out and leapt on the October wind from one wood-frame building to another. Proud Ten Mile Avenue rose in pillars of flame. Firefighters struggled to supply a bucket brigade from trickling autumn stream flows. Much of Kokomo suffered complete devastation from the blaze. A Robinson family came over to view Kokomo's remains and found only a scorched safe still standing on ruined Ten Mile Avenue. Damage estimates ranged between $300,000 and $500,000.

Kokomo businessmen and homeowners reeled from the ravaging fire's destruction. Then they regained their high spirits and began to rebuild. But their new shops, offices, hotels, saloons and the rest went up in Recen, Kokomo's twin town. For a while, the expanded community used the name Kokomo-Recen, and the distinction still persists, but finally the merged towns became commonly known as Kokomo.

Life goes on, and Kokomo's high life resumed with gusto. A year later, in 1882, James Brooks' Miner's Restaurant was serving frog's legs for Christmas, prospectors were bellowing for more beer at the Svea and other saloons, Father Fertaur, pastor of Robinson's Catholic Church was promoting a Recen parish, and W. P. Pollack had launched his Boss Bakery and Grocery Store.

(W. P. Pollack, for whom a Kokomo street was named, was probably the same W. P. Pollack who pioneered as Breckenridge's first Summit County clerk and recorder in the early 1860's. Pollack also served as Kokomo's 1882 notary public.)

D. T. Mitchell acted as Kokomo's postmaster. Victor Hills offered engineering and surveying services. Baugher & Company sold hardware. Rhone and Scott hung out a lawyers' shingle as did McDonald and Howard. And the Bergen House Hotel opened on Pollack Avenue. These were just a few businesses flourishing in new Kokomo-Recen.

Women's liberation sparked life in old Kokomo with the same controversy it caused across America almost a century later. Robinson's Summit County *Circular* reported on February 18, 1882:

> There was a suit at Judge Morrison's court on Wednesday, over some wearing apparel, in which all the frail females of Recene and a majority of those from Robinson participated. Some of the tallest swearing it was ever a justice's lot to listen to, was indulged in by the witnesses.

In 1881, Kokomo received rail service on the Denver & Rio Grande's Blue River Branch from Leadville. The town's businessmen and mine owners breathed a communal sigh of relief. Fare to Denver was $11.55, according to Crofutt's 1885 *Gripsack Guide*. Kokomo's Summit County *Times* in April, 1882, reported: "The average travel to Kokomo per day foots up to about 40 persons. Kokomo receives two cars of merchandise daily, by the D. & R. G." But Kokomo's rail depot, in old Recen, lay out in "the suburbs" and passengers had to haul their luggage uphill into town.

The Denver, South Park & Pacific Railroad, which had pushed its way over Boreas Pass to Breckenridge coveted a route to Leadville. This narrow-gauge line would eventually lay its track side by side with the Denver & Rio Grande through the Ten Mile Canyon to Leadville. At Kokomo, the rival lines raged in dispute over right-of-way. Finally, the D. S. P. & P. built two trestles, long remembered by Kokomo residents, and rode right over the D. & R. G. track. A sizeable rail spur at Kokomo went to the Kimberly-Wilfley Mill in Searles Gulch. Ties, spikes, broken ore cars and machine parts mark this site.

By 1885, Kokomo-Recen had a city hall, a fire department, the rail depot and a police department. R. Morrison served as justice of the peace and police magistrate. W. P. Pollack, agent for the Recen Town Company, was Recen recorder and treasurer, while A. E. Chase acted as Kokomo clerk and recorder, so the towns had not yet fully merged. The 1885 *Colorado Business Directory* lists enough saloons to slake an army's thirst, plus one hotel, the Clifton House (Mrs. Emily Anderson, proprietor). Crofutt's 1885 *Guide* mentions the Western (H. S. Strong, proprietor) and the Summit as Kokomo's principal hotels. The town then had a bank, two smelters, the White Quail and the Greer, plus both a daily and a weekly newspaper.

Kokomo kicked up its silver-cleated heels throughout the 1880's. Rich mines riddled the nearby mountains. Jacque Mountain alone had 200 claims, according to Kokomo surveyor Victor Hill's 1882 map. Sheep Mountain had at least 50. Elk, Tucker, East Sheep and Fletcher had hundreds.

Then came the Panic of 1893. Silver's price plummeted. Kokomo, hard hit, struggled to survive until 1903, when rising silver prices prompted a resurge in area mining. During that lean decade, 1893-1903, Kokomo had some tense times.

The incredible Big Snow Winter of 1898-99 cut Kokomo off from the outside world. The railroads gave up, and Kokomo waited out the winter-long storm, praying for spring.

Snow depth reached rooftops. Elizabeth McDonald Giberson remembered jumping from the upper windows of Kokomo's landmark two-story hilltop schoolhouse onto the snow. That winter Kokomo stepped up its tradition of checking on miners high in the nearby hills. At a set time soon after dusk, the miners all placed lamps in cabin windows facing town. If a lamp failed to appear, rescuers snow-shoed in with aid.

When spring finally came (snow remained through July in the high places), summer brought new challenges. In August, 1898, gun-slinging bandit Pug Ryan and his gang held up Breckenridge's classy Denver Hotel game room and hightailed it over the range to their "Robbers' Roost" hideout — in Kokomo. A bloody gunbattle between Ryan's gang and law officers ensued, killing a beloved Kokomo resident, Sumner Whitney. Kokomo went wild over the incident and didn't settle down for weeks. Ten years later, Kokomo children uncovered Ryan's buried loot. (See Chapter 17 on Pug Ryan.)

Kokomo gained fame in mining history when A. R. Wilfley invented his hallmark "Wilfley Table" there in 1895. The big Kimberly-Wilfley Mill dominated the turn-of-the-century Kokomo landscape.

When the twentieth century dawned, Kokomo's population had dropped to 350. William Adams enforced the law as 1900's constable, W. P. Swallow was postmaster, and G. R. Thompson assayer. Mrs. "Ma" Buffington mothered her guests at Kokomo's prestigious Mountain House Hotel. The Ten Mile Mining District's exclusive Sulphide Club had its first banquet in "Ma's" posh parlors. G. W. Quackenbush ran another local hostelry. The Arnold Meat Market and J. E. Riley's groceries provided foodstuffs while J. W. Dowd's Ten Mile Mercantile attempted to supply everything else. Well-known Ten Mile Canyon mine owner Peter Breene headquartered his big Colonel Sellars Mine at Kokomo. W.

Cramer began an 18-year stint as Kokomo schoolmaster in 1900. "Blackie" Biggens became Kokomo's most famous bootlegger during Prohibition.

Stubborn and tough, Kokomo refused to succumb to a twentieth century that made ghost towns of its neighbors. Kokomo had survived a destructive blaze, persevered the 1893 Silver Panic, and would endure cessation of its lifeline rail service in 1937.

Kokomo held on — as a wartime mining center in the forties when the Lucky Strike, Kimberly and Wilfley reopened to supply base metals for the military effort, and as a 1950's 200-population employee community for the Climax Mine. A March 2, 1958 *Rocky Mountain News* feature article highlighted Kokomo's skiing schoolmarm, Miss Emma Sawyer, who like her students skied daily to her Kokomo school classroom. Internationally-known skier Magnus Bucher, a former Kokomo teacher, had instructed Miss Sawyer in the sport. Her one-story brick schoolhouse is the only building left at Kokomo today.

The American Smelting and Refining Company mined several million dollars worth of lead and zinc near Kokomo between 1945 and 1950, the November 6, 1952 Denver *Post* reported. And Walter Byron re-opened the Recen boys' old Queen of the West Mine, discovered by them in 1878.

But death leered at the historic Ten Mile Canyon town. By fall, 1959, Climax had purchased much of Kokomo for future use as a tailing pond. The post office closed in October, 1965, after 86 years of service. Kokomo residents moved their 100-grave cemetery in 1966. In July, 1971, during the Climax vacation shutdown, the historic buildings in the twin towns of Kokomo and Recen were torn down and burned.

Today, Kokomo is gone. Only its site remains on the terraced hillside above the Ten Mile Creek. Foundations are scattered here and there around the mouths of Kokomo and Searles Gulches. Though the Climax Molybdenum Company has an ambitious plan for restoring the upper canyon to a natural state, the Kokomo scene today is grim. A chalk-gray dam for Climax's lower tailings pond looms large beside the century-old townsite, soon to be buried in molybdenum tailings.

Robinson

Robinson, Summit's biggest 1880's silver town, streaked to success. Its meteor rise once rivaled even the nearby silver mecca, Leadville. But tragedy punctuated Robinson's history. Incredible silver strikes precipitated untimely deaths. Lucky prospectors unearthed bonanza riches while others endured the harsh winters, hard work and privation for nothing. A crowded and colorful community history paled under the deathblow of silver's 1893 price plunge. Ten Mile's shining star city, Robinson, finally succumbed, like its neighbor, Kokomo, to ignominious burial in a tomb of tailings from the Climax molydenum mine.

On Sheep Mountain's eastern slope, Robinson straddled Ten Mile Creek at 10,778 feet, two miles above Kokomo in the silver-rich upper Ten Mile Canyon. Prospectors knew the area's mineral richness. In 1860, miners discovered a mind-boggling fortune in placer gold at nearby McNulty Gulch, below Fremont Pass. When McNulty placers played out in 1862, the pick 'n pan influx scrambled back over the range, leaving the upper Ten Mile Canyon to pristine silence.

Sixteen years later, in 1878, a Leadville merchant named George B. Robinson grubstaked (for half-ownership in the discoveries) two miners to prospect the Ten Mile around McNulty Gulch. The two, Charles Jones and John Sheddon, struck it rich with ten dazzling silver mines in what became the famous Robinson Group.

". . . its permanency does not admit of question", said the Jan. 1, 1884 *Rocky Mountain News*, referring to Robinson, with its rich mines.

Robinson quickly bought out the two prospectors' share of the brilliant discoveries. Then he shined his shoes and bumped by horseback, rattling stagecoach and lurching rail car to visit New York City bankers. There profit-hungry financiers helped him raise $100,000 to organize the Robinson Consolidated Mining Company.

News of Ten Mile silver soon reverberated against the steep mountain walls of Leadville's Collegiate peaks. Hordes of prospectors swept over Fremont Pass from that town, 17 miles from Robinson, to search for silver. Elk Mountain's stunning White Quail and Wheel of Fortune Mines were soon discovered. Carbonateville at the base of Fremont Pass one mile southeast of Robinson boomed to a log metropolis with more than 60 businesses listed in an 1879 directory. Kokomo sprang into an instant city in spring, 1879. And Robinson, originally called Ten Mile City, the last of the three silver-studded "cities" in the upper Ten Mile, quickly snowballed in size, soon outdistancing its neighbors.

The Robinson Consolidated Mining Company "yielded extraordinary profits", according to 1890's historian Frank Hall. And George B. Robinson used his mining monies to build a gem of a town. A. J. Streeter had already erected the first building on Robinson's townsite along Ten Mile Creek. But Robinson would not be content with haphazard growth. He harbored big plans for his namesake town. This enterprising Coloradan set out in 1879 and '80 to create an outstanding community, which blossomed into the thriving hub city of Summit County. He erected the Robinson Hotel, helped to establish the Ordean, Myers and Company bank, began to build an extensive smelting and milling works and encouraged a number of local businesses to flourish. The Bonanza Hotel, the Robinson *Tribune*, launched in December, 1880, four sawmills, various stores and a telegraph office soon lined the prim wooden sidewalks of Robinson.

By October, 1880, Robinson had completed his smelting and milling works, "one of the largest" in the Colorado mountains, according to Crofutt's *Guide*. The big main building measured 120 by 56 feet.

George Robinson, the former Leadville storekeeper, had become a huge success. Though he was only a two-year Colorado resident, a tidal wave of popularity swept Robinson to election in November, 1880, as state lieutenant governor — but, to the shock of Coloradans, the man died before November's end.

At the pinnacle of his career, Robinson became embroiled in a dispute with Captain J. W. Jacque and others over the ownership of the rich Smuggler Mine. Armed conflict threatened to erupt. Robinson had placed rifle-bearing guards at the Smuggler Mine with strict orders to fire on intruders.

Robinson, alarmed by a rumor of a 100-man posse ready to capture the mine during the night of November 27, 1880, heard a disturbing second rumor — that a guard at the tunnel's mouth had deserted his watch. Accompanied by Robinson mine manager, J. C. Brown, Robinson went up to inspect the Smuggler property. The guard, Patrick Gillan, was on duty. He heard Brown's voice warning Robinson to stay away from the mine door. "I simply want to see if everything is all right," said Robinson, preceeding Brown along the narrow

252

path. He advanced to the door and shook it. Gillan cried out, "What do you want?" Not hearing Robinson's reply, the guard immediately shot through the door. The bullet caught Robinson as he turned to leave. He died November 29.

Legend says that a wounded Robinson gave the guard a $1,000 payment from his deathbed, the reward promised for killing the first intruder to threaten the disputed mine.

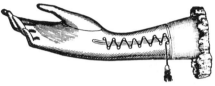

Georgia Burns Hill, daughter of the man who had taken Robinson's place at his Leadville store, retold this version of the lt. governor's death in "Memoirs of a Pioneer Childhood", published in the State Historical Society's *Colorado Magazine*, volume 32. Her father accompanied Robinson's body to Denver for burial. Then Burns moved his family from Leadville to Robinson to help look after Robinson's new store until the dead man's affairs were settled.

Georgia's memories of early Robinson reveal the character of life in the growing town. "The miners' cabins were built on the mountainside," she wrote, "the backs of them against it, and the fronts on high stilts, with snow piled up under them."

The Burns' first Robinson home stood among these miners' cabins. A muddy trail led down the lower slopes of Carbonate Hill to the town's business center in the valley where Mr. Burns managed Robinson's store, the largest in town, "nearest the mine".

A saloon-dance hall was already thumping out discordant music at all hours. Homes filled up with new families as soon as they were built. And a new set of noisy neighbors had just moved in:

> Not long after we had moved to Robinson we heard an unusual noise at the side of our house. And looking out of the window, we saw a group of small donkeys with uplifted heads, braying with all the strength of their lungs.
>
> "Why are they standing there making all of that noise?" mother wanted to know.
>
> "They're hungry," Father said. "Miners rode them before the railroad came and then they were abandoned to shift for themselves."
>
> Mother, who could never bear to think of anything going hungry, gathered up what scraps she could find and we children carried them to the little animals.
>
> Mother came to be sorry that she fed the burros as they became regular morning visitors, waking the neighborhood. But Madgie and I had lots of fun with them. They were gentle as could be and we rode around on their backs wherever they chose to take us, for we never learned to guide them.

Burros abandoned by prospectors were a common sight in the old camps. Many a Summit resident lost a night's sleep due to a braying burro outside his window.

Like Kokomo, early Robinson brought out the greed in a group of hooligans that flooded the early camp. "There was a great deal of claim-jumping in those days," reported Anna F. Robison, who lived in Robinson during the raw winter of 1880. Jesse McDonald, later a Leadville mayor and early 1900's Colorado governor, worked as a struggling young lawyer in the Ten Mile town. McDonald was almost killed by claim-jumping hoodlums when he attempted to straighten out some tangled Robinson mine ownerships. J. A. Thomas, who witnessed the murder attempt, "was quick enough with his gun" to get the angry claim-jumper, according to Ed Auge in the Summit County *Journal*.

Despite growing pains, Robinson expanded. Five hundred and ninety residents voted in the November, 1880 elections (no women) and male population totaled 850 at year's end.

For the growing town of Robinson, 1881 proved a banner year. On New Years Day, the Denver & Rio Grande railroad had steamed into town, to the intense joy of a boisterous welcoming crowd. The Rio Grande had hacked its way over Fremont Pass from Leadville encountering punishing problems enroute. "Much of the grading and most of the track-laying were done under a heavy fall of snow, the range being crossed in mid-winter," wrote Ernest Ingersoll in his 1883 *Crest of the Continent*. ". . . a striking instance of the energy and contempt of obstacles characteristic of Western railroad builders."

In 1881, Robinson received its school, in Summit School District No. 6, with 66 students in the 1881-82 school census. Miss Hamilton, a cultivated and mysterious lady who arrived in Robinson to play the piano for a local dance hall, became the first teacher.

Georgia Burns Hill remembered:

> By midsummer there were several families with children in Robinson so it was decided that a school should be opened. At father's suggestion, Miss Hamilton was chosen to teach it. She was an excellent teacher. The school house was just a mere shell of a building put up on the hillside opposite to the one where we lived.

In 1881 Robinson received its second newspaper, the *Ten Mile News*. Like its competitor, the Robinson *Tribune*, the *News* published until 1883.

For Georgia Burns' family, 1881 stood out as a year of sorrow. Georgia's beloved brother, four-year old "little Harry" had been pale and sickly that year. Though Mrs. Burns had older children and two babies to look after, she wore herself thin caring for little Harry, who desperately needed regular medical attention. ". . . it was impossible to get a nurse in the camp and the only doctor was off on a drunk," Georgia wrote. The family persuaded a Leadville doctor to vist the boy during illnesses. Georgia and her sister quit school to help with the babies.

The tragedy struck:

> Steadily now was little Harry losing ground. In late October when a blizzard swept down on us and the trains stopped running, the Leadville doctor could not get up to Robinson. The local doctor could not be found. Blood poisoning set in and on the first day of November, 1881, little Harry died.

To Mother it seemed the end of all things. We were all heart-broken. From the little window in my parents bedroom I watched them light a big fire on the snow. They kept it going until they could get a grave dug under it. A metal casket was sent up from Leadville in which the little body was placed. A preacher had come to the camp and he held church services and Sunday School in a store building on Main Street. He conducted the funeral services.

I cried my heart out because they took my little brother out in the cold and left him all alone in a hole in the ground . . .

Mrs. Burns' dying wish years later in Georgia was that little Harry's cold metal casket be removed from Robinson's frozen ground and placed beside her own grave in her native Georgia.

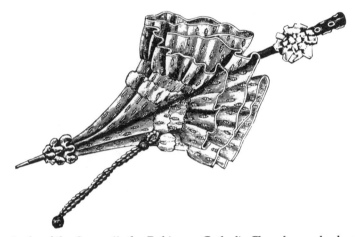

"Our Lady of the Snows", the Robinson Catholic Church, reached completion under Father Fertaur in 1882. A rollicking party initiated the new church building, with a sunny storm of fiddling music never to be outdone by the more stately hymns to resound there later. Fiddler Frank Boltz, second fiddler, Jim McCarnagie and piano-thumper George Pomroy played lively music for the high-stepping party-goers. The trio, long-remembered for frisky music-making at Kokomo, Robinson, Dillon and Frisco celebrations, were old-time favorites. Boltz rested the fiddle on his knee, instead of holding it beneath his chin in the normal positon, "and to see him manipulate it in this fashion was worth the price of admission," Ed Auge wrote in the Summit County *Journal*.

Prosperous local mine owner Peter Breene was asked if he would donate a chandelier for the new church. Giving testimony to the thought that too much music may have christened the church, the puzzled Breene replied, "Well, if somebody knows how to play it, I will."

By 1885, Crofutt's *Gripsack Guide to Colorado* listed Robinson's population as "about 1,000". Two railroads then served the bustling silver capitol, lauded as Summit's leading town. The Denver, South Park & Pacific railway had battled its way up the Ten Mile Canyon from Frisco, embroiled in a continuing right-of-way dispute with its competitor, the Denver & Rio Grande, all along the route. The D. S. P. & P. finally surmounted legal snaggles, arriving in Robinson in 1884. (But 1884 ranked as one of Summit's stormiest winters and the struggling D. S. P. & P. set off to a bad start on its Ten Mile extension.) Denver-Robinson passenger fare on the D. & R. G.'s 294-mile route via Leadville was $13.95. The D. S. P. & P.'s shorter route, 131 miles over Boreas Pass via Breckenridge and Frisco cost passengers $11.75.

The railroads helped to settle confusion over the town's official name. Early residents referred to the camp as both Robinson and Ten Mile. But after George Robinson's death, they pushed for Robinson as the town's official name in his honor. Crofutt's 1885 *Guide* still listed the community as Ten Mile, but asserted that the town "is called Robinson by the railroad companies". The railroads' name stuck.

Robinson's busiest streets, Main Street, Palmer Street, Ballou Street, Fairfield Avenue and Morgan Avenue were lined with businesses bustling in 1885. John Knox's Central Hotel, John Lapin's Eureka Hotel, D. H. Morris' Bonton Hotel, S. S. Morrow's Palmer House and Joseph Spencer's boardinghouse all provided lodgings, but the Robinson and the Bonanza ranked as the town's finest hotels.

Saloons dotted downtown Robinson. Saloonkeepers G. W. Dere, P. G. Foote, D. H. Gallagher, O'Leary and P. Peterson all doled out spiritous drink. Elizabeth McDonald, who grew up in 1880's Robinson, remembered her afternoon trips to her uncle's saloon for her father's daily bucket of beer.

The 1885 *Colorado Business Directory* also lists several grocery stores in Robinson, plus Burris' meat market, Christ Prichtle's bakery and W. H. Foote's restaurant.

Mine offices included the Robinson Mines headquarters (C. C. Moore, superintendent), Felicia Grace Mine (J. Meagher, sup't.), the Homestead (G. McCloskey, sup't.) and the Richmond (James Stewart, sup't.).

J. K. McDonald was Robinson's watchmaker in 1885; Frank Staery was the blacksmith and W. H. Woodford the notary and justice of the peace.

Life in 1880's Robinson had its high points. Children recalled with delight being able to make ice cream in July. They dug out snow that lingered in the shed or beneath the woodpile under the high porches to freeze the delicious treat. Robinson residents enjoyed an unparalleled mountain view. Georgia Burns wrote, ". . . we could look down and see the trains coming and going, with two engines attached when they went up and around a curve. Off in the distance was the Mount of the Holy Cross with the snow shining on it." Young Miss Burns also enjoyed the delicious and exotic wares supplied by Robinson's Italian fruit vendor. She missed a birthday party in punishment for this stolen pleasure: "I had taken advantage of Father's absence in St. Louis and had run up a bill with the Italian fruit stand man for California peaches and pears which I had long desired, but which Father had told me were too expensive for us to buy."

A certain Mr. E. H. Primrose also savored life in 1880's Robinson — especially after he began placer mining Robinson's slag-paved streets at handsome profit.

The Denver *Republican* featured the profit-minded Mr. Primrose in 1887:

> It seems that during the balmy days of Robinson, when the Robinson smelter was running at its zenith, that one of the streets of the town was paved about four feet deep with slag from the smelter. The process used at the smelter was not a very thorough one and the result was that thousands of dollars worth of silver ran off with the slag and was dumped in the streets for paving purposes. Mr. Primrose lately made the discovery that the slag contained a large quantity of silver and assays were made, returns ranging fron $50 to $100 per ton.

Robinson town fathers rose up in righteousness against Primrose's destruction of the town's thoroughfares, but after negotiation they simmered down. Primrose paid them 20 percent in royalties from his pavement placer operation.

Ironically, author Ernest Ingersoll had earlier raved about the area's ores, because they were so easy — probably too easy — to smelt. "Much of it is so admirably constituted that it 'smelts itself' — that is, it requires little or no addition of lead, iron and other accessories to its proper fluxion," Ingersoll said in his 1883 book.

Mr. Primrose wasn't the only Robinson resident having fun. 1880's social life kept a lively pace. While Fr. John Lewis Dyer was traveling to Robinson on weekday evenings to preach sobriety, Robinson's revelers were scrambling over the Ten Mile Range to Breckenridge, to attend some less-than-sober sprees held at Firemen's Hall, right next door to staid Fr. Dyer's church.

By 1890, most of the high-grade ore around Robinson had played out. The Wheel of Fortune's huge mill stood idle. The 1893 silver devaluation struck a death blow to area mines. In 1910, the *Colorado Business Directory* listed only a handful of Robinson businesses and a 150 population. Father Alger, the Catholic priest in 1892, numbered 15 Catholic families in Robinson and five single believers. Collections averaged a slim $5 per week.

In the 1920's, Ten Mile Creek began to swamp, sucking at foundations and rotting the city's fine wooden sidewalks.

In the 1930's, the town's only family stripped the big Catholic church down, board by board, for lumber and firewood.

The swamp overflowed the road into town. Robinson was only a corpse when the Climax Mine furnished it a mucky mausoleum — a silted tailings pond.

The Cast of Characters

"Roughing It": Lord Gore's Summit Safari

In 1855, four years before the Colorado gold rush began, a wilderness Summit County abounded with game. Herds of huge buffalo, numberless elk, deer and antelope, burly bears and a multitude of small game roamed verdant timber forests. Streams flashed silver with trout. Except for nomad Ute Indians, only a handful of hardy trappers had ever viewed the virgin land.

Enter: Colorado's most incredible tourist, Sir St. George Gore, a man with a crazy gleam in his noble eye, an Irish baronet who launched a hunting safari unparalleled in the history of the West.

"Lord Gore", as the American frontiersmen called him, strode onto the western scene trailed by a 40-man retinue of personal servants, marksmen, stockmen and guides. Gore, the Eighth Baronet of Manor Gore, County Donegal, Ireland, dispersed at least $250,000 on his three-year American adventure. (More than $1,850,000 in today's dollars.) This amounted to a drop in a silver-studded bucket for the $200,000-a-year landed Irish gentlemen. (Roughly a $1.4 million yearly income today.)

Behind the well-heeled huntsman rolled 28 vehicles — an elegant personal carriage, 21 handsome Red River carts, four sturdy Conestoga prairie wagons and two large freight wagons. Horses — 112 of the finest geldings — and oxen — 20 yoke — plus cows and pack animals followed. Fifty purebred hunting dogs yipped alongside, 18 of them blueblooded Irish staghounds and 32 sleek greyhounds. In Gore's personal attendance were two wigged and livried British valets, servants, mountaineers (among them the West's famous Jim Bridger), dog handlers, an expert fly-tier, trappers and voyageurs.

Seventy-five hand-carved custom-made rifles, 12-15 shotguns and countless pistols provided firearms for the hunt. And hunt they did! Lord Gore's three-year, 6,000-mile safari massacred for sport a generation of game — 2,000 buffalo, 1,600 elk and deer, 100 bears and countless antelope, small game and fish.

Jack Roberts, in his well-written, keenly-researched book, *The Amazing Adventures of Lord Gore*, introduced much of the history of the lordly huntsman. Roberts detailed the origins of Gore's grand American sojourn.

Sir St. George Gore began his adventure when he sailed from the seaport of Southampton in 1854, bound for New York, Pittsburgh and the outfitting post of St. Louis. With him, planning to accompany Gore as far as Fort Laramie, came William Thomas Spencer Wentworth-Fitzwilliam, scion of the richest family in British nobility. "Lord Fitzwilliam," an amateur astonomer, added scientific credibility to the unprecedented safari.

Gentried friends, Fitzwilliam's own American expedition and the paintings of western wilderness artist Alfred Jacob Miller had whet Lord Gore's appetite for a grand hunt in the American West.

Earlier arrangements with the London office of the powerful American Fur Company put that organization at the disposal of the expansive Gore. The St. Louis office would exchange American currency for drafts on Gore's bulging London bank account, serve as an employment agency for his retinue, counsel the baronet on his expedition and provide the latest maps for routing the journey. All this followed a policy ordained by St. Louis company president Pierre Chouteau, Jr., who encouraged explorers, scientists and missionaries to penetrate the untamed West.

When Gore's legendary cargo arrived at the Planter's House in St. Louis, the first ripple of a coming tidal wave of talk, gossip and rumor that would mark his safari began. St. Louis buzzed about the fold-up solid brass bedstead, the oval steel bathtub, embossed with the Manor Gore coat of arms, the flawless French carpets, pewter goblets, leather-bound first editions of classic literature, cases of vintage wines and liquors — plus a fur-lined commode with removable chamber pot!

The baronet's personal gun collection created its own wave of comment. England's prestige gunsmiths — Purdy, Westley Richards, Joseph Manton — had crafted custom pistols, rifles and shotguns, all percussion cap muzzle-loaders, for the highborn huntsman. These craftsmen carved fine English walnut for the gun stocks, then inlaid the wood with engraved plaques studded with bone, ivory and mother of pearl. All metal parts displayed intricate scrollwork designs. Rifle plaques depicted horse-mounted hunters, stags and hounds, while bird guns boasted detailed carvings of pheasant and quail.

Despite the mind-boggling cargo that Gore had transported to St. Louis, he launched a buying spree that curled the chin-whiskers of the frontier outfitting town's citizens. Gore's shopping list included 21 Red River carts, with genuine oak hoops and sturdy canvas covers. These high-wheeled, one-horse carts, enameled bright red, glided easily over rough terrain. Gore ordered four Conestoga wagons to haul his epicurean food supply, blacksmith equipment and tools. He bought 500 gallons of rotgut trade whiskey to smooth diplomatic relations with hostile Indian tribes. (Artist Charles Russell said: "If you could drink trade whiskey, you could get shot and killed, but you wouldn't die till you sobered up.") Gore also purchased food for his crew, stock animals and countless other supplies.

The baronet's new and luxurious yellow-wheeled carriage, with plump leather cushions, answered the high-rolling gentleman's requirement for easy travel, despite a bumpy, rutted, rock-strewn track. High wheels and specially designed running gear also made the carriage a perfect transport for the traveling aristocrat's collection of instruments — delicate chronometers, sextant, refracting telescope, compasses, thermometers and a cistern barometer.

By mid-June, 1854, the elegant entourage made its incongruous debut on the Santa Fe Trail (heading for the Oregon Trail cut-off), a caravan of carts, wagons, hunting hounds, and saddle horses and stock animals, guides and huntsmen, all led by the master's plush carriage. (Gore's transport trailed a two-wheeled odometer designed to measure what would become a 6,000-mile westward jaunt.)

Well-known guide Henry Chatillon led a three-man vanguard charged with the selection of campsites and the snaring of what little game was available on the much-traveled Oregon Trail. (Later, Henry's brother, Joseph Chatillon, would replace the guide.) Perched atop the baronet's carriage, in the driver's seat, lounged famous hunter-trapper, Jim Bridger, mountaineer who had penetrated the isolated reaches of the Rocky Mountain wilderness, Lord Gore's personal guide. The baronet, Oxford-educated, fluent in languages and conversant in the classics, took a huge liking to Bridger. Bridger, who signed his name with an X and quaffed his "Taos Lightning" without a quiver, referred to the courtly Gore as "That thar big Dutchman".

Gore's caravan crossed the prairie toward its destination, Ft. Laramie. Laramie would provide a staging ground for mountain hunts in Colorado, where Gore left his name on the craggy Gore Range, 9,000-foot Gore Pass, crystal Gore Creek and more. Lord Gore hunted in "New Park" where the Blue River flows into the Colorado, in the territory of what later became Summit County, Colorado. (Adjustments of county boundaries since diminished the size of this early ample county designation.)

Late summer in this untrammeled Colorado mountain park provided Lord Gore a huntsman's paradise. He arrived at the beginning of the annual buffalo mating season when the huge animals gathered in bands up to 500 in secluded areas along the lower Blue River to breed. Gore shot at anything that "walked, bawled, squawked, flew or swam", but the danger of the buffalo hunt fulfilled his dreams of adventure.

Astride "Steel Trap", the baronet raced into the wild crush of the hunt. The baronet himself had trained Steel Trap to respond to the pressure of the nobleman's knees during the fury of the chase. The huntsman's horse learned to

barrel into the melee of the stampeding herd, head for the right shoulder of the moving prey — and be alert to skirt an attack by an enraged wounded mammoth.

The rider had to fire and reload at a wild run, which meant pouring out the double charge of powder, loading the ball in the muzzle and pounding the butt to "seat" the ball, then capping the charge — all at breakneck pace. Lord Gore's critics maintain that the titled sportsman proved himself not only a poor marksman, but also refused to reload his own firearms, allowing a harried retainer to dash behind him reloading as fast as the baronet could empty the charge.

Hunting had become for Lord Gore the main activity of a leisured life — an avocation. His affluent cronies, all sportmen, spent their years in the same way. To imagine Gore as a poor marksman or a lazy hunter seems incongruous. But to level against him the charge of reckless slaughter of thousands upon thousands of American game animals for private pleasure is more valid. Sir St. George Gore toted home some trophies — prize pelts, racks and skins, but left behind him a monumental trail of animal corpses, a ghastly tribute to his love of "sport".

The idea of roughing it never clouded the baronet's patrician outlook. Unparalled camp luxury marked his move through the West.

Author Roberts described the baronet's peerless camp accommodations: Workmen preceeded Gore to the campsite where they shoveled a smooth plat on the rocky turf. There they would assemble the baronet's portable castle. After leveling the site, they dug a drainage ditch around the graded area. Then they set up Lord Gore's gay green and white striped tent. A large India rubber pad covered the ground and upon this workmen laid the handwoven French carpet. Then the crew lugged in the baronet's camp stove, rigging the stove pipe through a roof jack. British campaign chests and fine leather trunks, the oval bath tub, folding table and chairs, guns and gun racks, leather-bound books and other personal appointments followed. The final luxury, the portable solid brass bed, was made up with goose-down mattress and pillows, pure Irish linen sheets and Hudson's Bay blankets. The outrageous fur-lined commode took its place at the foot of the bed.

The baronet and Jim Bridger enjoyed a late gourmet dinner. Lord Gore's servants, wigged and grandly attired, prepared and served fresh game and epicurean side dishes. Rare vintage wines accompanied the repast. Sir St. George savored a snifter of brandy with his rugged companion and read to him from the works of William Shakespeare. (Bridger later critiqued Shakespeare's efforts as "too high falutin' for me".)

Lord Gore viewed with disdain the thought of rising early. While the slow-moving wagons set off promptly in order to reach the next camp before the pampered huntsman, the baronet preferred to sleep till 10 a.m. At 9, his valet tiptoed into the green and white tent to build a fire in the camp stove. Then he hauled in water to simmer for the master's daily bath. He removed the chamber pot from the commode, scoured it and freshened it with a spritz of lime. Quietly, he cleared the dishes from the sybarite's late dinner. Then he laid the tarpaulin and hoisted upon it the magnificent embossed bath tub.

When Sir St. George awoke from princely slumber at 10, the tent was toasty warm and the hot bath water stood ready to mix with cold for a luxurious bath.

Later, the baronet donned his hunting costume. No buckskin for the Eighth Baronet of Manor Gore! He wore corduroy breeches and linen gaiters over stout leather hunting boots. His pleated Norfolk jacket boasted bellows pockets for small game or ammunition. A deerstalker hat, the kind worn by the fictional sleuth Sherlock Holmes, capped his well-trimmed blond hair. He regarded his image in his camp mirror — a handsome, well-muscled sportsman, with luxuriant honey-colored sideburns and noble visage. The lord called for breakfast, anticipating the adventure of the day's hunt ahead.

Lord Gore's unruffled calm would be disrupted. During a later sojurn to the Black Hills, ferocious Sioux Indians robbed him of his equipment and stripped the clothes from his back. Lord Gore and his men were forced to walk barefoot and naked for weeks in burning sun, wind and rain till they finally found shelter with a hospitable Indian tribe.

(The baronet later distinguished himself by becoming the only private individual ever to offer his services to the United States government to raise an army for the extermination of the Sioux on a cost-plus contract basis.)

In June, 1856, Gore's cook wounded Big Plume, the Indian brother-in-law of Alexander Culbertson, the American Fur Company trader at Fort Union. And Gore's men managed to cause a disastrous forest fire that destroyed Indian land and game. Both Indians and fur company officials learned to hate Gore for his prodigal waste of timber and wildlife. Federal government agents Cumming and Maypenny initiated punitive action against Gore, planning to recover his pelts, antlers and other trophies, sell them and return the money to the Indians. But the market for hunting trophies proved poor. The plan failed.

Before leaving for his return to Ireland, the baronet offered his aristocratic supplies for sale to the disgruntled trader, Culbertson, at Fort Union. Culbertson's low offer stung the baronet's well-nurtured pride. The lord felt anger flooding his blue ·blooded. veins. Rage seized the Irishman. In its grip, he directed his men to haul his expensive supplies and equipment to a spot before the gate of the walled fort. Biographer Jack Roberts detailed Gore's orgy of destruction: He ordered the oxen unyoked, and then set the fine Conestogas and Red

River carts aflame! He heaped the green and white tent onto the fire. Campaign chests, French carpets and commode, linen sheets and leatherbound books, brass bed and bath tub fed the bonfire.

Lord Gore, who as a gentleman never drank to excess, began popping corks from his charcoal-aged bourbon bottles and quaffing the contents. As the fire roared, he opened his casks of trade whiskey to gaping onlookers. To the hated Indians, he gave his oxen and cows. (Better than the blackguard Culbertson!)

Delicate instruments melted into metal globs. Fuel for lamps exploded before the incendiary baronet. With a wild laugh, he lunged for his precious violin and hurled it in the greedy blaze. He pitched to the fire first editions of Dickens, Irving, Thackary and Scott. He unearthed the leather case containing his credentials, personal letters and his journal from his remaining clothes and belongings and lobbed it high above the conflagration, to watch it tumble through the heat haze into the flame.

The acrid smell of burning India rubber from his six-compartment rubber raft and the noisy explosions of fuel containers punctuated a bizarre scene. Firelight gleamed red on the drunken face of Sir St. George Gore. At the conclusion of this final tribute to a philosophy of waste, he ordered the debris from the fire to be pushed into the river so that no salvage would remain.

Madman? No. Lord Gore returned to Ireland to resume his life as the self-indulged Irish landlord. (He even perpetrated another hunting safari upon the exotic birds of Florida in the 1870's.) But, by today's standards, Lord Gore appears at least eccentric. His pampered camp life denied the reality of its untamed wilderness locale. His lavish use of funds for personal pleasure, his reckless slaughter of wildlife, stand today as criminal waste. To Gore, the typical 19th century gentleman, these vast resources existed for his pleasure.

Sir St. George slew everything with claws, paws, wings or gills — the only quarry the baronet failed to snare was his namesake's legendary dragon.

The Silverthorn Family

Breckenridge's pioneering Silverthorn Family stands out above the frenzied crowd of 1860's gold-seekers as unique. Why? Because in the face of brash excitement and bizarre events, the Silverthorns remained sane and steady. In a raw camp society of rootless male prospectors, the Silverthorns stood together as a strong family unit. In a rough-and-tumble time of greed, the Silverthorns emerged as community servants, performing acts of kindness, working to create a community in a camp populated by a bunch of strangers.

The miners loved Mrs. Silverthorn so much that they lugged a sled up Boreas Pass to meet her when she returned to Breckenridge from Denver each spring. They trudged to the top of the range on snow shoes, met Agnes Silverthorn "with loud hurrahs, and hats tossing in the air", and escorted her in style on the sleigh to Breckenridge. "How the boys loved her," an early Breckenridge resident told 1884 authoress Alice Polk Hill. She "was called the mother of the camp, the good Samaritan to all in trouble and distress".

Breckenridge remembered "the old Judge" at his 1887 death for "hundreds of kindly acts". He was "always ready to assist in any public work or to aid his neighbors . . ."

The Breckenridge *Daily Journal* eulogized the Silverthorns with this flowery tribute: "Scarcely a man ever spent a season on the upper waters of the Blue, or its branches, from 1860 to 1880, but has the remembrance of some kindly act by the deceased couple graven upon the tablets of his heart, to be effaced only when that organ ceases in life-giving beats."

Who were the Silverthorns?

The Judge, a spry, wrinkled, gnome of a man and his wife, Agnes, "a broad, buxom matron", had two "black-eyed beauties of daughters", Martha and Matilda. A Pennsylvania family, they were transplanted by circumstance to a lusty, squalling, newborn Breckenridge, Utah Territory. As hotel keepers, they would greet America's great traveler-authors who toured the Colorado gold and silver camps and remembered the Silverthorns in their books.

Marshall Silverthorn

Marshall Silverthorn, age 48, came to Colorado in late-winter 1859 to regain his health. He was so sick that traveling parties on the Kansas western border refused to allow "that old man" to join them, fearful he would die on the prairie. Yet the feisty Pennsylvanian displayed more spunk and energy than the most strapping Argonaut. When a departing gold rush group turned him down with "No graveyard deserters for us", Silverthorn saw red. He ripped off his coat, put up his dukes and danced around like a fighting rooster challenging the group's biggest, brawniest member to a fisticuff duel. Marshall Silverthorn didn't get his duel, but he did win passage with the Denver-bound party. They were impressed by the wiry little bantam — but they stowed some planks, suitable for a coffin, in the wagon bottom, just in case.

He was a tough, knotty little man, a leprechaun, with twinkling, merry eyes, grizzly gray hair and beard. He chewed tobacco constantly. He arrived in the tent and shanty camp of Denver, May 17, 1859. Colorado's dry, sun-scrubbed air returned Silverthorn to health. Less than a year later, in March, 1860, he was back in Pennsylvania, launching the return trip to Denver with Mrs. Silverthorn, and three young children. (The Silverthorn's youngest, son James, died at age five in 1863.)

Years later Martha Silverthorn's daughter wrote the story of her mother's trip. This portion of "The Story of a Colorado Pioneer" and other portions quoted later are written in Martha's "voice":

> In Council Bluffs we outfitted for the trip across the plains. We did not travel on Sundays. Mother devoted this day to washing, baking and cooking for the following week. Twice during the trip the Indians were determined that my father should trade my mother for some of their ponies. The last time they were inclined to be rather ugly about it and Father had quite a time with them.

Marshall Silverthorn and family arrived in Denver May 18, 1860 and lived one year in that brawling camp. Gunfights occurred regularly in Denver's Larimer Street nucleus. They decided to leave the scrappy frontier city and seek the family fortunes in Summit's gold-rich Georgia Gulch. But the Silverthorns stopped in Breckenridge — and there the Silverthorns stayed.

Mr. Silverthorn rented a house built by Breckenridge's first postmaster, O. A. Whittemore. Whittemore had converted his house to a supply store in spring, 1860, a year before the Silverthorns arrived. He sold the building because he saw new opportunities in mushrooming Parkville, where he opened a new store on the first floor of the just-completed two-story Masonic Lodge.

The Silverthorns' Breckenridge home was primitive:

> The floor of the kitchen was made of very old sluice boxes that had been worn until the knots stood out, caused by constant washing of water and gravel. As a rule these boxes were burned and the ashes panned for gold that would collect in the knots and crevices. The front room has a dirt floor with shelves and a counter running along one side. Father took a team and hauled sawdust from an old mill above town and covered this dirt floor to the depth of six inches. Mother sewed burlap sacks together and made a carpet . . . All the dust sifted through so it was easy to keep clean. In this room we made three beds, end to end, on the floor, by placing two logs one on top of the other. The enclosure was filled with hay, then feather beds that had been brought from Pennsylvania were placed on this.

Marshall Silverthorn plunged into placer mining and soon gained the recognition of his fellow prospectors. Silverthorn had served as a county legislator in Pennsylvania and as party delegate to Pennsylvania state conventions. Early Summit residents soon tapped his talents, appointing Silverthorn Judge of the

Miners' Court, the only local government available in the young Colorado camps.

"Judge" Silverthorn became the feisty public conscience of old Breckenridge. In 1887, members of the Princeton Scientific Expedition reported:

> While we were ridding ourselves of our numerous packages, the Judge disappeared. We found on going down that a drunken fellow had been behaving unseemly in the street, and that our little shrivelled up judicial authority had made out a warrant, served it himself, and seizing the prisoner by the back of the neck, had kicked him up the side of a hill to the calaboose, although he had complained of being very ill a few minutes before.

"The Judge" was tough.

Rules of procedure and court decorum never slowed the Judge in his swift dispensation of justice. Bayard Taylor, in Breckenridge to lecture, had his first introduction to the Breckenridge halls of justice in 1866:

> I noticed two individuals entering the building. One was middle-aged, and carried a book under his arm; he wore "store clothes." The other, a lively young fellow, with a moustache, sported a flannel shirt. The latter reappeared on the balcony, in a moment, and proclaimed in a loud voice,
> "Oh yes! Oh yes! The Honorable Probate Court is now in session!"
> Thereupon he withdrew. The announcement produced no effect, for he immediately came forth again, and cried
> "Oh yes! Oh yes! The Honorable Probate Court is now adjourned!"
> I waited, to see the Honorable Probate Court come forth, with the book under his arm; but, instead of that, the lively young man made his appearance for the third time, with a new announcement,
> "Oh yes! Oh yes! The Honorable Commissioners' Court is now in session!"
> How many other Courts were represented by these two individuals, I am unable to say; but the rapidity and ease with which the sessions were held gave me a cheerful impression of the primitive simplicity and peace of the population.

Court Week kept Judge Silverthorn hopping. Not only did the court remain in session all week, but fiddlers and an organist played up a merry storm for the annual Court Week Dance and spry Judge Silverthorn cut up with the friskiest party-goers.

Alice Polk Hill, the 1880's Colorado authoress whose personality combined elements of famous Hollywood gossip columnist Louella Parsons and a Dowager Queen, visited Breckenridge on the new narrow-gauge railway over Boreas Pass in 1883. Tracking tales for her book on Colorado pioneers, she contacted a Breckenridge resident, a writer himself, who regaled her about Breckenridge's best-loved pioneer.

> You must see Judge Silverthorn; he loves to talk of the old times. He came here in '59, and was judge of the Miners' court. He is a diminutive man, almost dried to a crackling, and has such a strange, weird look that you couldn't help wondering to what age or order of human beings he belongs. His hair and beard are grizzly gray, and he chews continually. When he tells a border tale his little keen eyes twinkle with humor and

intelligence, then he goes into convulsions of laughter and kicks up his feet until he resembles a jack-knife half open — forming a picture altogether grotesque. But he is the soul of honor and goodness, with a heart so large that it is continually running over with kind deeds and comforting words.

Mrs. Hill visited Breckenridge the year Mrs. Silverthorn died. Perhaps that is why she gives no indication of having met the Judge or his wife personally. She stayed not at the Silverthorn Hotel, but at the fashionable Grand Central Hotel.

That Marshall Silverthorn regained his health in Colorado is an undisputed fact. Any middle-aged man who could survive injuries from a trampling by runaway horses, as the Judge did, has to be in robust health. He also suffered a punishing fall, according to Bayard Taylor:

They, (Summit residents) have very little sickness of any kind, and recover from wounds or hardships with a rapidity unknown elsewhere. I was informed that the Honorable Probate and Commissioners Court once tumbled down a fearful precipice, and was picked up a mass of fractures and dislocations — yet here he was, good for several sessions a day!

Judge Silverthorn had attained some level of prosperity in Pennsylvania, but the 1857 recession reduced his means. In Breckenridge, however, his hotel, placer mining and other business interests gave him a measure of affluence. He used his new income to boost Breckenridge — and his own earnings. In 1880, Judge Silverthorn loaned $2,000 at a walloping 18 percent interest to the backers of a new Fireman's Hall, to house the newly-organized Breckenridge Fire Department. One of the new firefighting team's first two calls was a November 16, 1880 blaze at the Silverthorn Hotel, which they extinguished "with little damage".

The Judge also made his hotel available for visiting and local preachers to conduct worship services. The much-traveled itinerant, Reverend John Lewis Dyer, enjoyed the Silverthorn's hospitality during rest stops on his mountain travels. Even when no preacher could come, the hotel dining room rang on Sunday with the old Moody and Sankey hymns. A worshipper would read a printed sermon. It marked the beginning of a long tradition of church-oriented society in Breckenridge.

Silverthorn housed the court and county records at his Silverthorn Hotel in the 1860's (after Breckenridge acquired the county seat from Parkville), and operated the United States postoffice, established January 18, 1860, in his busy front room. The postoffice cancelled mail with a Utah Territory stamp — until February 28, 1861, when a new designation, Colorado Territory, became official.

In 1869, just when things began to get dull in old Breckenridge, when placer gold ran out and unemployed miners lounged in the streets, "Captain" Sam Adams stepped off his spirited saddle horse and into Judge Silverthorn's life.

Over cigars and barrel whiskey, Captain Adams confided his mission to the Judge and other Breckenridge leaders. Remaining on the books of the U.S. government was a provision for a sizeable bounty to be paid to anyone who found a Northwest Passage. Breckenridge, Adams explained, had the Northwest Passage route flowing outside its cabin doors — the Blue River began a network of navigable rivers flowing all the way to California.

To share in the cash reward, all Breckenridge had to do was build four boats and furnish supplies for the voyage.

The town jumped at the chance to throw off its boredom and embrace new hope. Carpenters hammered boat nails while ladies appliqued a huge banner reading: "Western Colorado to California — Greetings!"

Marshall Silverthorn gave a speech to christen the maiden voyage. He presented Captain Adams with a dog, to serve as naval mascot, and some of Mrs. Silverthorn's homemade bread.

Adams launched his Breckenridge Navy and immediately encountered a series of disasters that included smashed boats in river rapids, a landlubberly crew that jumped ship and the inglorious demise of the canine mascot.

With the Breckenridge Navy "down the drain", tiny Breckenridge returned to its sleepy lifestyle.

Judge Silverthorn made all the wheels turn in early Breckenridge. The Breckenridge *Journal* pinpointed it with: "At times, in the early days, he was the principal, and sometimes the only, business man in the camp. He was storekeeper, postmaster, justice of the peace, blacksmith and landlord by turns or all combined."

In the years following his wife's 1883 passing, Judge Silverthorn lived in Denver with his daughter, Matilda, who had become Mrs. Joseph C. Wilson in 1887. The merry old gentleman, who acquaintances said looked the same age for 25 years, refused to perch in a rocking chair. His idea of rocking was far more lively. At a September 14, 1887 Denver soiree, Judge Silverthorn was, as usual, the life of the party, "singing and romping about as gay as the youngest young lady in the party," according to a *Rocky Mountain News* story reprinted in *Blasted, Beloved Breckenridge*. He enjoyed an hour's romp with the children that evening. Then the Judge announced, "I'm feeling as young as any one of you, and if I see tomorrow, will be 79 years of age." A friend offered congratulations; the Judge warned him to wait 24 hours.

Then Judge Silverthorn strolled to one of the windows, gazed out momentarily and fell to the floor. A doctor rushed to the scene and found him dead. Cause of death was a common 1880's killer: Apoplexy.

(Actually, Marshall Silverthorn, born in 1811, died just before his 76th, not 79th, birthday, an error by the *News*.)

Five hundred mourners followed Judge Silverthorn's hearse to the cemetery, an indication of his popularity.

Agnes Ralston Silverthorn

Beloved Mrs. Silverthorn tacked muslin over her window openings in lieu of glass, sewed burlap bags together for carpeting, battled inflated camp prices (flour: $42 a barrel), baked pies for hungry miners — and still found time to play mother-hen to a wild and woolly prospector population.

Saturday was the week's busiest day for Mrs. Silverthorn. Mail from the East arrived that day. Although two other mails came in weekly, Saturday's mail drew in miners from the gulches outside Breckenridge.

". . . mother was asked to bake pies to sell the day the men came down for the mail," Mrs. Silverthorn's granddaughter wrote, "and on Saturday morning she would bake between 40 and 50 pies, and a 100-pound sack of flour was very often used in this baking. They were sold with a quart of milk, paid for in gold dust . . ." Mrs. Silverthorn made thirty or forty dollars on mail day.

Agnes Ralston Silverthorn proved herself to be proud and resourceful. Though she gladly served hungry miners, she refused to capitulate to the demands of Indian leader Colorow, who made a career of intimidating scared settlers into catering his meals. "Old Chief Colorow at one time threatened to kill mother and burn Breckenridge down because she would not cook extra meals for him and his squaws."

Though most white women in 1859 feared the Indians, Agnes Silverthorn faced them with unshakable grit. The Indians "stole everything", especially soap, bluing and sugar from the Silverthorn's first Colorado home at Denver's 14th and Larimer Streets. This pilfering Mrs. Silverthorn endured. But when a squaw stole young Martha's brand-new bonnet, Agnes grew angry. She had just finished the sun-bonnet, a fine affair "made with casing and pasteboard run in called slats". Martha identified the thieving squaw from a street crowd. Mrs. Silverthorn confronted the Indian. Had she taken the bonnet? "No" came the reply.

As a murmuring crowd gathered, Agnes took the squaw by the elbows, raised them and shook the woman till the bonnet fell out from her clothing! Trembling whites whispered "We'll all be killed over this." But Agnes Silverthorn had her daughter's bonnet.

Silverthorn Hotel (center), built in 1860, appears in very early Main St. photo.

Breckenridge had long coveted the county seat, and finally seized it from a declining Parkville in 1862. But Mrs. Silverthorn realized the precarious nature of this new-found position when she noticed the county clerk packing up the records in a burlap sack. ". . . when he had been called out for a while, she hid the sack and so doing saved the county seat for Breckenridge," wrote her granddaughter.

Agnes Silverthorn, plump, smiling and kindly, provided the kind of hospitality that made the Silverthorn Hotel her own personal success. A trip-worn, saddle-sore, bone-weary visitor, Bayard Taylor was "greeted like an old friend" by Mrs. Silverthorn. He thought sleeping on Mrs. Silverthorn's featherbeds, with gleaming white sheets and pillow cases, like dying and going to heaven:

> Mrs. Silverthorn kept her promise. When the artist and myself found ourselves stretched out in a broad featherbed, with something softer than boots under our heads, we lay awake for a long time in delicious rest, unable to sleep from the luxury of knowing what perfect sleep awaited us. Every jarred bone and bruised muscle claimed its own particular sensation of relief, and I doubted, at last, whether unconsciousness was better than such wide-awake fullness of rest.

Samuel Bowles, Springfield, Massachusetts *Republican* journalist, commented in 1869: "There is a good hotel here; of logs to be sure, with a broad buxom matron, and black-eyed beauties of daughters, to whom, after dinner, we consigned Governor Bross, with warning against his fascinations."

Bowles traveled with a party that included U.S. Vice President Schuyler Colfax and Illinois Lt. Governor William Bross, who was the long-lost brother of Summit's colorful Stephen Decatur.

And William Brewer, arriving a few years later, regretted missing Mrs. Silverthorn's hospitality:

> As I reined up to the first "hotel", we saw a fat, good-natured woman come to the door, and with her such a troop of women and girls (some of the latter decidedly pretty), that I feared the room was too little in that house for all of them and my troop of young men, so I went onto the next. Alas, I had not read what Bowles had said of Judge Silverthorn and his pretty daughters.

Brewer, accompanying a young, male college group, stopped at Rankins Hotel, "an equally good house". The group missed a "big party" at the Silverthorn's.

Rocky Mountain News Editor William Byers, touring Summit County to report for his new publication, the Tarryall *Miners Record* in 1861 chimed: "The Breckenridge Hotel, store and postoffice, three in one and one in three, is the best place to stop on the Blue."

In 1862, the Silverthorns added a two-story wing to their popular hostelry. Editor Byers capped their growing reputation for fine service when he praised a most patriotic July 4 celebration:

> After an Independence Day ceremony, the audience retired to Silverthorn's . . . they partook of one of the finest and most complete dinners ever served on the Western Slope of the Rocky Mountains. Here we found

the table spread with all the luxuries, from the oyster beds of the Atlantic to the silvery rivulets of the Western Slope, in which the speckled trout so greatly abound.

Music, "numerous toasts" and dancing at the Colorado House across the street worked up renewed appetites, later satiated by a sumptuous midnight supper. Thus refreshed, the party ably celebrated the national holiday till dawn.

For more than 20 years, the Silverthorns added a measure of grace to the budding Breckenridge cultural scene and permeated the town with their kindly spirit. When Agnes Silverthorn, then 63, died in 1883, the Silverthorn Hotel floundered.

Matilda Silverthorn Wilson

Early Breckenridge residents named today's Peak 8 ski mountain "Peak Tilly Ann" after Tilly Silverthorn and Ann Remine, the first two girls who climbed to the 13,005 summit. Tilly, a pretty dark-eyed miss lived through some hair-raising days as a child in Colorado's feverish gold camps. While living in Denver in 1860, the Silverthorn children attended Miss Ring's school. One day their teacher saw a suspicious character outside in the schoolyard. She warned the youngsters: "Children, I am afraid there is going to be trouble, so I will open the window and you crawl out and run home just as quickly as you can."

The man, George Steele, was gunning for William Byers to force him to retract certain damning statements about Steele.

"Mother wrapped sister, brother and myself in buffalo robes and put us in the attic so no stray bullets could touch us, since friends of Steele had gathered close to our home, prepared to fight for him." Steele died in a gun battle soon after.

Matilda and her sister Martha suffered the loss of their little brother, James, in 1863. That same year, the girls attended school in Denver. Their mother took Matilda and Martha over the range from Breckenridge in the fall. They studied at a private school in Denver's St. John's Church Rectory at 14th and Araphahoe Streets. The Silverthorns purchased a home in Denver, also on Araphahoe Street, near the tramway loop.

In 1867, Matilda traveled with her family across the Indian-infested plains for a Silverthorn reunion back East. (The girls decided to bring an Indian chief's jacket, trimmed with a macabre fringe of 204 human scalps, to show the folks back home what the West was really like.) During their trip, the Silverthorns reinforced their own ideas on "what the West was like". Story material to tell the folks back home included an Indian attack and theft of their horses. Matilda watched wounded men die. A last-ditch telegram for help against Indian massacre was answered in the nick of time by a troop of concerned friends from Denver. Matilda watched her seemingly tough father break down and cry openly, "I did not know I had so many friends."

Matilda, who died at age 28, must have passed away soon after her father's death in September 1887. Her young niece, Ada, was laid beside her grave in Riverside Cemetery in January, 1888.

271

Martha Silverthorn Finding

Growing up in an 1860's Colorado mine camp provided Martha Silverthorn with steel-like character strength. She had to be unflappable as an adult — she had "seen it all" as a child.

Young Martha witnessed her share of violent and tragic deaths. The notorious George Steele, whose presence sent the children scurrying out that Denver schoolroom window, was shot and killed in a gunbattle two blocks from the Silverthorn cabin. About the same time, a drunken Denverite, Jim Gordon, killed a young German, but was acquitted of the crime on a technicality. Denver Germans retaliated by hanging Gordon in July, 1860. "I witnessed this hanging," said Martha.

During their 1867 trip East, Martha watched as two young soldiers, wounded badly in an Indian skirmish, died in her camp. "They were dying and calling for their mothers," she remembered. Mrs. Silverthorn and another woman tended the delerious young men. "The boys died at daybreak, happy in the thought that their mothers were with them."

Later a young telegraph officer died in a gunbattle within Martha's earshot and that night an Indian was killed while his band stole her traveling party's horses. Martha Silverthorn lived through the Sand Creek Massacre, the Hungate Family Massacre, the Denver flood and the Denver Indian scare, events that punctuated the years from 1864-67. She grew up no stranger to violence and death.

Today's children must watch for cars when crossing streets; yesterday's children faced the hazards of wild animals seeking prey. Mountain lions and bears populated Summit forests, but one of Martha's closest calls came from an irate buffalo:

> One summer I was sent down to the Placer Mine to take father's lunch to him. I walked slowly along, picking strawberries and wild flowers and had been home only a few minutes when one of the men came running up and asked mother if I was home. A large buffalo had come along very angry and had torn up all the sluice boxes and followed my trail up, crossing the river just before he reached town, which was all that saved me.

Pioneer children never learned of the easy life. Life in raw mine towns meant hard work. In spring, 1862, the Silverthorns moved to a new house. Martha hauled heavy buckets of rock and dirt to help her father excavate the cellar and also worked to build a fireplace. Then she attacked the job of wallpapering — with old newspapers.

Martha Silverthorn grew up a beauty. She married Charles A. Finding in January, 1873. The Finding's first child, a daughter, Agnes, arrived November 23, 1873. Agnes, too, landed midstream in high country life. Martha wrote of traveling over Boreas Pass by foot: "...the next year was the last we were compelled to walk over the range. I carried our little baby (Agnes) in my arms, a distance of 15 miles."

272

Two more daughters blessed the Finding family: Ada (Sister) in 1875 and "Tonnie" in 1877. Sister died tragically at age 12 and Tonnie at age 28. Agnes lived to be Breckenridge's "Grande Dame". She died at 82 in 1955. The Finding girls carried on the tradition of caring, concern and service that marked the Silverthorn Family. When Agnes became engaged to Duane Miner, the *Blue Valley Times*, April 26, 1913, glowed: "The bride is one of Breckenridge's most beloved native daughters. Her name is linked with almost everything that has been undertaken in the line of charity and moral advancement in the town since her girlhood."

Her father, Charles Finding, had prospered. He served as Breckenridge postmaster and town mayor. In spring, 1885, he built Finding's Hardware on Main Street across from the Silverthorn Hotel. The building capped an already thriving business in hardware and mining supplies. He needed four large warehouses to hold his ample stock.

Finding's Hardware became a credit to Main Street, the only stone building in Breckenridge, with the finest native stone and lumber, plus red sandstone trim. Today, Finding's Hardware store still stands as the Summit County Investment building.

Charles Finding had built a beautiful home for Martha on north Main Street. She lavished its interiors with 1880's opulence, including windows elegantly swagged, even framed photographs festooned with floppy bows. The first floor boasted a library, parlor, music room, dining room and kitchen. Bedrooms occupied the second floor. Fancy floral-pattern wall-to-wall carpet spread through parlor and music room; hand-loomed patterned area rugs overlaid the carpet. Tiny and fragile Victorian tables contrasted with the grandiose parlour stove, heavily cast in ornate swirls. Outdoors a fence enclosed the large, grassy yard with its Victorian bird bath. An elegant carved gate marked the entrance.

Agnes Finding grew up in this fashionable home. When she married Duane Miner, the home became hers. In more recent years, the Finding-Miner home housed the Mine Restaurant, but the historic home succumbed to destructive fire in January, 1971.

The Silverthorn Hotel stood on its original location — midway between Lincoln and Washington Avenues on Main Street's west side (next door to the Greenhouse) — until summer 1957. Agnes Finding Miner had sold the building to Jay Cooper and Cooper moved to Salida. Vandals stole historic items and damaged the structure. Cooper finally decided to raze the almost century-old Silverthorn Hotel.

The Judge's old Silverthorn Placer was located on the lower flank of Buffalo Mountain in Salt Lick Gulch. A town sprang up to house early 1960's Eisenhower Tunnel construction workers. Residents named the new town "Silverthorne", adding an extra "e", after the Summit pioneer.

Breckenridge declared at the Judge's death that it would never forget Marshall Silverthorn. For his love and loyalty to his new high-country home, Summit County must remember him too.

273

Commodore Stephen Decatur

Samuel Bowles, famous traveler-author of the late 1800's called him "the prince of prospectors, the character of characters".

"Commodore" Stephen Decatur, indeed a character and perhaps a prince, ranks as one of Colorado's most colorful pioneers.

Decatur, who spent a lifetime suppressing the mystery of his bizarre past, pioneered early Georgetown, Colorado, founded the Summit County mining community of Decatur at the base of lofty 13,132-foot Argentine Pass, and organized a company to build a much-needed wagon road over Argentine. He represented Summit County in the Colorado Territorial Legislature and served as the infant State's commissioner to the 1876 Centennial Exposition in Philadelphia. A gallant soldier, acclaimed orator, and crusty newspaperman, Decatur

was also an undisputed bigamist, leaving wives and families scattered behind on his westward path. An inveterate drinker, he ultimately drowned in an alcoholic quagmire.

But paramount to the Stephen Decatur story is the puzzle that bewildered frontier townsfolk in Iowa, Kansas, Nebraska, New Mexico and Colorado, all places Decatur touched with his creative and quizzical character. Was Decatur really the long-lost brother of Illinois Lieutenant Governor William Bross? Bross, who bore a close physical resemblance to Decatur, traveled to Colorado in 1868, having information that his brother remained alive in this mineral-rich western territory. Bross stood ready to renew filial bonds with this missing brother, whom the family had believed a victim of murder. In a Denver hotel, Bross recognized Decatur as the errant sibling and fell on him with joy. Decatur, horrified, disentangled himself from the Governor's embrace. He refused to acknowledge relationship between the two.

He continued to reaffirm, with indignant voice, banging fist and a flash of formidable eyebrows, this emphatic denial. ". . . the name Bross would set him afire in a moment," the Georgetown *Courier* years later reported. Yet, curiously, Decatur took a huge liking to Bross' daughter and took her to the mountains to camp along the Blue River.

It was only after his death in June, 1888, that the Georgetown, Colorado, *Courier* published full details on the mysterious life of the West's peripatetic pioneer, Stephen Decatur.

Commodore Stephen Decatur, reported the *Courier, was* Stephen Decatur Bross, born in Sussex, New Jersey in the early 1800's. His father, Moses, was a shoemaker and taught the trade to his second son, Stephen, during the boy's early life at the family's next home near Milford, Pennsylvania. But though Decatur would fall back on his craft, the bright young man craved more intellectual pursuits. He attended Massachusetts' Williams College and became a teacher. The ambitious and eloquent Decatur soon snared a position as principal of New York's Chester Academy.

Life took its prosaic course. The proper young educator was quite properly wed to Miss Evalinda Hall in the 1830's. His bride soon bestowed upon Stephen a little daughter and gave him the expectation of a second child to come. Life's familiar pattern was repeated. When Evalinda was six months along, staid Stephen departed for a brief business trip to New York City.

His family never saw him again.

Relatives pursued every thread of evidence in their search to find Stephen. They believed him murdered. Evalinda, sorrowing young widow, gave birth to a son, who she named Stephen Decatur Bross in honor of his departed father.

And where was the missing Stephen Decatur Bross? Was his body hidden in some gloomy back alley of New York's crowded tenements? No! His body, still connected most vitally to soul and psyche, had "gone West". The lure of the erupting Mexican War seduced him to leave his mundane and predictable Eastern life. Assigned to the famous Doniphan's Regiment, Stephen (now Stephen Decatur) participated in Colonel Stephen Kearney's storied march to Sante Fe and Chihuahua. One of his commanders, Colonel Clay Taylor, remembered Decatur as "a gallant soldier".

The Mexican War ended. Decatur roamed with the Indians, and took a squaw wife to his fireside. He quickly cultivated the Indian's talent of treading silently on moccasined-feet, even through the crisp October forest. This talent enabled Decatur to sneak silently from his tipi, leaving another unwitting wife and family behind, when the familiar yen to go West arose again.

He traveled with a contingent of Mormons and enjoyed the Mormon custom of plural marriage with gusto enough to drive any proper Victorian lady to copious inhalations of smelling salts. The Latter Day Saints finally expelled Decatur, possibly due to his weakness for spiritous drink.

Stephen Decatur next lived along the Missouri River and around 1851 ran a ferry at Council Bluffs, with a sideline shoemaker's business in his ferry house. The journal of Stephen's friend, Rudolph Frederich Kurz, indicates on June 4, 1851, that Decatur had stopped there enroute to the California gold fields. "Two months ago, he served as a sailor on a ship, but owing to the illness of his comrades on their way to California, he got stuck fast in this region," Kurz's feathery script relates.

Perhaps the whimsical Mr. Decatur seized upon the title "Commodore" from these riverboat/ferryman stints.

During this period he earned a reputation as respected citizen, educated man and much-pursued orator. It was during a speech near Omaha that one of Decatur's former students, David H. Moffat, recognized him as the missing "Professor Bross". Decatur was headed for the first of several embarrassing encounters with former family members.

Stephen bristled at the young man's claim. He stoutly denied it. Nevertheless, Moffat contacted Decatur's second brother John A. Bross, a prominent Chicago lawyer (later killed on a Civil War battlefield), and John Bross started at once for Nebraska.

"Colonel Bross met Decatur and at once identified him as his brother," the 1888 Georgetown *Courier* related. "Decatur . . . professed great surprise and indignation at the claim made by John A., who returned to Chicago thoroughly satisfied that the lost brother has been found."

Restless, Decatur required constant change. He alternated between respectable and rapscallion lifestyles with pendulum regularity. In 1856, he married again and fathered three children as a prosperous farmer in the rural Nebraskan community of Decatur. (He also left behind another namesake, Decatur, Kansas.)

But rumors of excitement and gold at Pike's Peak in 1859 fanned the embers of Decatur's nomad yearnings. Shortly after the Colorado gold rush began, Decatur again vanished — leaving bereft wife and forlorn children behind.

Lusty, thriving, bold and beginning, territorial Colorado provided just the challenge Commodore Stephen Decatur always sought. Here lay the adventure of the gold fields, the brawling excitement of the mine camps, the stimulation of a new territory flourishing around him. Decatur stepped boldly upon this new soil, enlisting in Colorado's historical Third Regiment, which attacked the Utes in the much-maligned Sand Creek Massacre. He later prospected around Georgetown and became a leader in the growth of that silver-studded city of the Rockies.

A born promoter, Decatur busily involved himself in Georgetown's mushrooming business life, developing a salt works, promoting new wagon roads and talking up the new town to all who would listen. His garrulous gift with language came into constant service. Georgetown citizens called upon him to preach a sermon, preside at a burial, present medals to little scholars, offer testimonials.

In fact, this secret sipper of grape and grain even inspired a Temperance meeting audience in Georgetown's McCoy Hall. The *Colorado Miner* later editorialized: "Commodore Decatur spoke for half an hour. If everyone should follow the precepts and advice of our speaker, there will be no drunkenness in the land."

Decatur, who could denounce drunkenness with eloquence, could also wax eloquent when raising a glass. His favorite toast: "Here's to our noble selves. There are few like us — and few like us."

The Commodore found his way over the chiseled peaks of the Divide and discovered the pristine country of Peru Creek and the Montezuma area, which he dubbed "God's Country". He always loved this Snake River country best, report his biographers, Inez Hunt and Wanetta Draper in their book, *To Colorado's Restless Ghosts*.

Though our 1800's social dropout had rejected Eastern civilization, he still relished the dainty fare that his Peru Creek cabin pantry couldn't provide. "Cream toast", swimming in melted butter, and mush with milk were treats that early prospectors had to forego.

But Stephen Decatur discovered the Georgia Ranch (probably the early dairy ranch close to today's Keystone Ranch golf course) and soon wallowed in the delights of a weekly bucket of butter and brimming can of fresh milk.

In 1868, he took Samuel Bowles to visit Georgia Ranch. Bowles described the dairy in his 1869 book, *Colorado: Its Parks and Mountains*:

> Away under a bluff, a speck in the distance, was a log cabin, — "the Georgia Ranch," towards which we now rode with freshened speed. Here in a cabin of two rooms, with a log milk-house outside, the only dwellers in this rich pasture park, were a man, his wife and daughter, their home

277

> and farm were in Southern Colorado, but they had come up here in the spring with forty or fifty cows, and were making one hundred and forty-five pounds of butter a week, and selling it to the miners . . . The dairy cabin was a "sight to behold," such piles of fresh golden butter, such shelves of full pans of milk, — there wasn't room for another pound or pan; and yet the demand far exceeds the supply . . .

Bowles packed a bottle of cream, filled his water canteen with milk, and received Decatur's Methodist blessing "May the Lord take a liking to you". With a hearty "Amen", he rode away down the valley beside the soda and mineral springs that bubbled up nearby.

In summer, 1870, J. B. Burns made a trip to the gold and silver-seamed Summit County mines with our promoter-pioneer as guide. Burns wrote to the *Colorado Miner* of June 7, 1870: "Under the guidance of Commodore Decatur I passed over the range from Montezuma to Breckenridge, the present principal mining towns of Summit County. Everybody in Colorado knows the Commodore . . . To ride and camp with him is to acquire a 'liberal education' of life in the mountains . . ."

The Commodore laid out the mining town of Decatur at the base of Argentine Pass in 1868. He became the town's lifeblood, promoting the rich ores, which assayed up to $2,000 a ton, and helped to develop the rich mines there, including the Delaware, Peruvian, Queen of the West, Revenue Tariff, and, in 1879, J. M. Hall's famous Pennsylvania Mine, a landmark which despite recent fires remains still partially standing. The discovery of the proud Pennsylvania, which yielded more than $3 million from its underground stores, launched the growth of the nearby town of Decatur. (Today, the $3 million would be worth more than $21 million, due to 100 years of inflation.)

Firmly ensconced as a Summit County resident, Decatur answered a call to serve in 1867 and '68 as Summit representative to the new Colorado Territorial Legislature, where his talent as an orator served him well.

By 1881, Decatur's town boasted a population of 300, a hotel (the Sautell), postoffice, homes and a school halfway between it and its neighbor, Chihauhua. The town, destined to a violent death, crumbled in the spring of 1898 when neighboring Gray's Peak let loose a massive avalanche that decimated almost the entire town in a single roaring crush of destruction. Some half-hearted rebuilding occurred. In 1956, Denver writer Thomas Hornsby Ferrill described the swaying buildings as "American jigsaw Gothic". Buildings with ornate drop cornices and hand-carved window frames were wall-papered with 1882 newspapers featuring silver king H. A. W. Tabor, Boss Tweed and railway tycoon Jay Gould, said Ferrill. Today only a graveyard of scattered foundation stone remains.

The rich Snake River Mining District, locked in by the ponderous wall of the Continental Divide mountains, could never prosper without a link to the Eastern Slope and the commercial coffers of Denver. Recognizing this, Decatur and eight associates formed the Snake River Wagon Road Company with the ambitious goal of constructing a toll road over America's highest Rocky Mountain road pass, 13,132-foot Argentine, a steep, rock-ridden, often snow-blocked link between the Snake River region and bustling Georgetown. Decatur managed to separate $10,000 from the bankrolls of his investors (among them Denver editor William Byers and future senator, Henry Teller) and began the work on the Pass' easier, less difficult Eastern ascent on June 8, 1867. By 1869, the road reached completion, but the hazardous western descent proved so arduous that work crews under Decatur's friend, Joe Watson, constantly quit and had to be replaced about every four weeks. Though the views from Argentine Pass (formerly known as Sanderson's Pass and Snake River Pass) ranked as spectacular, the narrow road clinging desperately to cliffsides, offered danger, and sometimes death, to those who traveled it. (And the wind blew so fiercely at the cyclonic summit that pedestrians often had to crawl on all fours in exposed areas of the Pass.)

After Argentine Pass, Decatur gave up on toll roads and became a journalist, serving as an editor of the *Colorado Miner* from 1869-73. His frequent forays over the Pass to Peru Creek provided regular reportage on the mining and social activities of the more remote Western Slope.

Journalist Decatur acquired the "nom de plume" of "Old Sulphurets". A fellow reporter described Sulphurets as "short, stocky, iron gray, bushy eyebrows and whiskers. Energetic, enthusiastic, sociable, a raconteur with an inexhaustable bag of stories, ready on a moment's notice to make a speech . . ."

Sulphurets could stir up a stew of verbiage as lethal as that from a witch's cauldron. One of his verbal peppercorns reads:

> For a mass of unintelligible hotch potch nonsense in the shape of correspondence from this place, we commend our readers to the *Lawrence Kansas Tribune* of the 20th inst. The concoctor of that mass of garbage should have the hole in his head filled with lard, or some material that will give truth at least to his emanations. For a consummate falsifier he is one ahead of any and all of the rubbish in the shape of correspondents, that ever visited this section.

But he could also make wildflowers bloom on the newspaper page, as with his July 20, 1872 poesy:

> Two smiling divinities, blue-eyed, fair-haired, intelligent young ladies, while pleasuring and sightseeing among the glens and canyons of the Rockies made us a social call and by their cheering conversation sent dull care whirling to the misty land of forgetfulness.

Jesse Randall, an editorial comrade on the *Miner*, was a lifelong friend to Decatur. He launched his own newspaper, the Georgetown *Courier* in May, 1877. For many years after Decatur's death there hung in Randall's *Courier* office a photo of Decatur and a sword belonging to the impetuous Old Sulphurets.

When in 1876 the United States celebrated in wild jubilation its Centennial Year and Colorado became the nation's Centennial State, Governor John L. Routt chose Stephen Decatur as one of two commissioners from the new state to the Centennial Exposition in Philadelphia. It proved a crowning moment for Decatur.

But the Commodore plummeted from this pinnacle of recognition and success with amazing speed. At the height of his career, the aging Decatur's weakness for whiskey became all-consuming. "He drank early and late," writes the *Courier* noting his death. "He drank constantly. Impoverished and without any means of livlihood, he drifted . . ." The Commodore "became a resident of Custer County (at Rosita, Colorado) and eked out a miserable existence as a Justice of the Peace and on the charity of friends." The neighbors always shared a pot of soup, or a wedge of freshly-baked pie.

Penniless, Decatur sought and finally received his long-overdue $1,000 fee for service to Colorado as Exposition Commissioner. This, and a small Mexican War veteran's pension, kept him going until his death in Rosita on June 3, 1888.

To his death, Decatur maintained his rigorous denial of any association with his puzzling past. "My name is not Bross", he would assert. To his intimate friend, and famous author of the day, Grace Greenwood, he did divulge the story of his early years, but that lady refused to share the tale. Frank E. Root, author of *The Overland Stage to California*, wrote that Decatur revealed to him at Old Latham Station in 1864 his real identity. This, and other clues, led friends to establish his true background.

Today, guarding the Commodore's beloved high valleys, are two soaring sentinels, Mount Decatur and, beyond the rocky sweep of the Divide, Mount Bross, as silent as their unreconciled namesake brothers.

Commodore Stephen Decatur adds his kaleidoscope personality to the colorful mosaic of the West's parade of pioneers.

Eastern writer Samuel Bowles, in his 1869 book, *Colorado: Its Parks and Mountains*, wrote a passage about this "Lord Byron" of Colorado's past:

> . . . the Commodore . . . kept me entertained with his original experiences, his keen observations on men and manners, and his quaint yet rich philosophies. He is an old Greek philosopher, with an American variation; as wise as Socrates, as enthusiastic as a child, as mysterious in life and purpose as William H. Seward or an Egyptian sphynx, as religious as a Methodist class leader; he ranks high among the individual institutions and idiosyncrasies of Colorado.

THE SCRIBBLER

Pug Ryan

Both saints and sinners paraded across the stage of Summit County's colorful past. But no one ranks higher on the roster of wrongdoers than the infamous Pug Ryan. Ryan stands as a robber, murderer and blackguard.

Some of Breckenridge's staunchest citizens played a role in the Pug Ryan affair. They were his victims, divested of their watches and jewelry while engaging in a little innocent gambling the night of August 11, 1898. The hold-up itself proved mild by the standards of the old West, but a violent gun-battle followed. The bloody deaths of two local men, both husbands and fathers, and two outlaws, forever stamped Pug Ryan's name on the memory of Summit residents.

The Scene: Breckenridge's well-bred Denver Hotel, where faro, roulette, crap and stud poker games amused patrons of the hotel's game room. Bartender Ed Brewer scurried about in white apron, serving foaming schooners of beer and other spiritous beverages. Chips clinked, cigar smoke wafted toward the ceiling, conversation buzzed, the bar bell rang.

The Action: Enter a band of four miscreants, masked and armed, bent on thievery. Their targets were a safe stuffed with cash, valuables and gold specimens, and also a rich old Hebrew clothing man who dozed nightly by the stove with his $600-$800 bankroll.

Their midnight entry through the hotel's rear door progressed according to plan. But the bandits' furtive approach to the game room was interrupted by an ear-splitting "Bang". One bungling burglar had accidentally discharged his sawed-off shotgun into the game room ceiling. Panic hit the robbers. Discovery loomed. With no time to spare, the robbers forgot the safe and ordered the gamesters to line up. Three men leveled guns at the victims, while a fourth relieved hotel owner Robert Foote, along with Ed Brewer and George Ralston, of

Clothier Charles Levy poses on plank sidewalk outside his store. Levy's bulging bankroll was robber Pug Ryan's special target.

Pug Ryan

their gold watches. (Ralston's watch, valued at $500, was a family heirloom.) "I certainly hate to lose that," moaned Foote as the bandit removed his watch. The thief glanced up, and noticed a dazzling $250 diamond stickpin, which Foote had borrowed from friend Charles Moessner to wear for the evening. That, too, disappeared into the robber's pocket. With $50 in cash from the faro bank and bar till, the gang made their get-away, ignoring in their haste the bulging pocketbooks of their victims and the several thousand dollars in the safe.

One of the thieves looked like a real thug. Thirty-two year-old Arthur L. Scott, alias Lewis A. Scott, alias J. C. Moore, alias Pug Scott, alias Pug Ryan, displayed a pug nose and a face scarred with a seamy history of barroom brawls and unsavory skirmishes. He stood 5-foot, 6¾-inches, with gray eyes and light hair. Pug Ryan's police "I.D." details a face road-mapped with scars:

> . . . scar on the right side of neck; small scar on right cheek; small scar on right cheek bone; jaggy scar on left side near eye; scar on outer edge of left eye; large scar on left top of head; two-inch long scar on left side of head; several scars on back of head; right little finger crooked; small scar at base of right thumb; . . . scar on back of left hand; scar on center of knee.

Ryan also had the letters P-U-G tatooed on his arm.

An 1892 brawl in a barroom on Denver's Larimer Street resulted in 40 head stitches for Pug, accounting for just one of his many scars. A man named Murphy attacked Pug with a billiard cue after Pug attempted to slice Murphy's jugular vein. The newspaper report of the incident labeled Ryan as a "West Denver tough".

Pug's special target that August 11, 1898 night was the rich Jewish clothier. But Charles Levy had retired early that evening and his hefty bankroll remained intact. The desperadoes failed also to notice Frank Roby who hid beneath the billiard table and William Passmore, who, awakened from sleep by the shot, stumbled from his hotel room upstairs, then quickly jumped under a bench when he viewed the robbery in progress. Mrs. Foote, wife of the proprietor, and several other ladies had thrown on robes and peeked out from bedroom doors to watch with horror the scene below.

Accounts differ on the actual number of robbers in the hotel. Ed Auge, who left the Denver Hotel game room with Charles Gilbert enroute to the Oro Mine, missed the hold-up by just ten minutes. He recounted the robbery in a 1938 Summit County *Journal* article, reporting the number of robbers as four. A gang member, Dick Manley, however, said only two of the four robbers had entered by the rear door. One of the thieves, a slim, light-complexioned 5-foot, 9-inch man with a long blond moustache, had sauntered through the game room shortly before midnight to "case the joint". He gave the o.k. to the boys waiting outside. This man, named Lewis, had worked for W. P. Knorr, whose gaming operation had been robbed in June.

Lewis remained behind while the other three bandits escaped on foot and scrambled in the dark up and over a steep trail surmounting the Ten Mile Range to Kokomo. There they holed up to sleep in a cabin one mile south of bustling Kokomo, a Ten Mile Canyon mining town.

Irate townspeople of Breckenridge organized. Sheriff Jerry Detweiler, who was serving his first year in office, appointed Breckenridge's Ernest Conrad as deputy. Robert Foote offered Conrad a $100 reward to apprehend the criminals. Conrad boarded the 4 a.m. freight train to Leadville, with plans to travel as far as Kokomo, where a gang of suspicious characters had reportedly taken up residence.

When he arrived at Kokomo, Conrad kept close-mouthed about his mission. A Kokomo newsman asked him whether he came to track the Denver Hotel robbers. Conrad brushed him off with a denial: He had been offered a reward to capture the bandits, but had refused it. He was in Kokomo on personal business. Conrad investigated, and later deputized local resident Sumner Whitney. About 2 p.m. that afternoon, August 12, 1898, Conrad and Whitney approached "Robbers Roost".

Inside with the bandits was "Broken Nose Charley", Charles Reilly, a "no-good Kokomo loafer" who, an August 20, 1898 news report said, had rustled "beer and grub for the hungry hyenas". Broken Nose Charley supplied tips to the robbers also, suggesting they hit Leadville's busy Pioneer Saloon the next night.

Conrad had assisted with Breckenridge law enforcement duties for years, but none of that experience prepared him for an encounter with the remorseless Pug Ryan.

A bungled decision would cost the two deputies their lives. Conrad and Whitney surprised Ryan and his men at Robbers Roost. The two law officers had seized the upper hand. But unsure in the face of Ryan's bravado, they concluded that they had made a mistake. Conrad and Whitney apologized and left the cabin.

Once outside, their common sense returned. They re-entered the cabin for a second inspection and demanded: "Boys, we must see what you have got under those blankets."

Suddenly, the scene exploded in gunfire.

Pug Ryan fired his pistol twice with deadly precision. He killed Ernest Conrad with a shot through the head and mortally wounded Sumner Whitney. Whitney managed to shoot bandit Dick Bryant and wound cohort Dick Manley.

Bryant lay writhing in death, gasping and rolling from side to side. He got hold of some window boards and wrenched them off in his pain. Whitney, though severely wounded, trained his gun on Bryant, ready to finish him off if necessary. Manley, bleeding from a serious bullet wound in his abdomen, ignored that trauma and screamed in pain over his finger, shot off as he attempted to escape through a door.

What happened to Pug Ryan? He escaped unscathed. But before he bolted, Ryan robbed his wounded partner, Dick Manley, and said, in formal farewell, "God damn you, son-of-a-bitch. I have a notion to kill you." Ryan kicked the defenseless Manley and left.

The bloody shootout at isolated Robbers Roost might easily have gone undetected. But John Barret, a Leadville man standing on a railside platform awaiting the Denver & Rio Grande train home heard the shots. He gave the alarm, and Kokomo residents rushed to the scene. First to arrive at the blood-spattered cabin was George Steve, who witnessed Pug Ryan's rifling the dying Manley's pockets. He later testified at Ryan's trial.

Pug Ryan escaped toward Jacque Ridge south of Copper Mountain. Kokomo residents in angry pursuit judged the trail to be "hot" when they found Pug's lighted cigar stump. But they never found Pug.

He made a clean getaway.

Summit County busied itself with cleaning up in the aftermath of the gun battle. And with mourning.

Dead lay 42-year old Ernest Conrad, loving husband and father of three young children. He was a respected longtime resident of Breckenridge. Fatally wounded was Sumner Whitney. D. & R. G. conductor Al McCurdy placed his Leadville-bound train at the disposal of Kokomo residents who transported the wounded Whitney to a Leadville hospital. This established Kokomo resident and married father of three children died there on September 7, 1898, less than one month after the shooting. Before he expired, Whitney identified Pug Ryan's photograph. He wrote across it: "This is the man who did the shooting," and signed his name.

Dying robber Dick Manley, a married man of 24, died shortly after the gunfight, despite emergency surgery. Manley was buried without ceremony in Kokomo. The outlaw came from a prominent Colorado family. His sister, Mrs. B. T. Birmingham, arrived in Kokomo to claim his body the Sunday following the shoot-out. When officers exhumed Manley's body, they discovered Ed Brewer's gold watch chain in the dead man's pocket.

Bandit Bryant died also. His body was claimed in jail by a brother and brother-in-law and transported to Leadville for burial.

Four men suffered violent death, yet the scoundrel Ryan remained unpunished.

Broken Nose Reilly, jailed in Kokomo, almost met his maker as well. Enraged citizens gathered in the street outside the jail rumbling of a "necktie party". Before the men could organize under a leader, authorities spirited the ill-fated Charley off to the Breckenridge jail.

All of Summit County arose in furor. Maddened residents jammed the streets of Breckenridge. Bob Etzler rode up and down Main Street on horseback with a rifle, ready to blast Ryan should he appear. Breckenridge sheriff Jerry Detweiler arrived in Kokomo with a posse soon after the battle. A special D. & R. G. train bearing more lawmen from surrounding counties and bloodhounds arrived to join this posse and follow Ryan's trail. Bloodhounds found nothing and darkness prevented further search. In Dillon, residents organized parties to scour the hillsides for the villainous Pug. They turned up no trace of the desperado. However, a Denver news report detailed the August 15 robbery of a camp near Slate Creek where Charles A. Finding and O. G. Mitchell were fishing. The two saw smoke and returned to their camp to find their tent ablaze. After dousing the flames, they discovered $15 missing from Finding's coat and $10 from Mitchell's pants pocket. The Denver *Times* concluded that there existed "little doubt it was Ryan".

Dick Manley had made a deathbed confession in the Breckenridge jail. It supplied the evidence for an all-points bulletin for Ryan's arrest:

> I, Dick Manley; being on my death bed, make the following statement, believing my end near and wishing to confess before going before my Maker . . . That I, Dick Bryan and Hugh Ryan started out from Victor about a week ago to do such work as we've been doing. We came to Breckenridge and got in with a tall, light complexioned, slim fellow about five feet nine inches, who steered us to the place we held-up last night . . . This man Lewis went ahead of us and came out and said all was well, and Bryan and Ryan went in. Bryan had a short shotgun and so did Ryan. One was quick on the trigger and it was fired accidentally. We got three gold watches and $50. We walked all night and came up to the cabin where the shooting of today took place. There we calculated to sleep . . . The officers came down to the cabin and talked awhile and went out and came back and said, "Boys we must see what you have got under those blankets," and the fellow that's dead, Dick Bryan, and Ryan jumped up and pulled their guns, and the officer that's dead was shot. They began shooting, and in the excitement and smoke I could not see who shot the other man, but I think the man that's dead did the first shooting.
> I went to run out and got my finger shot off as I was going out the door. This is the truth gentlemen . . .
>
> (signed) Dick Manley

Authorities launched a nationwide search for Pug Ryan, with plenty of incentive for the headhunters. The State of Colorado offered a $250 reward for Ryan's capture and conviction. Summit County posted $100 in reward money and El Paso County, also desirous of Pug's return, offered $500. The City of Chicago wanted Pug back for a visit too, with a $1,000 prize for his capture.

The slippery Ryan eluded his captors for four long years. Finally, in April,

1902, Seattle, Washington police picked up a tramp. The scar-faced vagrant protested that he was an innocent Seattle resident, J. C. Moore. But police discovered the letters P-U-G tatooed on his arm and identified the protesting Mr. Moore as murderer Pug Ryan.

An April, 1902 news clip was recently discovered by local Ryan-researcher Peter Fredin in early Denver Detective Sam Howe's scrapbook. It reads:

> Seattle, Wash., April 15. J. C. Moore, alias "Pug" Ryan, alias L. A. Scott, who is wanted in Summit County, Colorado for murder and who is suspected of complicity in the hold-up of a saloon at Franklin, Washington, during which Martin Johnson, bartender, was shot dead, was arrested here last night.

A writ of extradition signed by Washington Governor Henry McBride allowed Breckenridge Sheriff Detweiler and Deputy W. P. Lindsey to pick up Pug Ryan in Seattle and finally return him to Breckenridge for trial.

Detweiler locked Ryan up tight in the Breckenridge jail. But housing a murderer made the sheriff nervous. Would Ryan escape? Besides, keeping a prisoner for an extended jail stay in Breckenridge was expensive. Better to transfer Ryan to the Leadville jail where cheaper rates of $1 per day board prevailed.

Ryan proved a model inmate at Leadville. The sole exception: One Sunday, June 1, 1902, he ungraciously failed to appear at dinner. A trustee serving the sabbath meal noticed that not only Pug, but four other prisoners as well, had sacrificed their Sunday dinner for the lure of freedom.

While the Leadville sheriff was off for an afternoon of fishing, the five fugitives had sawed off a padlock on the sewer trap door and escaped through the watery outlet. A June 1, Leadville news bulletin reported: "Pug Ryan, a noted desperado charged with two murders and alleged to have commited numerous highway robberies, escaped with four other prisoners from the county jail this afternoon . . . A posse of 50 armed men is in pursuit."

Pug enjoyed a summer mountain hike from Leadville to Marble Junction, then opted for a train trip to Granite, Colorado. From Granite, he walked to Independence, where he paid a social visit to a friend named Jolles. Feeling relaxed, freed from the confining atmosphere of his jail cell, a nostalgic Pug decided to return to his hometown, gold-rich Cripple Creek. There he consulted his attorney, J. Maurice Finn, who tried to persuade Ryan to turn himself in.

The Cripple Creek excursion proved to be a fatal mistake. Night Marshall Nicholas Williamson recognized Pug lounging on a street corner at Third and Bennett Saturday night, June 7 around 10 p.m. Williamson promptly arrested the surprised Pug, who claimed to be a vacationing Denverite, Tom Davis, a stationary railroad engineer. But the tatooed P-U-G again provided the giveaway.

All of Breckenridge turned out for Pug Ryan's trial beginning June 14, 1902 at the big G.A.R. (Grand Army of the Republic) Hall, Breckenridge's social center. Ryan played to a packed house — people in Sunday clothes brought lunches to avoid losing a prized courtroom seat. Young girls ogled the impenitent felon and swooned, to the shocked dismay of their elders.

Defended by his attorney, Maurice Finn, who was assisted by James T. Hogan, Pug Ryan testified on his own behalf. His sister, Carrie Scott, had stated that Pug spent the time of the Kokomo murders with her in Cripple Creek. She had testified that the two were shocked to read the report of the Robbers Roost gunfight in the August 12 newspaper over breakfast.

Pug took the stand and contradicted his sister, affirming under oath that he was in Creede when he heard of the shooting. His squeaky, mouse-like voice proved a definite disappointment to the spectacle-minded Breckenridge audience. A criminal should sound criminal, after all.

Pug's defense attorneys argued mistaken identity. Their client, Arthur Lewis Scott, they contended, bore no resemblance to the blackguard Pug Ryan, a tall, stout, dark-haired rascal.

But the prosecution, under District Attorney Frank E. Purple, assisted by Sam Jones, shot the defense alibi full of holes. George Steve testified to witnessing the defendant Ryan rifle cohort Manley's pockets, kick and curse him. P. H. Chisholm, a Kokomo man who had agreed to accompany Conrad and Whitney to Robbers Roost, explained that he had ridden up late, after a delay, and heard shots. As gunsmoke poured out cabin windows, Pug Ryan had emerged and escaped, Chisholm stated. He positively identified the defendant as Ryan.

The widowed Mrs. Sumner Whitney affirmed Pug Ryan's identity before a hushed courtroom audience. She testified that she served Pug a meal from her own table in June, 1898. Mrs. Whitney, surprisingly, was no stranger to Ryan. She had known him ten years, even visited him in jail in 1895, and later in a penitentiary.

A jury, quickly selected the first day, consisted of twelve Summit County men:

H. C. Smith, foreman, Dillon	George Truax, Breckenridge
Carl Fulton, Swandyke	William Robinson, Breckenridge
J. H. McDougal, Swandyke	George Louage, Breckenridge
E. M. Cox, Lakeside	H. L. Shane, Slate Creek
William Lawyer, Montezuma	Robert H. Lee, Breckenridge
Ed Dwire, Montezuma	John Laskey, Lakeside

Carl Fulton, Swandyke postmaster, protested to Judge Owers: "I live in Swandyke and not in Breckenridge, therefore I know nothing about the case." The Judge smiled and remarked that he needed twelve men just like Fulton.

The jury couldn't help being moved by Sam Jones' passionate closing plea:

I see a beautiful happy home up Main Street, three young children, a loving mother and a loving husband and father. Suddenly, a mist came over this home. Sam Jones pointed to the defendant and continued, "Oh! Pug Ryan we got you. Four long years but at last. We cannot give you the gallows, but we will give you the nearest to it."

The trial ended Tuesday evening and promptly the next morning, after one hour's deliberation, the jury delivered its verdict: Guilty of murder in the first degree.

Canon City Prison Records Chief Ray Pitman reported that Pug Ryan was locked up there to begin a life sentence on July 17, 1902. This time, the miscreant found no escape route. He spent 29 years at Canon City, an "unruly, vicious and uncooperative" prisoner. His record reveals incidents including fighting in prison lines and in the chapel, striking a prison officer and possession of drugs in his cell. In January, 1920, doctors pronounced Pug "insane by reason of lunacy". Pug Ryan died on June 14, 1931 of renal cardiac disease and was buried in a rough pine casket at the prison's Woodpecker Hill graveyard.

Even after Pug Ryan's conviction, Summit County couldn't forget him. A surprising event ten years after the Breckenridge robbery added fuel to the Ryan legend. During the summer of 1908, Allie Carlson and her two cousins, Bertha and Bryan Murrell, picnicked and played on a mountainside near Kokomo. Beside a large log, they discovered the revolver and loot Pug Ryan had buried in a handkerchief there during his escape a decade before. The Summit County *Journal* printed this story:

> On Monday afternoon, a bunch of Kokomo children held a luncheon on the summit of Jacque Mountain . . .
> There on the mountainside the Carlson children picked up an old watch and chain. Directly another gold watch was found. Of course the children were excited and naturally ran home with their treasure . . .
> . . . (Their father) found the first clue to ownership of one of the watches in the monogram, R.W.F., which it bore.
> He called up the Journal by phone and said he had R. W. Foote's and another gold watch and a pearl-handled revolver and narrated how he came into possession of them.
> A morning later Mr. Foote was appraised of the recovery of the forgotten time piece. He took in the situation at once and said, "My diamond is on that hill too; it will be found where the watches were picked up, and I shall take the morning train to Kokomo."
> Sunrise next morning found Mr. Foote and Chet Acton knocking at the door of the Carlson home in Kokomo. The children were aroused and they led the way to the lone treasure spot. Acton scratched in the dirt at the spot pointed out by the children and in an instant uncovered the big diamond, to the great joy of him who was ruthlessly deprived of it ten long years before. The second watch proved to be the property of Ed Brewer then residing in Glenwood Springs.

Charles Moessner, who had moved to Hastings, Nebraska, arrived in July 1908, for his regular summer visit to Breckenridge and retrieved his diamond stickpin. Ed Brewer's watch had remained in perfect running condition and ticked away happily when wound. Robert Foote's Elgin responded to a cleaning and oiling job that restored it to proper function. The watch remains today in the possession of Breckenridge-area resident Robin Theobald, Robert G. Foote's great-grandson. The pearl-handled .38 caliber six-shooter that killed Conrad and Whitney was displayed for years in the Denver Hotel curio cabinet.

Even today Summit County refuses to let Pug Ryan's memory fade. Local newspapers print feature stories about his exploits. A restaurant in Dillon bears his name. The Pug Ryan story lives on.

The Man Who Brought You The Rock Piles: Ben Stanley Revett

In 1893, an aggressive Englishman, Ben Stanley Revett, marched his ample frame onto the Summit County scene. Dressed in flawless three-piece suit and white Stetson hat, the respected mining authority harbored a persistent dream: To dredge-mine the Swan River Valley's gold-rich bedrock gravels 40-feet below stream level. Against steep odds and frustrating failure, the determined Mr. Revett achieved his dream. Dredging kept Summit County alive through the grim 1900's until World War II. But it left an unlovely legacy of barren rock piles to mutilate a once-beautiful Blue River Valley.

Born in Calcutta, India around 1858 (the date is disputed), Ben Stanley Revett claimed direct descendancy from Scotland's Robert Bruce through his mother, Isabel Bruce. Revett's father served as chaplain to the British Army in India. When he chose mining as his career, Revett disappointed his music teacher, who planned to train the excellent young tenor for the opera.

Belle Turnbull, local Summit County author and one of the beloved "French Street Ladies" with writer Helen Rich, wrote an article about the intriguing Englishman published in 1962. She reported that Revett graduated from London's Royal School of Mines. But dredge boat historian Erl Ellis, who also chronicled Revett's career, could unearth no such record from London's Royal School of Mines. Ellis consulted members of the Revett family, who believed most of Revett's schooling took place in Scotland. The young Britisher did work as an apprentice on Scotland's River Clyde for ship-builders Rankin & Blackmore, Ltd.

Revett travelled to the little-known Colorado town of Granite in 1884 to assist a British company in its placer mining operation at Twin Lakes above Leadville. The young mining engineer worked under Captain Charles Harvey for the Twin Lakes Hydraulic Mining Syndicate for five years, then became mine manager in 1889. The dynamic Revett pioneered the use of hydraulic machinery at Twin Lakes Placer and, in supplanting slow manual labor, cut costs per cubic yard in half.

According to Belle Turnbull, Revett visited Breckenridge in 1889 and heard news of a dazzling strike at the Ontario Mine on a saddle of gold-rich Farncomb Hill. His interest in Breckenridge gold kindled.

Revett spent a few more years at Twin Lakes Placer, then left Colorado to return to Britain early in 1892. But the lure of Colorado gold had gotten under Revett's proper British skin. John Campion, successful Leadville mine owner who had begun his mining career in Nevada, offered Revett a manager's post at Campion's Wapiti Mine on Farncomb Hill. Revett snapped up the opportunity to work with the successful Campion, who had acquired considerable mining property around Breckenridge and would play an intriguing role in the town's history.

Campion incorporated his Wapiti Mining Company on February 26, 1894, with Ben Stanley Revett directing daily operations. The little town of Wapiti sprang up just below the top of Farncomb Hill. A postoffice opened there on March 16, 1894.

Fate influenced Revett's interest in dredging. He had seven years shipbuilding experience. And mining colleague Samuel S. Harper joined Revett that first year at Wapiti. Harper came fresh from managing a gold dredge operation at Bannock, Montana, successfully pioneering the use of a Bucyrus-built gold boat there. A cautious individual, Harper often served as a brake to Revett's bounding enthusiasm.

Revett's dredging plans percolated. On April 14, 1894, he purchased the Bedrock and Williams placers on the Swan. He further whet his zeal for bedrock gold in 1895 when he drilled a shaft to bedrock on the Swan River at the mouth of Galena Gulch. Water swamped the shaft and the endeavor proved unsuccessful. But the resourceful Revett used an oil drill to test the glacier-deposited gravels, probably "the first application of such an implement to prospecting in Colorado," according to mining authority Leslie Ransome in 1911.

Revett continued to make Campion's Wapiti property a success, taking out quantities of gold. He showed off some Wapiti nuggets during an 1894 visit to Leadville and that town's *Chronicle* newspaper fluttered on February 19: "The display of gold is still at the bank, nothing like it having been seen in the state for richness or beauty." The *Chronicle* reported Revett's gold "weighs 50 ounces or almost $1,000".

Dapper Mr. Revett (left) drives famed matched grays off Farncomb Hill.

Revett paused in late 1896-early 1897 to journey to Salmon City, Idaho where he managed a placer operation on Bohanan Bar. According to Erl Ellis, an 1897 register of Breckenridge's Denver Hotel shows the signature, "Ben Stanley Revett, from Salmon, Idaho".

The enthusiast Revett was a born promoter. His excitement over dredge-mining proved contagious to moneyed Bostonian investors. By September, 1897, Revett had organized the North American Gold Dredging Company with Boston capital.

He turned over the management of the Wapiti Mine in 1897 to San Francisco brothers Frank and Maurice Griffin, recent Harvard graduates and Revett's personal friends. Then he launched the first attempts to achieve his dream. Revett supervised the creation of two mammoth "gold boats", constructed in 1898 near the mouth of Galena Gulch and the mouth of Gold Run Gulch in the Swan Valley. Designed to parallel the pioneering gold-dredge boats first introduced in New Zealand, these dredge machines were developed by San Francisco's Risdon Iron Works, which built machinery for America's first gold boats. (Revett's dredges were the third and fourth constructed in the U.S.) Risdon built the vital machinery, shipped it by standard rail to Denver, then narrow-gauge railway to Dickey and ox cart to the lower Swan Valley. There Ben Stanley Revett supervised construction of wooden hulls and assembly of Colorado's first gold dredges. When he completed his pioneering gold boats, Revett crowned each with an exquisite hand-worked silk pennant, bearing the figure of a swan, which floated atop the dredge.

The enormous floating barges, equipped with buckets on a revolving line, were designed to scoop gold-bearing gravels from bedrock 40-90 feet below the surface. (See Chapter 8 on how dredges work.) To the dismay of Mr. Revett (and probably his Bostonian investors as well), the much-hailed dredge boats crumpled under the stress of Summit County's deep, coarse "gravels", sometimes six-foot boulders. Revett's light dredges simply couldn't handle the damaging assault of huge rocks and incredible depth to bedrock. The dredges bucked at 30 feet, when bedrock at the Swan River sites lay 30-50 feet below. The dumpers failed to operate properly as well, and tailings piled up beneath the boat itself.

To make matters worse, Revett's comrade Samuel Harper had thrown up his hands and departed Summit County, leaving Revett to face failure alone.

None of this deterred the dauntless Mr. Revett one bit. He reorganized his company under the new name of the American Gold Dredging Company of Boston. He obtained a lease on the valuable Jessie Mine in mineral-pocketed Gold Run Gulch. He remodeled the 40-stamp mill there and added concentrating tables. And he chose a bride, Miss Mary Griffin, sister of the Griffin brothers managing Wapiti.

Revett met Mary when she visited her brothers from San Francisco, where her family was prominent. Revett, a staunch bachelor, fell hard for Mary, and few young ladies could withstand the magnetism of the chubby but irresistable Britisher, Revett.

The bridal pair celebrated their wedding on New Years Day, 1898. Ben Stanley

Revett personally designed an elegant manor house for Mary, stately "Swan's Nest". Built on the old Kimball Placer, the house overlooks the Swan River where it courses northwest before flowing into the Blue. When he learned that notable guests planned to visit, the impatient Revett set construction workers to labor day and night to finish Swan's Nest before the visitors arrived. The house, completed on time in June, 1898, became the scene of elite social gatherings.

The new Mrs. Revett barely had time to hang up her bonnet at Swan's Nest before her "Stanley" in 1899 whisked her away to California. He deposited her in San Francisco, then departed for Oroville. He directed a dredge operation on the Continental property at Oroville, again financed by Boston backers. After several months the Revetts returned to Summit County, Stanley afire with new dredge mining enthusiasm (and new investment money). Immediately, he dismantled the defunct Swan River dredges and built new boats capable of processing 2,500 cubic yards of gold-bearing rock per day. By the end of 1899, Revett had two new dredges gobbling up gold in the Swan. One was a Risdon dredge, built by the San Francisco company; the other, a Bucyrus dredge, produced by a Milwaukee dredge-building concern.

Revett poured personal funds into the development of gold dredging. His dollars, along with his dreams, were dashed. Investments like the new Bucyrus dredge, improved with increased steam power and a new stacker that measured two times longer in order to improve dumping, never proved successful. Too much gold went into the dump. Revett was "hard put to find money for running expenses", according to winch man George Robinson. The tenacious Britisher continued to transfer large sums from his personal bank account to offset dredge losses. Friends later said Revett had "made and lost three fortunes". Nothing, including money, would stand in the way of his dream.

A competitor entered the dredge scene in 1899: The Blue River Gold Excavating Company launched two gold boats on the Blue River two miles north of Breckenridge. Both eventually failed.

Meanwhile, our peripatetic promoter busied himself around 1900 buying up placer claims in fabulous French Gulch, where rich gold strikes dazzled an American public. By 1904, Revett owned 320 acres of placer ground in French Gulch, including the Jackson, French Gulch, Magnum Bonum and Corkscrew placers. And, under the auspices of the Reliance Gold Dredging Company, Revett was designing the ultimate in gold boats, a double-lift dredge constructed according to his personal specifications. The new steam-driven "Reliance" dredge became Colorado's first successful gold boat, the culmination of hard years of frustrating trial by Ben Stanley Revett. Launched July 14, 1905, the 500-ton, $90,000 Reliance began working about 600 feet west of where the Gold Run Flume crossed the French Gulch wagon road. The 44-bucket dredge, capable of deep digging, featured a hull built from iron-like Oregon timber, for no local wood would withstand the tremendous shaking and strain that dredge boats had to undergo. The Taylor Iron Works of High Bridge, New Jersey built the Reliance machinery under the direction of Revett's engineer, Ed L. Smith. Dredgemaster Julius Butchick, operating the Reliance at full capacity, could dredge 3,000 cubic yards per 24 hours. In its first seven months of operation, the Reliance, termed "a grand success", netted about $50,000.

By 1908-09, the Reliance dredge worked through the winter, a feat formerly considered impossible. (For one thing, stream flows diminished about November; for another, the dredge pond froze solid as bedrock.) In summer, 1909, workers overhauled the Reliance and converted it to electricity, which increased the dredge's profit record.

Even before the success of the Reliance dredge, Ben Stanley Revett had emerged as an internationally-known mining expert. He traveled to Siberia in 1900 to consult on a mining operation and in 1901 departed for Africa's Ivory Coast where he worked to introduce new mining techniques until his return in July, 1902.

He journeyed to Mexico (the year is unknown) to explore mineral possibilities there. In 1905, the busy year he debuted the Reliance, Revett served 70 days as consultant to a gold dredge company working Alaska's rich Nome River.

The dapper Mr. Revett could emerge from a grimy mine tunnel as spotless as he emerged from his dressing room each morning. His impeccable white Stetson crowned golden hair. He wore a full golden moustache to accent his large and nobly-featured face. Revett, called "magnetically attractive to women", stood five feet and seven inches tall and was almost that wide! But he carried himself with dignity. During his high-level prospecting trip to Mexico, a Mexican laborer working in a cemetery glimpsed Revett's ample figure and swore, "Holy Mother of God, when this hombre meets his death, may it be near the graveyard."

"For all his smooth facade," wrote Breckenridge's Belle Turnbull, "he was a bulldog for tenacity, and unlike the bulldog, he was resourceful and persuasive."

A natural salesman, Revett attracted investors. But, unlike some promoters, Revett stood for reliability and honesty, Turnbull affirmed. Unfortunately, the affluent Britisher proved himself no manager of large sums. His accounts, muddled by his sporadic shifts of personal funds in and out of corporation coffers, could appear suspicious. His compelling personality usually caused investors to overlook these accounting discrepancies. And Revett refused to do business with milktoast types, or those who would nitpick about his accounting practices. He dealt only with "strong people".

Poor Mrs. Revett probably viewed her globe-trotting husband as the white-hatted hero who continually rode off into the sunset. Though she herself departed a snow-bound Swan's Nest each autumn for the cultural haven of San Francisco, she must have missed her "Stanley" who was in Siberia when their baby daughter Frances was born in 1900. At least she could enjoy the summertime comforts of Swan's Nest, a mansion that remains today as the Campbell residence at Tiger Run. When Revett completed Swan's Nest, the Summit County *Journal* gushed: "Revett's house is the most elegant and most elaborate in this part of the state . . . The original design of the house was by Mr. Revett, an artist of no small ability."

A semi-circular design imitating a swan with wings extended, the curving showplace consisted of a large main building flanked by two-story wings on each side. Five large dormer windows interrupted the line of its steeply-pitched red roof. A long veranda curved along the front exterior, showing off its fancy rail of peeled log, shaped in an intricate geometric design. Beyond lay a croquet court, tennis court and sun dial with pathways of dredge rock crisscrossing the grounds. Views were less than spectacular — huge piles of dredge rocks blocked the panorama of the Ten Mile Range.

Revett ordered extra-large doors to accommodate his extra-large girth. They protected not only his massive midsection, but also his ego, from harm. The three-foot doors were built, according to Belle Turnbull, "so the dignity of its owner need not suffer by his having to pass through a door sideways".

One entered into a typical British "hall", a large room dominated by a huge dredge-rock fireplace. Visitors commented on the fireplace's intriguing hand-painted tiles. These tiles, the work of Mary Revett, depicted Indian scenes and famous American Indians. A large chair near the hearth was also built from dredge stones. An elaborate crystal chandelier hung from the ceiling. A woman neighbor who passed by Swan's Nest regularly described the chandelier as glittering "just like diamonds".

Eminent guests enjoyed lavish continental dinners in Revett's elegant dining room. Choice wines complimented each course. (Revett himself ate and drank legendary amounts.) Gentlemen smoked $1 Havana cigars in the library following the classy repast.

Male guests would later adjourn to Revett's billiard room, on the south wing's first floor, where a costly single slab of slate covered an expanse of floor. Or, all would gather for an evening of music, highlighted by the host's mellow tenor voice. Few high-country homeowners had telephones in the early 1900's, but Ben Stanley Revett did. On music nights, the stately Britisher telephoned the bar of Breckenridge's Denver Hotel, four miles away. The bartender then announced, "Gentlemen: Mr. Revett will now sing for you from Swan's Nest." The telephone receiver dangled as bar patrons enjoyed the operatic vocal style of the talented Mr. Revett.

Later, the Revett family retired to personal quarters in the mansion's four family bedrooms. The house boasted two indoor bathrooms. One featured an oversized tub with electric lights mounted above to create a steam bath, a welcome creature-comfort in chilly Summit County!

(Servants bedrooms in each wing, for the Japanese household staff, did not feature such amenities.)

The library in the north wing offered a warm mood with its tongue and groove wall and ceiling paneling and shelves of books. A similar paneled room in the south wing served as Revett's office. Nearby stood a stone vault with double steel doors where Revett secured gold nuggets and dust.

Little Frances Revett spent early childhood summers at Swan's Nest. But her mother feared the rugged mine community atmosphere would corrupt her little daughter's budding sense of refinement. Mary Revett was right. A five-year old Frances accompanied a distinguished guest to a nearby spring which failed to yield a cooling drink to the child's tin cup. "Not one damn drop!" cried the little miss. She threw down the cup in disgust. When the amused guest repeated the story at the dinner table, Mary Revett reacted with shock and dismay. She began to hate her husband's "rough country" home. She found life at Swan's Nest boring and unsophisticated.

An excellent horsewoman who showed thoroughbreds in Oakland as a girl, Mary drove her buggy to Breckenridge regularly to deliver dredge gold to the bank. In 1909, a buggy accident resulted in Mary's being thrown from her conveyance and injured. She spent some months recuperating, first in California, then in Denver while Frances attended her second year at Wolcott School there. Mary missed two winters in cosmopolitan San Francisco and grew more dissatisfied with churlish mountain life. Protesting a heart ailment, she finally left Revett and took Frances to San Francisco to live around 1913. Swan's Nest stood empty.

Ben Stanley Revett saw his fortune diminish. Forced to sell his beloved Reliance dredge to the Tonopah Placer Company in 1913, he became a consulting engineer to that company in 1915. (Tonopah was formerly the Gold Pan Mining Company, a venture in which Revett had a hand.) Revett later left Summit County and managed to maintain his capitalist lifestyle in the posh clubs of Denver and San Francisco on the generosity of wealthy friends.

In 1919, a burglar looted Swan's Nest of every remnant of its fine furniture and lavish accessories, leaving only a dress suit hanging in a closet. The thief, J. G. Collins, was later apprehended with his accomplice wife and convicted. But many Swan's Nest treasures disappeared.

Swan's Nest sold for $800 in back taxes and later served as the main lodge building for Rice's Hidden Valley Boy's Camp.

Frances Revett married Bradley Lewis Wallace, son of a prominent San Francisco attorney in a 1921 bay city ceremony. Her father, basking in continued repute as a mining authority, lived in semi-retirement at the Denver Club, still talking about his scheme to rework the rich tailings created by early, inefficient dredges. Ben Stanley Revett died in 1929.

His memory lives in two monuments of his creation. One is Swan's Nest, faithfully restored by Tiger Run's Campbell family with the help of Frances Revett Wallace. The other is a rocky trail of desolation, worm-form tailings that wind like the gray corpse of some giant prehistoric snake along the river beds of the Swan, French and Blue. While the noisy clanging dredges that Revett brought to Breckenridge penetrated the lives of local residents with their relentless racket, the dredges also produced paychecks and tax dollars to keep Summit County alive after the demise of traditional placer and lode mining.

Ben Stanley Revett, a man who rose to challenge, left a challenge for today: What can we do with the rock piles? This scar on the face of Breckenridge and its environs cries out for a new crusader to restore its gentle beauty. The job will require men with the bulldog resolve of a Ben Stanley Revett.

Colonel James H. Myers

Virginia-born Civil War Colonel James H. Myers left his spirited stamp on Summit history. Author, mining expert, newspaper editor, promoter par excellence, crusader and longtime local resident, Myers stands out from the crowd that peopled a colorful 1900 Summit County scene.

Myers' mining savvy went into his book, *Rudiments of Geology and Prospectors' Guide*, published in 1905. Besides being a seasoned mining expert, Colonel Myers turned his promotional talents to advancing Summit's silver mines.

Myers provided the brains behind the powerful King Solomon Mining Syndicate. The Syndicate invested its Eastern-raised resources mostly in the lower Ten Mile Canyon near Frisco, where the King Solomon Tunnel led a dazzling list of mine properties. The Syndicate was Myers' baby. He founded it way back in the post-Civil War 1860's with his best cronies, James Whitlach and J. H. Haverly. The trio came together from the most diverse backgrounds imaginable.

James Whitlach, from a Virginia "cracker" family (they lived on cracked corn and wild game secured by the "crack" of a rifle) entered the Confederate Army as a freckle-faced, red-haired, 14-year old kid. He soon became the best shot in the brigade, and rose swiftly from there. After the War, he headed for the Rockies and storied success as a prospector.

The second partner, J. H. Haverly, suffered the loss of his parents soon after his birth in the Pennsylvania mountains. He ran away from his guardian at 12 and sold newspapers, fast becoming a junior entrepreneur. When war broke out, Haverly peddled his newspapers aboard the rails to news-hungry travelers. Later, a smash success in the theatrical business paid him more than $500,000 per year.

James H. Myers, unlike his cohorts, was born into luxury's soft lap. His father was the largest slave-owner in Prince Edward County, Virginia, where slaves outnumbered whites five to one. A well-known scholar, the elder Myers valued his library more than his wealth and hoped his son would excel in the academic.

But the Civil War changed everything. The South's young men, those who survived, "bade farewell to the scenes of their childhood and the happy dreams of their boyhood days, and started for the mining regions of the Rocky Mountains to try and regain their lost fortunes," said the Montezuma *Prospector* in a 1906 Myers profile.

Colonel James H. Myers relaxes from hectic promoter's schedule among typical 1890's office furnishings — rolltop, spitoon, swivel chair.

> Among these pilgrims was Colonel Myers, who enjoyed the distinction
> of being the youngest man in the Confederate army who had ever received
> a commission of colonel, which was given him by special request of Gen.
> Robert E. Lee.

Whitlach, Haverly and Myers formed a sinewy triumverate after the war. "To these three men nothing seemed impossible," said the *Prospector*. "They were trailblazers and pioneers."

Reaching age 70 in 1906, Colonel Myers was the last surviving partner of an original syndicate that had once included many famous investors. Myers had focused his energies on silver-rich Summit County, where he lived first in 1880's Chihuahua, then Montezuma. His King Solomon Mining Syndicate headquartered in Frisco and Denver. Myers' son, James H. ("Dimp") Myers, Jr., managed the Ten Mile Canyon's King Solomon ventures, and later continued his father's promotional activities in Montezuma.

Despite his age, Myers remained the energetic promoter, the scrappy infighter. He organized backers to build the big Lenawee Mill at the mouth of the Lenawee Tunnel near Montezuma. He had his hand in mining companies all over the Ten Mile and Montezuma districts. He pushed the extension of the railroad beyond Keystone to eventually meet the Vidler Railroad Tunnel through Argentine Pass. (Despite his persuasive talents, none of these railroad dreams came to fruition.) He battled early environmentalists who threatened to encroach on miners' freedom to claim public land. As the Montezuma *Prospector's* crusty editor, he boosted the Montezuma area with boundless enthusiasm and attacked, with equal vigor, the empty promises of promoters like those behind the North Ten Mile's Square Deal Mine. He scored unscupulous mine-stock peddlers with his published "Sermon to Promoters".

Summit's silver mines never had a booster like the inveterate prospector-promoter, Colonel James H. Myers. He is truly one of "the cast of characters".

The Old Newspapers:

Journalism Yellow As Summit Gold

The old newspapers of Summit County, especially those published during the bustling 1880's and '90's, reflect the dizzying spectrum of life in gold rush days.

A kaleidoscope of mine town life — the tragic deaths of two baby sisters on Peru Creek, a ravaging fire at Kokomo, Breckenridge's white-glove social gatherings, outlaw Pug Ryan's escapades, a 13-pound gold nugget discovered on Farncomb Hill and the record-breaking snows of 1898 — played vivid color across the printed page. This human record remains almost a century later to provide an intriguing glimpse into Summit County's rich past.

The editors who printed these stories, feisty, flamboyant men of their times, felt none of the restraints imposed by modern standards of objective reporting. On the contrary, they wallowed in the subjective — emotion, opinion, and personal comment punctuated the news. These bushy-browed editors, with their bristling moustaches and more bristling copy pencils, took advantage of the news columns to lambast one another! The venom of rivalry mingled freely with their printers ink.

A Look At Some Old Newspapers And Their Editors:

Kokomo: Silver-studded hub of the upper Ten Mile Canyon in the 1870's, Kokomo produced the county's first newspaper, the Summit County *Times*, on September 27, 1879. "The World's Highest Newspaper" was published each Saturday by Thomas Gowenlock, who served also as Kokomo town mayor. Gowenlock regularly reminded his readers of their good fortune in having an expert in the editor's chair. Calling himself an "old hand" in mining, Gowenlock pontificated: "Patrons of the Summit County *Times* will receive the benefit of the information gained by our experience." He foresaw "stagnation and death" for townsfolk who failed to support the newspaper. And he cast a bitter eye toward powerful Leadville, whose newspapers, he complained, "belittle and ignore" Summit County.

Breckenridge: The capitol of the Blue River mining district debuted the county's second newspaper, the Breckenridge *Daily Journal* on July 22, 1880. Its editor, Jonathan Cooper Fincher, with his rapier-sharp quill, gained local prominence. Reverend Mark Fiester's book, *Blasted, Beloved Breckenridge*, contains an information-packed chapter on "Ye Editor". Fiester writes of Fincher: "'Ye Editor' wielded strong influence and power, second to no other in the community."

When Fincher railed about the eyesores on Breckenridge's Main Street, town fathers listened. Regarding an 1881 mud puddle at Main and Washington Streets, Fincher wrote: "The town trustees ought to look after it or someone will be drowned." In 1882: "There should be an ordinance against making our Main Street a receptacle for refuse, glassware, empty tin cans or bunches of bale wire." 1888: "The surveyors who originally laid out the plat of this town must have been knock-kneed, cross-eyed, left-handed and stuttered like sin, for there are no four blocks in the town on the same lines."

Jonathan Cooper Fincher crusaded against his rival newspaper with a poison-dart sting of the editorial pen. He called the two-man editorial staff of Breckenridge's Summit County *Leader*, first published July 31, 1880, "a fool and a liar, both cowards", and their newspaper "the breech clout from the cesspool on Lincoln Avenue".

Chihuahua grave remembers Clancy family's little daughters. Summit's old newspapers chronicled life and death a century ago.

Dillon: But Dillon *Enterprise* editor O. K. Gaymon bore the real brunt of Fincher's relentless barrage. He labeled the *Enterprise* the "Dillon Crossing Foghorn" and Gaymon its "assinine editor". Fincher recommended Gaymon be "spanked and put to bed until he learns to open his mouth without putting his foot in it". He charged that Gaymon, an "irresponsible idiot", printed only "foul rot".

When Gaymon entered politics, Fincher reported (Jan. 1, 1898):

> Piccolo-voiced Gaymon was up from Dillon Sunday trying to explain why he betrayed the silver republican candidates at the last election . . . the Dillon political blotch and Summit County's disgrace should in all decency keep quiet, for there is a disposition on the part of some to inquire into his acts while disgracing Summit County as senator.

Fincher compared Gaymon to a feisty dog: ". . . the meanest of its kind and is composed of fleas and barks — get out, you cur."

Cantankerous? Yes! But Fincher was also dedicated. With the help of his three daughters, editing, type-setting, doing heavy press work and job printing, "Ye Editor" kept his newspaper alive during years of "continued doubt and fear" for its financial survival. The National Editorial Association expressed in September, 1887, "surprise that the little *Daily* was so tenacious of life and admitted that its equal under all circumstances was not published in the United States".

Fincher's tenacity paid off. His Breckenridge *Daily Journal* was joined by a sister publication, the weekly Summit County *Journal*, in July, 1883. The *Daily* ceased publication in July, 1888, leaving the *Journal* to stand alone. Endowed with its creator's determination to survive, the 97-year old *Journal* still appears each Thursday in Breckenridge.

Ironically, Gaymon took over Fincher's *Journal* in 1897, after J. W. Swisher quit the editorial post. Fincher's ghost may well have sought to retaliate by mixing up the letters in Gaymon's type box and puddling ink on his journalistic copy. Before Gaymon quit in September, 1909, he managed to consolidate the Breckenridge *Bulletin* and the *Journal* to forge a single, strong newspaper.

Montezuma: A solid day's hike from Breckenridge, lay the crow's nest cliffs of Montezuma Canyon. There, in the hub town of Montezuma, James R. Oliver debuted his newspaper, the Montezuma *Millrun*, on June 24, 1882. Oliver, an experienced newspaper man from Central City, seemed to resist the lure of yellow journalism more than his colleagues and published a gazette bursting with mining news, social reportage and a myriad of personal items. In fact, the *Millrun* had to occasionally request the Breckenridge paper to credit mining news stolen from its columns. By September, 1887, Oliver was ready to sell the newspaper to J. W. Swisher, one of Montezuma's first town officials. After the demise of the newspaper, nine months later in May, 1888, Swisher left Montezuma. But he returned to newspapering in 1892 when he bought Jonathan Cooper Fincher's *Journal* in Breckenridge.

Colonel James H. Myers edited the weekly Montezuma *Prospector* from 1906 to 1909 in the firebrand style of the day. His special target: The Square Deal Mining Company's operation on North Ten Mile Creek near Frisco. Though Square Deal president Frank E. Wire proclaimed the company "'short' on promises and long' on fulfillment", Myers called the company a fraud. He labeled the enterprise the "Crooked Deal Mining Company" and nicknamed its hot-air president "Windy Wiggles". Myers headlined one of his weekly diatribes against the Square Deal with: "Wind and Bluff Don't Go". "Come on, tell the truth and shame the devil," Myers remonstrated. Show the public one certified copy of a bill of lading to verify ore shipments, he challenged. On May 5, 1906, he ran this front page ad:

> THE MONTEZUMA PROSPECTOR WILL PAY ANYONE A REWARD OF TWENTY-FIVE DOLLARS IN CASH IF THEY WILL FURNISH THE PROSPECTOR WITH RETURNS FROM ANY ORE BUYER, SAMPLING MILL OR SMELTER, SHOWING THAT THE SQUARE DEAL MINING COMPANY EVER SHIPPED A POUND OF ORE FOR WHICH THEY RECEIVED ANY PAY. THEY WILL ALSO PAY THE SAME REWARD FOR EVIDENCE THAT SAID COMPANY EVER HAD AT ANY TIME PREVIOUS TO THIS DATE ANY LEGAL TITLE TO THE HENDERLITER RANCH.

Though Myers ran a fire and brimstone "Sermon to Promoters" in the *Prospector*, the old Civil War colonel was himself a past master in the promoter's art. The *Prospector* chimed in praise of Myers' own mining ventures, the King Solomon Mining Syndicate and the Lenawee Mining and Reduction Company. Testimonials to the unassailable integrity and amazing progress of these mining ventures often appeared.

Even men of the cloth came under Myers' editorial fire. The Denver Methodist preacher, Brother Wilcox, drew a barrage of criticism for his holier-than-thou hypocrisy. "Well, now, the Methodists may be saints without so much as a blotch or stain upon their saintly robes; they may get up a little closer to the throne to twang their little harps . . .", said Myers, but they can't match a miner in "blue overalls and hob-nailed shoes" for closeness to the Creator.

A Look At The Old News

Along with a liberal dose of opinion, the columns of the old county newspapers also carried some national news. The Summit County *Journal* on December 11, 1897 reported the struggles of the Argonauts during the Yukon's Klondike Gold Rush. On February 5, 1898, the *Journal's* new editor, Gaymon, reported on Colorado men fighting the Spanish-American War: "The Colorado Boys were the heroes at the fall of Manila, all hail the home guards in Blue."

G. A. R. Hall stage, festooned for 1890's graduation, snared a headline.

Dillon's *Blue Valley Times* reported on April 26, 1912 the loss of 1,700 lives in the sinking of the Titanic. The great San Francisco earthquake and fire made the pages of the Montezuma *Prospector* on April 21, 1906.

But the brittle leaves of old newspapers, starched and yellowed like ancient lace, entice the reader more with their local news reports, the personalities and the passing scene of old-time Summit County.

Breckenridge's Summit County *Leader* reported on Christmas Eve a strike at the Ontario Mine, the size of which caused a teetotaler to celebrate with whiskey. "John Baylor, superintendent of the mine said last evening, 'I do not often take anything, but tonight I feel so good, I guess I will . . . Nothing but a five-foot vein of solid gold will beat what we opened up . . . at the Ontario today!'"

Early in 1910, when the Summit County courthouse addition began to take shape, local ladies demonstrated pre-lib power in their campaign for a women's room to be included in addition plans. The *Journal* provided an editorial boost by printing this verse:

> The rest-room is an assured fact.
> Why, of course they'll have a rest-room,
> That is what the smiling ladies state.
> Everyone will do her duty —
> It is sure to be a beauty,
> For Breckenridge is always up to date.

303

EARLY SUMMIT COUNTY NEWSPAPERS

Kokomo

The Summit County *Times*: September 27, 1879-1881
The Ten Mile News: 1881-1883
The Summit County *Herald*: 1881-1883

Robinson

The Robinson *Tribune*: December, 1880-1883
The Summit County *Circular*: 1881-1883

Montezuma

The Montezuma *Millrun*: June 24, 1882-May 26, 1888
The Montezuma *Prospector*: April 14, 1906-1909

Frisco

The Successful Miner: 1907-1908

Dillon

The Dillon *Enterprise*: April 14, 1882-1889
The Blue Valley Times: April 26, 1912-October 31, 1914

Breckenridge

The Breckenridge Daily *Journal*: July 22, 1880-August, 1888
The Summit County *Leader*: July 31, 1880-1892
The Summit County *Journal*: July, 1883-present
The Summit County *Democrat*: 1888-1889
The Bi-Metallic: 1892-1893
The Breckenridge *Bulletin*: March 5, 1898-October 2, 1909
The Summit County *Miner*: 1902-1903
The Breckenridge *Herald*: February 10, 1917-1918
The Summit County *Star*: 1918-1921
The Summit *Gazette*: 1926-1927

Another newspaper-aired crusade focused on a female issue, that of "tight lacing". While the New York Cash Store advertised Glove Fitting Corsets in the *Journal*, its editor mourned the death of a young lady from Silver Plume who expired while dancing at a ball there. Cause of death: Tight lacing. "Those corsets should be done away with, and if the girls can't live without being squeezed, we suppose men could be found who would sacrifice themselves."

On August 29, 1891, the *Journal* reported undertaker M. H. Huntress' receipt of Summit County's first hearse. The funeral vehicle displayed "all the essentials necessary to impress the beholder with the solemnity of its mission".

The much-heralded Denver, South Park & Pacific Railroad provided transportation for those still living, among them one Prince Phillip Ernest Furst zu Hohenlohe Schillingsfurst. The Prince was accompanied by his sister, Princess Elizabeth and a count. The royal party, guests of gold-dredge king, Ben Stanley Revett, received gifts of Breckenridge gold nuggets, according to a May 28, 1904 Breckenridge *Bulletin* report.

A pert little miss, Ella Foote, rode sidesaddle in 1898. Social news, personals, filled *Journal's* columns in affluent 1890's.

"Enjoy the Italian breezes of Dillon for at least a day," invited the Montezuma *Millrun* on November 17, 1883. (Italian meant balmy or resort-like to 1880's readers, a feature especially appealing to the chilly residents of 10,200-foot Montezuma.) The *Millrun* was encouraging readers to attend "A grand Thanksgiving celebration in Dillon on the 29th . . . complete with horse racing and target shooting. There will be a grand ball in the evening in the newly finished school house and an elegant supper is promised at the De Becque House . . ."

"A Felon's Love", serialized in the 1898 Summit County *Journal*, competed with another romance, "The Love Potion", for the dime-novel reader audience. "Home-Made Philosophy", one of the departments, warned, "It's better to treat the devil like a neighbor, than to treat a neighbor like the devil."

Spring, 1912, blossomed and the *Blue Valley Times* reported that Miss Ella Foote, escorted by J. A. Theobald, enjoyed an auto ride to the lovely burg of Dillon. The social note postscripted the news that Mrs. R. W. Foote had gone along to chaperone the ride.

Another motor car, the first to go to Montezuma, arrived August 30, 1912, according to the *Times*. The driver, Henry Albers, took his Ford touring car next day to scale Boreas Pass. The grade proved almost too steep, the *Times* said.

Advertisements provide another rich source for insight into old-time Summit County life. Patent medicine ads promised cures for ailments ranging from bad bile or warts to female troubles. ("I owe everything to Miss Lydia Pinkham and her Vegetable Compound," a young lady's testimonial reads.) "Dr. Witt's Little

Early Risers are famous little pills for constipation, biliousness, indigestion and all stomach and liver troubles," stated an 1897 ad from Stephenson's Pharmacy in the *Journal*.

Piso's Cure for Consumption, Mother's Friend, Dr. Gunn's Onion Syrup, and Shiloh's Cure, a catarrh remedy, all competed for reader attention in an 1893 issue of the Breckenridge *Bi-Metallic*.

With all these miracle cures available, it seemed ironic that pharmacist Snyder, "the new drugstore pill mixer", should be "laid up with a bad cold and an attack of biliousness this week," according to an 1898 *Journal* Personals column.

Charles Levy's store announced a clearance sale on beaver skin shawls and all-wool fascinators (35c each, cash only) in an August 20, 1898 *Journal* ad. And C. F. Frey advertised a Freighting Office & Stables at Keystone Ranch in an early issue of the *Blue Valley Times*. (There's a new ranch for golfers at Keystone today.) That same issue advertised the opening of a new City Market in Dillon. (Today's City Market opened in the nearby Summit Place shopping center in late 1976).

Young ladies sallied forth on summer berry-picking expeditions. Miners were maimed in grisly dynamite accidents. A four and one-half foot trout was caught at Haywood, near Keystone. Pug Ryan's gang shot and killed three peace officers at Kokomo. The Colorado Dredge Company expected to retrieve three-quarters of a million dollars in gold from a rich bedrock section in the Swan Valley. Yet another child died when a beloved 12-year old, Ada (Sister) Finding succumbed to croup. All of this life leaps from the cracked pages of the old newspapers, a vivid diary of gold rush days.

White Gold:  Early Days of Summit Skiing

Skiing dates to at least 2,500 B.C. in Siberia. Apparently, this neolithic ski craze caught on, because archeologists have also unearthed ancient Scandinavian ski fragments in recent digs. Norway had a ski troop in 1747. Norwegians later nurtured the birth of skiing in the U.S., officially introducing skiing by 1841 and establishing it as a transportation means in the California Sierras during the 1849 gold rush there. Snowshoe Thompson, whose mother was Norwegian, carried the mails in the high Sierras from 1855 to 1869. His 12-foot, one and one-half inch thick skis weighed around 15 pounds. But they always got the mail — and Snowshoe Thompson — safely delivered.

Breckenridge miners made a big gold strike in February, 1860 by using "snowshoes" to penetrate Gold Run Gulch. By the 1880's, Crested Butte was staging ski races popular enough to close the school for the day, and skiing miners were whooping it up on Aspen Mountain. Teddy Roosevelt skied in 1884 in the Dakota Badlands.

Breckenridge's Eli Fletcher was steaming wooden boards and curving their tips around a peeled log to fashion skis for friends in the 1880's. After a drying spell before the fire, the boards, often spruce, would retain their curved tips. He attached a cleat to the ski, which held the wearer's everyday boot. To this, the Summit skier would add a long, heavy pole, used to push off, steer and brake. Could the skier turn those weighty boards? "Turn?", said one old-time skier. "Sure, you could turn, if you wanted to. But the skis wouldn't turn — no way!"

A young Norwegian named Eyvind Flood dazzled Montezuma and Sts. John residents with his skiing expertise in the early 1900's. A mining engineer at Sts. John under British manager Mumby, Flood could "swoop down the hill from Sts. John in nothing flat," according to an awed Elizabeth Rice Roller. Flood was the "first expert skier we had known. He had professional equipment and his daring exhibitions on our wintry slopes made him a model and hero for all our boys . . ."

Peter Prestrud, who arrived in Frisco from Hamar, Norway in 1910, brought with him a boundless enthusiasm for ski jumping. Prestrud led a group of young local ski buffs to build an ambitious ski jump at Dillon. Located above Old Dillon on the present Dam Road, near today's scenic overlook, the jump was lovingly constructed and maintained. It was no amateur's stuntboard. The cut for the on-run can be seen high above the reddish rock outcrop overhanging the Dam Road. The first street in Old Dillon had to be closed so skiers could run out their jumps.

The Dillon Jump, renamed Prestrud Hill in 1954 to honor its creator, became the scene of a world-famous jump.

Anders Haugen, born and raised in Telemark, Norway, surprised Dillon old-timers when he traveled all the way to Colorado during an American sojourn and scrambled over difficult Loveland Pass to appear in Summit County. His goal: To attempt a little-known ski jump rumored to be located at Dillon. Haugen readied himself for the jump with little local flurry. The Norwegian skier took the jump and soared an amazing 213 feet in 1919 to establish a brand-new world record! The next year, he beat his own record on the Dillon Jump by sailing 214 feet.

Recognition was late in coming to the hapless Haugen. He finally received his Olympic medal 50 years later in Chamonix, France for the world record set in Dillon in 1920.

Dillon jump team, 1919 or 1920. Front: Eyvind Flood, Peter Prestrud. Rear: Hans Hanson, Carl Howelson, Anders and Lars Haugen.

Colorado skiers were making their first, snaking tracks in the state's abundant powder, but a sleepy Summit ski scene failed to waken. A coterie of Denver skiers created the Arlburg Club at "West Portal", the slopes rising at the Moffat Tunnel's west opening, which later became Winter Park. While Steamboat introduced its cumbersome boat tow in 1934 (skiers sat on the boat's sides and piled their skis in the middle) and Aspen drew skiers in the late 1930's (50 cents per night for a room at the Hotel Jerome), Summit struggled along with no organized skiing. There was plenty of snow. A small ski area on Hoosier Pass existed, but snow-clogged passes prevented outsiders from using it. In 1936, for example, all Summit passes remained snowblocked from January 25 till April 22.

Across the county line on Fremont Pass, Climax opened its Chalk Mountain ski area with a double rope tow around 1936. A handful of local skiers used it.

Meanwhile, across the U.S., a kindling interest in skiing fired into flame. Alta, Utah opened as a working ski area before World War II. Sun Valley also had lifts in pre-war days. Cannon Mountain, Franconia, New Hampshire, among others in the East, operated during the war. And both Ogden and Brighton, Utah had appeared early on the ski scene. Soon after the war, California's Mount Waterman, Mount Baldy and others quickly sprang up.

With ski enthusiasm spreading across the nation, Summit County, blessed with ski terrain unrivaled in the country, plodded along, devoting its time to shopkeeping, ranching and small business. No one, except those who refurbished the Dillon Jump for an infrequent meet, cared one bit about skiing.

But the ski boom that would catapult Summit County into a position as Colorado's number one skiing destination in the 1970's was waiting to detonate. Its spark would come from World War II's famous Tenth Mountain Division, U.S. Army ski professionals trained at nearby Camp Hale below Tennessee Pass. "The Tenth" was on its way home.

These men would bring change. Among them returned Peter Siebert, Earl Eaton and Robert Parker, key figures in Vail's development. And C. Minot ("Minnie") Dole, founder of the U.S. Ski Patrol. Friedl Pfeifer, who teamed up with the late Walter Paepcke, Container Corporation of America board chairman, to launch Aspen. Steve Bradley, longtime Winter Park executive director. Gordy Wren, instrumental at Winter Park and Steamboat Springs. Larry Jump, Arapahoe Basin investor. And Slim Davis, U.S. Forest Service Arapaho National Forest head ranger, who helped prompt a reluctant Forest Service to allow Colorado ski areas to use national land.

These and many other Tenth Mountain Division skiers, experts toughened to handle weather extremes and World War II battle conditions, made a tremendous impact on skiing in Colorado and the U.S. "They started the industry, really," said Joe Jankovsky, former Araphahoe Basin owner. Broader praise came from veteran Colorado skier John Rahm: "The Tenth Mountain Division made a significant impact on skiing in Colorado and all over the world."

The Tenth's impact on Summit County came in 1945 with Arapahoe Basin.

Just beneath the stony spires of the Continental Divide where Loveland Pass peaks drop steeply toward the west, lies a mountain-rimmed bowl, its raw rock clothed each winter in a mantle of dry Rocky Mountain powder snow. Over a century ago, silver miners poured over the Divide toward this big mountain bowl to seek out its precious mineral stores. They sunk their questing holes in the rocky ground.

Nearly 80 years later other men crossed the range and discovered this bowl. One was Max Dercum who in 1941 developed plans for a ski area in the big basin. World War II interrupted his dream. Another was seasoned skier and Arapaho National Forest ranger, Slim Davis, the Tenth Mountain Division Army skier who saw the glistening basin's potential in the early 1940's.

It was Davis who in 1945 directed comrade Tenth Mountain Division skier Larry Jump and ski racer Sandy Schauffler to the big basin. The two were conducting a ski area survey for the Denver Chamber of Commerce. Larry had skied Loveland Pass as a member of the Tenth Mountain Division and had stayed at Dillon's old Wildwood Lodge. Sandy Schauffler, a Navy pilot, had raced for the Colorado ski racing team and was an FIS (Federation Internationale de Ski) Olympics candidate in the early '40's. The two-man survey team spent four months looking at potential ski area sites in Colorado.

Hot gear and skiwear chic had yet to appear on Summit ski scene.

Arapahoe Basin

The peaks of the Continental Divide blazed white in the sunshine the day the Arapahoe Basin plan crystallized. A boisterous crew of skiers — among them Larry Jump, Denver ski manufacturer Thor Groswold and ski pioneer Max Dercum — had hiked or hooked rides up Loveland for a skylarking race down.

310

Larry Jump paused and looked up to view the dazzling bowl, as big and beautiful as Slim Davis had described it.

The big bowl became Arapahoe Basin, the first ski area in Summit County.

To obtain Forest Service approval for the land provided the developers' first challenge. But Max Dercum, one of the five Arapahoe Basin partners, owned land at midway, a five-acre mill site that he had picked up for back taxes, after his arrival in Summit county from the East in 1942. After the Forest Service finally granted its approval, the five partners were told, "Now we will have to open the area for bid, as we did at Berthoud." Five faces dropped. Max Dercum, Larry Jump, Thor Groswold, Sandy Schauffler and competitive skier Dick Durrance, the fifth partner who had been a member of the invincible 1939 Dartmouth ski team, exchanged panicked looks.

"You can't do that," Larry Jump gulped, grasping at a straw. "We own five acres halfway up that hill." Happily, Forest Service representatives relented. "And we sealed the deal," said Jump.

Ingenuity, bargain-sleuthing, scrap-mongering, jerry-rigging and bulldog determination marked the building of Arapahoe's first ski lifts.

Jump turned out to be a master at scrounging up old Army and Navy surplus equipment. And he transformed his "finds" into ski equipment for Arapahoe Basin.

Exuberant ski novice Bertha Tate enjoys first Summit powder, Fall, 1920. Her delight foreshadows Summit ski boom. Today, Summit leads all Colorado ski destinations.

He scooped up a bargain surplus steel tram from the Army at Camp Hale. He asked Heron Engineers in Denver to fabricate the tram into Arapahoe Basin's first chair lift. Heron said, "Yes, as a matter of fact, we've just received our first chair lift orders from the Aspen and Berthoud ski areas." Heron used cables and pulleys "liberated" from old mines around Glenwood Springs and Silverton and designed the same makeshift, but workable, lift for all three fledgling ski areas.

"Everything at Arapahoe Basin in the early years was jerry-rigged," recalls John Bailey, a later Basin manager. "We needed timber and it was hard to come by. So Larry picked up a portable sawmill, cheap."

The sawmill was fine, but it lacked power. "So Larry bought an old Army surplus motor, the kind mounted on sectional barges for amphibious use." The huge, heavy and bulky motor, complete with propeller, was designed for use in sea water. "We had to put in an irrigation system from the creek to cool it," said Bailey.

The motor was never intended for use on a sawmill. "Every time a log went in, the motor slowed down. When the log came out, the motor raced," said Bailey. To counter this problem, the indefatigable men of Arapahoe Basin built a governor, consisting of a flap which hung on a bailing wire connected to the throttle. The flap was positioned so that it could be blown by a fan on a fly wheel connected to the motor. When the motor raced, the air from the fan would blow the old tin flap out, which yanked on the bailing wire and shut down the throttle. The engine stopped racing.

"Later, we got an ex-Navy portable generator — a huge thing — which had served in Guadalcanal," remembered Larry Jump. "Max would have to hike through the snow to midway every morning to start the generator. Fortunately, it blew up one night — and with the insurance money, we were able to buy a better one!"

"Larry Jump bought an old Army weasel and went all over that mountain," chuckles John Rahm. "The only problem was that the weasel was supposed to operate in swamps, mud and muck." The ups and downs of the weasel in snow provided plenty of laughs for Arapahoe Basin-watchers.

Lift tower foundations had to be dug by hand in those years. The tedious and back-breaking labor of building a chairlift halted the first winter at Arapahoe (1946-47) when an early storm, pushed by stiff winds and punctuated by below zero temperatures, made further work impossible.

"So we used a rope tow and jeep to haul skiers," recalls Jump. "We had 1,200 skiers that winter. At $1 per ticket, that meant we took in $1,200.

The partners wheedled some additional cash from investors during the 1947 summer, and opened for the '47-'48 season with not one, but two single chairlifts, using the Army surplus tram and old mine pulleys to whisk skiers all the way to Arapahoe Basin's 12,500-foot summit.

John Bailey helped dig the foundations for those lift towers. And he's got plenty of stories to tell. Here's one:

"We had a bunch of D.U. football players working with us in August that year in an attempt to get into shape for the football season. They didn't share our feeling of pressure to get the lifts built. As we struggled to dig the foundations for the lift towers — a tough job in that rocky country — they busied themselves building a dam on the creek. The next morning, they further amused themselves by blowing it up with dynamite.

"We were sweating, six feet down in the hole, digging and throwing the dirt up. Up top, the sides of the hole were banked up another three feet from our diggings. Suddenly, one of the D.U. guys threw three sticks of dynamite into the hole — with fuses lit. We shot out of that hole without ever touching the sides." The pranksters, the men later discovered, had simulated dynamite by carefully cutting pine branches to size.

"After we got over being mad," says Bailey, "we each tried to climb out of that nine-foot hole without help — and no one could do it."

Business dribbled in slowly those early years at Arapahoe Basin. People came from Colorado, from Chicago and the Midwest. Those who tried it became a loyal core of dedicated skiers. The growth of Arapahoe Basin and Dercum's warm, welcoming Ski Tip Ranch were intimately linked.

Ski Tip, a rambling collection of intriguing miners' cabins and add-ons, held a unique charm for guests. "Ski Tip developed as one of the great ski lodges of the West," said Larry Jump. For a long time, Ski Tip remained the only ski lodge in the county. "If Ski Tip had 20 guests," Jump remembers, "that's all Arapahoe Basin would get all day. Some days we'd have two or three skiers. Once we had only one skier. But our big day in the early years was the day we had 300 skiers. The lifts would handle 300 per hour. There was a 40 minute wait that day."

But early skiers were used to waiting, according to Jump. And lift tickets cost only $3.

Dreams more than money held the Basin together in the early years. Men like Larry Jump, Sandy Schauffler and Max Dercum were so in love with skiing that they thought the whole world would soon be smitten too. When the cash cupboard went bare, as it often did, the partners simply peddled more stock — at $1 per share.

Unexpectedly, Arapahoe developed its own dozen disciples who spread the good news about the top-of-the-nation ski area. The "St. Peter" of the group turned out to be famous traveler-author Lowell Thomas. "Lowell was an old friend of Sandy and me," says Larry Jump. "He was our guiding spirit. He gave Arapahoe Basin a high recommendation wherever he went."

And ski film-maker John Jay boosted the Basin by including its mountain footage in his yearly films.

Arapahoe grew. By 1948, the partners were ready to install their first ski school director. Their choice: Germany's Willy Schaeffler. Schaeffler is now legend in Colorado skiing, with years as Arapahoe Basin ski school director and his post as 1960 Squaw Valley Olympics coordinator. As D.U. ski racing coach, Schaeffler led the team to 14 National Collegiate Championships.

Schaeffler introduced many European and American celebrities to skiing the Basin's lavishly powdered runs. Ethel and Robert Kennedy were Arapahoe Basin apostles, frequently with Willy Schaeffler as their guide. Former U.S.

Senator Peter Dominick (a stockholder) and former Colorado governor John Love, plus the Denver *Post's* late Palmer Hoyt and the *Rocky Mountain News'* Jack Foster, helped spread the word. Merrill Hastings, *Colorado Magazine* publisher, made his start in Colorado ski country cutting timber at Arapahoe Basin. A long string of Hollywood celebrity skiers added luster to the Basin's name.

More and more skiers came over Loveland Pass to Arapahoe and many sallied forth to explore the tourist attractions of Summit County. Some encounted a hard core resentment from locals. "Skiers were the 'hippies' of that era," a Summit resident remembered. This local skier dropped into a Frisco cafe for dinner and was refused service because he wore ski boots. "It took four or five years after Arapahoe started before some businessmen realized the potential of skiing in Summit County," said John Bailey. "They were glad to take their money — but they didn't like skiers."

Despite snubs from Summit merchants, the early Basin skiers were having fun. For one thing, the mountain offered acres of fresh, deep powder. Groomed slopes were unheard of in those days. "Everyone skied on Thor Groswold's wood skis — racers, ski school directors, everyone," said Edna Dercum. "We bought our Groswold skis for $10 in the East before we came out here."

Groswold had the first ski factory in the Rocky Mountain West, according to the Dercums.

"I think Groswold made the best wood skis ever made, at least for powder skiing," said John Bailey.

While the skis were great, the bindings offered problems aplenty. Working skiers, instructors and patrol members, all suffered from achilles tendon prob-

Undaunted by dirth of chairlifts, this 1912 ski party at Lund Ranch, 12 miles north of Dillon, readies for day's first run.

lems caused by front-throw "bear-trap" non-release bindings. But these annoyances didn't keep them off the slopes.

Arapahoe Basin became a seedbed for the Colorado ski industry. "Arapahoe
was a training ground for ski patrols and ski schools all over," said Jump. Many
new Colorado areas staffed up with former Arapahoe Basin employees. "I can
think of half a dozen ski areas right now where the executives and mountain
managers started at Arapahoe Basin."

Not all of the bright young men stayed around Arapahoe long enough to
learn. One employee arrived at work after the big Christmas storm of 1952 to
witness the rush and roar of a gigantic avalanche distressingly close to where he
stood. The shaken young man went inside for a roll and coffee to recover his
composure. "As he sat eating," Larry Jump recalled, "'Little Professor' let go
and roared across the road and parking lot, leaving a depth of 16 feet of snow
behind. The young man paled, collected his gear from the office and scrambled
off over the slide. We never heard from him again."

Those were the early days at the Basin. In 1972, Joe Jankovsky and other
investors purchased the ski area from the original investors. In 1978, the Basin's
neighbor, Keystone, bought the mountain operation and launched a multi-
million dollar make-over that included lift replacement, base lodge remodeling
and new water and sewer facilities.

With a base elevation of 10,800 feet (parking lot elevation equals that of Aspen
Mountain summit) and a soaring 12,500-foot mountain, Arapahoe Basin enjoys a
spun-out season that can start in early November and last through late June.
Late spring snow base usually totals six to seven feet and the Basin has dry
powder in May.

The big Basin still stands as a reminder of the earth's awesome creative power.
There's hardly a skier who does not pause at the top of the world up there to
view the soaring peaks and sculpted bowls and give Mother Nature a silent
"thank you".

While Arapahoe Basin, with its dizzying heights, attracted ski experts and
vacationing celebrities, another ski hill catered to locals. The Cemetery Ski Hill
was, its owner John Bailey laughs, "a ridiculous operation". Located above the
old cemetery in old Dillon, the area featured a rope tow and a 150-foot vertical
drop. The tow ticket ran skiers $1 each, but not many turned out for the bargain.

"We offered night skiing with six or eight flood lights," chuckled Bailey.

"We used the motor from an old Studebaker to run the rope tow," said Bailey.
"We had to burn oil in coffee cans beneath the motor to warm it enough to start.
Every third or fourth time, the motor caught fire."

The Cemetery Ski Hill lasted only one season, 1949-50.

Of course, skiers also used the Dillon Jump and the Breckenridge baseball
diamond east of the present elementary school, where a rope tow hauled
youngsters as part of the school's weekly Tuesday-Thursday afternoon ski lesson. As a ski instructor, along with John Bailey and Public Service Company's
Earl Ganong, Edna Dercum worked hard to promote skiing as a school sport in
Summit County. "We had a running battle with the principal. He was a basket-

ball coach. Even if a youngster was five feet, five inches tall, he had to be on the basketball team." There were only 35 or 40 high schoolers, so all the boys were needed to make the basketball team. And they were not allowed to ski.

Tempers flared over the school's refusal to support skiing. A teacher and two school board members lost their jobs as victims of the squabble.

"The kids had terrible equipment," Edna Dercum recalled. Horrible seven-foot skis, painted white, were surplus from the Tenth Mountain Division.

Nevertheless, they were the good old days. John Bailey remembers: "In the early days, skiing meant powder. No 'packed' slopes. Early skiers were *skiers*, not sliders, used to snow conditions that would never go now. We could ski all day at Arapahoe Basin in deep powder."

Nostalgia for the long, uncrowded powder snow days long before the mani-cured slopes era still lingers among these trail-blazing Summit skiers. But downhillers like Larry Jump, Sandy Schauffler, Slim Davis, Max and Edna Dercum, John Bailey and others displayed the kind of contagious enthusiasm that touched off Summit's present ski boom.

Breckenridge

Today, Summit leads all Colorado contenders, including famous Vail and Aspen, in state skier counts. Breckenridge, the county's busiest ski area, opened December 18, 1961 with a chairlift and T-bar built by Rounds and Porter, a Wichita, Kansas-based lumber company with large Breckenridge land holdings. Since then, Aspen Ski Corporation and, today, California's Twentieth Century Fox conglomerate, have guided the rapidly-growing ski complex on Peaks Eight and Nine to success.

Keystone

Summit ski pioneer Max Dercum saw a 25-year old dream come true when his "baby", Keystone Mountain, opened to skiers in November, 1970. Keystone, with its long, sweet, meandering runs, since teamed up with its neighbor, challenging Arapahoe Basin, to offer both sweet and sassy ski terrain. Food industry giant, Ralston Purina Company, owns the two ski areas today. Under Ralston Purina's cultivated wing, Keystone has emerged as a sophisticated mountain resort.

Copper

The Colorado ski world waited a long time for the right people to come along and transform powder-carpeted Copper Mountain, with its nearly natural runs, into a major ski area. Even the U.S. Forest Service gushed uncharacteristically in its much-quoted praise: "If ever there was a mountain that had terrain created for skiing, it would be Copper mountain."

Yet securing Copper's base land and finding the capital to finance Copper Mountain's creation proved as challenging as skiing Copper's new and mogully A-lift runs. After long effort, Copper finally received backing from Colorado's Fulenwider Management and Development Company. And the project schussed to success, opening with two feet of fresh powder, and plenty of skier enthusiasm, in November, 1972.

Almost ninety years before, a Denver newspaper had pinned down an activity that then became a passion in Summit County. On December 25, 1882, the *Rocky Mountain News* commented:

> No matter what may be a man's profession or intentions, he is irresistably drawn into mining as soon as he becomes a citizen of Summit County. The merchants here are miners, the doctors are miners, the lawyers are miners and in short everyone mines in Summit County.

Today, the *News* could substitute the word "skiing" for "mining" and aptly pinpoint the passion that now holds Summit County in its inviting grip. A dozen decades after miners discovered gold along the Blue River, a new gold fever had consumed Summit's citizens. But this time the treasure is crystalline, frosty powder snow — White Gold!

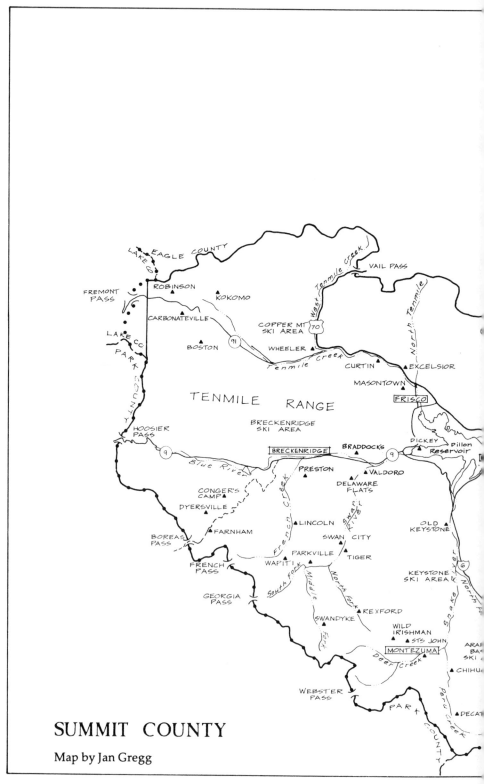

SUMMIT COUNTY

Map by Jan Gregg

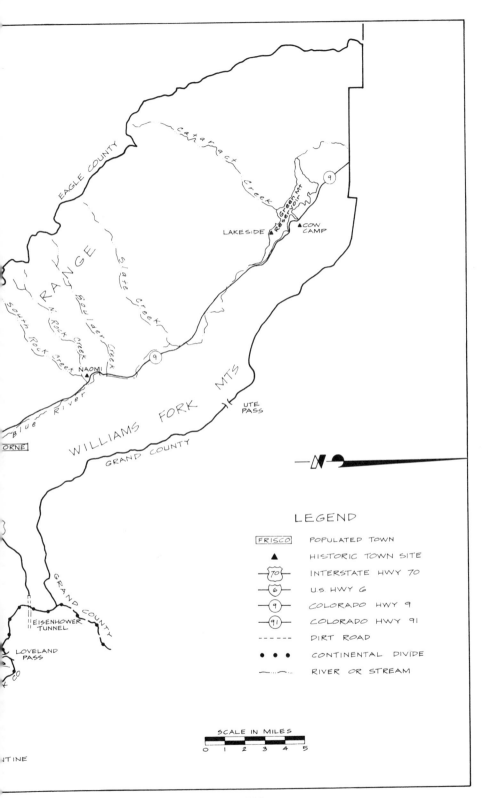

EAGLE COUNTY

Cataract Creek

RANGE

Slate Creek

Boulder Creek

N. Rock Creek

South Rock Creek

Green Mt. Reservoir

LAKESIDE ▲

▲ COW CAMP

(9)

(9)

NAOMI ▲

Blue River

WILLIAMS FORK MTS

UTE PASS

GRAND COUNTY

ORNE

GRAND COUNTY

EISENHOWER TUNNEL

LOVELAND PASS

CO

NTINE

N

LEGEND

FRISCO	POPULATED TOWN
▲	HISTORIC TOWN SITE
(70)	INTERSTATE HWY 70
(6)	U.S. HWY 6
(9)	COLORADO HWY 9
(91)	COLORADO HWY 91
- - - - - -	DIRT ROAD
• • •	CONTINENTAL DIVIDE
—··—	RIVER OR STREAM

SCALE IN MILES

0 1 2 3 4 5

BIBLIOGRAPHY

Books

Annual Colorado State Business Directories, 1875-1900.

Athearn, Robert A. *The Coloradans*. Albuquerque: University of New Mexico Press, 1976.

Bancroft, Caroline. *Colorful Colorado*. Denver: Sage Books, 1959.

Bird, Isabella. *A Lady's Life in the Rocky Mountains, 1879-80*. New York: Putnam's Sons. (Republished by the University of Oklahoma, 1960.)

Black, Robert C. *Island in the Rockies*. Boulder: Pruett Publishing Company, 1969.

Bowles, Samuel. *Colorado: Its Parks and Mountains*. New York: Bowles and Company, 1869.

Brewer, William H. *Rocky Mountain Letters, 1869*. Denver: Colorado Mountain Club, 1930.

Brown,Robert L. *Colorado Ghost Towns*. Caldwell, Idaho: Caxton Printers, Ltd., 1972. *Jeep Trails to Colorado Ghost Towns*. Caldwell, Idaho: Caxton Printers, Ltd., 1963.

Business Directory of Leadville, Kokomo and Carbonateville. Clark, Root and Company, 1879.

Carter, William. *Ghost Towns of the West*. Menlo Park, California: Lane Publishing Company, 1978.

Champion, Ruth. *Breckenridge Gold!* Fort Collins, Colorado: Old Army Press, 1977.

Chappell, Richardson and Hank. *The South Park Line*. Colorado Rail Annual Number 12. Colorado Railroad Museum, 1974.

Conner, Daniel Ellis. *A Conference in the Colorado Gold Fields*. Norman: University of Oklahoma Press, 1970.

Crofutt, George. *Crofutt's Grip Sack Guide of Colorado*. Volume II. Omaha: Overland Publishing Company, 1885. (Republished by Cubar, 1966.)

Dallas, Sandra. *Gaslights and Gingerbread*. Denver: Sage Books, 1965. *No More Than Five in a Bed*. Norman: University of Oklahoma Press, 1967.

Dorset, Phyllis. *The New Eldorado*. New York: MacMillan and Company, 1970.

Dyer, John Lewis. *Snowshoe Itinerant*. Cincinnati: Crawston and Stowe, 1891. (Republished by the Father Dyer Methodist Church, Breckenridge, 1975.)

Eberhart, Perry. *Guide to the Colorado Ghost Towns*. Denver: Sage Books, 1959.

Ellis, Erl. *The Gold Dredging Boats Around Breckenridge, Colorado*. Boulder: Johnson Publishing Company, 1967.

Emore, Anna B. *Dillon, Blue River Valley Wonderland*. Dillon,Colorado: Summit Historical Society, 1976. (Booklet).

Fiester, Mark. *Blasted, Beloved Breckenridge*. Boulder: Pruett Publishing Company, 1973.

Fosset, Frank. *The Gold and Silver Mines of Colorado*. New York: C. G. Crawford, 1880.

Greeley, Horace. *An Overland Journey from New York to San Francisco in Summer, 1859*. New York: C. M. Saxon, 1860.

Griswold, Don. *Colorado's Century of Cities*. Published by Smith Books for the author, 1958.

Hafen, LeRoy. *Colorado: The Story of a Western Commonwealth*. Denver: The Peerless Publishing Company, 1933.

Hall, Frank. *History of the State of Colorado*, Volume IV. Chicago: Blakely Printing Company, 1895.

Henderson, Charles W. *Mining in Colorado*. Washington: Government Printing Office, 1926.

Hill, Alice Polk. *Tales of the Colorado Pioneers*. Denver, 1884. *Colorado Pioneers in Picture and Story*. Denver: Brock-Hoffman Press, 1915.

Hollister, Orvando J. *The Mines of Colorado.* Springfield, Mass.: S. Bowles and Company, 1867.

Horner, John Willard. *Silver Town.* Caldwell, Idaho: Caxton Printer, Ltd., 1950.

Howbert, Irving. *Indians of the Pikes Peak Region.* Glorieta: Rio Grande Press, 1914.

Hunt, Inez and Draper, Wanetta. *Colorado Crazy Quilt.* Colorado Springs: HAH Publications, 1971. *To Colorado's Restless Ghosts.* Denver: Sage Books.

Ingersoll, Ernest. *Crest of the Continent.* Glorieta: Rio Grande Press, 1883.

Jocknick, Sidney. *Early Days of the Western Slope of Colorado.* Glorieta: Rio Grande Press, 1913.

Kindig, R. H., Haley, E. J., and Poor, M. C. *Pictorial Supplement to the Denver, South Park and Pacific.* Denver: Rocky Mountain Railroad Club, 1959.

King, Otis A. *Gray Gold.* Denver: Big Mountain Press, 1959.

La Baw, Wallace. *Nah-oon-kara, the Gold of Breckenridge.* Denver: Big Mountain Press, 1965.

Libbey, William, Jr. *Diary of the Princeton Scientific Expedition.* New York: 1879.

Look, Al. *Utes Last Stand.* Denver: Golden Bell Press, 1972.

Lovering, Thomas S. *Geology and Ore Deposits of the Montezuma Quadrangle, Colorado.* U.S. Geological Survey Professional Paper Number 178. Washington: Government Printing Office, 1935.

McConnell, Virginia. *Bayou Salado.* Denver: Sage Books, 1966.

Muench and Pike. *Rendezvous Country.* Palo Alto, California: American West, 1975.

Parkhill, Forbes. *Mr. Barney Ford.* Denver: Sage Books, 1963.

Poor, M. C. *Denver, South Park and Pacific.* Denver: Rocky Mountain Railroad Club, 1949.

Poor, M. C. *Memorial Edition: Denver, South Park and Pacific.* Denver: Rocky Mountain Railroad Club, 1976.

Ransome, Frederick L. *Geology and Ore Deposits of the Breckenridge District, Colorado.* U.S. Geological Survey Professional Paper Number 75. Washington: Government Printing office, 1911.

Roberts, Jack. *The Amazing Adventures of Lord Gore.* Silverton, Colorado: Sundance Books, 1977.

Rockwell, Wilson. *The Utes, A Forgotten People.* Denver: Sage Books, 1956.

Ruxton, George Frederick. *Ruxton of the Rockies.* Norman: University of Oklahoma Press, 1950.

Sandoz, Mari. *The Beaver Men.* New York: Hastings House, 1964.

Sharp, Verna. *A History of Montezuma, Sts. John and Argentine.* Dillon, Colorado: Summit Historical Society, 1971.

Smith, Duane A. *Rocky Mountain Mining Camps.* Bloomington: Indiana University Press, 1967.

Sprague, Marshall. *The Great Gates.* Boston: Little Brown, 1964.

Stoehr, Eric. *Bonanza Victorian.* Albuquerque: University of New Mexico Press, 1975.

Taylor, Bayard. *Colorado: A Summer Trip.* New York: Putnam, 1867.

Ubbelohde, Benson and Smith. *A Colorado History.* Boulder: Pruett Publishing Company, 1972.

Ubbelohde, Carl. *A Colorado Reader.* Boulder: Pruett Publishing Company, 1962.

Villard, Henry. *Past and Present of the Pikes Peak Gold Region.* London: 1860. (Republished by Princeton University Press, 1932.)

Walter, Douglas S. *Historic Sites in Summit County, Colorado.* Masters Thesis: College of Environmental Design, University of Colorado.

Watkins, T.H. *Gold and Silver in the West.* Palo Alto, California: American West Publishing Company, 1971.

Wislizenus, Adolphus. *Journey to the Rocky Mountains in 1839*. Glorieta: Rio Grande Press, 1969.

Wolle, Muriel Sibell. *Stampede to Timberline*. Denver: Sage Books, 1974. *Bonanza Trail* Bloomington: Indiana University Press, 1966. *Cloud Cities of Colorado*. (by Muriel V. Sibell) Denver: Smith-Brooks Printing Company, 1934.

Articles and Pamphlets

Burkey, Elmer. "The Georgetown-Leadville Stage". *Colorado* Magazine. September, 1937. (*Colorado* Magazine is published by the Colorado State Historical Society.)

Hall, John N. "Letter from the Blue River Diggings". *Western Express*. July, 1967.

Hastings, John Irving. "A Winter in the High Mountains. *Colorado* Magazine, Volume 27.

Hill, Georgia Burns. "Memories of a Pioneer Childhood". *Colorado* Magazine, Volume 32.

Keables, A.E. "Goldfields of Summit County, Colorado". (Pamphlet) April 20, 1905.

Lewis, Penny. "A Place Where Men Never Get Old". *Mountain Living* supplement to the Summit County *Sentinel*. September 26, 1977. "A Brief Historical Survey of Kokomo-Recen".

Low, J.B. "Robinson Mines Report". Leadville. (Pamphlet) September 3, 1879.

Miner, Agnes F. "Story of a Summit County Pioneer". Summit County *Journal*.

Opinions. A newsletter published by the King Solomon Mining Syndicate. Frisco, Colorado. 1905.

Parker, Dr. B.H., Jr. "Gold Placers of Colorado". *Quarterly* of the Colorado School of Mines, Volume 69. July, 1974.

Roller, Elizabeth Rice. "Life in Montezuma, Chihuahua and Sts. John." *Westerners Brand Book*. August, 1964.

Sharp, Verna. "Law and Order Come To Montezuma". *Colorado* Magazine, Volume 39. "Montezuma and Her Neighbors". *Colorado* Magazine, Volume 33.

Turnbull, Belle. "Gold Boats on the Swan". *Colorado* Magazine, Volume 39.

Widmar, R. "Blue River Gold Fields and Metal Mines". (Pamphlet) circa 1905.

Newspapers

Key newspaper sources used for this book were the old Summit newspapers, listed in Chapter 18. Also used were early editions of:
Rocky Mountain News
Denver *Post*
Denver *Daily Tribune*
Tarryall *Miners Record*
Georgetown *Courier*
Georgetown *Colorado Miner*
Georgetown *Herald*

Summit County history is highlighted in the following Summit County *Journal* articles:
Ed Auge article, March 29, 1935
"Nuggets" Series, 1938
"E.C. Peabody Remembers" Series, March 26-April 30, 1954

Research Materials

The files of the Summit County Historical Society supplied some research papers, including John Daugherty's "Survey of Historical Sites", prepared for the historical society and the U.S. Forest Service.

INDEX

For mines and mining, consult geographic listings.

Orleans, 156; Mark Twain, 154; Marlin, 154; More Work, 155; Morgan, 148; New York, 149: Old Settler, 149; Orphan Boy, 157; Peary, 157; Pennsylvania, 158; Peruvian, 159; Potosi, 155; Quail, 149; Queen of the West, 160; Radical, 153; Red Light, 161; Rothschild, 157; Ruby Mountain Group, 159; Sarsefield, 149; Shoe Basin, 158; Silver King, 150; Silver Wave, 151; Star of the West, 153; St. Cloud, 155; St. Elmo, 154; Sts. John, 154-55; Tariff, 157; Tiger, Tiger Extension, 155; Washington, 149, 157; Waterloo, 149; White Sparrow, 157; Wild Irishman, 155; Windsor, 155; Winning Card, 156

Mines, Ten Mile Canyon, Aborigine, 141; Aftermath, 141; Annie Lisle, 142; Atlas, 143; Augustine, 143; Baby, 142; Balahoo, 143; Ballarat, 142; Big Giant, 142; Big Horn, 142; Black Dragon, 142; Blackstone, 143; Bledsoe, 141; Boulder, 143; Boston Group, 143; Breene, 141; Brook, 143; Capitol Lode, 142; Checkmate, 142; Climax, 141; Cloudy Placer, 139; Colonel Sellars, 141; Colorado, 143; Crown Point, 142; Curious, 143; Eldorado, 142; Esmeralda, 143; Excelsior, 136-37, Felicia Grace, 142; Grand Union, 142; Gray Eagle, 142; Hard Cash, 143; Hard Luck Group, 139; Hidden Treasure, 142; Incas, 143; Ino, 143; International, 142; Invincible, 142; Justice Lode, 140; Keyes, 143; King Solomon, 138; Kitty Innes, 139; Little Carbonate, 142; Little Giant, 142; Lucky Boy Placer, 139; Mary Verna, 139; Masontown, 136; McNulty Placers, 143; Merrimac, 143; Mint, 136; Monroe, 139; New York, 142; North American, 139; Olympic, No. 2, 143; Ophir Tunnel, 136; Oro Fino, 143; Osage Group, 139; Pauline, 142; Pirate, 142; Polygon, 143; Pool Placer, 139; Queen of the West, 141; Recen, 141; Reconstruction, 139; Rhone, 142; Rising Sun, 141; Robinson, 142; Robinson Group, 136; Ruby, 142; Selma, 141; Seventy-Eight, 142; Shady Placer, 139; Sherman, 141; Silver, 142; Silver Chain, 141; Silver Queen, 141; Silver Tip, 142; Smuggler, 142; Square Deal, 136; St. Regis, 143; Storm King, 139; Summit Group, 139

Mining, Breckenridge area, American Ditch, 120
American Gulch, 37, 121
B & B Mines Company, 119
Barney Ford Hill, 131
Boreas Pass mining 131-34
Brown's Gulch, 37
Buffalo Flats, 117
Buffalo Ditch, 125
Campion, John, 121
Delaware Flats, 118
Farncomb, Harry, 122
Farncomb Hill wire gold, 121-22
Fuller Placer Company, 121
Galena Gulch, 118
Georgia Gulch, 37, 102, 120, 183, 230
Gibson Hill, 126-27
Gold Pan Mining Company, 128
Gold Run, 36, 125-26
Gold Run Ditch, 125
Illinois Gulch, 37, 131
Indiana Gulch, 171
Johannesburg Mill, 125
Moody, E. C., 125-26
Oliver filter, 126
Ransome, Leslie, 132
Reiling dredge, 123
Rexford, 119
Royal Tiger Mines Company, 118
Shock Hill, 127
Swandyke, 119
Tiger, 118
Tom's Baby, 122
Tonopah Placers Company, 128-29
Traylor, John, 119
Wakefield mining area, 131
Weaver, Balce, 125
Mining District, 113
Mining, gold, production 1859-1878, 116
Mining, lode, blasting, 109-10; definition, 113; financing, 110; Jessie Mill, 111; Jumbo Mill, 111; lode milling, 110-13, smelters lll, 115; tunnels, shafts, chambers, 109,115

Mining, Montezuma area, altitude, 145;
Bolivar Mill, 150
Boston Silver Mining Association, 154
Candler, Colonel, W. L., 154
Chihuahua, 156
Cinnamon Gulch, 157
Coley, John, 146
Deer Creek area, 152-53
Filger City, 156

330

332

PHOTO CREDITS

1. New York Mine, Author's Collection. 4. Montezuma, Summit Historical Society. 11. Beaver Men, Denver Public Library, Western History Department. 12. George Ruxton, Denver Public Library, Western History Department. 17. Ute Crossing, Denver Public Library, Western History Department. 26. Tipi Building, Denver Public Library, Western History Department. 27. Chipeta and Ouray; Cradle Board, Denver Public Library, Western History Department. 31. Colorow, Denver Public Library, Western History Department. 34. Main St., Breckenridge, Summit Historical Society. 37. Breckenridge View, Summit Historical Society. 43. Bayard Taylor, Denver Public Library, Western History Department. 45. Saloon, Summit Historical Society. 48. Breckenridge School, two views, Denver Public Library via Summit Historical Society. 50. Rev. John Lewis Dyer, Summit Historical Society courtesy the United States Forest Service. 52. Watson Store, Summit Historical Society courtesy the United States Forest Service. 53. Snow Tunnel, Summit Historical Society courtesy the United States Forest Service. 60. Edwin Carter, Denver Public Library via Summit Historical Society. 65. Montezuma, Summit Historical Society. 68. Saloon, Denver Public Library via Summit Historical Society. 71. Montezuma School, (A) Author's Collection, (B) Edna Dercum Collection. 75. Franklyn House, Summit Historical Society. 76. Barbershop, Edna Dercum Collection. 78. Main St., Dillon, Summit Historical Society. 85. Tip Ballif, Summit Historical Society. 90. Hamilton Hotel, Summit Historical Society. 91. Main St., Dillon, Summit Historical Society. 95. Frisco School, Summit Historical Society. 97. (A) Frisco, (B) Wagon, (C) Mount Royal Cabin, all Summit Historical Society. 100. Jail, Author's Collection. 103. Sluicing, Summit Historical Society courtesy United States Forest Service. 106. Risdon Dredge, Summit Historical Society. 110. Chautauqua Mine, two views, Summit Historical Society. 116. Cashier Mine, Denver Public Library, Western History Department. 117. Sled Train, Postcard. 120. Hydraulic Mining, Summit Historical Society. 123. Reliance Dredge, Summit Historical Society. 129. Dredge, Summit Historical Society. 130. Jessie and Tiger, Author's Collection. 131. Jumbo Mill, Author's Collection. 133. Erickson Mine, Toledo Tunnel, New York Mine, Author's Collection. 137. Square Deal Mine and Tunnel, courtesy Howard Giberson. 138. Excelsior Mine, courtesy Howard Giberson. 140. Kimberly Mill, courtesy United States Forest Service. 147. Bullion Mine, Summit Historical Society. 152. Cashier Mine, Summit Historical Society. 159. Peruvian Mine, Summit Historical Society. 163. Montezuma, 1876, Summit Historical Society. 167. Gravestone, Author's Collection. 169. Boston, two views, Author's Collection. 173. Argentine, Denver Public Library via Summit Historical Society. 177. Entertainer, Denver Public Library, Western History Department. 180. Prospector, Postcard. 181. Curtin, Summit Historical Society courtesy United States Forest Service. 186. Tiger, Denver Public Library via Summit Historical Society. 191. Pack Train, Summit Historical Society. 193. Lumber Train, Summit Historical Society. 195. Toll Gate, Summit Historical Society courtesy United States Forest Service. 197. Ore Wagon, Summit Historical Society. 201. Wagon, Summit Historical Society. 207. C & S Wreck, Summit Historical Society. 209. Rotary Plow, Summit Historical Society. 210. 1898 Train, Summit Historical Society courtesy United States Forest Service. 215. Boreas Station, Summit Historical Society courtesy United States Forest Service. 221. Rotary Plow, Denver Public Library via Summit Historical Society. 222. Uneva Lake, Summit Historical Society. 225. Rail Wreck, Summit Historical Society. 236. Sts. John, 1979, Author's Collection; Sts. John, 1880's, Summit Historical Society. 238. Sts. John Mill, Summit Historical Society courtesy United States Forest Service. 239. Smelter, Summit Historical Society. 241. Smelter, Summit Historical Society. 242. Sts. John, Author's Collection. 243. Kokomo, Summit Historical Society. 251. Robinson, Denver Public

Library, Western History Department. **269.** 1860's Breckenridge, Denver Public Library via Summit Historical Society. **274.** Stephen Decatur, Denver Public Library, Western History Department. **281.** (A) Charles Levy, (B) Pug Ryan, Summit Historical Society. **290.** B. S. Revett, Summit Historical Society. **297.** J. H. Myers, Summit Historical Society. **300.** Gravestone, Author's Collection. **303.** G. A. R. Hall, Summit Historical Society. **305.** Ella Foote, Summit Historical Society. **308.** Ski Team, Summit Historical Society. **310.** Skier, Summit Historical Society courtesy United States Forest Service. **311.** Bertha Tate, Summit Historical Society courtesy United States Forest Service. **314.** 1912 Skiers, Summit Historical Society courtesy United States Forest Service.